INTRODUCTION TO THE SYNOPTIC GOSPELS

Introduction to the Synoptic Gospels

Pheme Perkins

WILLIAM B. EERDMANS PUBLISHING COMPANY

GRAND RAPIDS, MICHIGAN / CAMBRIDGE, U.K.

Published 2007 by
Wm. B. Eerdmans Publishing Co.
2140 Oak Industrial Drive N.E., Grand Rapids, Michigan 49505 /
P.O. Box 163, Cambridge CB3 9PU U.K.

Printed in the United States of America

12 11 10 09 08 07   7 6 5 4 3 2 1

Library of Congress Cataloging-in-Publication Data

Perkins, Pheme.
    Introduction to the synoptic gospels / Pheme Perkins.
        p.   cm.
    Includes bibliographical references.
    ISBN 978-0-8028-1770-9 (cloth: alk. paper)
    1. Bible. N.T. Gospels — Criticism, interpretation, etc.
    2. Synoptic problem.   I. Title.

    BS2555.52.P47   2007
    226′.061 — dc22

                                2007012412

www.eerdmans.com

Contents

Abbreviations

AB	Anchor Bible
ABD	*Anchor Bible Dictionary*, ed. D. N. Freedman (5 vols.; New York: Doubleday, 1992)
Adv. Haer.	Irenaeus, *Adversus Haereses*
Adv. Marc.	Tertullian, *Adversus Marcionem*
Asc. Isa.	*Ascension of Isaiah*
BG	Berlin Gnostic Papyri
CBQ	*Catholic Biblical Quarterly*
C.E., B.C.E.	common era, before the common era (= A.D., B.C.)
ExpTim	*Expository Times*
Gos. Heb.	*Gospel of the Hebrews*
Gos. Judas	*Gospel of Judas*
Gos. Mary	*Gospel of Mary (Magdalene)*
Gos. Pet.	*Gospel of Peter*
Gos. Ph.	*Gospel of Philip*
Gos. Thom.	*Gospel of Thomas*
Gos. Tr.	*Gospel of Truth*
Hist. Eccl.	Eusebius, *Historia Ecclesiastica*
JBL	*Journal of Biblical Literature*
JSNT	*Journal for the Study of the New Testament*
JSNTSup	*Journal for the Study of the New Testament* Supplement Series
LCL	Loeb Classic Library

LXX	Septuagint
NHC	Nag Hammadi Codices
NHL	*Nag Hammadi Library in English,* ed. J. M. Robinson (fourth edition; Leiden: Brill, 1996)
NIV	New International Version
NRSV	New Revised Standard Version
NTS	*New Testament Studies*
OTP	*Old Testament Pseudepigrapha,* ed. J. H. Charlesworth (2 vols.; Garden City: Doubleday, 1983, 1985)
P. Berol.	Berlin Papyri
P. Oxy.	Oxyrynchus Papyri
P. Ryl.	Rylands Papyri
par.	and parallel(s)
PL	*Patrologia latina,* ed. J. P. Migne
NRSV	New Revised Standard Version
VC	*Vigiliae Christianae*
Vis.	*Visions (Shepherd of Hermas)*
WBC	Word Biblical Commentary
ZNW	*Zeitschrift für die neutestamentliche Wissenschaft*

General Bibliography

Primary Sources For Ancient Texts

Elliott, J. K. *The Apocryphal New Testament.* Oxford: Clarendon, 1993.

Hedrick, Charles W., and Paul A. Mirecki. *Gospel of the Savior: A New Ancient Gospel.* Santa Rosa: Polebridge, 1999.

Meyer, Marvin, ed. *The Nag Hammadi Scriptures.* New York: Harper Collins, 2007.

Robinson, James M., Paul Hoffmann, and John S. Kloppenborg, eds. *The Critical Edition of Q.* Minneapolis: Fortress, 2000.

Robinson, James M., ed. *The Nag Hammadi Library in English.* New York: Harper and Row, 1988, third edition.

Schneemelcher, Wilhelm, ed. *New Testament Apocrypha,* vol. 1: *Gospels and Related Writings.* Trans. R. McL. Wilson. Louisville: Westminster/ John Knox, 1991.

Stroker, William D. *Extracanonical Sayings of Jesus.* SBL Resources for Biblical Study 18; Atlanta: Scholars, 1989.

General Reference Works

Freedman, D. N., editor. *Anchor Bible Dictionary.* 6 volumes. Garden City: Doubleday, 1992.

Keck, Leander E., editor. *The New Interpreter's Bible,* vol. 8. Nashville: Abingdon, 1995.

McDonald, Lee Martin, and James A. Sanders, eds. *The Canon Debate.* Peabody: Hendrickson, 2002.

Trebolle Barrera, Julio. *The Jewish and Christian Bible.* Trans. Wilfred G. E. Watson. Grand Rapids: Eerdmans, 1998.

Introduction

Several years ago Allen Myers wrote asking if I might be interested in writing a book on the Synoptic Gospels for Eerdmans. Conversation among editors at the press had suggested a lacuna in the available literature. General readers cannot find the kind of information about how the Gospels were written, their sources, their preservation, and their individual characteristics that ministers and seminary students get in textbooks and introductory courses. Even those who have some professional training for ministry are at a loss when discoveries of new Gospel manuscripts or discussions of Gnostic Gospels hit the news. Those who have been out of school for a while may have learned to analyze a particular Gospel text using the basics of source and form criticism but not to consider its relationship to the Gospel in question as a literary whole. And most students, then and now, brushed over the sections on text criticism. Yet without the careful study of what actually survives on fragments of papyrus and in codices there would be no text for the translator or Bible for the reader. A healthy dose of text-critical common sense is also a good antidote for the dizzying hype that accompanies any newly published text.

Churches whose cycle of readings devotes a year to each of the Synoptic Gospels often take the Gospel in question for their Bible study. Although there are a number of recent commentary series for the serious lay reader, those volumes cannot explain the how or why of our approach to analyzing the Gospels. "It's as though the ministers have a secret they won't share with the rest of us," my sister-in-law often complains. I've never asked how she could feel that way after reading so many of the books and articles that I and other scholars have written for general audiences.

Many adults who enroll in master's level courses in theology and religious education or who take weekend ministry formation courses are not much better off. When teaching courses and workshops at that level, I often provide students with a list of recent books by well-known scholars and ask for a critical review of any one the student chooses. Despite the fact that these are mass-market trade books of interest to the readers, most students have a difficult time figuring out how the authors arrive at the claims they make about passages in the Bible. It's all a mystery, so students simply latch on to statements which strike them as particularly insightful or objectionable.

This book has taken on the challenge of explaining the what and why of the methods used by scholars when we approach the Gospels. Some of the more radical claims often featured in the news or in TV documentaries will be mentioned as proposals or hypotheses, not as majority opinion. Since there are limits on what we actually know about the various Gospels and their origins and transmission, one should not be surprised at disagreements among investigators. On the other hand those who claim that the disciplines of careful, historical study of the Gospels developed over the past three centuries are bankrupt are themselves either unwilling or unable to consider the evidence. There is a great deal which twenty-first-century scholars now know that was not known even in the early twentieth century. As in every other mature field of academic investigation, even as certain facts become established, new areas of investigation open up. Because this book is not for scholars, the focus has been on broad-scale consensus. Points of uncertainty or debate that frequently make the news will be flagged. My students can testify that I never saw a footnote that I didn't like (or read), but I have restrained that inclination in this book. The few footnotes provided will enable curious students to track down additional information. Readers can ignore them without peril to understanding.

The first two chapters treat more general questions about what a Gospel is and how the Gospels came to be considered official, apostolic testimony about Jesus. Although some scholars consider the Gospels to be closer to historical fiction, epic, or foundational myth, most would concur with the position that the Synoptic Evangelists intended to present what an ancient audience would consider a biography or life of Christianity's founder. Some of the differences between the Synoptics and ancient literary biography result from the influence of Jewish Scriptures in early Christian life and worship. Other elements in the depiction of Jesus are similar to lives of philosophers. However neither the Gospels nor ancient lives meet the standards of history that modern readers associate with biographies.

With the majority of scholars, we find the proposal that Matthew and Luke have rewritten and supplemented Mark to be a firmly established result of scholarly investigation. The reasons that ancient Christian authors came to assign the Gospels to specific apostles and to consider Mark an abridgment of Matthew made sense in their context. Throughout this book we will present examples in which comparing the Gospels with each other produces examples that support the view of Markan priority. At the same time we will situate the composition and transmission of the Synoptic Gospels within the context of a Christianity which continued to produce and circulate books about Jesus. Some are known only as titles or are represented by a few quotations in the works of early Christian authors. Some survive only in fragmentary texts whose content is clearly material about Jesus. The imperfect preservation of such remains makes it impossible to tell what sort of book they come from.

Chapter three expands the study of relationships between the Synoptic Gospels into the search for the sources employed by the Evangelists. Earlier scholars recognized a collection of Jesus' sayings behind material common to Matthew and Luke. After the discovery of a sayings collection that had been translated into Coptic, that hypothesis gained additional support. Recent scholarship has witnessed a movement to transform the sayings source into a "Gospel" in its own right. New editions and commentaries on the *Gospel of Thomas* and the so-called "Q" collection pop up in chain bookstores regularly. The extensive discussion of Q in this chapter reflects its prominence in current scholarship. Final sections of the chapter treat the forms in which individual units of tradition are cast and the question of an independent passion narrative. Each of the chapters dealing with the text of the Gospels concludes with consideration of related noncanonical gospel traditions. Chapter three discusses the relationship between the *Gospel of Peter* and the Synoptic passion narratives.

Each of the next three chapters is devoted to one of the Synoptic Gospels. They follow a common format that begins with the Gospel's overall narrative and its literary features, discusses characters, the figure of Jesus, and the implied community, and concludes with consideration of related apocryphal gospel material. Although these chapters do refer to what has been discussed in earlier sections of the book, they are sharply focused on the text of the Gospel in question. Bible study groups should be able to use an individual chapter to gain a perspective on the Gospel they are studying in a particular year. Study of Matthew and Luke benefits by comparing what each Evangelist does with the Markan narrative that he inherits, so some glances back into that Gospel will be in order. Since Luke followed the volume which contained his Gospel with another, the Acts of the Apostles, we will be referring to Acts to illustrate some of Luke's literary techniques and theological interests.

Though Mark was of considerably less interest to second- and third-century Christians than the revised versions produced by Matthew and Luke or than John, it was not lost. The same period exhibited considerable imaginative and theological diversity in producing other Jesus traditions. Our concluding chapter discusses additional apocryphal gospel material, both fragmentary papyri and Coptic codices that contain such now famous Gnostic Gospels as the *Gospel of Mary*. We argue that much of this material was created by the growing prominence of the four-Gospel canon in Christian life and worship. It does not contain much first-century Jesus tradition. Nor should the adoption of a Gospel canon for Christian worship and instruction be viewed as an example of ecclesiastical repression.

CHAPTER ONE

What Is a Gospel?

The Greek word translated "gospel," *euangelion*, did not refer to a type of literature or to a book in the first century. It had a more dynamic meaning, a proclamation of an event of major importance. For us that might resemble the breaking news headline that promises a story to follow. For the inhabitants of an ancient city, the word evoked the excitement of a messen-

---

Suggested Reading

Aune, David E. *The Westminster Dictionary of the New Testament and Early Christian Literature and Rhetoric.* Louisville: Westminster/John Knox, 2003.

Bockmuehl, Markus, and Donald A. Hagner, eds. *The Written Gospel.* Cambridge: Cambridge University Press, 2005.

Bonz, Marianne Palmer. *The Past as Legacy: Luke-Acts and Ancient Epic.* Minneapolis: Fortress, 2000.

Burridge, Richard A. *What Are Gospels? A Comparison with Graeco-Roman Biography.* Cambridge: Cambridge University Press, 1992.

Burridge, Richard A. "About People, by People, for People: Gospel Genre and Audiences," in R. Bauckham, ed., *The Gospels for All Christians: Rethinking Gospel Audiences.* Grand Rapids: Eerdmans, 1998, pp. 113-45.

MacDonald, Dennis R. *The Homeric Epics and the Gospel of Mark.* New Haven: Yale University Press, 2000.

Thomas, Christine M. *The Acts of Peter, Gospel Literature, and the Ancient Novel: Rewriting the Past.* New York: Oxford University Press, 2003.

ger racing into town with news of the latest battle, or news that a new ruler had assumed the throne in a distant capital. The Jewish historian Josephus reports that when Vespasian became emperor of Rome "proclamations" (Greek *euangelia*) led to feasting and civic rejoicing (*War* 4.618). The Greek translators of the Hebrew Bible used the cognate verb, *euangelizesthai,* for the announcement of God's impending deliverance. A participle from this verb refers to the bearer of that message in Isaiah (40:9; 41:27; 52:7). Therefore "gospel" was a key term for Paul to speak of God's new, definitive deeds of salvation in Jesus Christ (Rom 1:1, 16).

As a designation for written works, the term "gospel" must be secondary to the accounts in which first-century Christian authors presented Jesus as the one who fulfilled such prophetic promises or as the "great king" in whom God's rule is embodied. Recognition that Gospels have been shaped by Christian faith in Jesus as God's Messiah continues to fuel debate over whether their authors had any interest in historical information about Jesus' life and teaching. Are we reading what is essentially a series of fictions about the founder of a new religious cult? Or do the Evangelists employ first-century ways of recounting the life and teaching of an important figure even as they make a case for believing Jesus to be the source of God's salvation? Comparing the Synoptic Gospels with other ancient "lives" makes a plausible case for regarding them as biographical rather than fictional in intent. That conclusion does not mean that they are investigative documentaries. Each author exercises considerable freedom in presenting the events of Jesus' life, his character, and his teaching. After presenting the case for the Gospels as ancient "lives," we will note two alternative views that consider Mark and Luke to have been shaped according to the model of ancient epics. A final note suggests that by the end of the second century most Christians accepted the four-Gospel canon as authoritative accounts of Jesus.

Ancient Biography

Mark 1:1 uses the word "gospel" in the Pauline sense of proclamation about Jesus. His Greek-speaking audience may have recognized *christos* as a translation for "Messiah" (= "anointed"). Or they may have considered "Christ" an additional name used to distinguish this Jesus from others called "Jesus." Some ancient manuscripts show that readers no longer recognized "Christ" as an indication of Jesus' dignity. Scribes add more familiar titles, "Son of God" or "Son of the Lord," to fill out the verse.

Mark's introduction could lead an ancient audience to expect a speech in praise of Jesus as Messiah or Son of God. Or they might expect an account of his great deeds such as one finds in inscriptions honoring the emperor. Neither a speech nor stories about deeds require a full biography, an account of the subject's ancestry, parents, education, and adult life. Whereas modern readers often look for problematic aspects of an individual's character in biographies, ancient readers anticipate idealized portraits of famous persons. Those familiar with Jewish Scriptures might compare this account of Jesus Messiah with depictions of famous figures like Abraham, Joseph, Moses, or Elijah. Some elements of ancient literary biography are not found in our Gospels. The author does not address the reader except in Luke's preface (Luke 1:1-4). Nor do the Evangelists defend evaluative judgments about their hero's deeds or teaching.

Should the Gospels be treated as a subcategory of the ancient literary genre "life" (Gk. *bios*)? Differences from other examples of the genre might be attributed to antecedents in oral proclamation or models in Jewish Scripture. Some scholars reject this solution. They either seek other examples in ancient narrative or treat the literary genre of the Gospels as *sui generis*. The pattern for subsequent Gospels was created by the first Evangelist who affixed a narrative containing deeds and sayings of Jesus to the passion account. Given the varied types of narrative in which lives of famous persons are recounted, it seems unnecessary to exclude the Gospels from the larger category of "life" or biography. Though modern readers value character development, the ancients assume that heroes exhibit a fixed character that embodies a philosopher's teaching or the values of a society.

Childhood stories demonstrate adult virtues. *Jubilees,* a second-century B.C.E. retelling of Genesis, has the teenage Abraham introduce an innovative plow design to save seed from being eaten by crows:

> And the seed time arrived for sowing in the land. And they all went out together so that they might guard their seed from the crows. And Abram went out . . . the lad was fourteen. . . . And he caused the cloud of crows to turn back seventy times in that day. . . . And his reputation was great in the land of Chaldea. . . . And they sowed their land and harvested in that year enough food.

3

> And in the first year of the fifth week, Abram taught those who were making the implements for oxen, the skilled carpenters. And they made implements above the ground facing the handle of the plow so that they might place seed upon it. And the seed would go down within it to the point of the plow, and it would be hidden in the earth. And therefore they were not afraid of the crows. (*Jubilees* 11.18-24, trans. O. Wintermute in *OTP* 2: 79)

Abraham first excels in the ordinary method of preserving the seed. He then displays unusual wisdom in devising a way to avoid the problem altogether. The latter falls in the realm of fiction. Farmers continued to spread seed from a basket and then plow it under.[1] Birds were an ever-present hazard, as Jesus' parable of the Sower indicates (Mark 4:3-8).

Philo (ca. 50 C.E.) describes the child Moses as more intelligent than teachers from both Egypt and the rest of the world:

> He did not conduct himself as a young child . . . but sought to hear and see whatever would benefit his soul. Teachers immediately came from different parts of the world. . . . But he repeatedly advanced beyond their abilities . . . and indeed he himself proposed problems that were difficult for them to solve. (*Life of Moses* 1.21, my translation)

Jesus demonstrates a similar ability to confound the wisest adults in Luke's tale of the twelve-year-old quizzing Torah experts (Luke 2:41-51). Jewish readers certainly knew that the tales of Abraham and Moses were not taken from Torah. Imaginative developments that expand on a subject's life are not inappropriate to retelling the biblical story. Just as Genesis 12 only introduces Abraham when he leaves his ancestral land to follow the Lord, Mark's Gospel opens the story of Jesus when he leaves Nazareth to begin his mission from God. Both Luke and Matthew provide additional stories which indicate that Jesus was prepared for that activity from birth.

Biographical narratives about famous philosophers exhibit other features comparable to the Gospels. Some contain letters or other summaries which present basic teachings of the philosopher, as in Diogenes Laertius's life of Epicurus:

---

1. See Philip J. King and Lawrence E. Stager, *Life in Biblical Israel* (Louisville: Westminster John Knox, 2001) 88, 93.

I will attempt to lay out his opinions in those works [a list of Epicurus' books] by quoting three of his letters which epitomize his whole philosophy. (Diogenes Laertius, *Lives* 10.28)

Epicurus to Menoeceus, greetings. The young person should not delay philosophizing, nor should someone who is old become tired of philosophizing. For it is never too early or too late to have a healthy soul. (10.122)

Diogenes concludes his account of Epicurus with a famous collection of maxims attributed to the philosopher. Either Epicurus, himself, or a follower had compiled a list of forty short sayings. These maxims may have been memorized by those engaged in philosophy to achieve happiness, for example:

2. Death is nothing for us, for when the body has dissolved, it has no sensations. And what has no feeling it is of no concern to us.

8. No pleasure is evil by itself, but the things that produce certain pleasures bring with them troubles many times worse than the pleasures. (10.139-54)

Episodes in the life of a philosopher or his manner of death also illustrated his message. Philosophers associated with the Cynic school were famous for poking fun at the pretensions of other philosophers. By training themselves to live without possessions, fine food, or social honors, these philosophers scorned the absurd behavior of most humans. They possessed as little as possible and wandered about preaching. Jesus' sayings on the homelessness of his disciples (Luke 9:57-62) might have reminded readers of the Cynic way of life. The conversion of a rich, young man, Crates, to Cynic philosophy provides other parallels to radical conversions in the gospel stories:

Antisthenes in his book, *Successions*, says that he [= Crates] was first inclined toward the Cynic philosophy when he saw Telephus in some tragedy carrying a small basket and being completely miserable. So he turned his property into cash — for he was from a prominent family. Then he distributed the proceeds, about 200 talents, among his fellow citizens. . . . Often some of his relatives would visit to try and get him to change his mind. He used to drive them away with his staff. He remained determined. (Diogenes Laertius, *Lives* 6.87-88)

5

Jesus' own disciples gave up their family ties and occupations to follow him (Mark 1:16-20). However, another rich young man is no Crates. He refuses to dispose of his property in order to follow Jesus (Mark 10:17-22). Crates' relatives failed to win him back from living and teaching philosophy. Jesus' relatives make a similar attempt (Mark 3:21-22, 31-35). Crates ends the encounter by using his staff, a Cynic trademark, to chase family away. Jesus' family cannot get near him because of the crowds. He resolves the situation by redefining family. The incident concludes with a saying which could stand on its own as a maxim: "Whoever does the will of God is my brother and sister and mother" (Mark 3:35).

If Jesus' teaching redefines what it means to "do the will of God" (Matt 6:10), then Jesus' death provides the culminating example of that message as one would expect. Jesus meets Peter's objection to a suffering Messiah by insisting that the cross is God's plan (Mark 8:33). He warns his followers that they too must suffer (Mark 8:34-37; Matt 5:11-12). Jesus' prayer in Gethsemane exemplifies appropriate submission to the will of God (Mark 14:35-36). Jesus' silence before those who taunt him by recalling the miraculous powers at work in his ministry (Mark 15:31b; Matt 27:41-43; Luke 23:35) shows the reader that he remains resolute.

Each Evangelist presents the story of those who taunt Jesus somewhat differently.[2] Mark has bystanders employ false accusations from the proceeding before the Sanhedrin, a supposed claim on Jesus' part that he will destroy the Temple and raise it in three days (Mark 14:57-59; 15:28-29). Only the high priests and scribes refer to Jesus having saved others (15:31b). Those crucified with him join in the mockery (v. 32c). Luke has the people watching, but only the high priests, the soldiers, and one of the two crucified with Jesus engage in mockery. The other crucified criminal rebukes his fellow, appeals to Jesus, and receives a promise of salvation (Luke 23:35-43). Luke's tightly scripted narration demonstrates the saving power of Jesus' death. Matthew adds an echo of Wis 2:17-18 to the end of his account (Matt 27:43). The high priests have become the wicked who kill the Righteous One because they find his very presence obnoxious. The mockery itself has a scriptural antecedent in Ps 22:8-9. Such details are invisible to readers unfamiliar with the Bible, but for believers they demonstrate that Jesus' death is part of God's plan for salvation.

---

2. For a detailed analysis of the passion narrative, see Raymond E. Brown, *The Death of the Messiah: From Gethsemane to the Grave* (New York: Doubleday, 1994) 982-1030.

Such allusions cannot serve as evidence for the disinterested reader even when the authority of Scripture is invoked to support the Evangelist's understanding of Jesus as in the presentation of Jesus as Son of David (Luke 20:41-44). They create additional difficulties for historians. Modern investigative history would tag details in the Gospels that seem to be fitted to passages from the prophets or Psalms as fabricated or at least uncertain. Since we lack records or firsthand testimonies about exactly what happened during Jesus' passion, historians must piece together bits of information from similar situations and look for the narrative and theological interests of each Evangelist. Raymond Brown exhibits a suitably cautious approach to the scene of Jesus being mocked by those crucified with him:

> There is no convincing reason to reject the assertion of the four evangelists that there were others crucified with Jesus, and it is not impossible that crude criminals would have expressed contempt for Jesus' religious pretensions. Yet Mark/Matt assign no direct words to this reviling of Jesus, and Luke 23:39 has one of the hanged wrongdoers use virtually the same words that appeared in the first and second mockeries. Surely then there was no precise memory about this reviling of Jesus and the dominant interest was to show the just maltreated by the unjust.[3]

Just as we argue about what is a plausible historical scenario, the Evangelists employed their knowledge of Scripture to supplement traditions about Jesus' life and death. A life of God's Messiah would be expected to conform to biblical patterns. It need not have the same elements as the life of a great statesman, an emperor, or a philosopher.

Echoes of Scripture serve the same function as the evaluations of the subject that one finds in other ancient biographies. Accounts of an emperor's death can be scripted according to the author's evaluation of him. Suetonius depicts the aged Augustus taking care of his appearance, then saying farewell to friends, and asking after a sick daughter and, just before death, his wife, Livia (Suetonius, *Augustus* 99). A brief moment of terror is reinterpreted by the historian:

> The only sign that his wits were wandering, just before he died, was his sudden cry of terror: "Forty young men are carrying me off!" But even

3. Brown, *Death*, 1028.

7

this may be read as a prophecy rather than a delusion because forty Praetorians were to form the guard of honor that conveyed him to his lying in state.[4]

Vespasian, depicted as a wit who could use a good line to deflect criticism, has an exit line for his own death: "I must be turning into a god" (Suetonius, *Vespasian* 23). Nero, by contrast, becomes increasingly confused, indecisive, and too cowardly even to commit suicide properly (Suetonius, *Nero* 47-49). Suetonius is the only source for the elaborate tale of Nero's last hours. The emperor's public self-display in the year prior to the revolt depicts what a recent biographer calls "an ever more resplendent aura of most unwarlike military glory . . . the celebration of art and athletics with the celebration of war, . . . a spectacle presented in a city turned for a day into a theater."[5] It is hardly surprising that this atypical Roman would not die with the nobility befitting an emperor. Suetonius has decked out the dry facts of Nero's end with a drama of panic, flight, and ignoble death. Only the slightest respect is accorded the emperor. His head was not severed from the corpse for public display.

Even though the death of a Jewish hero such as Moses was set down in Scripture (Deuteronomy 34), later Jewish writers supplemented its sparse details. Philo of Alexandria suggests that as Moses was on the point of death, God transformed his soul and body into a single, pure being of mind. Moses' burial place was unknown because God exalted him into heaven — the appropriate end for one who was "king, lawgiver, high priest, and prophet" (Philo, *Moses* 2.288-91). In the first-century *Testament of Moses,* Moses is described as "that sacred spirit, worthy of the Lord, manifold and incomprehensible, master of leaders, faithful in all things, the divine prophet for the whole earth, the perfect teacher in the world" (11:16).[6] Alan Segal concludes that by the first century Moses was widely thought to have been enthroned above the angels, as close to being deified as possible for any Jewish figure.[7]

An ancient biography could thus conclude with a death scene that

---

4. Suetonius, *The Twelve Caesars,* tr. Robert Graves, revised Michael Grant (Baltimore: Penguin, 1979) 110.

5. Edward Champlin, *Nero* (Cambridge: Harvard University Press, 2003) 234.

6. J. Priest, "Testament of Moses," in *OTP* 1:933-34.

7. Alan F. Segal, *Life after Death: A History of the Afterlife in Western Religion* (New York: Doubleday, 2004) 510-11.

provides a summary evaluation of the subject's life. Nero's disgraceful exit reflects the end of the Julio-Claudian line and stands in sharp contrast to the Roman nobility of Augustus. Moses, a friend of God, not only has the attributes of one who has founded a great nation, he remains closer to God than any other human. Vespasian appears to mock the customary divine honors conferred upon a deceased emperor. His penchant for the humorous may have served him well at life's end, but it seems a bit short of the noble *gravitas* in the story of Augustus. From a very different perspective Philo depicts a Moses in process of transfiguration at life's end.

The ancient biography is much less complex than its modern counterpart. Destiny is often conferred by god(s) at birth. A person's achievements mirror those virtues celebrated as fixed in one's character. Individuals do not create themselves and their public life stories as in modern versions of self-fashioning. Plutarch's parallel lives of famous Greeks and Romans highlight character while Suetonius shows an eclectic interest in anecdotes about his subjects.[8]

Would an ancient reader have considered the Gospels to be biographical narratives? An outsider accustomed to more stylized, literary treatments accorded such famous figures as Augustus or Moses might have hesitated to think an obscure Jew executed by a Roman prefect had done anything worth recording. He would appear to be a figure popular with the masses thanks to an ability to delude them with magic or to needle public authorities much like Cynic philosophers. Without an appreciation for the Jewish Scriptures and hopes for salvation that the Evangelists find fulfilled in Jesus, the importance given Jesus would not be as evident as it is to believers.

Only two of the Gospels, Matthew and Luke, begin with the family and birth of their subject. John 1:1-18 replaces the biographical family origins with Jesus' divine origin as the Word sent from the Father. Though one eventually learns in Mark that Jesus' family origins are obscure and even an obstacle (e.g., Mark 3:20-21, 31-35; 6:1-6a), that narrative opens as he emerges on the public stage.

The Gospels are also thin on chronology. Luke remedies that gap in his sources by pegging Jesus' birth to the Roman history of the region

8. Simon Swain, "Biography and Biographic Representation in the Literature of the Roman Empire," in M. J. Edwards and Simon Swain, eds., *Portraits: Biographical Representation in the Greek and Latin Literature of the Roman Empire* (Oxford: Clarendon, 1997) 23-24.

(Luke 2:1-5)[9] whereas Matthew has the family return from Egypt to resettle in Galilee at the time of a different major event, the death of Herod the Great (Matt 2:19-23). Since Herod's son Archelaus ruled Judea until replaced by a Roman prefect in 6 C.E., Luke's Jesus could be a decade younger than Matthew's. A more secure tradition fixes Jesus' death under Pontius Pilate, who governed Judea from 26 to 36 C.E. Determining which years admit of a Passover feast beginning just before the Sabbath has its own difficulties. Either 30 or 33 C.E. can be defended. Brown concludes that in the former case Jesus was about 36 and had spent somewhat less than two years as a public figure. In the latter, Jesus was about 40 and had been active for some four years.[10] In either case, the brevity of Jesus' public ministry does not require a more detailed coordination with events on the larger historical stage.[11]

The brevity of Jesus' career and the insignificance of his family origins did not provide much scope for the author of a life. Without the story of what came after his disciples discovered that Jesus, not Moses, had been raised, transfigured, and exalted at the right hand of God, there would have been no reason for anyone to compose a biography. Jesus of Nazareth would have rated no more than a brief notice such as John the Baptist receives in Josephus's history (*Antiquities* 18.116-19). The persistent scholarly debate over whether the Gospels should be considered a subcategory of the biography genre often focuses on which ancient texts are used to define the category rather than on the short period of time during which Jesus was active as a public figure. Some scholars prefer to see the Gospels as biographic narrative or encomium formulated to defend Christian beliefs.[12] Even more elaborate theories have been proposed that push the Synoptic

9. Luke also gives a standard dating formula for the beginning of John the Baptist's activity, the fifteenth year of the reign of Tiberius Caesar, possibly August-September of 28-29 C.E. (Brown, *Death*, 1374).

10. Brown, *Death*, 1374-76.

11. Raymond Brown argues that scholars mistakenly attribute the sort of turmoil associated with the death of Herod the Great or the period after the brief rule of Agrippa (41-44 C.E.) to the period of Jesus' ministry. In fact Pilate's extended term of office appears to have been quite uneventful from the Roman point of view (*Death*, 677-79).

12. See M. J. Edwards, "Epilogue: Biography and the Biographic," in Edwards and Swain, eds., *Portraits*, 227-33. Edwards insists that once the non-canonical Gospel literature is included in the mix, it is evident that Gospels are not biographies (p. 230). He employs a tightly restricted group of texts in defining what counts as a biography in the ancient context.

Gospels closer to Jewish fictional works, in which biblical figures are presented in roles similar to those of heroes in Hellenistic novels, than to history or biography.[13]

Such proposals are less persuasive than the view that the canonical Gospels are intended as a type of biography or biographic narrative. They do not fit the mold of more developed literary examples for two reasons. First, the Gospel authors and audiences are attuned to the biographical elements in the Jewish Scriptures. Hence the significance of a subject's life in God's plan of salvation is central to the story. Second, the public career of Jesus of Nazareth was very short. Hence the account of his death and resurrection comes to dominate the story in a way that is not typical of other biographies.

Whereas the more erudite Greco-Roman historian or biographer may identify himself, the sources used and even his own evaluation of divergent reports about an incident, the Evangelists do not do so. Even Luke, whose use of a prologue and chronological markers brings his Gospel closer to Greco-Roman biography, never identifies himself directly or speaks to the reader in the first person. Burridge rightly insists that authors and audiences bring expectations about the genre of a work to their understanding of it. The Gospels employ Jesus' teachings and deeds in order to explain the Christian faith, which their readers share. Like other lives, the Gospels focus on an individual subject, Jesus of Nazareth. They provide a picture of who Jesus is.[14] They are not designed to present the doctrines of a philosophical school or to provide entertainment as a novel might.

Gospels and Apostles — A Key Combination

Since the Evangelists remain in the background as anonymous narrators, their works provide no direct evidence of authorship. By the middle of the second century C.E. Justin Martyr refers to the "memoirs" of the apostles as Gospels (1 *Apology* 66). However, he provides no titles and little information about their content. He wishes to demonstrate that the eucharistic formula is based on reliable tradition and that alleged parallels in other

13. Michael E. Vines, *The Problem of Markan Genre: The Gospel of Mark and the Jewish Novel* (Leiden: Brill, 2002).

14. Burridge, "About People, by People, for People," 120-27.

cultic meals are demonic imitations of the truth. Justin next describes the activities of Christians, who gather on Sunday, the day of Jesus' resurrection. Their worship includes reading "the memoirs of the apostles or the writings of the prophets" (*1 Apology* 67). He uses such phrases as "the Gospels," "his words, when he said" or "the memoirs of the apostles" (*Dialogue* 100) to introduce words of Jesus or claims about him. One might infer that the "memoirs" in which sayings of Jesus are recorded constitute a single book, since Justin cites Matt 4:9-10 as recorded in the memoirs and, shortly after, Luke 23:42, 44 as "in the memoirs which I say were drawn up by his apostles and those who followed them" (*Dialogue* 103). However, the reference to disciples of the apostles suggests that more than one volume is in play.[15] How many memoirs Justin knows and who the authors were said to be remain unclear.

Justin's remarks show that he considers the Gospels to be such apostolic memoirs. His references to events in the passion narrative and to Jesus' baptism as attested by those sources include Matthew, Luke, and probably Mark. Whether Justin knew John's Gospel as part of this group remains contested.[16] Justin's generic way of speaking about the authorship of his Gospel collection remains puzzling. He does not preface citations with the kind of name and title formula, "from the Gospel according to," that Christians associate with liturgical proclamation. When Justin refers to the vision of the millennium and universal judgment in Revelation, he gives the name of the prophet, "John, one of the apostles of Christ" (*Dialogue* 81.4), but does not speak of John as author of a book containing those prophecies. Thus it appears that the emphasis on recorded apostolic memoirs served to guarantee the reliability of Christian traditions about Jesus. Concern for identifying the author of each individual Gospel was not as pressing.

The situation has changed with Irenaeus, writing a generation later (ca. 180). The Gospels are Scripture along with the prophets (*Adv. Haer.*

---

15. See Graham N. Stanton, *Jesus and the Gospel* (Cambridge: Cambridge University Press, 2004) 100.

16. Stanton (*Jesus,* 100-102) argues for the affirmative. He does not think Justin used any apocryphal Gospels or written sayings collections. An even more vigorous defense of the view that, though there are no explicit citations of John in Justin, Justin depends on John for his christology and considers it one of the apostolic memoirs suitable for reading and exposition on Sunday can be found in Charles E. Hill, *The Johannine Corpus in the Early Church* (Oxford: Oxford University Press, 2004) 312-42.

2.27.2), though Irenaeus rarely uses the phrase "Scripture says. . ." to introduce a saying of Jesus.[17] He justifies the fact that there are four Gospels, neither fewer nor more, by appeal to quaternity in cosmic structure (*Adv. Haer.* 3.11.8-12). By Irenaeus's time the identities have been established for the authors of the Gospels:

> . . . and the Lord Himself handing down to His disciples, that He, the Father, is the only God and Lord, . . . it is incumbent on us to follow, if we are their disciples indeed, their testimonies to this effect. For Matthew the apostle — knowing one and the same God . . . and Luke likewise. Then again Matthew. . . . (*Adv. Haer.* 3.9.1-2)

> Luke also, the follower and disciple of the apostles, referring to Zacharias and Elizabeth. . . . (3.10.1)

> Wherefore also Mark, the interpreter and follower of Peter, does commence his Gospel narrative: "The beginning of the Gospel of Jesus Christ. . . ." (3.10.5).

> John, the disciple of the Lord, preaches this faith, and seeks by the proclamation of the Gospel, to remove that error which by Cerinthus had been disseminated. . . . (3.11.1)

Irenaeus counters the theological innovations of his Gnostic opponents by quoting the explicit testimony of four reliable witnesses. Jesus did not proclaim a different God and Father from the one known in the Hebrew Scriptures. Two of the witnesses are apostles, Matthew and John. Two are followers of the apostles, Mark and Luke. In short, by the time Irenaeus writes, Christians routinely refer to known disciples of Jesus or their followers as the Evangelists.

During the second century stories about the composition of each Gospel supported these identifications. Irenaeus employs this tradition in refuting Gnostic claims to possess secret traditions received from the risen Lord that are not found in the four Gospels (*Adv. Haer.* 3.1.1). Since his opponents rely on esoteric, post-resurrection tradition, Irenaeus points out that the apostles did not begin their public preaching until they had received the Spirit at Pentecost. They waited even longer before committing

---

17. Stanton, *Jesus*, 106.

their teaching to writing. Therefore one cannot suspect them of being deficient in knowledge. Each author speaks to a different audience and area of the early Christian mission:

> Matthew also issued a written Gospel among the Hebrews in their own dialect while Peter and Paul were preaching at Rome and laying the foundations of the Church. After their departure, Mark, the disciple and interpreter of Peter, did also hand down to us in writing what had been preached by Peter. Luke also, the companion of Paul, recorded in a book the Gospel preached by him. Afterwards, John the disciple of the Lord, who also had leaned upon His breast, did himself publish a Gospel during his residence at Ephesus in Asia. (*Adv. Haer.* 3.1.1)

This neat chronological and geographical pattern fits into the next peg in Irenaeus's argument. The apostolic succession of bishops in major sees guarantees the truth of what is taught in the churches (3.3.1).

The fourth-century church historian Eusebius collects several variants of these traditions about the Evangelists, including the text from Irenaeus (*Hist. Eccl.* 5.8.2-4).[18] Matthew is consistently described as composed in Hebrew for Jewish Christians. At one point, Eusebius suggests that Matthew composed his Gospel in Hebrew for those to whom he had been preaching when he was about to depart for elsewhere (3.24.5-6). "Matthew collected the oracles in the Hebrew dialect and each one interpreted them as well as he could" (3.39.14). Origen's version of the Matthew tradition refers to the story of the tax-collector's call to be a disciple in Matt 9:9 (6.25.4). Since Luke is depicted as the companion of Paul who wrote down Paul's gospel for Gentiles, the name must have been taken from the Pauline letter tradition (Col 4:14; 2 Tim 4:11: "Luke alone is with me"). Origen derives the special relationship between Peter and Mark's Gospel from the reference to Mark in 1 Pet 5:13 (6.25.5). While the Origen tradition asserts that Mark wrote in accord with Peter's instructions, Eusebius cites other versions which tell a different story. Irenaeus, as we have seen, thought that Mark wrote after the deaths of Peter and Paul in Rome. Eusebius cites a tradition which claimed that those who had heard Peter were dissatisfied with "a single hearing" or "unwritten teaching of the divine proclamation" and so persuaded Mark to provide a written text.

18. See Philip Sellew, "Eusebius and the Gospels," in Harold Attridge and Gohei Hata, eds., *Eusebius, Christianity, and Judaism* (Studia Post-Biblica 42; Leiden: Brill, 1992) 110-38.

Peter allegedly approved it for use in the churches (2.15.1-2). Though Eusebius attributes this tradition to both Clement of Alexandria and Papias, it does not match his citations from those authors. Papias, Eusebius's earliest source on the origins of the Gospels, is said to have derived his information from "the elder," but he says nothing about apostolic ratification (3.39.15). Clement of Alexandria explicitly denies that Peter approved the Gospel (6.14.7).[19]

These examples indicate that by the mid-second century it was no longer sufficient to set apostolic memoirs alongside the prophets. The apostolic authority of the Gospels read and studied in the church had to be firmly established. Apostolic authorship was supplemented with an account of the circumstances that produced each Gospel. As churches possessed more than one written Gospel, they needed titles to distinguish them. The title format "Gospel according to . . ." appears in late-second-century material.[20] It is not always possible to tell whether Irenaeus intends the phrase "in the G/gospel" to refer to one of the canonical Gospels, to the single gospel message which has been given four written expressions, or to oral proclamation that is grounded in apostolic succession.[21] The Evangelists themselves had no need to press their credentials as individual authors. Audiences would recognize the correspondence between the Gospel being read and what was being preached in the churches, as Luke's preface suggests.[22] The geographical spread of Christianity, decreasing availability of eyewitness oral traditions and diversity among teachers generated an explosion of books in the second century, which required clarification concerning the Gospels and their authors. The majority of

---

19. Sellew, "Eusebius," 116-17.

20. As in P[66] and P[75]; Harry Gamble, *Books and Readers in the Early Church* (New Haven: Yale University Press, 1995) 153-54. Annette Yoshiko Reed, "ΕΥΑΓΓΕΛΙΟΝ: Orality, Textuality, and the Christian Truth in Irenaeus' *Adversus Haereses*," *VC* 56 (2002) 20, n. 33, observes that except when contrasting canonical Gospels with those deemed heretical, Irenaeus often introduces a quotation with "the one according to . . ." rather than "the Gospel according to." Thus Irenaeus suggests that there is a single Gospel that has been presented by four different authors.

21. Reed, "ΕΥΑΓΓΕΛΙΟΝ," 30-38, 46.

22. On the importance of a relatively stable oral tradition concerning Jesus' life and teaching in the four decades between the death of Jesus and the composition of the Synoptic Gospels see Martin Hengel, "Eye-Witness Memory and the Writing of the Gospels: Form Criticism, Community Tradition and the Authority of the Authors," in Bockmuehl and Hagner, *The Written Gospel*, 70-96.

early Gospel manuscripts only contain a single work. A title provided not only a clue to the content of a work but also association with a revered apostle, which indicated the antiquity and truth of its tradition.

The Eusebius traditions also show that second-century Christians had little information about how the Gospels originated. They acknowledge that the apostles spread the message through oral proclamation, the original meaning of the word "gospel." The written texts are secondary to that endeavor. There was considerable uncertainty even in the second century whether the apostles whose teaching was set down by others initiated the process or approved the final product. Mark and Luke could have responded to demands for a written account after the apostles had died. Similarly the tradition which Eusebius reports concerning Matthew, a composition in "their language (Hebrew)," does not correspond to the Greek Gospel to which his name is attached. Yet all later authors including those who report the tradition of an Aramaic (Hebrew) Matthew cite the Gospel only in Greek. Eusebius' account also infers that Matthew's impending departure (death?) led him to leave a written text behind for Jewish Christians.

The ancient sources are uncertain about the chronological order in which the Gospels were composed. Some assume that Matthew's Hebrew Gospel would have been the first, others that Mark's record of Peter's teaching prior to the apostle's death was the initial Gospel. Each written Gospel emerges in a different region, so the question of temporal priority is not one of literary influence of one on the other. The modern argument for the chronological priority of Mark argues from comparative analysis of the texts, a difficult task in a manuscript culture. For Irenaeus, as we have seen, the key point is not such chronological or literary relationships but the fact that the four apostolic Gospel books attest to a single truth preached by the apostles and handed on to their successors. While most scholars today would agree that Mark appears to be our earliest written Gospel, some still push as earlier Gospels works for which there are no ancient manuscript remains such as an Aramaic Matthew or a sayings collection (Q), promoted as "the Q Gospel." The former is popular among very conservative Christians, the latter among those liberal believers who imagine Jesus as a teacher of universal wisdom. We will have more to say about these views later.

Mark's Innovation: Framing the Ministry and the Passion

Paul's letters written in the 50s C.E. show that evangelization required telling the story of Jesus. Jesus' death on the cross figured prominently in Paul's own preaching (e.g., Gal 3:1; 1 Cor 2:1-2) as did testimony to his resurrection (1 Thess 1:10; 1 Cor 15:3-5). The communal meal remembered Jesus' words at his last meal with the disciples (1 Cor 11:23-26). Christians in Paul's churches were familiar with such prominent figures as Peter (Gal 1:18; 2:7-14; 1 Cor 9:5), James, the Lord's brother, and John (Gal 1:19; 2:9). They had also heard of Jesus' teaching, probably in the form of brief stories and sayings (e.g. 1 Thess 4:15; 1 Cor 7:10).

Our shortest written record, Mark's Gospel, combines stories of Jesus' deeds and teaching with a narrative about his last days and death in Jerusalem. The story it tells can be performed by an actor or storyteller in an evening. Second-century Christians imagined Mark fixing familiar oral traditions in writing. Some modern scholars think that his text reflects a tradition of Christian storytelling. Writing does not spell the end of oral tradition in the ancient world. A text may even serve as the script which generates further oral retelling of its story. Mark writes in a choppy style that often jumps from one episode to the next. There are sharp edges to his characters and elements of conflict between Jesus and his disciples not found in the other Gospels. Some of these features may enhance the powerful impression that the Gospel makes on an audience when it is performed orally.[23]

Scholars disagree over whether we can discern earlier written sources in Mark. A continuous account of Jesus' passion and death would seem to be the most likely candidate for such a pre-Markan written tradition. However, reconstructions of such a passion account have not converged toward a consensus. Raymond Brown rejects the whole enterprise in his study of the passion.[24] Smaller collections of Jesus material may have included miracles, parables, stories of Jesus' controversies with opponents, and the apocalyptic prophecies in Mark 13. These could have circulated as open-ended notebook collections carried by traveling missionaries.

23. See Joanna Dewey, "The Survival of Mark's Gospel: A Good Story?" *JBL* 123 (2004) 495-507.

24. Brown, *Death*, 53-57; also see Appendix IX by Marion L. Soards, "The Question of a Premarkan Passion Narrative," pp. 1492-1524.

Mark establishes Jesus' extraordinary power as miracle worker and teacher at the beginning of his story. Jesus cannot go anywhere in public without being pressed by crowds from all over. Midway through the story, Jesus' closest disciples learn his identity as Messiah (Mark 8:27-30) and Son of God (9:2-8). At that point, Jesus predicts his impending suffering and death in Jerusalem (8:31-33, repeated at 9:30-32; 10:32-34). The dramatic arc of the story comes into focus as Jesus' disciples resist the way of the cross. Although Jesus predicts his resurrection, the Gospel originally ended with women fleeing from the empty tomb in fear (16:1-8a). Matthew and Luke each supplement the empty tomb story with other resurrection traditions. The women will no longer flee in fear and silence. They report to Jesus' disciples as instructed. Eventually Christian scribes formulated additional endings for Mark's Gospel as well.

Matthew and Luke Improve on the Model

As we have seen, Irenaeus used the close similarities among the Gospels as evidence against those like the Valentinians who claimed that Jesus had given secret teachings to select disciples. He insisted that there was only one gospel taught by all the apostles. In other words, the unity of the Gospels lies at the level of apostolic preaching, not in their dependence on common written sources. By the fourth century it was evident to St. Augustine that there must have been a literary relationship between Matthew and Mark. By that time Matthew had come to dominate early Christian worship and teaching.[25] So Augustine concluded that Matthew was prior to Mark. Mark provided nothing more than a condensed version of Matthew (*De consensu evangelistarum* 1.2; PL 34:1044). This view of Mark ensured that it would remain peripheral reading among Christians to the end of the eighteenth century.[26]

In the past century and a half most scholars have come to think that Augustine got the relationship between the two Gospels backward. Mark created the basic pattern for a life of Jesus, an account of the public ministry followed by a narrative of the passion. This innovation was so popular that

25. E. Massaux, *The Influence of the Gospel of Matthew on Christian Literature before Saint Irenaeus*, ed. A. J. Bellinzoni (Macon: Mercer University Press, 1993).
26. Francis J. Moloney, *The Gospel of Mark* (Peabody: Hendrickson, 2002) 1.

within two decades other Evangelists used Mark as the basis for revised versions of the story. Such reuse of earlier material was quite normal. It occurs throughout the biblical material. The Chronicler reshaped material from Kings. The Greek versions of parts of the Hebrew Bible such as the Psalter and Daniel are longer than the canonical Hebrew text. Writings which scholars refer to as "rewritten Bible" that diverge even further from the Hebrew Bible were found among the Dead Sea Scrolls. Luke's preface (Luke 1:1-4) states that the Evangelist used earlier written work to compose his Gospel.

Since it is possible to find ancient examples for both expansion and abbreviation of a source text, Augustine's guess that Mark abbreviated Matthew was not foolish.[27] But other known abbreviations are for works that ran to several volumes. Furthermore, Mark's text often contains awkward Greek, repetitions, misquotations, and misunderstandings of Jewish customs that Matthew or Luke get right. It is not impossible to assume that Mark took a clearer and better written text and made a mess of it, but it is simpler to assume that Mark provided the initial model. With that in hand the other Evangelists sought to produce better versions. The relative neglect of Mark from the third through the eighteenth centuries shows that Matthew and Luke succeeded in that task.

Some scholars have suggested filtering our earliest Gospel manuscripts to see what they tell us about Christian use of Gospels in the second and third centuries.[28] Seven papyri of Matthew were probably written before the mid-second century. On the basis of the data regarding these papyri presented in the table on p. 20, Stanton proposes revising the standard view that the Gospels were copied by scribes used to dashing off business and legal documents, products of a community that was too poor to afford better. Most of these scribes could write in a hand suited to literary works.[29]

---

27. A minority among scholars continues to come up with ingenious arguments in favor of the priority of Matthew or even to argue that Mark was abbreviating both Matthew and Luke. They can show that the actual process of composition, scribal alteration, and cross influence was more complex than the basic theory would suggest. But these theories have not proven helpful in reading and analysis of the Synoptic Gospels as we have them. Readers curious about the current debate from an evangelical point of view can read the essays in David Alan Black and David R. Beck, eds., *Rethinking the Synoptic Problem* (Grand Rapids: Baker Academic, 2001).

28. Stanton, *Jesus,* pp. 192-206.

29. Stanton, *Jesus,* pp. 197-200. Most of the papyri to which Stanton refers were published in 1997 to 1998.

Papyrus	Contents	Comments
P¹	Matt 1:1-9, 14-20	midway between handwriting of everyday business (documentary) and that of a good book copyist
P⁴⁵	parts of the final chapters of Matt: 20:24-32; 21:13-19; 25:41–26:39; also parts of Mark, Luke, John, and Acts	written by a competent scribe
P⁵³	small fragment, parts of Matt 26:29-40	
P⁶⁴ + P⁶⁷	fragments of Matthew 3, 5 and 26 from the same codex as P⁴, which contains extensive fragments of Luke 1, 3, and 5	a four-Gospel codex in two columns per page, written in a good book hand; format suggests liturgical use; would have been expensive
P⁷⁷	small fragment of Matt 23:30-39	delicate handwriting, some evidence for chapter division, punctuation, and breathing
P¹⁰³	small fragment of Matthew 13 and 14	elegant handwriting, very similar to P⁷⁷
P¹⁰⁴	small fragment of Matthew 21	elegant handwriting

Such carefully made copies suggest that by the late second century Gospels were not considered popular, second-rank writings or handbooks for private use by teachers. The evidences for expensive, well-made codices are signs that the Gospels had an authoritative public function. Stanton finds that remains of John's Gospel, ten examples from the same period, show features similar to those of Matthew.

The situation with respect to Mark is much different. Only one text, a Chester Beatty codex that contained parts of all four Gospels and Acts (P⁴⁵), can be dated prior to the mid-third century. The other two papyrus copies of Mark are from the fourth (P[88]) and sixth (P[84]) centuries respectively. The five early papyrus copies of Luke put it well ahead of Mark, though well behind John and Matthew.[30] Of course, the distribution figures may change as papyri continue to be identified, dated, and published. However all known papyri show a similar pattern. Matthew and John are more frequently copied than Luke and Mark. So the material remains coincide with data based on early quotations or allusions. Stanton thinks that the second-century views on authorship of the Gospels are largely responsible for the statistical difference. Matthew and John are apostles, but Luke and Mark are merely followers of Paul and Peter respectively.[31]

We will analyze each of the Synoptic Gospels in later chapters. Even though Matthew's book is twice as long as Mark and Luke's nearly so, one can still discern a narrative skeleton that resembles Mark's Gospel. By adding material on Jesus' family and birth, Matthew and Luke have brought the story closer to what readers might have expected in a biography. Each also connects Jesus with historical figures of the time through the infancy stories. Mark 6:1-6a highlights the insignificance of Jesus' Galilean origins by depicting Nazareth as a place of disbelief. Matt 13:53-58 repeats the story in almost the same words. Slight changes in detail could be Matthew's way of clarifying or correcting the account. Jesus is "son of the carpenter" whose "mother is called Mary" (Matt 13:55), not "the carpenter, the son of Mary" (Mark 6:3). We may not be sensitive to such details, but Matthew's genealogy traces Jesus' claim to be the promised Davidic Messiah through Joseph (Matt 1:16). Mark asserts that Jesus could not do any miracle in Nazareth because of their disbelief and then remarks that he did heal a few people (Mark 6:5). Matthew drops the awkward retraction and simply says that Jesus did not do many miracles there because of their disbelief (Matt 13:58). At that point one might see Matthew acting as a good editor. He has expressed what Mark meant in simpler form.

A tradition about Jesus being rejected in Nazareth is seen in Luke's Gospel, but not in this form. Instead Luke has Jesus begin his public ministry in the Nazareth synagogue. He announces that he has come to fulfill the promise of Isaiah (61:1-2; 58:6). This speech, not Jesus' miracles, causes people to ask "Is this not the son of Joseph?" (Luke 4:22). Jesus then turns the crowd against him by referring to miracles that Elijah and Elisha

30. Stanton, *Jesus*, 200-203.
31. Stanton, *Jesus*, 204.

worked on behalf of persons who were not Israelites. The crowd's hostility is even stronger than that in the story told by Mark and Matthew. People want to throw Jesus off a cliff (Luke 4:29). Luke's talent as a master story-teller is on display throughout his work. Many of our most loved parables, the Good Samaritan, the Prodigal Son, the Rich Man and Lazarus, are found only in his Gospel.

This example highlights other techniques employed in fashioning new versions of Jesus' life on the Markan frame: shifting the order of events, substituting a different but related story, and increasing the density of scriptural allusions. Luke's preface mentions the need to reorder what the Evangelist found in his sources (Luke 1:3). Matthew and Luke both substitute the story of Jesus' testing in the wilderness (Matt 4:1-11; Luke 4:1-13) for Mark 1:12-13, which says nothing about how Satan tempted Jesus. Their new version includes dueling Scripture quotations. Thus Jesus emerges as the verbal master of Scripture before he ever steps into debate with the religious teachers of his day. Such debates with authorities are more prominent in Matthew and Luke than in Mark. Most of the additional material included in those Gospels involves Jesus teaching. Thus the revised temptation story provides a demonstration of an aspect of Jesus' ministry that Mark's version did not. Mark tells readers that Jesus teaches with an authority unlike that of the scribes (Mark 1:22) before giving any examples of his actual teaching.

When Matthew and Luke revise or supplement Mark, they are engaged in a natural process of filling out the story. Luke's preface explains that he intends to tell the story in a way that will provide a basis for the message about Jesus that is being preached. Matthew also has the needs of the Christian community in view. He gathers teaching material into five discourses. The first, a compendium of basic teachings known as the Sermon on the Mount (Matthew 5–7), is the best known. It is often printed and commented on as a separate work. The conclusion to that sermon warns a Christian audience not to be deceived by appearances. Some will claim to believe in Jesus but not put the teachings into practice. No one can expect salvation without following what Jesus teaches (Matt 7:21-23). Careful observations of the way in which each Evangelist tells the story of Jesus provide a valuable window into the faith of the first two Christian generations. Each Evangelist highlights those features of the tradition that are most important for his audience.

Note: Alternate Suggestions for Genre

We are convinced that Mark intended to compose a biographical narrative. The revisions made by Matthew and Luke indicate that they understood the Gospel to be such a life. Some scholars remain unconvinced. They have proposed other literary models as the basis for Mark's composition. Three suggestions frequently appear in books or popular media: apocalyptic historical monograph,[32] Jewish novel,[33] or a reverse imitation of Homer's epic tales.[34] Each of these hypotheses leads to the further conclusion that the Evangelists have no interest in representing historical persons or events as they might have occurred.

Both Daniel and Revelation refer to the persecution of God's faithful ones. Mark's readers must expect to suffer as Jesus does (Mark 4:16-17; 13:9-13). Mark 13:19 echoes Dan 12:1 LXX. In Daniel, the day of tribulation is predicted for the future. Mark makes a subtle shift. The great tribulation has never been seen *until now*. In other words, Mark expects his readers to recognize that they are now living in the last days.[35] Daniel's apocalyptic symbolism reflects historical events at the time of the Maccabean revolt. The Temple was destroyed, defiled by Antiochus with a pagan altar (Dan 9:26-27; 11:31-33; 12:11). Mark's Jesus predicts the impending destruction of the Temple (Mark 13:1-2). The "abomination" from Daniel is converted to a "he" (Mark 13:14), possibly referring to the zealot leader Eleazer, who employed the Temple as headquarters (Josephus, *War* 4.151-57, 182-83, 201, 388).[36]

The opening chapters of Mark have another feature typical of apocalyptic writings, conflict with the demonic. In this case, Jesus appears as an exorcist who has come to destroy the hold which Satan has over human life (Mark 3:22-30). His activity is not limited to Israel. Jesus drives out a demon with the symbolic name "Legion" (5:9) from a non-Jew as well (5:1-20). The 2,000 pigs driven off the cliff underline the magnitude of the evil

---

32. Adela Yarbro Collins, "Is Mark's Gospel a Life of Jesus? The Question of Genre," in A. Y. Collins, *The Beginning of the Gospel: Probings of Mark in Context* (Minneapolis: Fortress, 1992) 1-38.

33. Michael E. Vines, *The Problem of Markan Genre: The Gospel of Mark and the Jewish Novel* (Academia Biblica/Society of Biblical Literature 3; Leiden: Brill, 2002).

34. MacDonald, *Homeric Epics.*

35. Joel Marcus, *Mark 1–8* (Anchor Bible 27; New York: Doubleday, 1999) 29.

36. Marcus, *Mark,* 35.

forces arrayed against Jesus. Perhaps the name "legion" also reminded Mark's readers of their Roman overlords. Thus Jesus' victory has cosmic significance. All people in the region will be freed from the evil powers which hold them in bondage.

One might expect an apocalyptic prophecy to end on a note of triumph as both Daniel and Revelation do. How can Mark be treated as part of that literary genre when its narrative ends with frightened women fleeing the tomb? Still, the apocalyptic images and ideas in Mark provide some basis for referring to apocalyptic prophecy as the Evangelist's model.

The categories of "Jewish novel" and Homeric epic have less textual support. MacDonald admits that Mark never uses actual quotations from Homer's poetry, despite its popularity in ancient schooling. To support the proposal that Mark has deliberately inverted themes from the *Odyssey* one must paint with a broad brush. For example, MacDonald matches the whole story of Odysseus and Circe from *Odyssey* 10 to Mark 5:1-20, the story of the Gerasene demoniac. Circe turns Odysseus's men into swine. He forces her to free them, but later in the story they drown. MacDonald invokes the popular representations of the encounter between Odysseus and the cyclops Polyphemus in *Odyssey* 9 as a further parallel to the savage behavior of the man possessed by Legion.[37] Though an audience familiar with Homer might have detected bits of familiar story patterns, nothing in Mark requires Homer as its model. Closer parallels to the wording of Mark 5:1-20 can be found in the Greek Old Testament story of God delivering Israel from the Egyptians in Exod 14:1–15:22.[38]

Marianne Bonz has adopted the hypothesis that the Evangelists had popular retelling of ancient epics in mind.[39] She does not assume that Mark was based on Homer. Instead she proposes that Luke employed echoes of Virgil in recasting the traditional material he had inherited. Virgil's narrative is not employed as the basis for content or even explicit storylines, as in MacDonald's proposals for the use of Homer in Mark.

---

37. MacDonald, *Homeric Epics,* 66-72. For a detailed discussion of MacDonald's project, see Karl Olav Sandnes, "*Imitatio Homeri?* An Appraisal of Dennis R. MacDonald's 'Mimesis Criticism,'" *Journal of Biblical Literature* 124 (2005) 715-32. Sandnes points out that MacDonald's literary parallels are very subtle. Other ancient authors who engage in similar echoing of earlier texts combine such muted background echoes with more explicit announcements of the relationship.

38. Marcus, *Mark,* 349.

39. Bonz, *Past as Legacy.*

Rather, Bonz argues that Virgilian patterns shape the way in which Luke-Acts crafts a foundation story for the divinely guided mission of the Pauline churches. Techniques familiar from Homer and Virgil crop up in Luke's work such as the catalogue of nations in Acts 2:9-11, which is similar in length and structure to the catalogue of conquered peoples in *Aeneid* 8:722-38.[40] Both lists appear haphazard but serve as proleptic evidence of a divinely ordained mission. Where Virgil has a remnant escape Troy and merge with the Latin peoples to reestablish the ancient line, Luke has a Jewish remnant expand through its assimilation of Gentiles. The church represents the true spirit of Israel in a new people of God.[41]

Bonz argues that Luke did not compose a Gospel based on Mark's literary model and later decide to supplement it with Acts. His intent from the beginning was to present the founding epic of the Christian movement in two books.[42] She draws political conclusions from the cordial, even supportive Roman officials in Acts. Although Luke presents Jesus, not the emperor, as the true basis for world peace, the Evangelist is not hostile to the Roman order. Instead, he anticipates a transformation from within through the conversion of Roman authorities.[43] This suggestion ignores the civic realities of Roman religious life. A Roman official or members of the local elite were more likely to act as benefactors to temples, private associations, and even synagogues than to adopt religious beliefs that exclude Rome's divine protectors.

Another approach to the Gospel genre that also highlights literary imagination compares the Gospels to fictional narratives. Scholars pursue this line of argument on the grounds that Gospels and books of acts, whether canonical or apocryphal, fail to meet a number of basic criteria for biography or historiography. They do not cite sources, construct a consistent chronology, or emphasize eyewitness information. The authors do not identify themselves or inform readers of their reasons for engaging in study of the past.[44] Such statements about why persons acted as they did or about the chronological sequence of events can be found in works of fiction as well as history. Most scholarly studies of the Hellenistic novel have focused on the romantic novels, which recount the adventures of sepa-

40. Bonz, *Past as Legacy,* 108.
41. Bonz, *Past as Legacy,* 128.
42. Bonz, *Past as Legacy,* 154-55.
43. Bonz, *Past as Legacy,* 182-83.
44. Thomas, *The Acts of Peter,* 3.

rated lovers. Fictional accounts of historical figures such as Alexander the Great are more appropriate parallels to the Gospels. In a Jewish context, one can find Greek expansions of the stories of Esther and Daniel, the book of Tobit, or the tale of Joseph's marriage to a converted Egyptian woman in *Joseph and Aseneth.*[45]

However, for ancient readers the distinction between history or biography and fiction depends on whether the narrative reports events that are claimed to have actually happened. When one reads a tale of some Jewish hero or heroine from the past that has been expanded with novelistic features, one is in a different world from the Gospels. The Evangelists are providing an account of the life and teaching of an individual who was nearly their contemporary. The Christian readers to whom the Gospels are directed consider Jesus of Nazareth the most important figure in human history, greater than Abraham, Moses, or David. Nonbelievers might take a different view since neither Jesus nor his followers could boast any great achievements in the first half century. Such readers might have been inclined to consider the Gospels a peculiar bit of Jewish fiction, even if the Evangelists themselves were not inventing a fictional character.

Note: The Four-Gospel Canon

Luke's work comprised two books. The first we describe as a "Gospel" modeled on Mark. The second, Acts, serves as an account of the deeds of the apostles. Those scholars who prefer the fictional genres of epic or novel as models for Mark or Luke can find more analogies to such ancient fiction in Acts than in the Gospels. Once Christians began treating the four Gospels as a well-defined group, Acts was displaced from its position as Book Two of Luke's work. Had Luke-Acts been copied as though it were a single literary work, the discussion of its literary genre would have developed differently. By the end of the second century, Irenaeus defends the "four-Gospel collection" as authoritative apostolic teaching. He wishes to exclude two possibilities by finding a rationale for the number "four": a reduction in the number and the open-ended formulation of new Gospels such as he finds among Gnostic Christians (*Adv. Haer.* 3.11.8). We have

---

45. For a study of these writings, see Lawrence M. Wills, *The Jewish Novel in the Ancient World* (Ithaca: Cornell University Press, 1995).

seen that he stresses the unity of the gospel as apostolic witness to Christian faith. But he does not have to defend the group of four Gospels itself.

How did this collection come into general use? Two other bits of evidence show that it was well established around 180 C.E.: the Muratorian fragment[46] and the anti-Christian tract written by Celsus. Introductory comments on Matthew and Mark must have preceded the discussion of Luke and John in the Muratorian fragment, which is anxious to affirm that despite their differences, the Gospels display the same Spirit. Origen reports that Celsus sought to undermine the credibility of Christianity by appealing to the existence of differences among the Gospels. By changing the text "three or four or several times" Christians have tried to insulate themselves from criticism (Origen, *Contra Celsum* 2.27). Celsus is familiar with all four Gospels. It is possible to find papyrus codices that contained the four Gospels together from the late second century as well.[47] Thus scholars are reasonably certain that Irenaeus is not innovating when he refers to a fixed collection of four Gospels as evidence for apostolic teaching. He is referring to a phenomenon that was already well-established in the churches.

Tracing the origin and use of such a four-Gospel collection back into the earlier part of the second century depends on evidence whose significance is contested. Some scholars reject the early dating of 125 for the earliest John manuscript, P[52], but in any case one cannot tell if the codex from which it came contained a four-Gospel collection. Justin Martyr's reference to liturgical reading from the memoirs of the apostles would certainly have included Mark, Matthew, and Luke, since he quotes those Gospels. But scholars remain divided over whether or not his use of "Word" to refer to Jesus reflects familiarity with John's Gospel. Eusebius does not provide quotations from Papias's work on the sayings of the Lord that refer to Luke or John, so many scholars have argued that Papias did not know the four canonical Gospels as a fixed collection in the early second century.

To employ Papias as evidence for such an early collection, other

---

46. A number of scholars have insisted that this text is not from the second century as it claims but is a fourth-century composition. See G. A. Robbins, "The Muratorian Fragment," in *ABD* IV, 929. For a concise argument against the revisionist view, see Stanton, *Jesus*, 69.

47. Stanton, *Jesus*, 71-75, points to P[75] and the more elegantly produced codex, possibly for liturgical use, P[64] + P[67] + P[4].

scholars have turned to various anonymous traditions (e.g., *Adv. Haer.* 5.34.2) as taken from Papias's book.[48] Hill proposes that Eusebius has drawn on Papias for his more extended account of the impetus behind John's composition (*Hist. Eccl.* 3.24.5-13).[49] That suggestion would allow us to push the existence of a four-Gospel collection back to the first quarter of the second century. The passage in question is an extended paraphrase of a source which considers the Synoptics an established group prior to John setting down his tradition in writing. The theological agenda pursued by Eusebius's source is not one of commenting on the sayings or teaching of the Lord as Papias was said to have done. The source is, rather, defending the unanimity of the four-Gospel testimony in the face of apparent contradictions between the Johannine and Synoptic accounts of the origin of Jesus, Jesus' relationship to the Baptist, and the beginning of Jesus' ministry. This demonstration appears to have been provoked by a challenge to Irenaeus's theological view of the four-Gospel canon. The chronological solution proposed, that John is describing a period prior to the Baptist's imprisonment that the others omitted, is characteristic of Eusebius's solution to such difficulties. Therefore, attractive as Hill's proposal seems, it does not definitively prove that a four-Gospel canon had been adopted early in the second century.

The apologist Tatian might serve as evidence for use of a four-Gospel collection around the middle of the second century if his *Diatessaron,* a harmonized version of the four, can be linked to his years studying with Justin Martyr in Rome. However, many scholars think that he did not compose the *Diatessaron* until he had returned to Syria around 170. That dating would make Tatian's work contemporaneous with Irenaeus. For these scholars, Tatian's turn toward radical asceticism and production of this alternate Gospel were probably connected. Though he may not have lapsed into heretical Valentinian sectarianism, his concern to fix the truth of Christianity in a new Gospel form could represent a break with the pluralism of mid-second-century Christianity in Rome. The *Diatessaron* served the Syriac church as its authoritative Gospel until it was replaced by the four-Gospel canon in the fifth century, but no copies or extensive cita-

---

48. As part of his extensive argument against the view that John was avoided by second-century orthodox Christianity because of its Gnosticizing taint, see Hill, *Johannine Corpus*, 385-96.

49. Hill, *Johannine Corpus*, 386-87.

tions of the *Diatessaron* have come down to us.[50] However, the technique of the Gospel harmony differs from rewriting or composing a new Gospel such as one finds in the second-century *Gospel of Peter*. A Gospel harmony involves retaining the words of the original texts. Therefore, Tatian's project can be viewed as an indication that the four-Gospel canon was firmly established by mid-second century.

Tatian's title, the Greek expression *dia tessaron*, "by means of four," indicates that he intends to represent the four Gospels in his work, not to replace them. Some scholars have detected an additional fifth source, a Syriac version of the sayings collection known as the *Gospel of Thomas*.[51] However, that hypothesis is debatable.[52] Given the overlap between sayings material in *Gos. Thom.* and the Synoptic Gospels, Tatian might have employed a Syriac translation of Synoptic material. In any event, he seems to have included in his harmony as much detail as possible from each of the four Gospels.[53] Thus the *Diatessaron* represents an alternate way of preserving the traditional apostolic canon, not a challenge to its authority.

The familiar title "Gospel according to . . ." also implies that more than one Gospel was circulating in Christian churches. Second- and third-century scribes would attach the designation "Gospel" to a number of other writings from Gnostic circles which do not belong to the same genre as the four canonical Gospels.

Many important historical developments have been aided by changes in media. For the early Christians, use of the codex rather than the

---

50. Scholars have extracted *Diatessaron* variants of Jesus traditions from later authors and Gospel harmonies. Such identifications face the problem of assuming what one would like to prove, that Tatian had recast the material to foster an Encratite theology. Emily J. Hunt, *Christianity in the Second Century: The Case of Tatian* (London: Routledge, 2003) 145-50, concludes that there is no solid reason to identify a heretical, Encratite sect in Syriac Christianity. Asceticism was a prominent feature of Christian praxis in that region. If Tatian left a legacy there, it was as a Christian philosopher, not as an Encratite teacher (pp. 154-56). For a detailed discussion of the *Diatessaron*, see William L. Petersen. *Tatian's Diatessaron: Its Creation, Dissemination, Significance and History in Scholarship* (Supplements to *VC* 25; Leiden: Brill, 1994).

51. See below, pp. 67-72.

52. Petersen rejects the dependence of Tatian on *Gos. Thom.* (*Tatian's Diatessaron*, 298-99). He entertains the possibility that Tatian's teacher Justin Martyr employed a Jewish Christian "harmony" that did not contain John's Gospel (pp. 1-3, 27-31).

53. F. Gerald Downing, *Doing Things with Words in the First Christian Century* (JSNTSup 200; Sheffield: Sheffield Academic, 2000) 196.

scroll made it possible to combine four Gospels in a single volume. That fact alone may have contributed to the rapid adoption of a four-Gospel canon. It would not be necessary to select only one as the "true Gospel" or to adopt some harmonized version. Even when Matthew's Gospel had become the runaway best-seller in terms of use and citation, as happened by the third century, churches retained Gospel books that contained all four.

CHAPTER TWO

Books and Believers in Early Christianity

Christians are so familiar with the Bible as the center of both individual piety and communal worship that they find it difficult to imagine religious

---

Suggested Reading

Alexander, Loveday. "Ancient Book Production and the Circulation of the Gospels," in R. Bauckham, ed., *The Gospels for All Christians: Rethinking Gospel Audiences.* Grand Rapids: Eerdmans, 1998, pp. 71-105.

Bauckham, Richard. "For Whom Were the Gospels Written?" in Bauckham, ed., *The Gospels for All Christians,* pp. 9-48.

Ehrman, Bart D. *Misquoting Jesus: The Story Behind Who Changed the Bible and Why.* San Francisco: HarperSanFrancisco, 2005.

Gamble, Harry Y. *Books and Readers in the Early Church: A History of Early Christian Texts.* New Haven: Yale University Press, 1995.

Haines-Eitzen, Kim. *Guardians of Letters: Literacy, Power, and the Transmission of Early Christian Literature.* New York: Oxford University Press, 2000.

Hengel, Martin. *The Septuagint as Christian Scripture.* Trans. Mark E. Biddle. Edinburgh: Clark, 2002.

Millard, Alan. *Reading and Writing in the Time of Jesus.* New York: New York University Press, 2000.

Morgan, Teresa. *Literate Education in the Hellenistic and Roman Worlds.* Cambridge: Cambridge University Press, 1998.

Snyder, H. Gregory. *Teachers and Texts in the Ancient World: Philosophers, Jews and Christians.* London: Routledge, 2000.

belief without a sacred text. Students are surprised to learn that most ancient religions did not have anything comparable to the Jewish or Christian Scriptures. They are often puzzled by the fact that there was no official version of the mythology associated with the Greek and Roman gods and goddesses. What counted were local customs, ritual practices, and the stories as told at a particular shrine or by individual reciters. Even the laws were less dependent on written formulation than on the presence of authorities who could determine what the law was in a particular case.

Since the literacy rate may have been as low as ten percent of the population, people depended on others when they had to deal with written material. It is possible to imagine disciples of Jesus spreading devotion to their master among fellow Jews in Galilee and Judea without resorting to written texts. He was the one predicted in the Law and the prophets with which Jews were already familiar. Jewish Christians continued to observe the religious rituals of their ancestors. As long as the Temple remained standing in Jerusalem, they participated in worship there and tried to persuade fellow Jews to believe in Jesus as the Messiah.

However, as St. Paul indicates in Romans 9–11 most Jews remained unpersuaded. The astonishing success of Christian evangelization came among non-Jews in urban centers, even in Rome itself. These believers spoke a common form of Greek, not the language of the literary classics. Whether through prior association with Greek-speaking Jews or thanks to Christian teachers, they must have gained some familiarity with Jewish Scriptures.

Our Gospels are part of an extraordinary outburst of new religious literature that took place in these churches. In this chapter we will explore the way in which books were created, copied, and preserved in the early centuries. Readers who wish to get on with analysis of the Synoptic Gospels may prefer to skip ahead to the next chapter.

Early Christianity as an Explosion of Texts

Texts played an important role in second Temple Judaism. Distinct forms of the Pentateuch separated Jew from Samaritan.[1] Traditions of Torah in-

---

1. Eugene Ulrich has pointed out that the Samaritan Pentateuch was not a peculiarly sectarian document, but with the Septuagint represents one of three text forms for the Pentateuch in circulation at the time. The Septuagint of Exodus 34–39 differs from the Maso-

terpretation and practice distinguished groups within the Jewish community. Such rewritten Scripture as *Jubilees* may have enjoyed near canonical status among the Essenes.[2] Greek-speaking Jews not only translated their holy books into Greek and interpreted them through the lens of literary and philosophical allegory but also composed new works. Judaism could express its heritage in the cultural language of the Hellenistic world.[3] The biblical texts found at Qumran demonstrate that even writings treated as canonical, the Torah, prophets, and Psalms, still circulated in different editions in the first century.[4]

We do not know how significant such differences were to first-century readers. Historians such as Josephus do not attempt to reconcile divergent accounts found in their sources. Josephus had scribes copy different accounts of the Temple (*War* 5.184-227; *Antiquities* 15.410-20) or differing ideological evaluations of Herod's building projects (*War* 1.400-428; *Antiquities* 15.266-76) into his histories without comment. Was Herod's building an expression of his piety or an example of cultural corruption? We cannot tell which view Josephus intends readers to hold.[5] We do know

---

retic Hebrew text in its description. The latter appears to have been revised later. Several Exodus and Numbers manuscripts from Qumran have versions of the text similar to the Samaritan Pentateuch. If we had the linguistic habit of referring to "Samaritan Jews" rather than "Samaritans," the significance of the Samaritan Pentateuch for the history of the biblical text might not be so easily overlooked. Eugene Ulrich, "The Qumran Biblical Scrolls — The Scriptures of Late Second Temple Judaism," in T. Lim, ed., *The Dead Sea Scrolls in Their Historical Context* (Edinburgh: Clark, 2000) 74-76.

2. Eugene Ulrich, "Our Sharper Focus on the Bible and Theology Thanks to the Dead Sea Scrolls," *CBQ* 66 (2004) 8-9. One finds at Qumran as many as 12 to 21 manuscripts of *1 Enoch* and over 14 of *Jubilees,* numbers comparable to the Pentateuch. *Jubilees* is cited as authoritative in CD 16.2-4 and 4Q228. Therefore Ulrich includes *1 Enoch* and *Jubilees* with the minor prophets and Daniel as "strong" scriptural authorities at Qumran. The only texts with more authority are the Torah, Psalms, and Isaiah. Even these were circulating in different editions.

3. Readers wishing a general survey of this literature should consult James VanderKam, *An Introduction to Early Judaism* (Grand Rapids: Eerdmans, 2001).

4. Ulrich, "Qumran Scrolls," 76-86. Ulrich points out that since almost all of the 800 biblical manuscripts attested in the Qumran finds have been copied by different scribes, they must not have been produced by the local community. They are more likely to have been brought to Qumran from elsewhere and so reflect text types in general usage, not sectarian scribal practices (pp. 81-84).

5. See E. P. Sanders, "The Dead Sea Sect and Other Jews: Commonalities, Overlaps and Differences," in Lim, ed., *The Dead Sea Scrolls in Their Historical Context,* 39 n. 66.

that by the mid-second century Justin Martyr must defend the Greek text used by Christians for such sensitive prophecies as Isa 7:14 ("virgin") or Ps 96:10 (LXX 95:10: "reigns *from the tree*") against other translations in use among Jews (*Dialogue with Trypho* 71.1–73.4). Justin claims that the Jews have edited the biblical text to exclude passages favorable to the Christian position. The Greek text used by Christians is the version whose authenticity is guaranteed by the miraculous agreement of the seventy elders (*Dialogue* 71).[6] Justin disputes details of wording and reference with alternative readings from the Jewish tradition to defend the Christian position that the Hebrew prophets speak about Christ. Just as the mid-second century produced a four-Gospel canon as an authoritative witness to Jesus' life and teaching, so Christians must establish their own claim to interpret Jewish Scriptures.

It would be hard to imagine that a new movement established itself in this Jewish milieu without expressing its identity in relationship to authoritative texts.[7] While those writings which would comprise the New Testament dominate the manuscript remains, Christians were composing and circulating other writings as well. In the first half of the second century they do not appear to have employed sharp distinctions between canonical and non-canonical writings. Their confusion over categories is evident in the story about Serapion (ca. 190) and *Gos. Pet.* When the Bishop of Antioch first visited the town of Rhossus, he thought that all members of the church held orthodox beliefs. He presumed that the Gospel they attributed to Peter supported that faith, and he did not bother to examine it. Later the bishop was told that this community held heretical views about Christ as only seeming to be human and die. Teachers of this heresy, "Docetists" (from Gk. *dokein*, to seem, pretend, imagine), were appealing

---

6. This legend concerning the translation made for Ptolemy II originally referred to the Torah (see *Letter of Aristeas* 3-5). Justin assumes that it encompassed also the prophets and Psalms. *Aristeas* 310-11 insists that no changes can be made to the text. The Jewish leaders' response to the reading of the Torah is "Since this version has been made rightly and reverently, and in every respect accurately, it is good that this should remain exactly so, and that there should be no revision." Then they command that "a curse should be laid . . . on anyone who should either alter the version by any addition or change to any part of the written text, or any deletion either. This was a good step taken, to ensure that the words were preserved completely and permanently in perpetuity" (R. J. H. Shutt's translation in *OTP* I, p. 33).

7. See Judith Lieu, *Christian Identity in the Graeco-Roman World* (Oxford: Oxford University Press, 2004) 27-48.

to *Gos. Pet.,* so Serapion engaged in more detailed study of the Gospel. He concluded that most of it was acceptable but that a number of spurious additions should be removed (Eusebius, *Hist. Eccl.* 6.12).

This example suggests that one should not treat composition of the apocryphal Gospels as a political or theological shot across the bow of an orthodox Christianity represented in the four-Gospel canon. For at least a century Christians probably did not make a sharp distinction between earlier gospel traditions and later recastings of the life of Jesus. Such later Gospels might focus on legends of Jesus' conception, birth, or childhood, as in the *Protoevangelium of James* (mid-second century) or the *Infancy Gospel of Thomas* (early second century). They might expand on a core collection of Jesus' sayings, as in *Gospel of Thomas* (early second century), or contain additional episodes from the life of Jesus, as in *Papyrus Egerton 2* (early second century). They might reflect the understanding of Jesus' life and mission current in Jewish Christian circles, as in *Gospel of the Hebrews,* the *Gospel of the Ebionites,* or the non-Gnostic *Gospel of the Egyptians* (all early second century). Or like what remains of the *Gospel of Peter,* they may have developed the stories surrounding Jesus' passion and resurrection, as also in the recently published *Gospel of the Savior* (late second century), the *Acts of Pilate* (mid-second century) or the fifth-century *Gospel of Nicodemus.*[8]

Scribes also gave the title "Gospel of . . ." to treatises by Gnostic Christians that are not associated with the category "Gospel," that is, presentations of the life and teaching of Jesus. Gnostics used dialogues between the risen Jesus and his disciples to place Gnostic myths and accounts of salvation in the mouth of Jesus. Most of these works are titled "revelation" or "hidden book." But one example of the genre was given the title *Gospel of Mary.* Mary Magdalene is a participant in the dialogue and recipient of revelation from Jesus, but she is not the fictive author of the work. Nor is *Gos. Mary* a source of Jesus tradition. Two other second-century compilations of Gnostic meditations that include some use of gospel material but are not formally Gospels also belong in this category of mislabeled works, the *Gospel of Philip* and the *Gospel of Truth.* The impression often given in the media that a wealth of Jesus material in first-century

---

8. For the list and dates of major Christian apocrypha, see Bart D. Ehrman, *Lost Christianities: The Battles for Scripture and the Faiths We Never Knew* (New York: Oxford University Press, 2003), xi-xii.

Gospels was suppressed by church authorities is not supported by any evidence.

Instead, we should recognize that in the early centuries of the Christian movement, believers read from a more extensive collection of sacred writings than one finds in the canon. Fragments of previously unknown Gospels will continue to be discovered as the thousands of unpublished papyri are deciphered and published.[9] In the case of small fragments of Gospel text, it may not be possible to distinguish between a "new Gospel" and a version of one of the canonical Gospels, for which there are already substantive variations in the text.[10] The persecution under Diocletian (ca. 303 C.E.) called for the destruction of the sacred books used by Christians. Both canonical and non-canonical Gospel books were handed over to authorities. Local versions of the four Gospels or of non-canonical texts were less likely to survive than the Gospel texts being used by churches in major cities like Alexandria, Antioch, or Byzantium. During much of the second century, Gospels circulated in individual copies. Codices containing the four Gospels make their appearance in the third century. In the first two centuries, then, the collection of books available for reading in one church was not the same as that used elsewhere. Many second-century communities may not have possessed copies of the four which make up what Eusebius refers to as "the holy foursome" (*Hist. Eccl.* 3.25.1). Writing in the early fourth century, Eusebius recognizes that churches still dispute the inclusion of James, Jude, 2 Peter, 2 and 3 John, and Revelation. He notes that a number of widely circulated early Christian writings such as the *Acts of Paul, Shepherd of Hermas, Letter of Barnabas, Apocalypse of Peter,* and *Didache* are no longer accepted in the canon. He comments that he would have identified the *Gospel of the Hebrews* as spurious but acknowledges that it is used among Jewish Christians. Unlike other Gospels such as those attributed to Peter, Thomas, or Matthias and other apocryphal Acts such as those of Andrew and John, *Gos. Heb.* has never been condemned as incompatible with Christian faith.

Eusebius provides a glimpse of the extensive body of literature which fourth-century Christians might encounter as representative of apostolic

---

9. See Ehrman, *Lost Christianities,* 23-51.

10. For detailed examples of the substantive differences among manuscripts of the canonical Gospels, see D. C. Parker, *The Living Text of the Gospels* (Cambridge: Cambridge University Press, 1997) 31-70.

teaching. Eusebius takes pains to explain the differences between John's Gospel and the Synoptic Gospels in both style and the narrative of Jesus' life. He treats John's three-year chronology for Jesus' ministry as a clue that John is recounting what happened in a two-year period prior to the Baptist's arrest. The other Gospels only begin with Jesus' ministry after that point (*Hist. Eccl.* 3.24). Eusebius inhabits a different world from that of the earliest Christians. The Roman emperor has adopted their faith. Codices containing the canonical Gospels are important liturgical objects (*Hist. Eccl.* 7.15). A visitor to Caesarea Philippi could see a statue of the woman with a hemorrhage kneeling before Jesus (Mark 5:25-34) as well as colored portraits of Jesus and the apostles Peter and Paul (*Hist. Eccl.* 7.18). Now that the Gospels have become sacred objects, gospel stories and apostles appear in visual as well as written form. Eusebius explains this transition to statuary and portraiture as the custom of Gentiles in honoring persons they consider saviors.

The emperor Constantine ordered elegant codices containing the entire Bible for use in the new churches being built to put the empire's official Christian religion on display. Converting an empire to Christianity would require transforming the imagination of a populace. The legends of the gods, goddesses, and heroes of mythology, epic poetry, tragic drama, and visual art did not vanish overnight. The creativity of Christian storytelling which preserved both the canonical Scriptures and the dramatic tales found in the apocryphal Gospels and Acts furthered the process of religious change. Today we see movie versions taking the Christian story as well as classical myths and heroes to a population that is often unfamiliar with the written texts.

How Books Were Written

Most Christians grow up thinking of the Gospels as part of a larger book, the Bible. Printing made that development possible. The great Bible codices of the fourth and fifth centuries had to be hand-copied by well-trained scribes. In the earlier period, one finds manuscripts in less careful handwriting. The codex format was used for drafts, notes, or writings that were not high literature. The scrolls on which the Jewish Torah or classical literature was copied were made by gluing together papyrus sheets. To create a codex papyrus sheets of 15 inches by 9 inches were folded down the middle

37

and glued together. Scribes would copy their text in ruled columns. The fourth-century biblical codex called Sinaiticus has columns 2.25 inches in width. Between those columns, it contains a helpful set of numbers introduced by Eusebius so that readers could locate the parallel versions of a story in the other Gospels.[11]

Of the 871 known second-century manuscripts containing non-Christian literature, only fourteen are from codices. The eleven known Christian papyri are all from codices. By the end of the fourth century, of approximately 172 biblical manuscripts only fourteen come from scrolls. Even non-biblical Christian literature was being preserved in codex form by that time.[12] Originally use of the codex may reflect the socioeconomic level of the Christians who wrote, copied, and circulated the Gospels. They could not afford the more expensive format. In addition codices would have been easier to transport and to consult. However, the sort of aids we use to navigate our Bibles — titles, prologues, and section divisions — do not appear until the fourth and fifth centuries. Ancient scribes did not put spaces between words and used little punctuation. Consequently, reading a text required prior familiarity with its contents. And since few people were literate, most Christians depended on hearing and memory for their knowledge of the Gospels.

The standard length of a book scroll was thirty to thirty-five feet, giving enough room for 10,000 to 25,000 words. The Gospels were standard-length books. Longer works were divided into scroll-length books. Luke employs that convention. His Acts of the Apostles forms the second volume of a work that began with his account of Jesus in the Gospel (Acts 1:1-2). An experienced reader could probably perform an entire Gospel in two or three hours.

Scribes are pictured standing to make short notes or sitting on a stool, bench, or the ground with the scroll or codex across their knees.[13] Most texts were copied one at a time. Among the elite, books might be borrowed from a friend for copying by a slave trained as a scribe. The earliest Christians may have gained their ability to read and copy texts as household slaves or as record keepers in commercial ventures. Most people em-

11. See Bruce M. Metzger and Bart D. Ehrman, *The Text of the New Testament: Its Transmission, Corruption, and Restoration* (New York: Oxford University Press, 2005, fourth edition) 1-96. A photograph of a page of Sinaiticus can be found on p. 66.

12. Metzger and Ehrman, *Text,* 14, count eighty-three codices to thirty-five scrolls.

13. Metzger and Ehrman, *Text,* 27-28.

ployed scribes to do the actual labor of writing. Paul distinguishes his hand from the work of the secretary who wrote down his words (Rom 16:22; 1 Cor 16:21; Gal 6:11; Col 4:18). Although most scribes were male, scholars have begun to collect evidence for the existence of female scribes, most of them working for female owners.[14]

Scribes who had been trained for commercial or bureaucratic purposes might also have composed some of the popular literary works of the time. Chariton of Aphrodisias, who identifies himself as secretary to the orator Athenagoras, composed the romance novel *Chaereas and Callirhoe*. Our only Christian example of such an author wrote the popular mix of allegorical visions and exhortation known as the *Shepherd of Hermas* near the end of the first century.[15] A version of *Hermas* was included after the New Testament in the fourth-century biblical codex Sinaiticus. In his second vision, Hermas sees an elderly lady reading from a small book. When she asks him to proclaim its content to God's elect, Hermas replies that he cannot remember that much. He asks her to lend him the book so that he can make a copy and return it (*Vis.* 2.1.1-3). Hermas' skills appear fairly rudimentary. He says that he had to copy the book out letter-by-letter because he had trouble separating the letters (*Vis.* 2.1.4). Children learned to write by copying out letters and sentences penned by the teacher. Such evidence as exists suggests that copying and memorizing set patterns and phrases was antecedent to reading. Students had notebooks of admirable passages to memorize and employ as needed. After learning to read, copy, and memorize, they might paraphrase literary texts.[16] Reading any text involved a complex process of analysis, prior familiarity, and interpretation. Hermas's letter-by-letter transcription of the book he has received in a vision shows a lack of familiarity with its content.

Since Hermas presents himself as the freed slave of a wealthy mistress who has become a prosperous householder in his own right (*Vis.* 1.1.1), he may have acquired his training as a household slave/scribe. The *Shepherd* includes a bit of evidence for how its text was put into circulation (*Vis.*

14. Haines-Eitzen, *Guardians of Letters*, 40-49.

15. Carolyn Osiek, *Shepherd of Hermas* (Minneapolis: Fortress, 1999). The endpaper reproduces a ceiling painting from the Catacomb of San Gennaro in Naples (second-third century C.E.) that illustrates one of the parables in the *Shepherd*, the tower of *Similitudes* 9.3.4-5.

16. See Morgan, *Literate Education;* R. Cribiore, *Gymnastics of the Mind: Greek Education in Hellenistic and Roman Egypt* (Princeton: Princeton University Press, 2001).

2.4.3): Hermas was told to produce two copies, one for Clement, possibly the author of *1 Clement,* an exhortation from a Roman bishop to the church in Corinth. Clement is to send it to other cities, whether a single manuscript to be copied and returned or copies made in Rome one cannot tell. A second copy was to be given to Grapte, a Christian woman in charge of instructing widows and orphans. Hermas himself was to read the revelation with the presbyters of the city. Whether they were to propagate the contents of the visions and exhortations orally or with the aid of further written copies or excerpts one cannot tell.

This example highlights the difficulty of assimilating the contents of a written text. If it is not familiar to the reader, some form of initiation by a teacher is required. One had to build up a store of vocabulary words, paraphrases of its content, and sections that had been analyzed in detail in order to read effectively. That process took the form of exchanges between teachers and students in philosophical and rhetorical schools.[17] Presumably the process by which Hermas conveys his work to the presbyters of the Roman church involves such discussion. How Grapte went about making sufficient sense of the text so that she could instruct widows and orphans we are not told.

We have no ancient evidence for how our Gospels were composed and circulated. The *Hermas* example provides a plausible model. Eusebius's description of the composition of Mark assumes that Christians at Rome urged Mark to write down what he had heard Peter preaching publicly. He did so and made it available to anyone who requested it (*Hist. Eccl.* 6.14.5). According to Clement of Alexandria, Peter accepted this development after the fact: "when Peter heard about this, he made no objection and gave no special encouragement." That comment fits a situation well-known among ancient rhetoricians and philosophers. Disciples might distribute preliminary versions of the master's work or copies of his speeches taken down by others without the teacher's permission. A teacher had two choices. Either accept the situation, as Peter is said to have done, or protest the validity of the copies in circulation and issue a new edition.

As we have seen, there would be new editions of Mark in very short order, namely the Gospels of Matthew and Luke. In addition, in the second and third centuries there were other attempts at revising Mark or compos-

---

17. See Snyder, *Teachers and Texts,* 2-5. Snyder describes teachers as "text-brokers" (p. 11).

ing further Gospels attributed to Peter. The need for private copying and informal distribution channels shows that Mark's Gospel was associated with a major Christian center. Otherwise, we have no way of explaining how it came to be so quickly taken up and revised by two different authors. The traditions known to Eusebius do not address this question, since they assume that each of the Evangelists wrote independently. Early Christian teachers like Clement of Alexandria, who read the Gospels against the backdrop of ancient biographies, presumed that the Gospels with genealogies, Matthew and Luke, were written first. The peculiarities of Mark and John had to be explained. Mark was treated as a disciple's notes based on his memory of Peter's preaching, and John was understood as a spiritual interpretation of the literal facts about Jesus recorded in the other Gospels.

How the Gospel Texts Have Come Down to Us

Our ability to produce thousands of identical copies of a work makes it hard for us to imagine the achievement of the earliest Christian writers. Writing, copying, circulating, and preserving their texts was a difficult process. In order for copies of a text to survive, it must have been widely used. Despite the small numbers of Christians in the first century or so, they were able to spread copies of the Gospels quite widely. Perhaps even more remarkable, the Gospels were known to outsiders who wrote against Christianity by the middle of the second century. Justin Martyr (ca. 150) reports that his Jewish opponent Trypho had read the Gospels (*Dialogue* 10.2; 18.3). In the third century, Origen rebuts an attack on Christianity composed by Celsus in the later second century. Celsus is certainly familiar with Matthew's Gospel and probably with John. Another second-century opponent, the court physician and philosopher Galen, does not appear to have read any of the Gospels. He responds to what he has heard about Christians. By the third and fourth centuries, the Gospels are the references for anti-Christian polemics.[18]

Ancient scribes introduced changes into the text as they copied it. Some modifications were unintentional. The eye or ear wandered from one line to the same phrase further along or misunderstood a particular sequence of letters. Other modifications may have been intentional, the in-

---

18. See John G. Cook, "Some Hellenistic Responses to the Gospels and Gospel Traditions," *ZNW* 84 (1993) 233-54.

troduction of a gloss or explanatory phrase or correction of what appeared to be awkward or unintelligible phrasing. Or a scribe familiar with the other Gospels might introduce another Evangelist's version into what he was copying.

By the early third century, the language base of Western Christianity had shifted from Greek to Latin. It was the end of the fourth century before Jerome's revision of the various Latin versions would provide those Christians with the Bible that would shape life and worship until the Reformation. After Jerome, there was no interest in copies of the Greek Bible in the West for over a millennium. Renaissance scholars had to use Byzantine texts for their editions of the Greek New Testament.[19] The quality of available manuscripts varied widely. Differences between the Greek texts and Jerome's Latin Vulgate also caused difficulties for these scholars.

When Erasmus in the sixteenth century lacked Greek manuscripts for New Testament material found in the Latin, he composed his own Greek text. He also corrected readings in his Greek manuscripts that appeared to be the result of errors in copying.[20] He produced four editions of his Greek text. With the second edition (1516) Erasmus also included his own Latin translation of the Greek. This innovation made it possible to see differences between the Greek and the Latin Vulgate. Luther employed this edition for his translation of the New Testament into German.

With revisions by further editors Erasmus's text came to dominate the market. For the next four hundred years, this Textus Receptus ("received text") was treated as the definitive Greek New Testament even though scholars had access to earlier, better manuscripts. His version became so fixed in the tradition of printed Greek Bibles that Calvin's successor, Theodore Beza (1519-1605), largely ignored the variant readings of two early manuscripts in his possession, Codex Bezae (fifth or sixth century) and Codex Claromontanus (sixth century). Beza's editions solidified the position of the Textus Receptus and served as the basis for the most famous English translation, the King James Version.[21] Modern translations

19. Metzger and Ehrman, *Text,* 137-52.

20. Metzger and Ehrman, *Text,* figure 23 (p. 144) illustrates Erasmus's corrections on the page of one of the Greek manuscripts used for his edition. The words "pray for those who persecute you" had been dropped out of v. 28 in Luke 6:20-30.

21. For a lively account of how the King James Version came about, see Alister E. McGrath, *In the Beginning: The Story of the King James Bible and How It Changed a Nation, a Language, and a Culture* (New York: Doubleday, 2001).

employ new eclectic editions of the Greek text, which seek to represent the evidence from the great codices of the fourth to sixth centuries, the thousands of earlier fragmentary manuscripts, and to some extent quotations and early translations of the New Testament.[22]

Latin translations originally represented a move to use the language of the people. The Reformers insisted upon a similar development. A linguistic barrier should no longer keep the Bible from the uneducated. Some vernacular translations were made from the Latin Vulgate. After the publication of the Greek text and of Latin translations of that text, other translators used Hebrew and Greek texts.

So our reception of the Gospels involves multiple problems of translation. Like all languages, Greek has a long history of development. The language spoken over much of the eastern half of the Roman Empire in New Testament times was not that of Homer or Plato. Grammatically it is simpler. Its lexicon includes new words and meanings. The literary elite sought to conform to classical Attic standards, but the Evangelists use the common language of their day. Scholarly interest in the New Testament has made study of that *koine* ("common") Greek a priority.[23]

When Texts Differ: What the Text Critic Contributes

The problems facing Erasmus and other Renaissance editors as they sought to establish a Greek text initiated the search for older manuscript witnesses as well as the collation of variant readings found in early quotations. For classical authors, editors only had a few manuscripts of any text along with some quotations in other ancient authors. The collections of papyri recovered since the nineteenth century have provided some additional evidence for classical authors. By contrast, today's student of the

---

22. The most widely used Greek text is Nestle-Aland, *Novum Testamentum Graece,* now in its twenty-seventh edition, also the text found in the United Bible Societies' *The Greek New Testament,* fourth edition. But readers who use the New International Version should be aware that it is based on a different Greek text prepared by Edward Goodrick and John Kohlenberger III. It can be found in Richard J. Goddrich and Albert L. Lukaszewski, *A Reader's Greek New Testament* (Grand Rapids: Zondervan, 2003).

23. The scholarly lexicon which incorporates the most recent research is Frederick W. Danker, ed., *A Greek-English Lexicon of the New Testament and Early Christian Literature* (Chicago: University of Chicago Press, 2000, third edition).

New Testament text faces a daunting list of thousands of witnesses and variants. D. C. Parker estimates that approximately 2388 manuscripts include Gospel material.[24] By examining all the variants, a text critic tries to describe the process which gave rise to them.

The first breakthrough in classifying the manuscripts saw identification of two major text families in addition to the Byzantine type used by Erasmus, the Western and Alexandrian or "neutral" text. The primary exemplar of the Western type is our oldest bilingual (Greek and Latin) codex, Codex Bezae. It often includes additional words and phrases and is ten percent longer than the other text types in Acts. Its variations include paraphrases, harmonizing, and addition of apocryphal traditions. This text type was widely disseminated. It figures in early Latin translations and in quotations in patristic authors from the second century on. The Alexandrian type appears in two major codices from the fourth and fifth centuries, Sinaiticus and Vaticanus, as well as in papyri (P^{66} and P^{75}) and quotations in Alexandrian authors. The tradition of copying, editing, and commenting on ancient texts developed in the famous scholarly center of Alexandria may be responsible for the care taken in preserving a stable form of the text through the centuries. Even in this type, the text preserved in Vaticanus and P^{75} appear to have undergone less modification and correction than other examples of this group. Although one would anticipate other text families originating in other localities, identification of such text types remains uncertain.[25]

Today text critics acknowledge that they cannot hope to recover an original text. One may even ask whether the concept of original text makes sense in the ancient environment.[26] Even an individual author might produce variant editions of a work. The goal of text criticism is to provide a Greek text which could be the basis for the actual forms of the New Testament text represented by our growing body of evidence. Text critics employ rules of thumb used in studying all ancient manuscripts.

No single codex or text family can serve as a base text to which corrections are added as needed. Instead all the evidence of variant readings

---

24. Parker, *The Living Text of the Gospels*, 9.

25. For a thorough discussion of these questions see Metzger and Ehrman, *Text*, 276-80.

26. Parker, *Living Text*, 4-5, evokes the comparable case of Shakespeare's plays, in which texts represent various stages of production. A rehearsal text and the performed version of a play may both differ from printed versions even today.

for each passage has to be collected and evaluated. In some instances everyone trained in the field agrees on the preferred reading. In others, the evidence and conclusions are mixed. For a simple example of the latter, consider Mark 1:1-2. The footnotes to the NRSV tip off the reader to the problem. V. 1 concludes with the phrase "Son of God," but a footnote points out that "other ancient authorities"[27] do not have the phrase. V. 2 introduces the quotation with "as it is written in the prophet Isaiah." The note mentions ancient authorities which read "in the prophets." The United Bible Societies publish a Greek text with ratings to indicate how confident the members of the editorial committee are about the text chosen in each place that variants are considered. The phrase "Son of God" receives only a "C" as the earliest reading of v. 1. In other words, the editors have little confidence that the phrase was not introduced by later scribes. By contrast, "Isaiah, the prophet" in v. 2 receives an "A" rating.

A brief look at the factors which go into these decisions will indicate the basic questions that scholars consider. In these cases, we are not dealing with the sort of changes which result from lack of attention, slipping to the same word further on, or misreading or mishearing the text being copied. Nor are we faced with a situation in which an awkward phrase or rare word appears to have been corrected by a scribe at some point in the copying process. Nor are we dealing with a case in which the scribe is so familiar with the expression from another Gospel that he or she has unwittingly introduced it into the text being copied. For an easy example of that shift, look at Luke 11:2. Luke has Jesus begin, "Father, hallowed be your name." The NRSV notes point to a number of other variants. It is easy to see that once the version of the Lord's Prayer used in worship conformed to Matthew's "Our Father in heaven" (Matt 6:9), scribes would shift to that form even when copying Luke.

That example illustrates the principle at work in our examples from Mark 1:1-2. Text critics will prefer a reading which is most likely to have given rise to the other variants. Why are scholars so confident about "Isaiah

---

27. Only the notes which begin with "other ancient authorities" refer to important variants in the Greek text. Other notes refer to alternative translation possibilities such as "gospel" for the NRSV's "good news" in Mark 1:1. English translations do not footnote all the various readings that students of the Greek New Testament find in their editions. They only represent those which reflect significant differences in meaning. Even so readers who pay attention to the bottom of the page will find at least one such reference for almost every chapter in the Synoptic Gospels.

the prophet" in Mark 1:2? Because "Isaiah the prophet" is more difficult to explain as a scribal correction than "the prophets" would be, since the quotation in v. 3 is not Isaiah alone but a combination of Exod 23:20; Mal 3:1; and Isa 40:3. A scribe who recognized the conflation might well have chosen to correct the introduction with the more general expression "in the prophets." Codex Alexandrinus prefers the more precise "in the prophets," as one might expect from a center accustomed to careful analysis of ancient texts. When Matthew composed a Gospel that incorporated much of Mark, he fixed the problem in another way. He only quotes Isa 40:3 (Matt 3:3).

"Son of God" in Mark 1:1 is a bit more difficult. The designation "Son of God" plays an important literary and theological role in Mark's Gospel. Jesus hears God's voice address him as "my beloved Son" at his baptism (Mark 1:11). Peter, James, and John hear that voice at the Transfiguration saying "this is my beloved Son" (9:7), about halfway through the narrative. Finally, the centurion who has just witnessed the events of Jesus' death exclaims "truly, this man was Son of God" (15:39). For some interpreters such considerations tip the balance in favor of including the phrase in the opening verse. For other scholars, the problem is explaining why it would fall out of the manuscript tradition in Sinaiticus as well as a number of early quotations and versions. The standard editions of the Greek text all beg the question by printing the Greek words for "Son of God" in brackets. What difference does the choice make? Clearly, Mark's Christian readers are prepared to confess that Jesus is "Son of God" whether or not the expression appears in v. 1. Adding the expression provides a way of highlighting the phrase as central to the Gospel's message right out of the box. The opening phrase, which might otherwise seem a simple heading to what follows, thus provides a clue to the theological significance of the narrative. Therefore it seems slightly more likely that the phrase "Son of God" was an expansion by Christian scribes familiar with the Gospel as a whole than that it had fallen out of the tradition represented by some texts.

Study of ancient educational practice has shown that texts have no life independent of their oral performance and interpretation. Most of the audience could not decipher them even if written texts had been more commonly available. Some papyrus fragments appear to have been used as amulets rather than reading material.[28] Text critics today are not simply cataloguing and picking over a mass of details of no interest to anyone else.

28. Parker, *Living Text*, 27.

Rather, they seek to understand what the variants have to tell us about the early Christians who produced them. Sometime differences provide a window into the theological concerns of Christians in the second and third centuries. Luke 22:43-44 in the NRSV is printed in double brackets. The note indicates that they are missing in other ancient versions. Many Christians will be familiar with the comforting angel and the drops of bloody sweat from pictures of Jesus praying in Gethsemane. So why the brackets? The verses do not appear in our oldest manuscripts, but they do appear in quotations from second- and early-third-century patristic authors. For those authors, these verses are part of an important theological debate about the human suffering of Christ. Some Christians in the second century did not see how the "Son of God" could experience pain. They claimed that Jesus only appeared to suffer. His inner divine self was untouched by the experience. This passage helped orthodox Christians refute that view just as it has shaped Christian visual imagination ever since.[29]

Today's text critics are no longer just providing the Greek text from which other scholars and translators work. They are contributing insights into the social and theological history of Christianity.[30] Even though most Bible students rarely give the text critic's efforts a thought, we would not have a text to translate without them. We will not be delving into details of text criticism further in this book.[31] These brief observations should enable readers of modern English translations to include those references to "other ancient authorities" in their Bible study.

The Septuagint: Scripture Cited in the Gospels

While returning to a Greek text as the basis for translation was a return to the original language of the Gospels, employing the Hebrew text as the basis

---

29. Metzger and Ehrman, *Text,* 285-86.

30. For some additional examples of these contributions, see Metzger and Ehrman, *Text,* 280-99; Eldon J. Epp, "The Oxyrhynchus New Testament Papyri: 'Not without Honor Except in their Hometown?'" *JBL* 123 (2004) 5-55; and Wayne C. Kannaday, *Apologetic Discourse and the Scribal Tradition: Evidence of the Influence of Apologetic Interests on the Text of the Canonical Gospels* (Society of Biblical Literature Text-Critical Studies 5; Atlanta: Society of Biblical Literature/Leiden: Brill, 2004).

31. A lively account of texts, versions, and theological reasons behind some of our variant readings can be found in Ehrman, *Misquoting Jesus.*

for Christian Scripture was not. Almost all of the Scripture quotations in the New Testament itself are based on the Greek translation of the Hebrew Scriptures known as the Septuagint (LXX). Legend had it that when Ptolemy II (285-247 B.C.E.) wanted a copy of the famed Jewish Torah for the library in Alexandria, he sent for seventy-two learned Jews to undertake the task. They are said to have each come to the same wording separately before completing the good copy for the king. The librarian was then asked to make another good copy to take back to the priests in Jerusalem.

Although the legend held that the translators had fixed every word of the translation so that it could never be revised, there were different Greek translations of individual books in circulation. In some cases, the translators employed Hebrew texts that differ from what would become the standard Hebrew text. In others, translators sought to produce a quite literal rendering of the Hebrew text. An individual New Testament citation may be closer to the Hebrew text than the commonly used Septuagint text for one of two reasons. An author such as Paul or Matthew might have introduced a correction based on his familiarity with a Hebrew or Aramaic version of the passage in question, or he might know a Greek translation that differs from those available in our surviving manuscript evidence.

Because we now employ translations of the Hebrew text as the first or "Old" Christian testament, a quotation in the New Testament may not match its source in our Bibles. Take the passage from Isaiah in Mark 1:3, for example. It reads, "the voice of one crying in the wilderness: 'Prepare the way of the Lord, make his paths straight'" (NRSV). Follow the footnote back to Isa 40:3 in the NRSV and we find, "A voice cries out: 'In the wilderness prepare the way of the LORD, make straight in the desert a highway for our God.'" One might think that Mark or an earlier Christian source had changed it so that "in the desert [wilderness]" was the location no longer of the highway but of the voice in order to fit the quotation to John the Baptist. But a look at the Septuagint shows that the Greek version of Isaiah is the basis for Mark's citation. It reads: "the voice of one crying in the wilderness: 'Prepare the way of the Lord; make the paths of our God straight.'" The parallel passage in Luke (Luke 3:4-6) extends the quotation through Isa 40:5. Thus the voice not only points to the Baptist's activity but to the gospel message itself: "and all flesh will see the salvation of God" (Luke 3:6). You will not find the reference to salvation in your Old Testament version of Isa 40:5. There it is "the glory of the Lord" that is seen by all people.

Early Christian writers also recognized the differences between the Hebrew text used by the Jewish community and the Greek Scriptures of their own tradition. Second-century Jewish revisions of the Greek changed the wording of Isa 7:14 from the Greek word *parthenos* ("virgin, unmarried girl") to *neanis,* which is more commonly used to translate the Hebrew word *'almâ.* Because *neanis* does not include the sense of "virgin" in its semantic range, Christians understood the revision as a Jewish attempt to deny that Isaiah had predicted the birth of Christ (Justin Martyr, *Dialogue* 43; Irenaeus, *Adv. Haer.* 3.21.1-2). After discussing the problem of different translations for the Hebrew word, Origen argued that whatever the translation, Isa 7:14 cannot refer to a descendant of King Ahaz as Jews hold (*Contra Celsum* 1.34-35). He compiled a six-column parallel version of the Old Testament, the *Hexapla,* which enabled scholars of his day to compare the Hebrew with four Greek versions. The first column provided a Hebrew text and the second its transliteration in Greek characters. The remaining columns contained the Septuagint and three second-century revised translations, those by Aquila, Theodotion, and Symmachus.

Origen acknowledges that the Septuagint is Christian Scripture. However, he insists that Christians should be familiar with the differences between their Bible and that of the Jewish community. It would be foolish to argue with Jews on the basis of a passage that is not part of their Scripture. Although the Septuagint originated among Greek-speaking Jews over two centuries before Christianity, by the third century C.E. it is the Christian Bible. Jews accept only the Hebrew text as sacred Scripture.

The greatest Christian scholar of the fourth and fifth centuries, St. Jerome, provided Latin-speaking Christians with a translation to replace the Greek that they no longer understood. At the same time, he recognized the importance of Hebrew for studying the Old Testament. His contemporary, St. Augustine, lacked Jerome's linguistic talents but was familiar with the problem of differences between Hebrew, Greek, and Latin versions. He discusses a famous example, the number of days before Nineveh would be destroyed in Jonah 3:4. According to the Septuagint, the city had forty days. According to the Hebrew and the more literal Greek translations, it had only three days. The three days that Jonah spent inside the fish (Jonah 1:17) had served as a popular Christian prediction of Jesus' resurrection (see Matt 12:40). Matt 12:41 mentions the Ninevites' repentance to condemn Jesus' generation. Augustine recognizes that some readers might insist that the Hebrew text should take priority over the Septuagint. He resolves the dilemma by suggesting that the spiritual meaning of the text admits both readings. "Three days" points to the resurrection of Christ while "forty days" indicates the time between the resurrection and ascension (Acts 1:3; Augustine, *City of God* 18.44). Both the Hebrew and Greek versions of Scripture are inspired, Augustine argues. Jonah the prophet is the source of the Hebrew. The seventy translators of the Septuagint owe their translation to the Holy Spirit. St. Augustine concludes, "I deem it right to make use of both as authorities, since both are one, and both divine."

The language of the Septuagint provided the Evangelists with religious meanings that words and phrases did not have in ordinary Greek usage. Most of these terms are so familiar that we hardly give them a second thought. The Greek word *angelos* simply means a messenger or envoy. However, thanks to the Septuagint, we know "angel" as a special kind of messenger, one from God. The word *ethnos* refers to any group of people or nation. For Jews, the word has a more specific sense. It designates those who are not Jewish, *goyyim* or "Gentiles." The disparaging use of the word in Matthew (e.g., 6:32) is one clue that the Evangelist is Jewish.

Luke is the best Greek stylist among the Evangelists, as Jerome recognized. He often adopts the vocabulary and style of the Septuagint. Some familiar phrases which would have provided the tone of "biblical speech" include "glorify God" (Luke 2:20; 5:25-26; 7:16; 13:13), "place in your heart" (1:66; 21:14); the figurative use of "son" (5:34; 10:6; 16:8; 20:34), and "go in peace" (7:50; 8:48).[32] Luke also adopts Hebrew grammatical constructions from the Septuagint. His narrative opens with "it happened in the days of Herod king. . . ." (1:5), and the events surrounding Jesus' birth are announced, "and it happened in those days a decree . . ." (2:1). The expression "and it happened in the days of" would be familiar from narrative passages in the Septuagint (Judg 14:15; Ruth 1:1; 1 Kgdms [=1 Sam] 3:2; 4:1). At the key transition in which Jesus turns toward Jerusalem and his destiny, Luke employs the biblical sounding idiom "And it happened when the days of his being taken up were fulfilled and he *stiffened his face to go to Jersualem*" (Luke 9:51; LXX Ezek 6:2; 13:17). Luke begins his Gospel with a complex sentence written in imitation of classical style favored by an elite audience, so his adoption of biblical words and phrases must be equally deliberate.

---

32. See Joseph A. Fitzmyer, *The Gospel According to Luke I-IX* (Anchor Bible 28; New York: Doubleday, 1981) 109-25. Most of the items identified as Hebrew or Semitic influences in Luke's Greek are derived from the Septuagint.

Even at the level of the language used to tell the story of Jesus, the Evangelist affirms the continuity between these events and the sacred traditions of Israel. "It was necessary that everything written in the law of Moses and the prophets and the psalms about me [Jesus] be fulfilled" (24:44).

We do not know how non-Jewish converts came by their copies of the Septuagint. Some may have been sympathetic to Judaism and even attended synagogue gatherings. Luke presents a charming tale of a highly placed Ethiopian eunuch returning from Jerusalem with a scroll of Isaiah in hand (Acts 8:26-40). Philip catches up to him and offers to explain the text from Isa 53:7-8. We have noted that in antiquity no one could just pick up a book and read it. Careful study and the guiding hand of a teacher would be needed to figure out something as complex and unfamiliar as Isaiah. Churches must have acquired copies of or selections from the Torah, prophets, and Psalms in order to provide instruction for non-Jewish believers.

Marcion and the Idea of a Second-Century "Canon"

As we have seen, Justin Martyr indicates that by the mid-second century Christians would hear either "memoirs of the apostles" or "the prophets" read and explained (1 Apology 67). In the same period, dissident Christian groups either demoted or rejected the authority of the Jewish writings. Gnostic groups held that the creator god of the Law and the prophets was the illegitimate offspring of a heavenly Wisdom figure. Human beings had an inner spark of true divine light which made them superior to the hostile creator. Once awakened by the Savior, the Gnostic race would return to unity with the divine world from which it had been separated. Since biblical texts from Genesis and proclamations of the Lord as sovereign creator in Isaiah figure in Gnostic mythology, some Gnostic teachers detect hidden inspiration behind some passages in the Jewish Scriptures. Another second-century teacher, often lumped together with the Gnostics, Marcion drew a sharp division between the Jewish god and the loving Father revealed by Jesus. He insisted that the Jewish Scriptures be read literally. They do not point toward Jesus as Messiah typologically or allegorically, as contemporary Christian teachers like Justin argued. When St. Paul spoke of Christ as the "end of the Law" (Rom 10:4), he meant just that. Believers have the gospel revealed by Christ. They should reject the writings of the Jewish covenant and the creator god who inspired them.

Standard treatments of Marcion in church history texts often depict him as the catalyst for the formation of a New Testament canon comprising the Gospels and epistles. He produced an edition of Luke's Gospel and of the Pauline letters for use in Marcionite churches. An additional work, the *Antitheses,* served the needs of Marcionite teachers. It began with a summary of Marcion's understanding of the gospel message. Then detailed analyses of the individual sections from the Gospel and epistles demonstrated the truth of that view while highlighting the contradictions between Christian revelation and the Jewish Scriptures. Marcion certainly did not understand Luke's Gospel as advocating continuity between the gospel and the Law, the prophets, and the Psalms. His edition of the Gospel and the epistles removed passages which suggested that the same God was worshiped in both the old and the new covenants (Irenaeus, *Adv. Haer.* 1.27.2; 4.12.3; 4.38.1-5; Tertullian, *Adv. Marc.* 4.6).

More recent studies of Marcion see him as more characteristic of early-second-century Christianity than the radical innovator who created the idea of a Christian canon that he has been portrayed as.[33] Justin Martyr's defense of the Christian reading of the Jewish Scriptures against the literal interpretations of a Jewish opponent in the *Dialogue* could serve just as well in a debate with Marcion. Marcion agrees with Justin's Trypho that prophetic oracles like Isa 7:14 are about the royal house of King Ahaz, not about Jesus as Messiah. The question of whether Christians will continue to treat the Scriptures inherited from the Jewish origins of the movement may have been more vigorously contested early in the second century than we ordinarily think. Of course, Marcion's followers would have had some familiarity with the Jewish Scriptures in order to understand those sections of his *Antitheses* that discuss the contradictions between those texts and the true gospel.

Did Marcion understand his edition of Luke and the Pauline letters to be a replacement Scripture? Most accounts assume that he did. John Barton argues that such a conclusion retrojects the fourth-century idea of a Christian canon too far back into the second century. The Jewish texts are "Scripture" because they represent a collection of ancient prophetic or-

---

33. For an excellent survey of both traditional and contemporary views of Marcion that supports a reinterpretation of his significance see John Barton, "Marcion Revisited," in Lee Martin McDonald and James A. Sanders, eds., *The Canon Debate* (Peabody: Hendrickson, 2002) 341-54.

acles. Allegorical interpretation was a regular element in the interpretation of inspired or revered texts. The Gospels were not perceived as such. They told a story that everyone knew and served more as memory aids for those who handed that tradition on.[34] Barton points out that Marcion's treatment of Luke and the Pauline letter collection fits a widespread pattern in dealing with texts. Removing spurious passages that had crept into the manuscript as it was copied is hardly a hostile act. It brings Marcion closer to the modern text critic than to the vicious heretic described by those who opposed his teaching. Barton suggests that Marcion could have appealed to Luke's preface in defense of his own correction or reediting of Luke's Gospel.[35] Had he been active some decades earlier, Marcion might have been considered an "Evangelist" or he might have established another family in the textual tradition for Luke's Gospel. Unlike Tatian, who combined four Gospels into a single narrative, Marcion adopted a single Gospel, perhaps because of Luke's traditional association with Paul (Col 4:14; 2 Tim 4:11). His apparent lack of interest in or use of other Gospels or Jesus traditions makes him more of a text editor than the author of a Gospel. The collection of writings prepared for his churches might be thought of as minimum requirements for a mid-second-century house church: a Gospel, apostolic letters, and a summary of the message and guide for interpreters of those texts. Most Christian groups would have some portions of the Jewish Scriptures and perhaps more than one Gospel as well as a collection of apostolic letters.

34. Barton, "Marcion," 345-50.
35. Barton, "Marcion," 348.

CHAPTER THREE

The Quest for Sources

Luke's preface suggests that the author was familiar with several earlier narratives about Jesus. These works embodied what had been handed on by those who participated in the events described, but are not firsthand records. As we have seen, the stories known to Eusebius in the fourth century acknowledged that written Gospels emerged several decades after the death of Jesus. They made available memories of the oral teaching and stories given by apostles from that founding generation. Unlike other historical accounts, Luke-Acts does not make any further references to documents or records in which the author found his information (contrast 2 Macc 2:1, 4, 13-15). Nor does Luke identify himself as having privileged access to the events in question as an eyewitness himself or to members of

---

Suggested Reading

Brown, Raymond E. *The Death of the Messiah.* New York: Doubleday, 1994.

Hultgren, Arland J. *The Parables of Jesus.* Grand Rapids: Eerdmans, 2000.

Kloppenborg Verbin, John S. *Excavating Q: The History and Setting of the Sayings Gospel.* Minneapolis: Fortress, 2000.

Mack, Burton L. *The Christian Myth: Origins, Logic, and Legacy.* New York: Continuum, 2001.

Scott, Bernard Brandon. *Hear Then the Parable: A Commentary on the Parables of Jesus.* Philadelphia: Fortress, 1989.

that generation. By contrast, the Jewish historian Josephus touts his participation in events associated with the Jewish revolt against Rome over against the hearsay evidence of others who had written before him (*War* 1.1).

Those scholars who consider the Gospels as modeled on legend or fiction might point to such deficiencies as evidence for their case. However, considering the situation of Christian books and readers in the first centuries, another explanation is possible. The scattered, loosely affiliated house-based communities that made up the church in various cities did not have archives, official records, or even a set collection of Christian texts. Most of what was known about the life and teaching of Jesus had been transmitted orally. Therefore, the only written text which Luke could presume to be known to an audience would be the Septuagint, which served as Scripture in Christian circles. Luke promises his reader an accurate, orderly account that will substantiate the gospel as taught in the churches of his day.

It is hardly surprising that scholars have gone looking for clues about the sources available to the Evangelists in the Gospels themselves. We have seen already that in the third and fourth centuries Christians had theories about sources for the Gospels, reminiscences of Peter in the case of Mark or an earlier Hebrew or Aramaic prototype for Matthew. Or, as Augustine surmised, one might consider Mark an abbreviation or epitome of the longer Gospel. Modern scholars have a much larger pool of manuscript data to consider, as we have seen. They also have tools that enable them to make detailed comparative analyses of the Gospels at a level unknown to these early exegetes. Yet in the end discussion of the sources employed by the Evangelists still depends on observations about the Gospels themselves.

Early Christian exegetes knew that the similarities of Matthew, Mark, and Luke were a scaffolding that supported numerous differences among them. Although Tatian's *Diatessaron* attempted to combine the four Gospels in a single work and Marcion adopted a single Gospel, Luke, most Christians were content to live with the differences. Each Evangelist had a different background and audience in view even though the four-Gospel canon was adopted as Scripture for the whole Church.[1] On the basis of the

---

1. For example, the anti-Marcionite prologue to Luke explains that although Matthew and Mark had already written Gospels for Judea and Italy respectively, the Holy Spirit inspired Luke, working in Greece, to write for Gentiles (see Joseph A. Fitzmyer, *The Gospel Ac-*

survival of manuscripts and citations in early Christian authors, Matthew came to be the Gospel most commonly read in Christian churches.

From a Synopsis: Comparing the Synoptic Gospels

Since most Christians learned what they knew of the Gospels by hearing them read, subtle differences between accounts of the same event were probably not apparent. Churchgoers today often cannot say which elements of the Christmas story come from Matthew and which from Luke even though those accounts are completely distinct from each other. Today such details provide scholars with important clues to the context that each Gospel addresses.

In the fourth century Eusebius created a set of paragraph numbers so that codex users could locate parallels to a Gospel episode in the other Gospels. But consulting such codices would have been difficult even for those who could read. Comparative analysis is much easier with corresponding sections of the different Gospels printed side by side on a single page. A book containing three or four Gospels laid out in this fashion is called a synopsis or harmony of the Gospels. Such a book makes it possible to hunt for verbal similarities and differences among accounts. Printing has also made it possible to draw more detailed maps for the sequence of episodes in each Gospel.

Scholars of the eighteenth century confronted the data gleaned from their study with different questions than those of a St. Jerome or St. Augustine. Aware of the immense differences between the modern world and the cultures of the ancient Near East, Greece, and Rome, students of ancient texts no longer considered them simple reports about persons or events. Detailed investigation of the sources of biblical material was required in order to figure out what sort of historical information it contained. Many biblical stories copied patterns from the folklore and myths that were turning up in newly discovered ancient Near Eastern literary remains discovered by archaeologists.

---

cording to Luke I-IX [Anchor Bible 28A; New York: Doubleday, 1981] 38-39). For a survey of the patristic views on the Evangelists and their audiences see Margaret M. Mitchell, "Patristic Counter-Evidence for the Claim That the Gospels Were Written for All Christians," *NTS* 51 (2005) 36-79.

By the latter half of the eighteenth century, scholars had the basic data concerning the relationships between Matthew, Mark, and Luke in hand. Many parallels are so close in wording that one of the three Gospels must have been the basis for the others. Since Luke states that he made use of other accounts (Luke 1:1-4), the debate over priority came down to choosing between Matthew and Mark. Since antiquity Matthew was thought to be the basis for an epitome or abbreviation made by Mark. However, Mark has some items in common with Luke not found in Matthew. Therefore Mark, if he was an abbreviator, must have employed both Matthew and Luke for his short version. Referred to as the Griesbach hypothesis after the eighteenth-century scholar who first formulated it, this position still has its advocates today.[2] Much of the popularity of this hypothesis derived from another assumption about Matthew's Gospel. Our extant Greek version of Matthew was considered either a translation of or a subsequent edition of the Hebrew or Aramaic Gospel referred to by Papias. Both Luke and Mark could be seen as moves away from the particularity of Jewish Christianity under the influence of Pauline universalism.[3]

Difficulties for the Griesbach hypothesis are raised by material in Matthew and Luke not represented in Mark. Both Matthew and Luke have additional material at the beginning and end of their Gospels which fill out the literary expectations of a "life." Readers are informed about Jesus' genealogy, miraculous conception, birth, and infancy. Matthew and Luke also take the story beyond the women's discovery of Jesus' empty tomb (Mark 16:1-8) to the resurrection. Jesus appears and reestablishes fellowship with the shattered disciples. Each of the two Evangelists has a unique set of traditions for these additions to the story. Even as they add material or omit items found in Mark both Evangelists continue to follow the structure of Mark's Gospel. Most of Matthew's departures from Mark's order occur in the first half of his Gospel. After Matthew 14:1 (= Mark 6:14), the Evangelist follows Mark quite closely. Luke changes the opening of Jesus' public ministry to encompass considerable activity in Nazareth and Capernaum prior to the call of the disciples. Peter's mother-in-law is healed (Luke 4:38-39 = Mark 1:29-30), and Peter himself witnesses a miraculous catch of fish before his call to discipleship (Luke 5:1-9 = Mark 1:16-18). Matthew provides a cita-

2. See William R. Farmer, "Modern Developments of Griesbach's Hypothesis," *NTS* 23 (1977) 275-95.

3. See the detailed discussion in Kloppenborg Verbin, *Excavating Q,* 271-94.

tion from Isa 9:1-2 to explain why Jesus' ministry began in Galilee (Matt 4:12-17; cf. Mark 1:14-15) but follows Mark's order in having the call of the disciples prior to Jesus' actual preaching (Matt 4:18-22 = Mark 1:16-20). Luke depends on Mark for about half of his material. Two large sections of Mark are not reflected in Luke (Mark 6:45–8:26; 9:41–10:12). Matthew does include parallels to these sections of Mark (Matt 14:22-36; 15:1-39; 16:1-21) with the exception of Mark 8:22-26. Since the birth stories, genealogies, and resurrection narratives all serve to establish Jesus' special relationship with God, it seems more logical to assume that Mark had no such traditions than that he dropped them in abbreviating the Gospels.

There are also about 230 verses, mostly sayings of Jesus, that appear in both Matthew and Luke but not in Mark's Gospel. This material begins with the preaching of the Baptist (Luke 3:7b-9 = Matt 3:7-10). It includes such familiar texts as the Beatitudes (Luke 6:20-23 = Matt 5:1-12), the Lord's Prayer (Luke 11:2-4 = Matt 6:9-15), and the parable of the Lost Sheep (Luke 15:3-7 = Matt 18:12-14). Sometimes this collection is referred to as the "double tradition," that is, material shared by Matthew and Luke, to distinguish it from the "triple tradition," that is, material common to all three Synoptic Gospels. However, it became customary to employ the capital letter "Q" to designate the set of passages involved.[4] This material concludes with sayings that warn hearers to be vigilant in view of the coming judgment (Luke 17:23-24 = Matt 24:26-27; Luke 17:37 = Matt 24:28; Luke 17:26-30 = Matt 24:37-39; Luke 17:34-35 = Matt 24:40-41; Luke 19:12-13, 15-24, 26 = Matt 25:14-15b, 19-29; Luke 22:28, 30 = Matt 19:28).

Q also includes some narrative elements such as the familiar three-fold temptation of Jesus (Luke 4:1-12 = Matt 4:1-11), quite unlike Mark's brief notice about the testing of Jesus (Mark 1:12-13). However, when one reaches the Synoptic accounts of Jesus' passion, death, and resurrection, one no longer finds examples of this double tradition. Matthew and Luke either parallel Mark or incorporate special traditions of their own. Therefore most scholars agree that Q was primarily a collection of sayings and episodes but not a precursor to the Gospel as a life of Jesus. Nor does that collection fit the concern with the death and resurrection of Jesus as the key to salvation, an emphasis reflected in bits of early tradition cited by

---

4. See James M. Robinson, Paul Hoffmann, and John S. Kloppenborg, *The Sayings Gospel in Greek and English with Parallels from the Gospels of Mark and Thomas* (Minneapolis: Fortress, 2002).

Paul (e.g., Phil 2:6-11; 1 Cor 11:23-26; 15:1-5). The prominent role of the passion in the four canonical Gospels suggested to some interpreters that the genre was crafted to support Christian belief that Jesus suffered and died for our salvation. Without the framework provided by the passion, the miracle traditions produce an image of Jesus as wonder-worker and the sayings traditions of one who is a wisdom teacher or a prophetic figure.

For over a century, most exegetes have agreed that some version of the "two-source" theory is the most fruitful interpretation of the data. Mark's Gospel was the basic framework employed by Matthew and Luke, who revised and expanded that account of Jesus with material from an early collection of Jesus' sayings (Q) and with additional material that is special to each Evangelist. Their revisions were completed within two decades of Mark's initial composition and appear to have been independent of each other. Given the variability of texts even when copied under the control of elite authors and their patrons, one cannot rule out the possibility that Matthew and Luke had somewhat different copies of Mark and Q. Because our Greek manuscripts are some centuries removed from the original work of the Evangelists, they were copied by scribes familiar with the other Gospels. So it is even possible that later scribes instinctively introduced elements from the other Gospels into Mark. Such harmonizing tendencies could account for the details noted by those exegetes who continue to hold that Mark is derived from Matthew and Luke.

As any scientist knows, a worthwhile hypothesis provides a best explanation of related sets of data. There always remain anomalies. Some of the oddball data will turn out to be insignificant. Some will generate further refinements in the basic theory. Some will eventually prove to be so critical that they become the key to quite a different theoretical construct. Some are puzzles for which we have proposed explanations that no one is entirely satisfied with. A comprehensive explanation for all of the data generated by detailed comparisons of the Synoptic Gospels would be more complex than the basic "two-source" model. It would have to include cases in which Mark appears to have been expanded or in which Matthew and Luke agree with each other over against Mark. Not all such examples can be accounted for as the substitution of a Q version for what is in Mark as clearly as can the Temptation story.

Such an explanation would also have to deal with the traditions unique to each Evangelist often designated simply by the letters "M" or "L" and with the ongoing oral tradition. Popular media often turn debates among scientists or scholars that are concerned with the difficulties of refining and expanding a theory into revolutions. Naive viewers or readers come away with the impression that mainstream scientists or exegetes are either idiots or ideologues.[5]

The test of any hypothesis or model is its ability to order existing observations and to generate new insights as it is employed in further investigation. On both fronts, the basic "two-source" framework for understanding the relationships among the Synoptic Gospels has proved its value. Although we do not have any explicit evidence from antiquity about the composition of the Gospels beyond Luke's brief comment in his prologue, two bits of external evidence can be introduced to support Markan priority. First, the observation that manuscript remains of Mark in the second and third century are as sparse as those of some non-canonical Gospels. During this period, Gospels usually circulated individually, not in codices containing the four canonical Gospels. Of some thirty known fragmentary Gospel manuscripts, only one is of Mark. Some five manuscripts contain partial remains of unidentified or non-canonical Gospels. This data suggests that Mark was less widely circulated after Matthew and Luke entered into circulation. If there had been a demand for an abbreviation based on Matthew and Luke, one would expect Mark to appear more frequently.[6]

Second, the suggestion that Matthew and Luke revised Mark by incorporating material from other sources fits the habits of composition observed in other writers of the period. There is no good evidence for an author disentangling a more complex text when producing an epitome as Mark would have had to do to get his Gospel out of Matthew and Luke. As the Jewish historian Josephus retells the history of Israel, he paraphrases, expands, gives a précis, or omits material from the Septuagint. When he has more than one account of the same event, he will often conflate the two. Josephus also takes more care to preserve wording from the Septuagint than from other sources. However, he uses a variety of words and phrases to convey the same meaning.[7] In the case of a historian like Josephus, the varia-

---

5. Readers who would like a detailed history of all the various theories that have been advanced to account for the relationships between the Synoptic Gospels can consult Kloppenborg Verbin, *Excavating Q*, 11-80.

6. Bart D. Ehrman, *Lost Christianities: The Battles for Scripture and the Faiths We Never Knew* (New York: Oxford University Press, 2003) 22-23.

7. F. Gerald Downing, *Doing Things with Words in the First Christian Century* (JSNTSup 200; Sheffield: Sheffield Academic, 2000) 153-66.

tions are deliberately chosen modifications of a familiar written text. In the case of the Synoptic Gospels, the situation is somewhat more complex. Neither Mark's Gospel nor Q was considered authoritative scripture when Matthew and Luke wrote their Gospels. In addition, oral traditions produced their own variants in stories about and sayings of Jesus. Therefore the process of Gospel composition is not simply based on a literary revision of earlier texts. The Evangelists have a close and dynamic relationship to the faith and practice of Christian communities, as Luke's prologue indicates (Luke 1:1-4).

The best test of any hypothesis lies in its use. A close reading of Matthew and Luke that begins with the premise that the Evangelist has employed Mark, Q, and his own special material provides exegetes with important insights. Consistent patterns in the modifications made by each Evangelist are clues to the perspective of each author. Since Matthew and Luke are each working with Mark, we can also gain some clues about how first-century Christians heard Mark. For example, compare the three versions of Jesus calming the sea presented on page 62. Both Matthew and Luke present a more concise story than we find in Mark. Matthew interrupts Jesus' progress to the boat with a group of sayings about the cost of being a disciple. Luke has that material in his next chapter (Matt 8:19-22 = Luke 9:57-62).

All three versions conclude with the disciples being astounded by Jesus' ability to command wind and sea. But Mark's way of telling the story introduces a jarring note. After calming the story, Jesus rebukes the terrified disciples: "Have you no faith?" Mark's disciples have questioned Jesus' concern for them as well: "Teacher, do you not care that we are perishing?" A stage director or an oral storyteller might well have this exchange performed as a harsh clash between Jesus and the disciples. Now look at the way in which the other Evangelists have scripted the same exchange. Jesus still comments on the faith of his disciples. That faith remains uncertain. Matthew's Jesus highlights their fear as evidence of a weak faith: "Why are you afraid, you of little faith?" Luke's suggests that in the terror of the moment, the disciples forgot the faith they had in Jesus: "Where is your faith?" Notice another shift that Matthew makes in telling the story. He has Jesus speak to the disciples about faith before performing the miracle, not afterward as in Mark and Luke. The miracle serves as a demonstration that is to bolster the faith of the disciples.

Notice another difference in Matthew and Luke that ameliorates the

Matt 8:18, 23-27 (NRSV)	Mark 4:35-41	Luke 8:22-25
Now when Jesus saw great crowds around him, he gave orders to go over to the other side. [+ vv. 19-22, Q sayings on discipleship]	On that day, when the evening had come, he said to them, "Let us go across to the other side."	One day he got into a boat with his disciples, and he said to them, "Let us go across to the other side of the lake."
And when he got into the boat his disciples followed him.	And leaving the crowd behind, they took him with them in the boat, just as he was. Other boats were with him.	So they put out,
A windstorm arose on the sea, so great that the boat was being swamped by the waves;	A great windstorm arose, and the waves beat into the boat, so that the boat was already being swamped.	and while they were sailing he fell asleep. A windstorm swept down on the lake, and the boat was filling with water, and they were in danger.
but he was asleep. And they went and woke him up, saying, "Lord, save us! We are perishing!"	But he was in the stern, asleep on the cushion; and they woke him up and said to him, "Teacher, do you not care that we are perishing?"	They went to him and woke him up, shouting, "Master, Master, we are perishing!"
And he said to them, *Why are you afraid, you of little faith?"*	He woke up and rebuked the wind, and said to the sea, "Peace! Be still!" Then the wind ceased, and there was a dead calm.	And he woke up and rebuked the wind and the raging waves; they ceased and there was a calm.
Then he got up and rebuked the winds and the sea; and there was a dead calm.	He said to them, *"Why are you afraid? Have you no faith?"*	He said to them, *"Where is your faith?"*
They were amazed, saying, *"What sort of man is this, that even the winds and the sea obey him?"*	And they were filled with great awe and said to one another, *"Who then is this that even the wind and sea obey him?"*	They were afraid and amazed, and said to one another, *"Who then is this, that he commands even the winds and the water, and they obey him?"*

62

harshness of the exchange between the disciples and Jesus: The disciples no longer question Jesus' concern for them. They cry out to him for assistance to rescue them. Luke also shifts the narrative order so that Jesus is said to fall asleep before the gale sweeps down the Sea of Galilee. Of course, Mark may have understood the story that way, if one had asked him to narrate the events in a strictly chronological order. Beginning a story and then sliding in a crucial detail just before it becomes necessary to the action is frequent enough in oral storytelling. In a film, the frame would shift from the disciples struggling at the oars to Jesus sleeping in the stern. So the variants in Matthew and Luke are like the changes in script or blocking that a director makes. The basic story remains, but the audience gains a different feeling for what is going on between the characters.

The next question to ask concerns the larger point of view. Does the rough-edged exchange between Jesus and his disciples represent a consistent pattern in Mark's Gospel? Do Matthew and Luke have a demonstrable tendency to soften Mark's depiction of the relationship between Jesus and his disciples? As it turns out, the answer to both questions is yes. For another example of the same tendency, consider the story of Peter's recognition that Jesus is Messiah in Mark 8:27-33 (= Matt 16:13-23; Luke 9:18-22). Once again, we find Matthew adding material in the middle of a Markan sequence. This time the additional verses concern the divine basis for Peter's confession, Peter's name, and Peter's future role in the community (Matt 16:17-19). These verses are based on Matthew's special tradition rather than on the sayings material from Q as in the earlier example. After telling the disciples not to reveal that he is the Messiah, Jesus predicts his passion (Mark 8:31 = Matt 16:21; Luke 9:22). In response, Peter objects to this destiny and Jesus slaps him down with "Get behind me Satan! You are a stumbling block to me; for you are setting your mind not on divine things but on human things" (Mark 8:33). Despite having just told readers that Peter is the solid foundation on which Jesus' church will be established, Matthew retains this exchange (Matt 16:23). Luke omits that part of the episode from his account completely. Luke has Jesus move directly from the passion prediction to the sayings about following Jesus.

Matthew may have been less concerned about retaining Jesus' reference to Peter as a reflection of Satan than Luke because he has shown readers that Peter has a larger role in God's plan. Neither Mark nor Luke explains how Peter was able to recognize Jesus as the Messiah. Matthew attributes Peter's confession to divine assistance: "Blessed are you, Simon son of Jonah! For flesh and blood has not revealed this to you, but my Father in heaven" (Matt 16:17). Peter's mistaken attempt to dissuade Jesus from the passion shows what happens without God's assistance. Another special Matthean tradition about Peter confirms the suggestion that the Evangelist portrays Peter as both a fallible human being and as an example of what faith can accomplish. Mark has a second story in which Jesus rescues his disciples from a violent storm at sea (Mark 6:45-52). This story apparently circulated in early Christianity attached to the feeding of the five thousand, since John's Gospel has the same pair (John 6:1-21). Luke only has the feeding miracle (Luke 9:10-17), not the second sea rescue. Luke may have omitted repetitious parts of Mark to make room for his longer narrative of Jesus' journey toward Jerusalem, or he may have known a version of Mark that did not have some of the episodes that are missing in his Gospel.

Matthew's version of Jesus walking on the storm-tossed waves (Matt 14:22-33) adds a famous scene, Peter's attempt to do likewise. Peter begins to sink as he lets the severity of the storm frighten him. Jesus rescues Peter but chides him as a person of "little faith." The Evangelist also modifies the conclusion of the story. Mark 6:51-52 makes a shocking statement that the disciples are hard-hearted. They do not recognize Jesus' true identity. In Matt 14:33, by contrast, as soon as Jesus gets into the boat the disciples confess that he is "Son of God." Thus there is a clear difference between the two versions in the portrayal of Jesus' disciples in general and Peter in particular. In Mark Jesus remains an enigma to his disciples. His words and deeds challenge their expectations about what God's Messiah will do. The disciples seem to become even more obtuse as they come up to Jerusalem for the passion. Matthew does not ignore the weaknesses of the disciples completely. Peter does lose confidence and begins to sink after all, but Jesus is there to reach out and save his struggling disciples. They are not "hard-hearted," only persons whose faith is weak or immature.

It is important to distinguish the textual evidence for differences between ways in which one Evangelist differs from the others and the speculative explanations that are suggested to explain an author's choices. Scholars can agree on the data and disagree heatedly over its meaning. The talking head shots of scholars in television specials often give the impression that wildly divergent theories are right there in the text. A professional exegete will know why a particular scholar either made the comments shown or must have been misrepresented by the editing process. A non-specialist pastor or teacher may not know what to say to the confused parishioner or student. When watching such documentaries, it is critical to distinguish information about what is in the text or has been found in the ground by archaeology from big picture theories of what it all means.

Take the problem of how the disciples are portrayed in Mark and Matthew as an example. There is no evidence about Jesus and his disciples outside the stories presented in the Gospels. Were relationships between Jesus and his disciples as difficult as Mark's narrative suggests? If so, then Matthew might be thought to have covered over their flaws in light of the role that the apostles later played in establishing the church. Protestant readers will see Peter as a model figure for the way in which ordinary men and women should build up their faith in Jesus. Catholic readers will think of Peter as the first in an ongoing tradition of popes. Fallible human beings are assured of God's guiding hand when they step into Peter's role. Since church historians know that for the first two centuries the diverse groups of Christians in Rome were not led by a single bishop, exegetes doubt that Matthew had the kind of papacy we see today in view, but he has enhanced Peter's position as an individual leader among the disciples.

The Peter example shows that interpreters can agree about how the Gospels are put together and still disagree over the meaning of those observations. Protestants and Catholics come to the stories about Peter with very different expectations. Even if one admits that Matthew writes from the perspective of a first-century Jewish Christianity that has little in common with either Protestant or Catholic churches as they came to be organized, one still has to figure out how Matthew's audience might have responded. To answer that question, scholars create an image of first-century Christians. Adult students today often find Mark's picture of disciples who are weak, fearful, and struggling to comprehend Jesus quite appealing. Sometimes they protest that Matthew (and Luke) should not have smoothed over the rough edges as they so often do. For a first-century audience, that objection would not carry much weight. Ancient rhetoric had three functions. Forensic rhetoric served the law courts. Deliberative rhetoric involved the political realm of choosing a course of action. A third form of rhetoric served those occasions in which a speech in praise of a person or a city was called for, an *encomium*. Of course, the lawyer or politician might employ a speech detailing the bad characteristics of an opponent, the opposite of an *encomium*. An ancient biography was expected to be a type of *encomium* for its central figure.

Mark's harsh treatment of the disciples only works as *encomium* if the audience perceives it as enhancing the figure of Jesus in some way. For example, Plato often pits the sharp questions of Socrates against an obtuse dialogue partner. Readers can be so carried away by Socrates that they overlook gaps and strange turns in his argument. Matthew and Luke were first-century readers of Mark. Given the care that each Evangelist has taken to revise Mark, it seems unlikely that they would have given such a positive explanation of the matter. Did the need for Jesus to explain the meaning of his parables point to a failure of understanding on the part of Jesus' disciples? Mark might give readers that impression (Mark 4:13, 34b), so Matt 13:51 has them affirm that they have understood Jesus' teaching. Luke 8:4-18 has omitted any suggestion that the disciples misunderstood, abbreviated the number of parables in the discourse, and relocated Jesus' words about his true family from its Markan position just prior to the parables discourse (Mark 3:31-35; also Matt 12:46-50) to its conclusion. Thus in Luke's narrative sequence Jesus' relatives have not arrived to intervene because his activity as an exorcist has led to suspicion about his character, as in Mark 3:20-30 (also Matt 12:22-32). They arrive, rather, at the edge of a large crowd that has been drawn together by Jesus' teaching (Luke 8:19-21). All who hear Jesus, the disciples, the crowd and his relatives, are invited to be part of Jesus' true family by putting the word of God into practice (Luke 8:21).

Eighteenth- and nineteenth-century scholarship often assumed that isolating the earliest sources in the Gospel material would provide a realistic portrait of the historical Jesus himself. In the mid-twentieth century, as scholars paid closer attention to the theological and literary features of each Evangelist, that assumption began to fade from the picture. Mark was as capable of recasting his sources as Matthew and Luke. He was not just an editor pasting together information received from others, as earlier Christians had thought. If Mark had some reason for casting Jesus' disciples in a somewhat unfavorable light, then Matthew's milder version could even be closer to the historical facts. Many different proposals have been offered to explain Mark's depiction of the disciples. Some interpreters have suggested that Peter and the other disciples represent a theological understanding of Jesus and his mission that Mark rejects. They point out that the disciples are devoted to the powerful miracles that Jesus performs. They try to drag him back to the masses in Capernaum (Mark 1:36-37; in

Luke 4:42 the crowds do this). Peter and the others resist Jesus' words about the cross and discipleship. The truth of the gospel message for Mark lies in the passion and death of Christ. Other scholars take a different approach to explain why Mark gives this picture of the disciples. Since Mark depicts suffering as a facet of life for believers, they suggest that Mark's audience would have seen this portrayal as encouragement. Mark's readers know that Peter, James, and John eventually gave their lives for the gospel. Stories of the weaknesses and repeated mistakes of these followers will enable Mark's audience to remain attached to Jesus even though they may have failed in similar ways.

Explanations for the observed features of a Gospel that depend on an exegete's best guess about the author's intentions or about particular characteristics of an audience can be difficult to adjudicate. Each proposal may be consistent with the set of assumptions about early Christianity that is employed to formulate a hypothesis. There may not be sufficient data to discriminate between different possibilities. First-century readers certainly would have assumed that any account of persons or events was intended to convey a message about its subject. They would expect another author or speaker to have a different point of view.

Since Mark did not make up the story of Jesus' ministry and death, the earliest Evangelist must have had sources as well. Some exegetes have attempted to re-create that level of pre-Markan tradition and even to distinguish between the theological orientations of such sources as miracle collections and of the Evangelists. Collections of shorter stories such as parables or miracles could have circulated orally or in notebook format. Some description of Jesus' trial and execution might have existed prior to Mark's Gospel as well. Those who detect the wording of a pre-Markan source within the Gospel depend on complex analyses that are disputed even among scholars. Non-specialists can appreciate ways in which Matthew and Luke have revised Mark by attention to the Synopsis.

From Q and the *Gospel of Thomas* to Sayings Gospels

The overlap in wording between Matthew and Luke made it possible for scholars to reconstruct a possible written text for the sayings source that the two Evangelists have in common. Familiarity with the individual style of each Evangelist also helped in selecting between the wording of Matthew and Luke when their versions differed.[8] Order in a collection of sayings is difficult to discern, as any reader of Proverbs knows. It is no surprise that Matthew and Luke show much more divergence in their incorporation of sayings material into the narrative order that they derived from Mark than in the larger sequence of episodes in the life of Jesus. Since Matthew's literary structure incorporates the teaching of Jesus into five extended discourses, scholars usually assume that Luke preserved the order of sayings in his Q source more often than Matthew did. The international committee which produced the new critical edition of Q tried to correct for any bias in that assumption by laying out the material in Matthew's order on one side of the reconstructed Q and Luke's on the other. In the end, they agreed with earlier studies that Luke provides the best overall sequence for the sayings.[9] Exegetes refer to Q passages by the corresponding chapter and verse references in Luke's Gospel.

Until the mid-twentieth century, the existence of a collection of sayings which lacked the biographical framework of Jesus' life remained a guess based on source criticism. Neither Matthew nor Luke could be shown to have taken the common sayings material from the other. Slender additional evidence that sayings of Jesus circulated among early Christians could be found in Paul's occasional references to "sayings of the Lord" (e.g., 1 Thess 4:15; 1 Cor 7:10). However, no such sayings collection had survived in the earliest manuscripts. When a collection of codices containing over fifty works that had been translated from Greek into Coptic was discovered in 1945, the situation changed. One of the works discovered was a collection of sayings of Jesus. It opened with "These are the secret sayings which the living Jesus spoke and which Didymos Judas Thomas wrote down."[10] The title given this collection in the codex is "The Gospel According to Thomas." Once the Coptic had been discovered, scholars recognized that some Greek fragments containing sayings of Jesus belonged to *Gos. Thom.* The Coptic codices were copied in the middle of the fourth century, but the Greek fragments have been dated in the late second or early third century. So we know

---

8. An international team of scholars has put together a Q synopsis which has proposed detailed reconstructions of the text of Q that also includes consideration of text-critical variants, traditions similar to Q in Mark and John, and the sayings found in the second-century *Gos. Thom.* See Robinson, Hoffmann, and Kloppenborg, *The Critical Edition of Q.*

9. Robinson, et al., *Sayings Gospel,* 9-10, 42-44.

10. See Robinson, *Nag Hammadi Library in English,* 126.

that at least one collection of Jesus' sayings remained in circulation for several centuries. Its first editors divided the text of *Gos. Thom.* into 114 sayings. Scholars use these numbers to refer to individual selections.

While *Gos. Thom.* confirmed the existence of sayings collections, it did not provide scholars with a second- or third-century edition of Q. There is no connection between the order of sayings in *Gos. Thom.* and Q. In addition to Q parallels, *Gos. Thom.* has variants of material from the traditions Matthew and Luke share with Mark and of the traditions unique to either Matthew or Luke. Almost half of the *Gos. Thom.* sayings have no Synoptic parallels at all, some of which are found in other early Christian authors. Once again, figuring out the relationship between a saying in *Gos. Thom.* and the parallel versions in the Synoptic Gospels is not a simple task. Only fragments of the Greek versions remain. The Coptic translator probably knew the Synoptic Gospels and could have introduced parallels to the language of the canonical texts. In some cases *Gos. Thom.* presents a shorter version of a saying or parable which could reflect the version that was reworked by one of the Synoptic Evangelists. Take the parable of the Rich Fool from Luke's special material (Luke 12:16-21) for example. *Gos. Thom.* 63a lacks the interior monologue, which is a stylistic feature of Luke's composition (see p. 219). Luke has incorporated this parable into a larger sequence against greed. Jesus tells the parable in refusing to resolve a dispute over inheritance (Luke 12:13-15). The additional maxim at the conclusion of Luke's parable returns to that issue.

Luke follows this piece of instruction with a group of sayings against anxiety about the future (Luke 12:22b-31 = Matt 6:25-33) derived from Q. Matthew incorporates the sayings against anxiety into the Sermon on the Mount, Jesus' first discourse in Matthew. One of the Greek fragments of *Gos. Thom.* (P Oxy 655 1-17) contains a shorter version of that Q tradition:

> Jesus says, "Be not solicitous from morning until evening or from evening until morning either for your sustenance, what you will eat, or for your clothing, what you will put on. You are worth far more than the lilies which grow but do not spin, and have no clothing. And you, what do you lack? Who of you can add to his stature/span of life? He will give you your clothing."[11]

11. From Joseph A. Fitzmyer, *The Gospel According to Luke (X-XXIV)* (Anchor Bible 28B; New York: Doubleday, 1985) 976.

Luke 12:16-21	Gos. Thom. 63a
Then he told them a parable, "The land of a rich man produced abundantly.	Jesus said: "There was a rich man who had much money.
And he thought to himself, 'What should I do for I have no place to store my crops?'	He said, 'I shall put my money to use
Then he said, 'I will do this: I will pull down my barns and build larger ones, and there I will store all my grain and my goods.	so that I may store, reap, plant and fill my storehouse with produce,
And I will say to my soul, Soul, you have ample goods laid up for many years; relax, eat, drink, be merry.'	with the result that I will lack nothing.'
But God said to him, 'You fool! This very night your life is being demanded of you. And the things you have prepared, whose will they be?'	Such were his intentions but that same night he died."
So it is with those who store up treasures for themselves but are not rich toward God.	

The Coptic translator condensed the tradition even further. Only the opening injunction remains. The poetic analogy with the lilies has been dropped completely: "Jesus said, 'Do not be concerned from morning until evening and from evening until morning about what you will wear'" (*Gos. Thom.* 36).

In this example Luke has combined the material from his special tradition with sayings from Q. Matthew used the same Q sayings in a different context at the opening of Jesus' ministry. *Gos. Thom.* confirms that the parable of the Rich Fool was not linked to the anxiety sayings in the pre-Lukan tradition. However, the contrast between our surviving Greek section of *Gos. Thom.* and the Coptic translation calls for a note of caution in using the Coptic to represent the text of an earlier Greek *Gos. Thom.* The Coptic translation does not provide an accurate representation of its own Greek precursor. Therefore, it cannot be alleged to provide an earlier, more immediate access to the words of Jesus himself than Q or the canonical

Gospels. Popular editions of *Gos. Thom.* litter the shelves of chain bookstores with claims emblazoned on the covers that they contain early or authentic words of Jesus. Not so. Each saying requires careful, critical study of its variants and tradition history.

Because the sayings in *Gos. Thom.* have not been reworked to fit a narrative account of Jesus' life and ministry, they may preserve some clues about the shape of the Q tradition before it was revised by one of the Evangelists. However, as the anxiety sayings demonstrate, the third-century Coptic translation also abbreviated familiar sayings and parables. In some cases, *Gos. Thom.* appears to do no more than epitomize material that was familiar from the Synoptic Gospels. It is even possible that in particular cases *Gos. Thom.* has lost the first-century setting and the biblical allusions of the Jesus tradition entirely. Joseph Fitzmyer's commentary on Luke 12:16-21 provides evidence for that conclusion. He says of *Gos. Thom.* 63: "In this form of the story, however, the rich man is not treated as a fool, and it has lost the cutting edge of the Lucan parable, viz. God's verdict."[12] The figure of the fool who ignores God or the requirements of Torah in absurd pursuits is a familiar motif in Israel's wisdom traditions (e.g., Ps 14:1; Prov 1:7; 9:10). *1 Enoch* 97:8-10 contrasts the folly of the rich, who pile up wealth in storehouses expecting to secure their life, with the judgment that awaits them: "Like water your life will flow away, for riches will not stay with you; they will quickly go up from you, for you acquired everything in wickedness and will be given over to a great curse."[13] The phrase with which the rich man concludes his interior monologue in Luke 12:19, "eat, drink, be merry," was a familiar expression in antiquity (Eccl 8:15; Tob 7:10; *1 Enoch* 97:8-9; Euripides, *Alcestis* 788-89; Menander, fragment 301).[14] *Gos. Thom.* 63 retains the skeleton of a tradition that condemns the rich for placing false confidence in piling up goods. It lacks the dramatic literary power of Luke's version. One cannot be certain whether it represents the early Jesus tradition as Luke received it or the Coptic translator's stripped-down abbreviation of a tradition originally closer to what we see in Luke. Perhaps its Greek archetype will turn up among the thousands of unedited papyri to provide a clue.

The international team which prepared the new critical edition of Q

---

12. Fitzmyer, *Luke X-XXIV,* 971.
13. Fitzmyer, *Luke X-XXIV,* 972.
14. Fitzmyer, *Luke X-XXIV,* 973.

creates a false impression of the relationship between the Coptic *Gos. Thom.* and Q by including a Greek text for all of the *Gos. Thom.* parallels to Q sayings in footnotes. The scholarly edition prints the Coptic text in a column of the synopsis. The student edition only has the Greek. In either case, users should be cautious about treating this Greek text as an authority for early Jesus tradition that is earlier than or independent of what is found in the Greek text of the Gospels.[15] The Q editors attempt to convey the uncertainties attached to their project by presenting their results as a fragmentary text. Where both the Matthean and Lukan versions of a pericope show signs of the Evangelists' editing, the Q text is presented as though scholars had filled in a gap in a fragmentary manuscript. The editors have also moved ten sayings to a position different from the order in which they are found in Luke and proposed including a few passages found in only one of the Gospels. The editorial team has even created Q fragments for material which it assumes must have been in Q, such as an opening sentence (cf. *Gos. Thom.* incipit) and references to the baptism of Jesus (cf. Mark 1:9-11 = Matt 3:13-17 = Luke 3:21-22) and Jesus' rejection at Nazareth (cf. Mark 6:16 = Matt 13:53-58 = Luke 4:16-30). Many scholars who accept the hypothesis of Q as a source are skeptical of such a detailed reconstruction. Even though most of Mark has been retained in one or both of the other Synoptic Gospels, such a comparative effort would not reproduce the text of Mark as we know it.[16]

The critical edition of Q does not limit its reconstruction to the material shared by Matthew and Luke that is without parallel in Mark. The editors also include sayings with parallels in Mark. The cases in which one finds both a Markan and a Q version in the same Gospel can be invoked to support this procedure. The examples on page 73 can be found in Luke.[17]

---

15. For a helpful chart that lists all the New Testament and early Christian parallels to each saying in *Gos. Thom.*, see David E. Aune, *The Westminster Dictionary of the New Testament and Early Christian Literature and Rhetoric* (Louisville: Westminster/John Knox, 2003) 467-72.

16. Michael Wolter ("Reconstructing Q?" *ExpTim* 115 [2004] 116-17) points out that Luke uses only 52% of Mark. The percentage of Mark drops to 43% in the section on Jesus' journey to Jerusalem, which has the heaviest concentration of Luke's special material. Of the 600 verses of Mark found in Matthew, only 320 are also in Luke. Without a copy of Mark, those verses would have been assigned to the special Matthean material. The result of this worst case estimate leaves a reconstruction of Mark almost 50% shorter than our surviving text.

17. See Fitzmyer, *Luke I-IX*, 81-82.

	Mark as source	*Q as source*
"anyone with ears to hear"	Luke 8:8c = Mark 4:9, 23	Luke 14:35c = Matt 11:15; 13:9
lighted lamp on stand	Luke 8:16 = Mark 4:21	Luke 11:33 = Matt 5:15
hidden to be disclosed	Luke 8:17 = Mark 4:22	Luke 12:2 = Matt 10:26
rules for those on mission	Luke 9:3-5 = Mark 6:8, 10-11	Luke 10:4-5, 7, 10-11 = Matt 10:10-12, 14
followers must deny self	Luke 9:23-24 = Mark 8:34-35	Luke 14:27; 17:33 = Mt 10:38-39
at judgment, Son of Man will reject those ashamed of him	Luke 9:26 = Mark 8:38	Luke 12:8-9 = Matt 10:32-33
welcoming child (Jesus) is to welcome Jesus (God)	Luke 9:48 = Mark 9:37	Luke 10:6 = Matt 10:40(?)
against scribes who love external signs of honor	Luke 20:46 = Mark 12:38-39	Luke 11:43 = Matt 23:6-7
confidence when put on trial	Luke 21:14-15 = Mark 13:11	Luke 12:11-12 = Matt 10:19-20

The Q presented in the critical edition also goes beyond including the Q version of such doublets to suggest a Q form for other passages. Scholars have long recognized that Matthew and Luke must have substituted the Q version of Jesus' temptation for the brief notice in Mark 1:12-13. Expanding that practice to sayings in which Matthew and Luke could just as easily reflect variants on Mark is more problematic. Many lists of Q will be more conservative, listing only the passages in which there is a clear verbal overlap between Matthew and Luke that has not been derived from Mark.

The list of Q passages on pages 74-80 has been derived from the critical edition and follows the proposed order there. The editors have divided the material into the smallest possible sayings groups rather than suggest any larger clusters of material or thematic units within Q.

	Luke/Matthew(Q)	Gos. Thom., Mark
Baptist appears preaching judgment	Luke 3:7-9/Matt 3:7-10	
Baptist speaks of the greater one to come after him bringing judgment	Luke 3:16b-17/Matt 3:11-12	Mark 1:7-8
[Baptism of Jesus]	[Luke 3:21b-22/Matt 3:16-17]	Mark 1:9-11
Temptation of Jesus	Luke 4:1-13/Matt 4:1-11	[Mark 1:12-13]
[Nazareth]	[Luke 4:16/Matt 4:13]	Mark 6:1
Blessed the poor, hungry, mourning	Luke 6:20-21/Matt 5:1-4, 6	Gos. Thom. 54 and 69.2
Blessed the persecuted	Luke 6:22-23/Matt 5:11-12	Gos. Thom. 68.1 and 69.1
Love your enemies	Luke 6:27-28, 35c-d/ Matt 5:44-45	
Do not retaliate against slap, lawsuit, conscription, borrower	Luke 6:29-30/Matt 5:39b-42	Gos. Thom. 95 (on lending)
Golden rule	Luke 6:31/Matt 7:12	Gos. Thom. 6.3 (= P. Oxy. 654)
Against loving only those who reciprocate	Luke 6:32, 34/Matt 5:46-47	Gos. Thom. 95 (on lending)
Be compassionate as God is	Luke 6:36/Matt 5:48	
Do not judge	Luke 6:37-38/Matt 7:1-2	
Blind leading the blind	Luke 6:39/Matt 15:14	Gos. Thom. 34
Student not greater than the teacher	Luke 6:40/Matt 10:24-25a	
Remove beam in your own eye before speck in neighbor's	Luke 6:41-42/Matt 7:3-5	Gos. Thom. 26 (= P. Oxy. 1, partially preserved)

	Luke/Matthew(Q)	Gos. Thom., Mark
Tree known by its fruit	Luke 6:43-45/Matt 7:16, 18; 12:33b-35	*Gos. Thom.* 45
Simply saying "master", not acting	Luke 6:46/Matt 7:21	(Mark 3:35a)
Foundation of sand or rock	Luke 6:47-49/Matt 7:24-27	
Healing centurion's child	Luke 7:1, 3, 6b-10/Matt 7:28a; 8:5-10, 13	
Baptist sends disciples to ask if Jesus is the one to come	Luke 7:18-19, 22-23/ Matt 11:2-6	
Baptist is more than a prophet	Luke 7:24-28/Matt 11:7-11	*Gos. Thom.* 78 and 46
[Divided response to Baptist]	[Luke 7:29-30/Matt 21:32]	
This generation's ambivalence toward Baptist/Jesus — Parable of children playing	Luke 7:31-35/Matt 11:16-19	
To would-be followers, homeless Son of Man	Luke 9:57-60/Matt 8:19-22	*Gos. Thom.* 86
Workers needed for harvest	Luke 10:2/Matt 9:37-38	*Gos. Thom.* 73
Disciples sent like sheep among wolves	Luke 10:3/Matt 10:16	
Take no provisions	Luke 10:4/Matt 10:9-10a	Mark 6:8-9
Conduct upon entering a house or town	Luke 10:5-9/Matt 10:7-8, 10b-13	Mark 6:10b-c, 12-13; *Gos. Thom.* 14.4
Responding to rejection by a town — it will be condemned at judgment	Luke 10:10-12/Matt 10:14-15	Mark 6:11

	Luke/Matthew(Q)	Gos. Thom., Mark
Woe against Chorazin, Bethsaida, and Capernaum	Luke 10:13-15/Matt 11:21-24	
Whoever takes in one of the disciples on mission does so for Jesus/ God	Luke 10:16/Matt 10:40	Mark 9:37
Thanksgiving for revelation to children of what is hidden from the wise	Luke 10:21/Matt 11:25-26	
Father known through the Son	Luke 10:22/Matt 11:27	*Gos. Thom.* 61.3b (? only a phrase)
Blessed eyes that see what you do . . . prophets and kings did not see it	Luke 10:23b-24/Matt 13:16-17	
Lord's prayer	Luke 11:2b-4/Matt 6:9-13a	
Prayer will be answered	Luke 11:9-13/Matt 7:7-11	*Gos. Thom.* 92.1 and 94
Against charge that Jesus employs power of Beelzebul	Luke 11:14-15, 17-20/ Matt 9:32-34; 12:25-28	Mark 3:22-26
[Robbing strong man's house]		[Mark 3:27] *Gos. Thom.* 35
One not with me is against me	Luke 11:23/Matt 12:30	Mark 9:40
[Hearing and keeping God's word?]	[Luke 11:27-28]	*Gos. Thom.* 79
Sign of Jonah given this generation	Luke 11:16, 29-30/Matt 12:38-40	Mark 8:11-12

	Luke/Matthew(Q)	Gos. Thom., Mark
This generation condemned: did not repent at greater sign than Jonah, Solomon	Luke 11:31-32/Matt 12:41-42	
Lamp placed on lampstand	Luke 11:33/Matt 5:15	Mark 4:21; *Gos. Thom.* 33
Diseased eye darkens body	Luke 11:34-35/Matt 6:22-23	*Gos. Thom.* 24 (= P. Oxy. 655)
Woes against the Pharisees	Luke 11:39, 41-44/Matt 23:1-2a, 6-7, 23, 25, 26b-27	Mark 12:38c-39; *Gos. Thom.* 89 (only phrase about washing cup)
Woes against interpreters of Torah	Luke 11:46b-48, 52/Matt 23:4, 13, 29-32	*Gos. Thom.* 39 (= P. Oxy. 655)
Wisdom condemns this generation for blood of prophets	Luke 11:49-51/Matt 23:34-36	
What is hidden will be revealed	Luke 12:2-3/Matt 10:26-27	Mark 4:22; *Gos. Thom.* 5.2 (= P. Oxy. 654); 6.5 (= P. Oxy. 654); 33.1 (– P. Oxy. 1)
Do not fear those who kill only the body	Luke 12:4-5/Matt 10:28	
Against anxiety: more valuable than sparrows	Luke 12:6-7/Matt 10:29-31	
At judgment Son of Man will acknowledge or deny those who did so to him	Luke 12:8-9/Matt 10:32-33	Mark 8:38
No forgiveness for speaking against Holy Spirit	Luke 12:10/Matt 12:32	Mark 3:28-29; *Gos. Thom.* 44

77

	Luke/Matthew(Q)	Gos. Thom., Mark
Against anxiety: Holy Spirit will aid those brought before synagogues	Luke 12:11-12/Matt 10:19	Mark 13:9-11
Store up treasure in heaven	Luke 12:33-34/Matt 6:19-21	Mark 10:21b; *Gos. Thom.* 76.3
Against anxiety: like ravens and lilies	Luke 12:22b-31/Matt 6:25-33	*Gos. Thom.* 36, shortened version of *Gos. Thom.* P. Oxy. 655
Watch: Son of Man comes like thief	Luke 12:39-40/Matt 24:43-44	Mark 13:35; *Gos. Thom.* 21 and 105
Parable of faithful/un-faithful slaves during master's delay	Luke 12:42-46/Matt 24:45-51	Mark 13:36 (warning against being found asleep)
Jesus' coming to divide families	Luke 12:49, 51, 53/Matt 10:34-35	Mark 13:12; *Gos. Thom.* 10 and 16
[Recognize the time]	[Luke 12:54-56/Matt 16:2-3]	*Gos. Thom.* 91.2
Settle with an opponent out of court	Luke 12:58-59/Matt 5:25-26	
(Parable of the Mustard Seed)	(Luke 13:18-19/Matt 13:31-32)	Mark 4:30-32; *Gos. Thom.* 20
Parable of the Yeast	Luke 13:20-21/Matt 13:33	*Gos. Thom.* 96
Enter narrow door; householder rejects those who knock on locked door	Luke 13:24-27/Matt 7:13-14, 22-23; 25:10-12	
Many from east and west included while you [this generation] rejected from dining with patriarchs in kingdom	Luke 13:28-29/Matt 8:11-12	

	Luke/Matthew(Q)	Gos. Thom., Mark
[Last shall be first]	[Luke 13:30/Matt 20:16]	Mark 10:31; *Gos. Thom.* 4.2 (= P. Oxy. 654)
Judgment against Jerusalem	Luke 13:34-35/Matt 23:37-39	Mark 11:9c (Blessed one comes in name of Lord)
[Humble to be exalted]	[Luke 14:11/Matt 23:12]	
Parable of the banquet guests	Luke 14:16-21, 23/Matt 22:2-10	*Gos. Thom.* 64
Disciple must hate family	Luke 14:26/Matt 10:37	Mark 10:29b; *Gos. Thom.* 55 and 101
Disciple must take up cross	Luke 14:27/Matt 10:38	Mark 8:34b; *Gos. Thom.* 55.2
Lose one's life to save it	Luke 17:33/Matt 10:39	Mark 8:35
Salt without flavor	Luke 14:34-35/Matt 5:13	Mark 9:49-50a
Impossible to serve God and mammon	Luke 16:13/Matt 6:24	*Gos. Thom.* 47.2
Kingdom of God since Baptist	Luke 16:16/Matt 11:12-13	
No stroke of Torah to be abolished	Luke 16:17/Matt 5:18	(Mark 13:30-31, permanence of Jesus' word; no Torah reference)
Against divorce, equivalent to adultery	Luke 16:18/Matt 5:32	Mark 10:11b-12
Against leading little ones into sin	Luke 17:1-2/Matt 18:6-7	Mark 9:42
Parable of the lost sheep	Luke 15:4-5a, 7/Matt 18:12-13	*Gos. Thom.* 107
[Lost Coin]	[Luke 15:8-10]	
Repeated forgiveness for repentant sinner	Luke 17:3-4/Matt 18:15, 21	

	Luke/Matthew(Q)	Gos. Thom., Mark
Faith like a mustard seed	Luke 17:6/Matt 17:20b	Mark 11:22b-23; *Gos. Thom.* 48
[Kingdom of God within]	[Luke 17:20-21/Matt 24:23]	[Mark 13:21, against believing false predictions] *Gos. Thom.* 3 (= P. Oxy. 654) and 113
Son of Man to come like lightning	Luke 17:23-24/Matt 24:26-27	Mark 13:21; *Gos. Thom.* 3 (= P. Oxy. 654)
Vultures gather around a corpse	Luke 17:37/Matt 24:28	
Judgement to come as in days of Noah	Luke 17:26-30/Matt 24:37-39	
One taken, another left	Luke 17:34-35/Matt 24:40-41	Mark 13:16; *Gos. Thom.* 61
Parable of servants entrusted with money by master on journey	Luke 19:12-13, 15-24, 26/ Matt 25:14-15b, 19-29	Mark 13:34 (tasks entrusted to slaves); Mark 4:25 (saying, to one who has, more given); *Gos. Thom.* 41 (saying: to one who has, more given)
You to judge 12 tribes of Israel	Luke 22:18, 30/Matt 19:28	

Some larger blocks of sayings can be discerned in the reconstructed Q if one assumes that Luke's blocks of material have followed his source. Like most such schemes, not all the sayings fit into the macro-categories.

John the Baptist's appearance and preaching	Luke 3:7-9, 16b-17
Temptation of Jesus	Luke 4:1-13
Jesus' inaugural sermon	Luke 6:20-49
Jesus on the Baptist, against "this generation"	Luke 7:18-35
Instructions to disciples sent to harvest	Luke 10:2-16
Blessing on those who respond to Jesus' preaching	Luke 10:21-24

On prayer	Luke 11:2b-4, 9-13
Jesus against his opponents	Luke 11:14-51
To disciples against being afraid of opponents	Luke 12:2-3(?); 12:4-31
Be vigilant, the Son of Man comes suddenly	Luke 12:39-56
Warning that many will find themselves excluded; judgment against Jerusalem	Luke 13:24-35; 14:23
To disciples on necessity of suffering	Luke 14:26-27; 17:33
To disciples, miscellaneous sayings and parables on conduct	Luke 14:34-35; 15:4-5; 16:16-18; 17:1-2; 17:3-4, 6
Further sayings and parables on coming judgment	Luke 17:23-24, 37, 26-30, 34-35; 19:12-13, 15-24, 26; 22:18, 30

The following items have been omitted from the editors' classification of Q segments, though in some cases they may be interpreted as part of the group to which they are closest.

Healing the centurion's child	Luke 7:1-10
To would-be followers, Son of Man is homeless	Luke 9:57-60
Lamp to be put on stand and darkness caused by diseased eye	Luke 11:33-35
Division within families	Luke 12:49, 51, 53
Settle with your opponent out of court	Luke 12:58-59
Parable of the Yeast	Luke 13:20-21
Kingdom of God since the Baptist	Luke 16:16

The only anomalous pericope is the lone miracle story. Most descriptions of Q skirt the difficulty by describing it as a statement about faith. For example, the editors of the critical edition entitle the section, "The Centurion's Faith in Jesus' Word."[18] Jesus' miracle working does not figure in any of the other sayings of Q or in the later *Gos. Thom.* Rather than attempt to make the healing of the centurion's son fit by stripping it of that element, one should consider alternate possibilities. This pericope could be a case of

---

18. Robinson, et al., *Sayings Gospel*, 90.

double tradition not taken from Q. The noun "faith" is rare in Q. The only other saying in which it appears is the grain of mustard seed (Luke 17:6/ Matt 17:20b), a text which has a parallel in Mark's sayings on prayer (Mark 11:22b-23). The only other reference to Israel in Q occurs in the concluding statement that Jesus' followers will judge its tribes (Luke 22:28, 30/Matt 19:28). Some scholars are uncertain about the inclusion of that judgment saying in Q.[19]

A possible explanation for the appearance of this healing in Q could be its attachment to the inaugural sermon at an earlier stage of that tradition. Luke's version of the sermon has been adopted by most reconstructions as the basis for the Q text. The critical edition, for example, takes its core Beatitudes as the opening of the sermon. It omits the woes against the rich (Luke 6:24-26), which have no parallel in Matthew. The ordinary procedures of source and redaction criticism would lead exegetes to treat Matthew's Sermon on the Mount as the Evangelist's revision of the Lukan sermon. Much of what Matthew's sermon adds can be found elsewhere in Q. However, other scholars see the substantial differences between the sermon in Matthew and in Luke as part of the evidence that each was dependent on a different form of Q.[20] Hans Dieter Betz appeals to the fact that each sermon is followed by the healing of the centurion's servant as evidence that the Evangelists were dependent on Q and not some other source for the sermon.[21] For other scholars, who think that Matthew and Luke have diverse oral and written sources for their double tradition, the sermon-miracle combination would be an example of such divergence.[22]

For the use of Q in a minimalist sense as a hypothetical source to explain how Matthew and Luke composed their Gospels, its exact parameters can be left indefinite. Sayings collections are so easily changed that the

---

19. See Aune, *Westminster Dictionary*, 394.

20. For the most detailed argument of this point, see Hans Dieter Betz, *The Sermon on the Mount* (Minneapolis: Fortress, 1995) 41-44.

21. Betz, *Sermon*, 43.

22. J. D. G. Dunn ("Altering the Default Setting: Re-envisaging the Early Transmission of the Jesus Tradition," *NTS* 49 [2003] 139-75) sees the love command section of the inaugural sermon (Matt 5:39b-42/Luke 6:29-30) and the Lord's Prayer (Matt 6:7-15/Luke 11:1-4) as examples of non-Q oral tradition. Also see Dunn, "Q1 as Oral Tradition," in Markus Bockmuehl and Donald A. Hagner, eds., *The Written Gospel* (Cambridge: Cambridge University Press, 2005) 45-69 on the importance of oral tradition in the early collections of Jesus' sayings.

multiple copies of a collection are more likely to differ in content or order than be identical. The overlap of written and oral traditions during the first and second centuries makes the mix of semantic overlap and variation that one observes in Q and *Gos. Thom.* inevitable.[23] It is possible to use the sections in which Matthew and Luke overlap as the basis for distinguishing between source material and the Evangelist's composition without knowing the exact wording or composition of Q. Commentaries on one of the Synoptic Gospels take up each section of the Gospel and analyze its sources individually. They include the *Gos. Thom.* versions of particular sayings or parables when *Gos. Thom.* appears to preserve a variant that has been less modified than those in the Synoptic Gospels or to suggest that one Gospel's version is older than another, as in the parable of the Mustard Bush (Mark 4:30-32 = Matt 13:31-32; Luke 13:18-19). The simple analogy in *Gos. Thom.* 20 may well reflect a version earlier than any of the Synoptics: "It [= the kingdom] is like a mustard seed. It is the smallest of all seeds. But when it falls on tilled soil, it produces a great plant and becomes a shelter for the birds of the sky."

As we have seen, *Gos. Thom.* sayings are not always earlier than the variants found in the Synoptic Gospels. The sayings preserved in the Coptic translation have been abbreviated, transmitted, and modified in a Christian environment in which the Synoptic Gospels were in circulation. If one looks, for example, for parallels to the Beatitudes which initiate the inaugural sermon, one finds some pale reflections in *Gos. Thom.* (see p. 84). The social conditions of those who suffer as poor, hungry, and mourning (cf. Isa 61:1-3) have faded in *Gos. Thom.* as we have it. Persecutors are not described as those who resist the prophetic word or the message about Jesus. Instead *Gos. Thom.* 69 has interiorized persecution as a necessary obstacle in the path to knowledge of God. By shifting the beatitude on hunger to the end of the persecution collection, *Gos. Thom.* 68-69 might be referring to hunger as an ascetic practice. *Gos. Thom.* 3 provides a key to the interpretation of kingdom sayings by the later believers responsible for the surviving Coptic version. Seeking the kingdom is not an external project to be realized in the communal relationships among human beings, as in the Synoptic beatitudes. It involves an inner quest to discover the true image of God. *Gos. Thom.* 3 concludes by interpreting poverty as

---

23. David M. Carr, *Writing on the Tablet of the Heart: Origins of Scripture and Literature* (New York: Oxford University Press, 2005) 280.

Q	Gos. Thom.
Blessed are you who are poor, for yours is the kingdom of God. (Luke 6:20)	Jesus says: Blessed are the poor, for theirs is the kingdom of heaven. (*Gos. Thom.* 54)
Blessed are you who are hungry now, for you will be filled. (Luke 6:21a)	. . . Blessed are the hungry, for the belly of him who desires will be filled. (*Gos. Thom.* 69.2)
Blessed are you who weep now, for you will laugh. (Luke 6:21b)	
Blessed are you when people hate you, and when they exclude you, revile you, and cast out your name as evil on account of the Son of Man. Rejoice in that day and leap for joy, for surely your reward is great in heaven; for that is what their ancestors did to the prophets. (Luke 6:22-23)	Jesus said: Blessed are you when you are hated and persecuted. Wherever you are persecuted they will find no place. (*Gos. Thom.* 68)
Blessed are you when people revile you and persecute you and utter all kinds of evil against you falsely on my account. Rejoice and be glad, for your reward is great in heaven, for in the same way they persecuted the prophets before you. (Matt 5:11-12)	Jesus said: Blessed are they who have been persecuted within themselves. It is they who have truly come to know the Father. (*Gos. Thom.* 69.1)

lack of spiritual insight: "But if you will not know yourselves, you dwell in poverty and it is you who are that poverty." Thus *Gos. Thom.* has its own story to tell about the meaning which second- and third-century Christians gave to the sayings of Jesus. Contrary to the impression often given in the media, *Gos. Thom.* should not be substituted for careful study of the Synoptic Gospels as though it were a suppressed voice of Jesus himself.

Q

Is It a Gospel?

Its editors entitled the student edition of Q *The Sayings Gospel Q*. A growing number of academic studies treat Q in the same fashion as the Synoptic Gospels. They argue for discernable strata, for theological emphases typical of the different redactions, and for a sociological description of its audience, the Q community.[24] Should a hypothetical text for which we have no ancient exemplars be referred to as though it were the earliest Gospel? Many exegetes still insist that it should not. The traditions about Jesus circulated in such a rich variety of oral and written forms that even the claim to have reconstructed the written text known to Matthew and Luke near the end of the first century is dubious, let alone the claim to discern earlier strata from the first decade or so after Jesus' death.[25] The Q Gospel project is more speculative than most of its advocates admit even in the scholarly literature. But new scientific insights do often emerge when scholars explore and debate what appears an unlikely sideline. In this field as in many others, the media often present hypotheses and partial results as revolutionary new discoveries of fact, so students of the Synoptic Gospels should be familiar with the "Q Gospel" discussion.

Should a collection of sayings be referred to as a "Gospel"? Collections of the sayings of sages from antiquity are designated "instruction" or "sentences" along with the name of the individual. A popular collection of maxims attributed to the philosopher Pythagoras that was copied and circulated up to the early modern period is known as the "golden verses."[26] Hans Dieter Betz argues that the summary or compendium of a philosopher's teaching like that of Epictetus known as the "principal opinions" best describes the genre of the Sermon on the Mount and Luke's counterpart, the Sermon on the Plain.[27] If that model is extended to Q as a whole, then the collection would have been perceived as a guide to Jesus' teaching. Since

24. See the history of Q scholarship, which justifies these developments on the grounds that they point forward to a more accurate picture of the historical Jesus, by James M. Robinson (*Sayings Gospel*, 11-66).

25. Dunn, "Altering the Default."

26. Johan C. Thom, *The Pythagorean "Golden Verses": With Introduction and Commentary* (Religions in the Greco-Roman World 123; Leiden: Brill, 1995).

27. Betz, *Sermon*, 72-80.

Gos. Thom. opens with "these are the secret sayings of the living Jesus," one might argue that "sayings of Jesus" would be a more apt title. The scribe who copied our Coptic version of *Gos. Thom.* gives it the title "Gospel of," but that title was not necessarily original. "Gospel of" was attached to a number of treatises in these fourth-century codices in order to claim apostolic authority for their contents. The concordance provided with the critical edition of Q indicates that the noun "gospel" is never used in the reconstructed Q, and the cognate verb only appears once, in Jesus' reply to the Baptist (Luke 7:22). We have no reason to assume that first-century Christians would have referred to a collection of Jesus' sayings as a "Gospel".

Of course, "Gospel" is a convenient marketing and database tool for the twenty-first century. It guarantees that a book or article on Q will pop up when readers are searching for information about the Gospels. But is there any sense in which Q might be said to belong to the same genus as the Synoptic Gospels? Those scholars who say that it does not emphasize two points: Q lacks narrative, and it fails to mention the death and resurrection of Jesus.

Those scholars who argue for referring to Q as a "Gospel" point to the vague definition of a "life" in antiquity. Some lives, especially of philosophers like the Cynic Demonax, known for pithy sayings, have as little narrative as Q.[28] They also point out that Q has more narrative structure and content than *Gos. Thom.* It opens with the preaching of John the Baptist, John's words about a greater one to come, and Jesus' temptation by Satan. It also includes one miracle story and ends with a group of sayings and a parable that refers to the final judgment. The Baptist reappears later in the collection when he sends disciples to inquire if Jesus is the one he has anticipated (Luke 7:18-19, 22-35). A single saying about the Baptist marking the transition between "the Law and the Prophets" and God's kingdom plundered by violence occurs later in Q (Luke 16:16). *Gos. Thom.* lacks any account of the Baptist's inquiry. It preserves short versions of two of Jesus' comments about the Baptist in separate places (*Gos. Thom.* 78.1-3; 46). It also lacks any version of the parable of children playing in the market, which concludes the second block of Baptist material in Q, and the final saying about the Baptist as transition to the kingdom. Those who repeated these sayings must have assumed that the audience knew who the Baptist was. *Gos. Thom.* has no interest in the Baptist's initial preaching or in the

---

28. Downing, *Doing Things,* 18.

subsequent interaction between John and Jesus. Therefore Q's two Baptist sections provide more narrative development than would be expected in a gathering of maxims, rules, or memorable sayings.

Similarly, although there is no explicit treatment of Jesus' death, several sayings point to the fact that Jesus died at the hands of persecutors on a cross: the beatitude on those persecuted (Luke 6:22-23), the woe against "this generation" for killing prophets sent by God (Luke 11:49-51), exhortations not to fear those who only kill the body (Luke 12:4-5) and to lose one's life for Jesus' sake (Luke 17:33), the promise of divine assistance when disciples are dragged before synagogues (Luke 12:11-12), and the requirement that a disciple take up the cross to follow Jesus (Luke 14:27). Still one must admit that none of these sayings speak directly of Jesus' death. If Jesus and his followers meet hostility and death as a consequence of their activities, their fate has been anticipated by the prophets and other righteous persons since Abel. The difference between these deaths and those earlier ones is timing. When the Son of Man returns in judgment, all will be repaid. The winners are to be gathered from east and west to feast with Abraham. The losers are condemned to eternal punishment.

How the "I" who speaks these words to his followers becomes the one who appears like lightning Q does not say. There is no hint of an Easter resurrection in these sayings. Nor is the death of Jesus a necessary condition of salvation or the basis for a new covenant between God and humanity. Yet Paul insists that the death and resurrection of Jesus lay at the heart of the message about Jesus from the beginning (1 Cor 15:3-5). Recalling those events belonged to the ritual meal which constituted the identity of Christian communities (1 Cor 11:23-26). Jesus' death shadows the narrative dynamic of all the canonical Gospels from early in the story.

This distinction between the canonical Gospels and Q has no significance if one considers Q simply a handbook of Jesus' sayings employed to instruct Christians. One would assume that the gospel preached to these Christians and their liturgical gatherings provided for the focus on the cross and resurrection as represented in Paul's letters. Paul wrote in the 50s, that is, at approximately the same time sayings collections began circulating among Greek-speaking Christians. But most of the scholars devoted to studying Q as a Gospel take a different position on the matter. They consider Q an independent theological view of Jesus' teaching and mission that rejects a Pauline view of the death and resurrection of Jesus as Son of God. Jesus speaks as a figure who embodies Wisdom or as God's envoy. Or, in some interpretations, Jesus is closest to the Cynic street preachers who mercilessly harangued audiences for their false cultural pretensions and anxieties. These scholars would argue that Q is not interested in christology but in the kingdom of God. This emphasis, they contend, brings one closer to the historical Jesus than the traditions of a vicarious death derived from Jewish martyr traditions.[29]

This sharp theological dichotomy reflects early-twentieth-century debates about the "Jesus of history" over against the "Christ of faith." The latter was attributed to the myth-making activities of a Hellenistic church. The historical Jesus, by contrast, was a first-century Jewish figure with minimal connection to what Christians made of him.[30] Most exegetes insist that there must be more continuity between early beliefs about Jesus and his actual life and teaching than reconstructions of this sort suggest. Admittedly, we lack early sources that provide clear evidence for the point at which Jesus' death was acknowledged as atonement "for sin" and therefore of more significance in God's plan of salvation than the Baptist's martyrdom, for example. Nevertheless, what happened to Jesus in Jerusalem must have been crucial to the story about him from the beginning. Even the tight link between the appearance of the Baptist, the coming of Jesus, and the new era of the kingdom of God that is evident in Q could not have been credible without some explanation of Jesus' execution. If people believed that the religious and political authorities were correct in condemning Jesus, they would not have been persuaded to follow his teaching.

Therefore, it is more reasonable to conclude that the lack of passion narrative in Q has more to do with the literary form of Q than with theological opposition to an early understanding of his death. Q served a more limited purpose in instructing believers about Jesus' teaching than did a Gospel like Mark, which seeks to provide an account of Jesus' life. Should the term "Gospel" be used for Q, then? The difficulty lies in the problem of definition. On the one hand, ancient scribes had no difficulty attaching the title "Gospel" to a wide variety of later compositions that contain Jesus traditions or tell stories about him. On the other hand, in the early first century the term "gospel" was not a literary designation but referred to the message preached about Jesus, as in Paul's letters and even the opening

---

29. Kloppenborg Verbin, *Excavating Q,* 353-408.
30. For the most thorough contemporary revival of that view, see Mack, *Christian Myth.*

verse of Mark. Q is not "gospel" in that sense. Nor does it fit the literary model established by Mark of a narrative account that links together the ministry, teaching, and death of Jesus. Some scholars would argue that Mark was not the first such narrative.[31] If the author of John's Gospel was not dependent on Mark, then he must have known a narrative of very similar structure, for example. Therefore the definition of "Gospel" can include a third entry limiting it to a subset of works which exhibit a central narrative framework comparable to Mark's. Q does not fit that meaning of the term either. It is only appropriate to refer to Q as a "Gospel" when using the word in its broadest sense as the scribe who gave *Gos. Thom.* its designation would have done.

Of course, those scholars who insist upon a minimalist use of the Q hypothesis will object to this semantic solution on methodological grounds. To ask whether Q is or was a "Gospel" presumes a stable textual object that does not exist. Indeed, it may be that the overlapping material in Matthew and Luke derives from different collections or from assemblages that were always in transition, due to their oral performance, and may never have existed in a stable form. *Gos. Thom.* illustrates the kind of collecting of Jesus' sayings that went into Q, but at no point can it be said to represent the double tradition employed by Matthew and Luke.[32] Until such time as actual manuscript evidence for Q is recovered, all discussions of Q as though it were a literary artifact remain speculative constructs based on a hypothesis that explains a much more limited data set. But, despite the reservations of colleagues, Q scholars are pursuing the task of analyzing the text as reconstructed. They continue to debate both the developmental stages of Q and the kind of Christian community which produced it.

---

31. Stephen Hultgren, *Narrative Elements in the Double-Tradition: A Study of Their Place in the Framework of the Gospel Narrative* (Beihefte zur *ZNW* 113; Berlin: Walter de Gruyter, 2002) 310-54.

32. Some Q studies have claimed that an early stratum of Q can be shown to be part of the *Gos. Thom.* Such assertions do not stand up to careful analysis, as April De Conick has shown ("The Original *Gospel of Thomas*," *VC* 56 [2002] 172-79). De Conick argues that Q is more appropriately referred to as a Gospel than *Gos. Thom.* because of its narrative elements (p. 179).

Strata in Q

Geologists and archaeologists rely on the existence of clearly defined layers in rock and sediments. Their ability to associate the strata with a chronology of ages or periods then helps them date items such as fossils, bones or human artifacts found in a particular layer. A number of scholars have begun using the imagery of archaeological strata to describe their attempt to take apart pre-Gospel traditions and produce a history of the Jesus movement. While scientific controls such as alternative dating methods exist in geology and archaeology, there are few such criteria in Q studies. Kloppenborg Verbin provides a list of four principles governing his analysis of stages in the development of Q:

   i. Consideration of the arrangement and order of the sayings.
  ii. Apparent additions of interpretive comments or glosses.
 iii. Recurring motifs, formulae, and echoes.
 iv. Detection of an argumentative progression in blocks of sayings.[33]

The complexity of applying any set of principles to Q has produced a number of different proposals about the growth and editing of the collection.[34]

     Kloppenborg Verbin points out that judgment sayings are worked into the sayings from the opening to the conclusion of Q:[35]

The Baptist preaches judgment	Luke 3:7-9
The Coming One will bring fire	Luke 3:16-17
Galilean towns threatened with a fate worse than Sodom	Luke 10:12-15
Against the Jerusalem Temple, its elite	Luke 13:34-35
Against "this generation"/"you"	Luke 11:31-32, 49-51; 13:28-29
Judgment to be sudden	Luke 12:39-40; 17:23-24
Judgment to be feared	Luke 12:42-46; 19:12-27

33. Kloppenborg Verbin, *Excavating Q*, 115.
34. Surveyed in Kloppenborg Verbin, *Excavating Q*, 135-63.
35. Kloppenborg Verbin, *Excavating Q*, 118.

He considers this motif of apocalyptic judgment to be a major redactional stage in the collection (Q2). He distinguishes it from an earlier layer (Q1), which was a compilation of six topical sub-collections aimed at instruction. These sub-collections are often spoken of as a formative wisdom layer in Q:

Inaugural sermon	Luke 6:20b-23b, 27-35, 36-45, 46-49
Harvesters on mission	Luke 9:57-60, (61-62); 10:2-11, 16 (23-24?)
On prayer	Luke 11:2-4, 9-13
Not to fear	Luke 12:2-7, 11-12
More sayings against anxiety, parables about the kingdom	Luke 12:22b-31, 33-34 (13:18-19, 20-21?)
Renounce family ties, take up cross	Luke 14:26-27; 17:33; 14:34-35

These groups include maxims along with second person imperatives, and they end with warnings or sanctions. The inaugural sermon is the most rhetorically complete discourse.[36] At the Q2 redactional stage, narrative elements were provided to introduce the sayings (Luke 3:3, 7a; 7:1, 18, 24; 9:57, 59; 10:21a; 11:14, 16, 29). Some are simple introductions: "he said to the crowds . . ." (3:7a). Others take the form of the chreia, a brief episode that illustrates the sage's wisdom by his reply to a question or challenge (e.g., 7:18). Though it can be viewed as such a chreia, Kloppenborg Verbin does not assign the temptation narrative to the Q2 layer but to a much thinner final stage that he associates with a more positive presentation of Temple and Torah than the earlier material. Angels are around the Temple to aid persons (Luke 4:9-12). The Torah is quoted positively (also 11:42c), and its eternity is affirmed (16:17).[37] Although the details assigned to particular clusters vary, the first two stages described are accepted by many Q scholars. The wisdom style clusters of teaching are thought to represent the earliest material. The emphasis on being prepared and watchful, on accepting Jesus and his emissaries lest one be excluded when the Son of Man comes in judgment, only arrives with the second level of redaction.

36. Kloppenborg Verbin, *Excavating Q*, 154-59.
37. Kloppenborg Verbin, *Excavating Q*, 160-61, 212.

Some scholars have pressed the analysis even further. Arnal suggests five stages for the development of the mission discourse, for example:[38]

oral core: proclamation of the kingdom	Luke 10:4ab, 5-6, 8-9
early oral, additional rules	Luke 10:2, 4c, 7
"official" version, pre-Q1: provision for rejection and rules about equipment	Luke 10:3, 8, 10-11
Q1: link to previous saying about harvest and conclusion; Jesus presented as unique authority but more pessimistic about the mission	Luke 9:57-62; 10:16
Q2: mission is past; Deuteronomic polemic — woe against Galilean towns for rejection	Luke 10:12-15

He proposes a similar progression of oral to written versions for other blocks of Q such as the Beatitudes.[39] It is easy to see that this reconstruction is more than literary analysis. A story about those who spread the Jesus traditions, their developing formal organization, and their responses to rejection by the larger populace in Galilee can be read off the proposed stages. Discussions of the so-called "Q community" are pursued as vigorously as those aimed at detecting strata in Q.

The Community Responsible for Q

Do the Gospels bear traces of the communities within and for which the authors wrote? Most studies of how the canonical Gospels have been edited make references to a community background in accounting for details peculiar to each Evangelist. But in recent years the assumption that sociological information about individual communities can be inferred from the Gospels has been challenged on two fronts, literary and historical.

Scholars who employ insights of modern literary theory point out that the audience which emerges from a text is not external to the reading process. Neither is the image of the author which readers form in their minds. Both "author" and "audience" are the result of a complex process

---

38. William E. Arnal, *Jesus and the Village Scribes: Galilean Conflicts and the Setting of Q* (Minneapolis: Fortress, 2001) 181.

39. Arnal, *Jesus*, 190.

of imagination. The actual author has embedded clues about the fictional author in the narrative. The situation becomes even more complex when the narrative employs a narrator's voice that turns out to be unreliable or ambiguous. Similarly, the "audience" is created by the complex set of narrative clues and the imagination of those who hear or read a text. Therefore exegetes must be cautious about treating texts as though they were mirror images of historical or social realities.

The historical challenge addresses the common assumption that each Evangelist spoke to a Christian community that could be considered distinct from other Christian communities. In fact, the jump from an audience inferred from the text to the audience as a first-century social reality to the audience as representative of a unique form of Christianity occurs without comment in many books on the Gospels. Those skeptical of this methodology on historical grounds point out that early Christians were a mobile group. Paul's letters provide evidence not only for his own movements but those of many unnamed Christians. In addition the conditions for survival of any ancient work in a manuscript culture and the independent revisions of Mark, Matthew, and Luke, which occurred within a short period of time, require an extensive network of communication among Christians across a wide geographical region.

Despite these challenges to their enterprise, scholars engaged in Q research claim that their investigations provide our best chance of understanding the historical Jesus and his followers. Many of the earlier studies began with the sayings that highlight a radical break with home and family. Jesus warns potential disciples that the Son of Man is even more homeless than birds or foxes. Animals have a home to which they return at night, but he does not (Luke 9:57-60). His followers must hate family (14:26; 12:51, 53). "Hate" refers not to emotional antagonism but to objective social behavior that refuses to honor the claims that others have on us. The combination of this depiction of Jesus and his disciples as persons without any place in the world and the instructions for itinerant missionaries leads to a description of the Jesus movement as two-pronged: wandering charismatics traveled around the towns and villages of Galilee announcing the kingdom. They relied on another type of believer, the sympathizers in the villages who listened to the word and provided for the wandering preachers but did not leave home.

Some scholars treated the wandering, charismatic lifestyle as a freely chosen break with society and its norms. They compared Jesus' followers

93

to the anti-social Cynic philosophers found in the cities of the Greco-Roman world. Other scholars were influenced by Marxism or liberation theology to describe a socioeconomic basis for the Jesus movement. They noticed that Roman authors often spoke of the urban poor as worse off than animals because the poor are homeless. When Jesus spoke of the poor, hungry, and mourning, he referred to rural peasants whose suffering had been caused by the rise of wealthy landowners associated with Herod and the Romans. Jesus was not a religious zealot hoping to oust the imperial powers. Only God could do that at the judgment. He and his followers had a message for the villagers about their relationships with each other.

More recent scholarship has dropped the wandering charismatic model from its account of early Galilean Christianity. The second person imperative used in many of the sayings suggests an interest in forming persons who belong to established local communities. The literary skills necessary to bring together the multilayered Q as one finds it also assume persons with a level of education beyond that of peasants. Village scribes might have been responsible both for the initial written collection(s) and for the final redaction of Q.[40] Appeals to the Cynic philosophers as models for the pattern of discipleship in Q depend on the hypothesis that the Hellenizing features of the new cities in Galilee such as Sepphoris would be sufficient to introduce urban, Greek cultural ideals to the larger populace. Yet neither Sepphoris nor Tiberias figures in Q, and even the larger Galilean towns, Capernaum, Bethsaida, and Chorazin are the subject of judgment oracles. Therefore more recent reconstructions by archaeologists have cast doubt on the claim that Sepphoris provides evidence for a Jesus movement influenced by Cynic philosophy as well.[41]

Peter Richardson has employed his knowledge of architectural and settlement patterns in first-century Galilee to ferret out "the Q community" on the ground.[42] Its household images fit the small rural towns of the north. Agricultural images are limited to crops grown in the lower part of Galilee that involve winnowing and threshing. One does not hear of the grapes or fishing that would be characteristic of villages in upper Galilee. The houses represented in archaeological finds do not have central court-

---

40. Kloppenborg Verbin, *Excavating Q,* 168-202; Arnal, *Jesus,* 163-73.

41. Jonathan L. Reed, *Archaeology and the Galilean Jesus* (Harrisburg: Trinity, 2000) 135.

42. Peter Richardson, *Building Jewish in the Roman East* (Waco: Baylor, 2004) 73-90.

yards or elaborate dining rooms. The banquets mentioned in Q can only be imagined to occur in a guest room on the flat roof that was the second story of a house or in some kind of communal space. Indirectly, this focus solely on sayings attributed to Q highlights the contrast between Q sayings and the Gospels for a picture of Jesus' ministry. No fishing? No storms on the sea of Galilee? In the canonical Gospels four of Jesus' core group of Twelve are fishermen. The busy fishing economy of the towns around the sea provides the basic transport for Jesus and his followers from one place to another.

Clearly the methods and results of searching for a "Q community" depend on such a limited database that a broad consensus will be difficult to obtain. Birger Pearson questions the presumption of a unique Galilean Christianity which finds its identity in Q. What evidence we have of Christian origins (e.g., Acts 2:7; also Gal 1:18) suggests that Jesus' Galilean followers spread out from Jerusalem. Further, since the old hypothesis of an Aramaic substratum for Q has been rejected on linguistic grounds by all scholars, the fact that its sayings are in Greek rather than Aramaic also raises a cautionary flag about an origin in the villages of Galilee. The fact that Galilee is the setting for these sayings has a simpler explanation: Jesus conducted his ministry there. Pearson finds a much more plausible scenario for the origin of Q by focusing on the fact that Q began as a collection of Jesus' sayings in Greek. He thinks that it was probably brought to Antioch from Jerusalem.[43] In addition, whatever that initial core collection was, it appears to have been modified as it was transmitted. Each version may have incorporated a different understanding of discipleship. Hans Dieter Betz has made the case, for instance, that the Beatitudes in Matthew's version are quite unlike those in Luke. For Matthew, the language of poor and rich translates into the moral categories of righteous and unrighteous. For Luke, poor and rich are ethical categories best understood in terms of Hellenistic moral philosophers. The woes serve as satirical commentary on the habits of the rich.[44]

Kloppenborg Verbin intimates that scholars who raise questions about the reconstructions of Jesus and his Galilean followers based on Q studies are motivated by theological anxieties. If Jesus is more like a Cynic philosopher, then his link to the Jewish tradition is broken or his unique

43. Pearson, "A Q Community in Galilee," *NTS* 20 (2004) 476, 490-93.
44. Betz, *Sermon on the Mount*, 572-73.

apocalyptic vision of God's reign cannot be defended. Or such critics fear undermining the belief that Jesus reached out to save humanity, not to challenge social conventions as a philosophical or political figure.[45] Yet even Q — or at least Kloppenborg Verbin's Q2 — presents a Jesus who emerges in connection with the apocalyptic religious excitement evoked by the preaching of John the Baptist. Q2 knows of, but has no place for, Jesus as healer and exorcist. If Q2 knows more about Jesus than it says, then asking critical questions about the various "Q community" proposals should not be treated as theological malice. Scholars who treat Q as a Gospel and as evidence for a Galilean form of Christianity which best mirrors Jesus' own ideals may come up with a revised account that answers the problems that have been raised. Or the current flurry of books and articles on Q may produce a fascinating array of variations with no generally accepted conclusions about how to put together the layers of editing in Q and the community context from which it emerged.

Form Criticism

The Shape and Function of Sayings and Stories

So far our quest has focused on the sources and editing of written texts. We have used categories such as beatitude, maxim, parable, miracle, and the like to describe units of content within those texts. Form criticism studies the shape of those smaller units within the Gospels.

Going to a mega-store to find a piece of music requires a knowledge of types and forms of music. The classical section or room is well-ordered. Find the composer, instrument, or orchestra. Then the subcategories follow clearly defined musical forms. With all other music the task is more daunting. Is the performer folk, country, or pop? Is the African crossover group "international," "world," or "pop"? What is the difference between "hip hop" and "rap"? At least if the CD is "hot" or new enough, it can be found on some other "top 50" or "new releases" rack in the general vicinity of its category.

Some of the categories are more helpful than others in describing the particulars of the music on a given CD. It is possible to listen to music without knowing anything about musical forms, just as many people read the

45. Kloppenborg Verbin, *Excavating Q,* 409-42.

Bible without thinking about the literary form(s) of the text they are reading. Familiarity with musical forms adds to the listening experience. Music appreciation courses explain the definitions. One learns things to listen for. Performing music requires a different sense of the form. Finally, the composer can use those elements of form to create a new piece of music.

Scholars began to classify units in the Gospels with the expectation that form and use or function in the life of the early Christian communities could be linked. Early-twentieth-century form-criticism, notably Rudolf Bultmann's *History of the Synoptic Tradition,* which appeared in German in 1921, pursued many of the same questions that Q scholars do today. By analyzing the forms of small units of tradition, one could discern the shape of the Jesus tradition as it was handed on orally before it had been fixed in writing. Understanding the rules for a particular type of saying or story would help one to discern accretions or modifications during transmission of the material. If a saying or story was formulated to explain or be used in a particular setting in the early church, as in the elaborate rules concerning the conduct and support of those on mission, then its claim to represent authentic words of Jesus was called into question. For most early form critics, the setting in the life of the community (German *Sitz im Leben*) was either liturgical, that is, baptismal or eucharistic, or didactic, having its place in the instruction of new converts. Such inner Christian categories bypassed a larger issue. If the forms in which the pre-Gospel traditions are cast and transmitted both orally and in writing are comparable to those found in other works in the larger Jewish or Greco-Roman environment, then the purpose of formulating particular types of material may depend as much on the larger cultural setting as on the religious needs of early Christians.

Although form criticism has been eclipsed in recent years by the questions of source, redaction, and literary criticism, some scholars are engaged in making up the deficit left by the earlier studies. Just as many of our newer orchestral composers mix the classical forms with influences from world music, so the Evangelists had a mixed set of resources. They could draw on familiar forms from the Hebrew and Greek Bibles or employ forms that are best attested in Greco-Roman legends, narratives, and sayings. Some collections of comparable examples treat only one side of the complex cultural mix, for example comparable parables in the Jewish tradition.[46] Others in-

---

46. Harvey K. McArthur and Robert M. Johnston, *They Also Taught in Parables: Rabbinic Parables from the First Centuries of the Christian Era* (Grand Rapids: Baker, 1990).

corporate comparable Jewish material into the more numerous examples of healing and nature miracles found in Greek and Roman sources.[47]

While the initial categories of form criticism were based on classification of the units of material in the Synoptic Gospels, more recent studies have turned to the Greco-Roman rhetorical handbooks. The latter have proven most significant as exegetes have extended form criticism to the Pauline epistles using rhetorical analysis. However, they also figure in studies of those narrative episodes in which Jesus resolves a question or evades the accusation in an opponent's question. This form of brief episode intended to illustrate a person's character was taught to schoolboys.[48]

The Gospels contain both sayings attributed to Jesus and stories about him. The two divisions overlap when a story about Jesus turns on what he says. The healing of the centurion's son (Luke 7:1-10/Matt 8:5-13) finds its way into the critical edition of Q because of the verbal exchange between Jesus and the centurion. Jesus concludes that this outsider (enemy) has greater faith than any Israelite. However, a different classification might put it among the other narratives in which Jesus heals a sick or deceased child. The miracle story can include faith in the healing power of an individual or deity as part of the genre for such story, though faith is not always present in ancient samples. The parables of Jesus also range from short comparisons such as the mustard seed (Mark 4:30-32/Luke 13:18-19/Matt 13:31-32/*Gos. Thom.* 20) to longer stories such as the great banquet (Luke 14:16-23/Matt 22:2-10/*Gos. Thom.* 64). While recognizing that particular episodes often mix categories, the distinction between saying and narrative remains a useful starting point.

Sayings Material

Scholars who distinguish an early layer in the sayings collection Q from a later one often appeal to the difference between wisdom and apocalyptic. Wisdom sayings make a general statement or observation about how human beings act. Or they incorporate maxims about how one should act to

---

47. Wendy Cotter, *Miracles in Greco-Roman Antiquity: A Sourcebook* (London: Routledge, 1999).

48. Ronald F. Hock and Edward N. O'Neil, *The Chreia in Ancient Rhetoric*, Volume I: *The Progymnasmata* (Atlanta: Scholars, 1986).

be happy or successful. Apocalyptic sayings carry the tone of warning, an appeal to repent before the judgment, or statements about the fate of persons or groups when God appears as judge. As we have seen, this approach to Q treats the wisdom material as earlier and more characteristic of Jesus himself. The strong apocalyptic tone that runs through the final collection reflects the shift in understanding during the decade or so after Jesus' death, by which time Jesus had been identified with the heavenly Son of Man, who will suddenly appear in judgment. Many scholars have questioned this simple chronological division between wisdom and apocalyptic sayings. They point out that Jesus emerged from circles that had formed around John the Baptist, who addressed a prophetic word about repentance in anticipation of God's coming judgment to Israel, as in the sayings which open the Q collection (Luke 3:7-9/Matt 3:7-10). There is no reason to weed out apocalyptic sayings from the earliest layer of the Jesus tradition.

Proverbs and other wise sayings about daily life migrated from one wise person to another in antiquity. Some of the material in the book of Proverbs can also be found in ancient Egyptian wisdom collections, for example. The fact that Jesus often uses proverbial sayings does not mean that he made them up. Take the Golden Rule, for example: "In everything, do to others as you would have them do to you" (Matt 7:12). In various forms that maxim is still taught to young children. Christians automatically think of it as a saying of Jesus. Others do not. The title "the Golden Rule" originated in the Middle Ages, but the maxim itself is very ancient and nearly universal. The ancient Greeks knew it, as did Confucius and ancient Hindu traditions. The philosopher Aristotle remarks that this maxim represents the opinion of the masses (*Rhetoric* 2.6.19). Matthew places it at the end of the teaching section in the Sermon on the Mount. He adds "for this is the law and the prophets." Of course, a maxim cannot substitute for the Torah and prophets or for the concrete examples of Jesus' teaching in the Sermon. Matthew opened the specific teaching section of the Sermon on the Mount by insisting that Jesus came to fulfill, not destroy, "the law and the prophets" (Matt 5:17-20). So he has employed this common maxim to make the same point at its conclusion.

Luke has the Golden Rule embedded in Jesus' words about non-retaliation (Luke 6:31), a set of sayings which began with the injunction "Love your enemies, do good to those who hate you" (v. 27). Non-retaliation and love of enemies sayings are treated as distinctive features of Christian ethics throughout the New Testament (Luke 23:34; Acts 7:60;

Rom 12:14, 17-20; 1 Cor 4:12-13; 1 Thess 5:15; 1 Pet 3:9). Often these principles are stated without Jesus being named as the authority. Although "do good to enemies, pray for the persecutor" do not accompany every example of the Golden Rule, Christians may have thought of these principles as equivalent. In an ideal case, one would prefer to receive good treatment from others. Both exegetes and philosophers have engaged in vigorous debates over the Golden Rule as an ethical principle through the centuries. Is it simply a moral commonplace? Or does it, at least in the positive form "do to others as you would have them do to you," provide the basis for all forms of altruism, including non-retaliation?[49]

That debate illustrates two important facets of wisdom sayings such as proverbs and maxims. First, they take on meaning from the specific contexts in which they are used. Second, they appeal to universal experiences, not to revelation or to the authority of a particular sage. What makes Jesus' use of wisdom traditions special cannot be either the form or content of such sayings. It must be the context in which he invokes particular maxims, or, in the case of non-retaliation and love of enemies, the larger discourse about moral obligations that he framed with the traditional maxim.

Another type of saying takes the form of a rule or law. Some laws are treated as cases with penalties attached. Others are stated as simple imperatives, as in the Ten Commandments or the rule against exacting interest on loans to the poor in Exod 22:25. Jesus does not create case law in the first sense. He does get credit for sayings which appear to be legal in the second sense. Paul considered Jesus' prohibition of divorce (Mark 10:2-12/Matt 19:1-12; Matt 5:31-32/Luke 16:18) a rule to be applied (1 Cor 7:10-11). However, like most laws, it did not cover all cases, so Paul also felt free to interpret it as inapplicable to some cases of Christians married to non-Christians (1 Cor 7:12-16). Among the examples of non-retaliation, Jesus included lending: "Give to everyone who begs from you; and if anyone takes away your goods, do not ask for them again" (Luke 6:30). And as an exhortation to love enemies, Jesus comments, "If you lend to those from whom you hope to receive, what credit is it to you? For even sinners lend to sinners, to receive as much again. But love your enemies, do good, and lend, expecting nothing in return" (Luke 6:34-35). Not only does Jesus concur with the law against usury in Exodus, he takes it one step further.

49. For a helpful summary of the discussion, see Betz, *Sermon on the Mount*, 508-19.

Lending is to be considered a gift to the ungrateful. Not only is it wrong to press for return of what has been borrowed, one should not anticipate any kind of repayment.

Formally, the sayings about lending appear to be stated as rules to be applied in all cases. Sayings advocating accepting loss rather than resorting to legal or other forms of retaliation must have been familiar to Paul. When he chastises the Corinthians for suing one another in court, he comments, "In fact, to have lawsuits at all with one another is already a defeat for you. Why not rather be wronged? Why not rather be defrauded? But you yourselves wrong and defraud — and believers at that" (1 Cor 6:7-8). In this instance, Paul does not refer to Jesus' words explicitly. Nor does he attempt to create an exception to the non-retaliation principle that might be said to embody its spirit. Instead he instructs the Corinthians to settle issues among Christians within the community, while admitting that such problems are a defeat. This solution represents an approach to legal sayings or rules that Christians still embrace. Even though Jesus begins with a form of speech that belongs to the category of laws or rules, he pushes for an ideal that is not practical. Laws have to deal with human beings who are defeated by conflicts which would not occur if human beings treated one another as their Creator intended. Courts have to protect the social order by intervening. So, as Paul admitted, Jesus painted a picture of how God intended people to act. Christians aspire to that reality. But the sayings of Jesus will not provide the rules or laws for negotiating the problems of life in a world that is far from the reign of God.

Other sayings provide rules which apply to Christian activities such as worship or the conduct of missionaries. Matthew's Sermon on the Mount collects sayings about the three pillars of Jewish piety, almsgiving, fasting, and prayer (Matt 6:1-18). Many churches read this Gospel to begin the season of Lent. During the forty days of preparation for Easter, Christians thus devote themselves to prayer, fasting, and charity. They recognize that some of the language Jesus uses, such as not letting the left hand know what the right is doing, does not constitute a rule. Much as in the spirit of the sayings about lending, those about piety undercut the human tendency to seek praise or admiration from others.

Matthew's Gospel concludes with the risen Jesus sending his disciples out to teach the nations. One of the sayings contains a rule for baptism. It is to be conducted "in the name of the Father and of the Son and of the Holy Spirit" (Matt 28:19b). Since our other New Testament references to baptism suggest that it was received in the name of Jesus (Acts 2:38; 8:16; Rom 6:3; Gal 3:27), this formula probably represents a somewhat later liturgical rule. It remains a requirement for valid baptism in most Christian churches.

The rules which required missionaries to take no provisions and rely solely on the hospitality of those in each town or village (Luke 10:4-9/Matt 10:7-13) could not be so easily retained. They presuppose short journeys between villages and towns as well as fairly limited stays in each place. That fits Jesus' activities but not the long journeys over land and sea between cities that made up Paul's missionary efforts. On reaching a destination Paul might stay in a city for months or even longer. Travelers had to bring their own provisions for long journeys, so Paul could not go from one place to another without a wallet, sandals, or change of clothes. To stay in a city for months or years at the first house to offer hospitality would have caused considerable hardship for his hosts. So Paul's strategy involved working at a trade, leather-working, and accepting occasional gifts from his other converts. This practice evoked negative comments about the apostle among Christians in Corinth. Paul's explanation in 1 Cor 9:3-23 shows that sayings of the Lord were part of the dispute (v. 14). Luke's Gospel resolves the problem of a divergence between Jesus' sayings and the later missionary practice by having Jesus change the rules at the Last Supper (Luke 22:35-36).

The Beatitudes have proven difficult to classify as either wisdom or apocalyptic sayings. They employ a consistent formal pattern of two lines. The first describes a particular type as "blessed" or "happy," and the second gives the reason. The Greek word *makarios* referred to a state of being like that of the gods, not subject to the sufferings of human life. Addressing persons as blessed in the second person plural, "you," could have had a basis in cults that promised initiates a blessed afterlife such as those associated with Demeter.[50] However, the Jewish use of beatitudes does not reflect that sort of ritual. Some examples fit the wisdom tradition in their praise for persons who observe Torah (Pss 1:1-2; 41:1-2). In that case, the beatitudes would be the introduction to a didactic discourse. They point to virtues that must be practiced by Jesus' disciples. However, the reversal of fate in the second clause does not appear to be a consequence of the individual's activity in the first. Instead it points forward to an apocalyptic reversal of fate for the righteous who suffer now. That orientation suggests that

50. See Betz, *Sermon on the Mount*, 92-104.

the Beatitudes in Matthew and Luke are a type of apocalyptic consolation rather than wisdom instruction.[51]

Individual sayings can be employed in diverse ways. Even rules and legal sayings were not always treated as such. Apocalyptic sayings may pronounce God's judgment on those who have rejected the gospel (as Luke 10:13-15/Matt 11:21-24) or console those who suffer now. The maxims and proverbs of wisdom tradition are even more fluid in their application. Other sayings of Jesus occur in a story form referred to as apophthegm or chreia. Such brief episodes were often used to demonstrate a philosopher's ability to vanquish the arguments of opponents. Or they might be collected to demonstrate the absurd teaching of a particular school to which the speaker is opposed. For example, a story attributed to one of Pythagoras's contemporaries was repeated to show how absurd that school's doctrine of transmigration of souls is:

> And once, when he passed by as a puppy was being beaten, they say, he pitied it and said these words, "Stop. Don't beat it for truly it is the soul of a friend: I recognized it when I heard it utter sounds." (Diogenes Laertius, *Lives* 8.36)

The powerful also may be the subject of short episodes that expose their pretensions.

Chreiai may be largely sayings, actions or a mixture of saying and action:[52]

> A Laconian when someone asked him where the Lacedaemonians consider the boundary of their land to be, showed his spear.

> There was a Roman knight drinking in the seats of the theater to whom Augustus sent word, saying, "If I wish to have lunch, I go home." The knight said, "Certainly, for you are not afraid to lose your place."

In their study of texts that instruct students of rhetoric to formulate such illustrative episodes, Hock and O'Neil find considerable variation even when the same chreia is retold by a single author. Students might be told to take a brief episode and expand it or a longer one and reduce it to

---

51. W. D. Davies and Dale C. Allison, *The Gospel According to Saint Matthew*, Volume I: *Matthew I-VII* (Edinburgh: Clark, 1988) 433-40.

52. Hock and O'Neil, *Chreia*, 27-32.

the brief one-liner. The story of Jesus cleansing the Temple provides an example of both an expanded and concise version:[53]

> Then they came to Jerusalem. And he entered the temple and began to drive out those who were selling and those who were buying in the temple, and he overturned the tables of the money changers and the seats of those who sold doves; and he would not allow anyone to carry anything through the temple. He was teaching and saying, "Is it not written, 'My house shall be called a house of prayer for all nations'? But you have made it a den of robbers." And when the chief priests and scribes heard it, they kept looking for a way to kill him; for they were afraid of him, because the whole crowd was spellbound by his teaching. And when evening came, Jesus and his disciples went out of the city. (Mark 11:15-19)
>
> Then he entered the temple and began to drive out those who were selling things there; and he said, "It is written, 'My house shall be a house of prayer'; but you have made it a den of robbers."
> Every day he was teaching in the temple. The chief priests and scribes, and the leaders of the people kept looking for a way to kill him; but they did not find anything they could do, for all the people were spellbound by what they heard. (Luke 19:45-46, 47-48)

One could not treat the expanded version as later than the concise one or vice versa based on the form of such stories alone. Since there are other reasons to think that Luke employed Mark's Gospel, he probably created the concise version and made a historical judgment about its significance as well. Mark's story links Jesus' prophetic gesture of cleansing and speaking out against commerce in the temple with the hostility that led to his death. Luke does not do so. The episode is an example of the sort of thing Jesus did, but religious authorities are hostile because of the general impact of Jesus' teaching on the crowds, not because of this particular incident.

The Synoptic Gospels contain many episodes in which Jesus' words are the focal point of the story. The temptation by Satan which Matthew and Luke took from Q (Luke 4:1-13/Matt 4:1-11) is somewhat unusual in having both parties to a hostile debate slinging Scripture citations at each other. More common forms involve questions put to Jesus (so Mark 2:18-20; 2:23-

53. Hock and O'Neil, *Chreia*, 36-41.

28; 12:28-34; Matt 18:21-22) or hostile authorities hoping to trip up Jesus (Mark 2:15-17; 3:1-6; 12:13-17, 18-27). Scholars have employed various subcategories to describe the brief stories which serve as settings for teaching by Jesus. Those sparked by opponents are referred to as controversy or conflict stories, those in which disciples seek instruction as school dialogues. An episode initiated by Jesus himself, like the temple cleansing, is sometimes given the generic designation "biographical apophthegm." Given the narrative variations typical of the genre as a whole, distinguishing Jesus' replies to opponents from those to anonymous questioners or disciples does not provide any information about the oral form of the episode. It only indicates how the Evangelist employs the story in the larger narrative frame of the Gospel.

Parables and Similitudes

English speakers will be familiar with phrases such as "lost sheep," "good Samaritan," and "prodigal son" even if they have never heard the parables to which those phrases refer. The Greek word *parabolē* can refer to a wide range of illustrative forms from single sayings such as proverbs or maxims to simple comparisons to extended stories illustrating larger concepts. As a translation of Hebrew *mashal*, "parable" can refer to riddles as well. This semantic range creates an awkward juxtaposition between treating Jesus' parables as hidden truth, a puzzle to be cracked (so Mark 4:10-12, 34), and considering parables as obvious truths, a way of clarifying his meaning by comparison or analogy (so Mark 4:33). If the parable is like a puzzle, then one has to find the key that unlocks its insights. If the parable is like a maxim or appeals to experience as other wisdom traditions do, then it should resolve a difficulty in understanding. A third possibility sees parables as similar to the popular fables of the period. In that case, the parable is a story constructed to illustrate an ethical point.

Many of the parables from Jewish sources which resemble those in the Gospels are used to illustrate specific teachings. As in many of Jesus' parables, a tale of the king and his subjects can stand in for the relationship between God and humanity. The following example resembles Jesus' story of guests invited to a banquet (Luke 14:15-24/Matt 22:1-10, 11-14):[54]

---

54. From Brad H. Young, *The Parables: Jewish Tradition and Christian Interpretation* (Peabody: Hendrickson, 1998) 282.

This may be compared to a king who summoned his servants to a banquet without appointing a time. The wise ones adorned themselves and sat at the door of the palace [for] they said, "Is anything lacking in a royal palace?" The fools went about their work saying, "Can there be a banquet without preparations?" Suddenly, the king desired [the presence of] his servants. The wise entered adorned, while the fools entered soiled. The king rejoiced at the wise but was angry with the fools. "Those who adorned themselves for the banquet," he ordered, "let them sit, eat and drink. But those who did not adorn themselves for the banquet let them stand and watch." (*Ruth Rabbah* 3.3, attributed to Rabbi Johanan ben Zacchai)

In addition to the parable about the banquet, a whole series of parables of Jesus employ the trope of wise (good) and foolish (bad) servants confronted by their master's sudden return. Since journeys of any distance could take months or even years, the long delay and surprise arrival were common experiences. Jesus' version of the banquet parable ups the stakes in the social insult category. None of the invited are wise. They all reject the summons to go about their business. Consequently, the host must round up guests among the poor, the homeless, drifters who would never see the inside of a rich man's house. Matthew's version of the banquet has the trope of the king finding some guests without suitable clothing attached to the conclusion of the story. This second ending seems unfair unless one recognizes that it probably came from another version of the story. Matthew's version also intensifies the social insult. The feast being refused is none other than the wedding banquet for a royal prince.

Almost a third of the teaching attributed to Jesus in the Synoptic Gospels takes the form of parables, similitudes, or comparisons. Some exegetes exclude from the category "parable" the short comparisons or proverbial statements and the stories formulated as ethical examples such as the Rich Fool (Luke 12:13-20). The semantic range of the term and the variability of story traditions suggest that similitudes and example stories are better seen as subtypes in the parable genre.

Parables appear at every level of the gospel tradition. The following catalogue assigns titles to help readers identify the passages in question. It is important to remember that a popular title may not be a complete or even appropriate description of the literary or theological points in a given story. For example, the familiar "Prodigal Son" does not end when the wayward youth is received back with great celebration. The father still has to address his elder son's anger over what appears to him as unjust disregard for his hard work (Luke 15:11-32).

	Mark	Matthew	Luke	Gos. Thom.
Parables in the Triple Tradition				
Sower's Seed	4:3-8	13:3-8	8:5-8	9
Interpretation of "Sower's Seed"	4:13-20	13:18-23	8:11-15	
Mustard Seed	4:30-32	13:31-32	13:18-19	20
Wicked Tenants	12:1-12	21:33-46	20:9-19	65-66
Parables in "Q"				
Lost Sheep		18:12-14	15:4-7	107
Wise and Foolish Builders		7:24-27	6:47-49	
Faithful (Wise) Slave		24:45-51	12:42-46	
Children Playing		11:16-19	7:31-35	
A Father's Good Gifts		7:9-11	11:11-13	
Great Banquet		22:1-10	14:15-24	64
Leaven		13:33	13:20-21	96
Slaves Entrusted with Money		25:14-30	19:12-27	
Parables in Mark and One Other Source				
Slaves Waiting for Master	13:34-37		12:35-38	
Seed Growing Secretly	4:26-29			57
Parables in Matthew's Special Material				
Unforgiving Servant		18:23-35		
Vineyard Workers' Wages		20:1-16		
Wise and Foolish Servant Girls		25:1-13		
Dragnet and Its Interpretation		13:47-50		
Final Judgment (Sheep and Goats)		25:31-46		
Treasure Buried in the Field		13:44		109
Pearl of Great Price		13:45-46		76
Two Sons		21:28-32		

	Mark	Matthew	Luke	Gos. Thom.
Parables in Luke's Special Material				
Lost Coin			15:8-10	
Prodigal Son			15:11-32	
Good Samaritan			10:25-37	
Rich Fool			12:16-20	63
Rich Man and Lazarus			16:19-31	
Pharisee and Tax Collector			18:10-14	
Building a Tower			14:28-30	
Going to War			14:31-33	
Unjust Estate Manager			16:1-8	
Two Debtors			7:41-43	
Friend at Midnight			11:5-8	
Barren Fig Tree			13:6-9	
Slave Minding the Door			17:7-10	
Unjust Judge			18:2-8	

Modern scholarship has challenged two common strategies for reading the parables: treating them as allegories or treating them as illustrations of a single point. The parable about the seed sown on various types of ground (Mark 4:3-9 par.) comes with an allegorical interpretation in the Synoptic Gospels (Mark 4:13-20). But *Gos. Thom.* 9 preserves the parable without an attached interpretation. Since the interpretation is presented as special teaching conveyed to the disciples, the Gospels themselves suggest that it did not circulate with the parable. Allegorical interpretation requires that elements in the story stand for something else, in this case different responses to hearing Jesus' preaching. If the allegorical reading was used as instruction, it could be seen as exhortation to those who began as enthusiastic disciples of Jesus but might be faltering. Without the detailed allegory, the story appeals to a familiar situation — not all seed yields fruit at harvest — to give the hearer an analogy for what Jesus is doing as he announces the reign of God.

A more pessimistic variant of the same analogy can be found in the late-first-century C.E. Jewish work 2 Esdras (= 4 Ezra). Writing after the

Roman destruction of Jerusalem, its author has the seer Ezra take God to task for creating humanity with a tendency toward evil and for failing to come in judgment despite declining numbers of truly righteous persons (7:45-48). His angelic dialogue partner replies that Ezra should not be any more concerned about the wicked who will perish than the farmer is about lost seed (8:41). Ezra will not be silenced easily. He points out that God is responsible for the timing of sun and rain, which have a crucial impact on the harvest (8:42-43). He also objects that human beings, made in God's image, are not comparable to the farmer's seed, so God should show them mercy (8:44-45). God responds by insisting that Ezra cannot love God's creation as much as the Creator does. The masses who will perish in the judgment chose their fate by rejecting God and the Torah and even perse-cuting the righteous. In any case, the timing of divine judgment is set and will come soon (8:46-62).

This extensive dialogue illustrates how a seed-harvest analogy func-tioned in first-century Jewish theological reflection. It indicates that the basic analogy employed in Jesus' various seed parables was as familiar to his audience as the king and subjects or master and slaves in other para-bles. However, unlike the 2 Esdras dialogue, Jesus' parables are not part of an extended theological dialogue or aids to Torah interpretation as in rab-binic examples. Luke's insertion of the Good Samaritan into a discussion of the love of neighbor command in Lev 19:18 employs the parable to illus-trate a point of Torah.

In some instances, the Evangelists use parables to illustrate an issue raised by Jesus' ministry. Fickle children quarreling over what game to play exemplify the peculiar reactions of popular opinion to the Baptist and Je-sus (Luke 7:31-35/Matt 11:16-19). Luke introduces a grouping of three para-bles with a reference to complaints among Pharisees and scribes that Jesus associates with sinners and tax collectors (15:1-2, followed by Lost Sheep in vv. 4-6, Lost Coin in vv. 8-9, and Prodigal Son in vv. 11-32). He picks up the note of rejoicing which concludes the parables with an additional saying in the first two cases (vv. 7, 10). The sayings leave no doubt about where God stands. God rejoices more over the one repentant sinner than a crowd of righteous persons who do not need repentance. This longer sequence and editing of a group of parables provides Luke's readers with a framework that indicates what the parables are about. Matthew applies the parable of the Lost Sheep to a somewhat different situation. It serves as a warning to community leaders not to despise or neglect the lowly in the community

(Matt 18:10-14). We have no way of knowing in what situation Jesus employed the figure of a shepherd dropping the others to seek a lost sheep.

In other examples, a brief analogy directs the audience toward the life-changing significance of discovering God's reign, a treasure or pearl (Matt 13:44-46). Or in the numerous servant parables in which the wicked or foolish are caught out by a master's sudden return, the parables serve as warnings to remain vigilant. Many of the longer parables exhibit unexpected twists in the plot line, which some exegetes consider a distinctive style in Jesus' own storytelling. We have already mentioned the insulting twist found in the Great Banquet: none of the invited guests even bother to come. The conclusion of the story has both a positive result, a party for unlikely guests, and a negative result, hostility between the host and those once his friends. The Prodigal Son ends without answering the question posed by the elder son's reaction. The audience has to decide on its own whether the young man has been persuaded by his father or not. The Unforgiving Servant (Matt 18:23-35) sets up an expectation of celebration when the king cancels an enormous debt only to have it swept away when the servant will not forgive a small one. Similarly, the Vineyard Workers' Wages (Matt 20:1-16) ends on a sour note. The owner dismisses the complaint of those who worked all day. They got what they signed up for. What the owner chooses to give others is none of their business. Without knowing the context in which Jesus used such parables, the reason for such shocking twists and dark conclusions remains a matter of speculation.

Parables used as example stories in ethical instruction such as the Rich Fool (Luke 12:13-20) or the Rich Man and Lazarus (Luke 16:19-31) treat the demise or post-mortem suffering of the central figure as appropriate to his behavior in life. The farmer with the abundant harvest acts out the stock part of a greedy person. Luke adds a saying to the end of the story, as he does with other parables. The reader should be able to figure out how the fool could have become "rich toward God" rather than himself. He should have recognized God as the source of his harvest and shared his good fortune with the poor. The Rich Fool also serves as an example of false anxiety about future provisions, the subject of a group of sayings from Q which follow the parable in Luke (12:22-32).

Although many of Jesus' parables pick up real-life situations, the Rich Man and Lazarus plays out as comic satire on the excesses of the rich. Similar stories in ancient Egyptian or rabbinic literature endow the poor man with qualities of piety or Torah devotion that the rich lack. They end when the fate of the two in the afterlife is revealed. So as a variant on the traditional example story, this parable should end with vv. 23-26. The rich man dies, finds himself in torment, and sees Lazarus with Abraham. But that traditional pattern only serves as a hook for the meat of the tale, the extended dialogue between Abraham and the rich man. Exegetes are uncertain how much of the exchange to attribute to Luke's artistry and how much came from his source. Minimally, the shift in the final exchange from listening to Torah to "one rising from the dead" suggests that the story has been expanded to allude to the resurrection of Jesus at some stage in its transmission.

Narrative parables with unusual twists or exaggerations in their plots seem to be characteristic of Jesus. Scholars have applied various methods of formal description derived from linguistics or literary criticism to the parables in the attempt to describe a unique pattern to Jesus' storytelling. Such an abstract formulation, it was thought, might provide a more scientific way of distinguishing authentic Jesus tradition from later accretions or allegorizing. While these methods have raised interesting questions about the parables, they have not resolved the larger question. Many exegetes insist that it is wrong to expect a unique, formal description of the parables of Jesus because Jesus employed traditional folklore patterns, images from the Hebrew Bible, and situations from everyday life in crafting his maxims and parables.

A more troubling question arises at the other end of the spectrum. Are some so-called parables simple allegories created to drive home a point? Two familiar stories raise such suspicion, the Wicked Tenants (Mark 12:1-9 par.) and the Wise and Foolish Servant Girls (Matt 25:1-13). The present form of the Wicked Tenants clearly picks up a metaphor from the Hebrew Bible, Israel as God's vineyard. Isa 5:1-6 depicts the Lord as a disappointed lover laying waste the unfruitful vineyard by withholding rain, tearing down the wall, and no longer tending the vineyard. So a story of disaster that concludes with violent action by a careful and patient landowner need not raise suspicions. Jesus simply transposes the poetic metaphor of God the owner and the vines of the vineyard to a story in which the vineyard is replaced by tenants who have leased it. The vines produce their fruit. The malicious and criminal actions of the tenants deprive the owner of his share of the harvest. Could this tale be an imaginative spin on a real-life situation? Documentary papyri from Egypt illustrate the sort of physical violence that can erupt when relatives or neighbors decide to move in on the plot or trees of a weaker party. The combination of an established image, Israel as God's vineyard, with an example drawn from the harsh side of daily life makes it possible to argue that Jesus told this story as an illustration of God's forbearance with an ungrateful people. Some exegetes who hold this view also think that Jesus was referring to the fate he anticipated for himself in the figure of the murdered son. However, the conclusion which Matt 21:41 has the crowd voice in response to Jesus' question about what the vineyard owner should do takes a different tack than Isaiah. The owner does not tear up the vineyard. He will punish those responsible and find tenants who will fulfill their obligations.

The parable as we find it in the Synoptic Gospels serves as a commentary on the death of Jesus and the emergence of Christian groups that are no longer subject to the Jewish authorities. Even Mark's version of the story has highlighted the correlation between the parable and the fate of Jesus. It has an awkward reference to the death of the Baptist, a servant who is struck on the head (Mark 12:4), and then expands on the number of emissaries who are beaten and even killed (v. 5). Matthew clearly understands replacing the wicked tenants with those who will give the owner his due in the same way that he understands the Great Banquet, which he has recast as a wedding feast for a king's son, adding a direct reference to the Roman destruction of Jerusalem in 70 C.E. (Matt 22:7). God has replaced a rebellious and hostile people (the wicked tenants) with the followers of Jesus. The interpreters who argue against considering the Wicked Tenants a parable of Jesus assume that it originated in Christian circles after the death of Jesus. It vindicated Christians in the face of on-going hostility from Jewish religious leaders.

Debate over whether the parable of the Wise and Foolish Servant Girls originated as a parable of Jesus follows a similar pattern. The generic division of "wise" against "foolish" behavior is typical of wisdom literature. In this story prudence consists in having enough oil in reserve to keep the lamps burning despite a long delay in the master's return. The wise also recognize that they cannot share with the foolish, or no one would have light. Though modern readers often stumble over that detail, the ancients would not have given it a second thought. Wisdom literature regularly warns the wise to have nothing to do with fools. Fools bring disaster on themselves and deserve wisdom's scorn (Prov 1:20-33). Although some commentaries patch together details from Tobit and rabbinic sources to defend the real-life situation in this parable, there is not enough first-century evidence to decide the question. Details of the Galilean wedding are often constructed on the basis of this parable. The story does have an element of exaggeration and the mixture of blessing along with a surprise disaster found in other narrative parables. The wedding banquet as an image of the happiness which the righteous are to enjoy with God would be quite familiar from the Jewish Scriptures. Jesus alludes to himself as the bridegroom (Mark 2:19-20/Matt 9:15). Therefore, some scholars consider the whole story to be the allegorical creation of early Christians. It addresses the concerns created by the delay of the parousia. Unlike the parable of the Wicked Tenants, which appears in the Synoptic Gospels and in an abbreviated form in *Gos. Thom.*, the parable of the Wise and Foolish Servant Girls only appears in Matthew's Gospel. Matthew provides a conclusion that is usually found in such contexts: "keep awake" (v. 13). This exhortation contradicts the storyline, since both groups fall asleep waiting for the bridegroom. The conclusion indicates the point that the Evangelist expects readers to take away from the parable. He does not indicate what the "extra oil" represents. Most exegetes assume that Matthew would understand it as deeds, carrying out the teaching of Jesus.

These examples illustrate the ambiguities which give rise to different interpretations of the parables. It is easier to fill out the meaning of a parable by appealing to the particular Gospel in which it is found than to treat it as an isolated story. The Evangelists have grouped parables together, added sayings at the ends of parables, or even given explanations of a few parables. Most books on the parables treat them as a separate corpus of brief images and narrative stories that reflect the preaching of Jesus himself. Some scholars classify parables by a formal characteristic such as the outcome, whether a central figure functions as a stand-in for God, or whether servants take part in the story. Others distinguish parables which draw the reader into a situation said to reflect how things are in God's reign from those which are allegories or are aimed at teaching a particular virtue. Another smaller group of parables deal with seeds and growth, nature rather than the actions of human characters providing the analogy for God's reign.

Some famous parables do not have a micro-plot line. Instead Jesus points the hearer's attention toward the way in which a particular individual responds to a situation, such as one who finds hidden treasure or a valuable pearl, one who prepares to build or for war, or one who looks for a lost sheep or lost coin. The underlying logic behind such brief presentations is typical of reasoning in many Jewish texts. If something is true in a less important case, how much more will it be true in this more important case. The principle can be worked in reverse as well. What is true of major cases must also apply to minor ones. In these brief parables the behavior of humans under special or crisis situations is the lesser case. The greater case might be response to God's reign, which is drawing near in Jesus. Or, in Luke's use of the Lost Sheep and Lost Coin, hearers are challenged to recognize that the effort expended to find what they have lost is nothing compared to what Jesus will exert to seek out the sinner.

Miracle Stories

Form criticism also provides categories for narratives about Jesus that do not lead up to sayings or parables. In some cases, such as birth legends or call stories, the category indicates that what is reported about Jesus matches the sort of story told about other important religious leaders, teachers, prophets, or political figures. Modern readers may prefer the "humble origins to greatness" biography. Ancient readers would not. An individual who changes human culture or history does not come into the world unannounced. Both Matthew and Luke provide appropriate legends about Jesus to support the Christian belief that he is Son of God. Each provides a different infancy narrative and genealogy, but most exegetes agree that these stories were in circulation before the Evangelists took them over. Great individuals also do not make up their destinies as they go along. Some form of divine call must also be part of the process. In Jesus' case, God speaks to him at his baptism (Mark 1:9-11 par.) and about him to his inner circle of three disciples at the Transfiguration (Mark 9:2-8 par.). Another stock storyline involves a quest or testing of the hero. Mark has a brief comment about Jesus in the wilderness while Matthew and Luke employ Q's temptation story, in which Jesus defeats Satan in a verbal duel.

The most striking narratives about Jesus during his ministry involve miracles. Sayings collections like Q are almost untouched by the large number of miracle stories that circulated concerning Jesus. Many modern readers find the miracle stories somewhat embarrassing. They prefer to supply naturalistic or sociological explanations for as many of them as possible. It is easy to find psychological explanations for most of the exorcism cases and perhaps even for cases of paralysis. The dead might merely be comatose. Eye diseases and blindness due to irritation, sun, and the like are not overly problematic. The sticking point involves nature miracles. Food multiplication has often been given a sociological explanation: that people who had been hoarding became willing to share turns up repeatedly in sermons. But controlling storms and walking on raging waters are another matter. One solution is to retreat once again to the broader narrative category of legend. Since the Hebrew Bible depicts God in control of the raging waters and striding across the sea, such stories could have been invented as legends. They provide a visual portrait in support of Christian faith that Jesus is the Son of God.

Such strategies are necessary for readers who are concerned that Christians not appear naive about how nature, medicine, and psychology work, but the miracle stories were problematic in the time of Jesus for quite a different reason. Since people had no other explanation for most of the natural and human disasters that happen than "the gods are behind it," they would not have been offended by the idea of miracles. For most people, prayer and traditional remedies were all they had. Some might make an arduous journey to a temple of the healing god Asclepius. The inscriptions and offerings of those who claim that the god healed them in a vision provide examples of many of the same diseases that Jesus heals. Jesus is not the only individual credited with the ability to heal. A few miracles were even attributed to the touch of the Roman emperors Augustus and Vespasian.[55] Neither the claim to work miracles nor the types of healing that Jesus performs were unknown in antiquity. Therefore most people even among the educated would have agreed that miracles can occur in principle.

Control over the powers of nature was not even limited to gods or human beings thought to be close to the gods. Magicians also claimed the ability to manipulate natural forces, to cause disease or to ward off the evil caused by others. Jesus' opponents accuse him of acting as an agent of Beelzebul, that is, of practicing magic (Mark 3:22 par.). In the exorcism stories, natural focus for such charges,[56] Jesus counters the accusation by depicting his activities as evidence for the opposite. God's reign is at hand, and Satan's control over humanity is clearly being broken up. Though the

55. For a comprehensive collection of miracle stories which provides parallels to the different types of miracle performed by Jesus see Wendy C. Cotter, *Miracles in Greco-Roman Antiquity* (London: Routledge, 1999).

56. See G. N. Stanton, *Jesus and Gospel* (New York: Cambridge University Press, 2004) 127-47.

controversy story in the Gospels has Jesus counter the accusation easily, it did not go away. Jewish traditions as early as the end of the first century presented Jesus as worthy of death because he practiced magic and deceived the people. Second-century opponents of Christianity were also familiar with these charges.

Therefore, miracle stories are something of a two-edged sword. On the one hand, they could support the claim that Jesus is God's beloved Son. On the other, they could provide ammunition for those who wanted to get rid of Jesus or his followers. Indeed, to attribute the ability to walk on water to a human being rather than a god or semi-divine being brings the category of magic into play. Legends about the Hyperboreans claimed that they had the magical powers to fly through the air or walk on the sea (Lucian, *Lover of Lies* 13). Or, to some first-century readers, the claim to walk on water might suggest the self-deification of Xerxes, Alexander the Great, Augustus, or Gaius Caligula.[57] Such insane hubris does not recommend these figures to an audience as great or admirable men. Nonetheless they were able to get masses of people to treat them as heroes or even demigods. If a person practiced magic arts, then he could also cast a spell over the crowds so that they would fail to see him for what he was.

The second-century apologist Justin Martyr argues with a Jewish opponent over the Christian understanding of Jesus' miracles. Justin points to the healing miracles as evidence that Jesus fulfilled what Isaiah prophesied of the Messiah (Isa 35:1-7). However, Satan has made it possible for both Jews and Gentiles to miss the evidence provided by the miracles and to call Jesus a false prophet, deceiver, and practitioner of magic arts instead. Among the Gentiles their own legends of healing gods like Asclepius and heroes like Hercules undermine faith in Jesus. Justin does not explain why Jewish leaders applied the condemnation of Deut 13:5 to Jesus. They should have accepted the correspondence between Jesus' deeds and prophecy (*Dialogue* 69).

The ancient examples show that claims based on miracle working could be contested. Even physical healing might elicit suspicions. Driving out demons and walking on water certainly brought the category of magic arts into play. While miracle stories could be circulated to support claims of divine power or favor, they were not accepted naively by all hearers even in the first century. The miracle-working neo-Pythagorean philosopher

---

57. See the examples in Cotter, *Miracles,* 155-59.

from the first century, Apollonius of Tyana, was compared to Jesus even in antiquity. Yet neither story would have been recorded in later biographies if the subject had been nothing but a miracle worker.

Just as sayings of Jesus circulated in collections, so also miracle stories. Mark's Gospel has Jesus repeat miracles in which Jesus calms a raging sea to rescue his terrified disciples (Mark 4:35-41; 6:47-52). He also feeds large crowds twice, first 5,000 (Mark 6:33-44), then 4,000 (8:8-10). Matthew follows Mark. Luke has only one feeding (5,000, Luke 9:10-17) and one storm miracle, the one with Jesus in the boat (Luke 8:22-25). John's Gospel, which is independent of Mark, has the same sequence as Mark 6: Jesus feeds 5,000 (John 6:1-14), then walks on water to rescue the disciples (vv. 15-21). Thus it appears that Mark may have derived his doubled miracle tradition from two different miracle collections. Luke may have had a version of Mark without the repetitions. By retaining doublets Mark faces the problem of explaining why the disciples do not appear any wiser the second time. He attributes these failures to a hardening of heart (Mark 8:17-18), accusations which put the disciples in the same category as Pharaoh or those Israelites who refused to hear the prophets.

As he does elsewhere, Matthew modifies this harsh judgment in reporting the episode. He drops the accusations of blindness, deafness, and hardness of heart in favor of one of "little faith" (Matt 16:8-9). Rather than conclude the episode with a challenge to understand what the two loaf miracles signify, as in Mark (Mark 8:21), Matthew has Jesus explain his warning against the leaven of the Pharisees and Sadducees: leaven stands for their teaching (Matt 16:12).

This example illustrates the importance of asking questions about the sources available to biblical authors even when the actual texts in question do not exist. Ancient historians also include doublets from earlier sources that do not always agree with each other. In this case Mark has combined variants of the same stories as sequential episodes in the plot. Doing so creates a more negative picture of how Jesus' disciples responded to the miracles than would have been the case in the miracle collections themselves. Since Luke's Gospel has only one version of the feeding and the storm, the issue of why the disciples did not understand the second time around does not arise. Matthew keeps the doublets found in his Markan source, but solves the problem differently.

The formal characteristics of a miracle story require an initial description highlighting the severity of the situation, some action on the part of the afflicted person (or petitioners acting in his or her stead), the words and/or actions of the healer, and the cure or rescue. Some healing miracles require that the petitioner engage in a specific action. Often the response of persons who witness the miracle serves to confirm that it has occurred. In the exorcism stories, exiting demons may damage objects on their way out. Exorcisms also require words or a set formula from the healer to force the demon out. Inscriptions from famous healing sanctuaries sometimes include another element found in the gospel stories, faith. Some of them highlight the sick person's initial lack of faith in Asclepius. Sometimes the god appears to a sick person in a dream demanding that he or she engage in a peculiar set of actions. In others, the god heals immediately. Neither the form nor the types of miracle attributed to Jesus in the Gospels are unusual in the first century. In physical healings, magical papyri rely more on formulas and elaborate potions than do the stories told about Jesus.

The Gospels also contain stories in which the healing is part of a debate about Jesus' teaching. For example, Jesus links healing with forgiveness in Mark 2:1-12. The conflict between Jesus and his opponents occurs because Jesus allegedly usurps God's authority to forgive sin. Notice that the "lesser to greater case" logic occurs in the reply. With some irony Jesus asks whether it is harder to say, "your sins are forgiven," or to tell the paralyzed to get up, pick up the stretcher, and walk (v. 9). Consequently, the miracle confirms Jesus' authority to forgive. As we saw above, the only miracle story attributed to the sayings source Q, the healing of the centurion's servant or son, turns on the contrast between this outsider's faith and the lack of faith of Jesus' own compatriots. Stories in which Jesus instructs those healed of leprosy to meet the requirements of Mosaic Law (e.g., Mark 1:40-45) could distinguish him from populist healers or magicians. Unlike populist healers, magicians, and the priests at healing shrines, Jesus does not receive money, goods, or other favors in return for his healing. Luke begins his account of Jesus' ministry with a sermon in which Jesus refers to Elisha's healing of a Syrian general of leprosy, which turns on the contrast between healing for money and God's gift through the prophet (2 Kgs 5:1-27; Luke 4:27). Clearly the narrative contexts in which the Evangelists report Jesus' miracles make it less likely that an audience will assume that Jesus was just another healer or magician than a simple collection of the individual miracles attributed to Jesus would have done. Readers of the Gospels should recognize that the miracles confirm Jesus' teaching and his close relationship with God. However, as Justin Martyr's argument illustrates, that Jesus was known as a miracle worker could still be turned against him by those determined to undermine the new faith.

The Passion Narrative

The death of the philosopher Socrates (399 B.C.E.) and the crucifixion of Jesus (ca. 31 C.E.) are the two best-known ancient stories of the trial and execution of an innocent man. No court records or transcripts exist for either case. Instead, accounts of their last days by students are responsible for the powerful images which have dominated western culture. Though others wrote about Socrates in antiquity, the defense speech *(Apology)* and dialogues *(Crito* and *Phaedo)* by Plato represent the death of Socrates as it would be remembered in western tradition for all time. In the case of Jesus, the passion narratives from the canonical Gospels have shaped our liturgical and artistic imagination.

Matthew's passion narrative adds a few incidents or details to the story as told in Mark. Luke's account diverges further from Mark than does Matthew's. John's Gospel goes its own way both in the chronology of the passion and in its portrayal of Jesus' trial and death. For example, the Synoptics have Jesus remain silent before Pilate. John's Gospel has a more dramatic scenario: Pilate shuttles back and forth between his exchanges with Jesus inside and with Jewish accusers outside. The Synoptics report that Simon of Cyrene was conscripted to carry Jesus' cross beam to the place of execution. John's Gospel insists that Jesus carried it himself. The Synoptic chronology has Jesus die on the day after the Passover meal in the evening. John's Gospel has him die on the day of preparation as the Passover lambs are being slaughtered in the Temple courtyard.

Naturally scholars attempt to get behind these famous trial accounts to what really happened to Socrates or Jesus as it might have appeared to a court reporter. They debate issues concerning legal proceedings and religiously motivated accusations. Socrates was accused of disregarding the traditional gods of Athens and spreading his beliefs among the young. Jesus was accused of blasphemy or, in later Jewish sources, of being a false prophet and practicing magic. Neither Socrates nor Jesus would have died if his teaching had not threatened powerful men in their respective cities. Jesus' situation is more complex since it involves two proceedings, an inquiry by Jewish authorities and execution at the hands of Roman soldiers.

Historical and legal questions aside, scholars have debated whether Mark's passion narrative was based on an earlier written account of the trial and death of Jesus. Some reconstructions attribute most of Mark's text to a pre-Markan narrative. Other scholars think that the lack of consensus in scholarly reconstructions proves that Mark was not editing an earlier written source. Skepticism over the existence of an extended passion narrative used by Mark does not imply that Mark made up the entire story. Traditions about Jesus' final meal with his followers, his trial before Pilate, and his crucifixion and resurrection were part of Christian evangelization from the earliest days (1 Cor 11:23-26; 15:3-5). The unresolved question is whether such oral traditions and confessional formulas had been brought together in written narratives. If so, did the narrative begin with the final meal, with the disciples and Jesus in Gethsemane, or only with the arrest? Did it end as the earliest manuscripts of Mark do with the women discovering the empty tomb, or did it include the resurrection?

The Jewish models for a story of the righteous person imperiled or killed by the wicked do not come from the death of Socrates but from stories in the Daniel cycle, stories about the deaths of prophets, and stories of the Maccabean martyrs. The servant songs of Isaiah, especially Isa 52:13–53:12, psalms about the afflicted (Psalms 22 and 69), and wisdom tales about the wicked seeing their victim's eternal life with God (Wis 2–5) provide both a narrative arc and details for telling Jesus' story. At some point the particular items being retold about Jesus must have been attached to the paradigm of the suffering righteous one. If his followers remembered that Jesus himself spoke about the suffering servant of Isaiah, then this narrative foundation for filling out or explaining Jesus' passion may have existed from the beginning. Extreme skeptics take the same building blocks from Jewish tradition as evidence that the entire passion narrative was the product of early Christian imagination. They insist that Mark or his narrative source actually knew nothing more than the bare facts that Jesus had been executed by Pontius Pilate and was seen as alive by Peter three days later. Most exegetes would assume that memories about Jesus' last days preserved more historical information than that.[58] Hence recon-

---

58. See the discussion of the skeptical views of H. Koester and J. D. Crossan by Raymond Brown, whose commentary argues that historical information is embedded in the passion narratives. Brown pays careful attention to the theological perspective of each individual Gospel as well (*Death of the Messiah*, 17-35).

structions of a pre-Markan passion narrative often play a role in historical reconstructions of the life of Jesus.

The *Gospel of Peter* and the Development of the Passion Narrative

Much as *Gos. Thom.* has been used to challenge the routine scholarly analysis of Jesus' sayings, so some scholars invoke another early-second-century apocryphal Gospel, the *Gospel of Peter,* as evidence for passion traditions earlier than the Synoptic Gospels. Those who take this position must distinguish the material alleged to be early from the remains of the second-century Gospel. Advocates for the priority of *Gos. Pet.,* such as J. Dominic Crossan and Helmut Koester, are skeptical about the historicity of the canonical Gospels. Koester argues, for example, that since the details in *Gos. Pet.* correspond more closely to early Christian exegetical use of Psalm 69 than those in the canonical gospels, *Gos. Pet.* is closer to the origins of the passion narrative tradition.[59] The same observations could support the opposite conclusion. Initially, remembrances of the passion were understood in light of the antecedent examples in the prophets and psalms. That perception shaped the retelling in a general way so that the confessional formulas which included "according to the Scriptures" made sense. Only as Christians were constrained to "prove it" or answer Jewish objections did the need for more precise correspondence between the passion narrative and Scripture arise. Consequently, exegetical corrections would have been introduced to bring an account closer to its scriptural antecedents.

Both sides of the debate over the value of *Gos. Pet.* for understanding the sources and structure of pre-Markan passion tradition(s) agree that *Gos. Pet.* is not dependent on the canonical Gospels or revising them. The details of sequence and wording of individual episodes are not close enough to indicate copying. Similarly, there are no cases in which the unique features of one of the canonical Gospels can be shown to depend on special tradition found in *Gos. Pet.* Such lack of contact adds to the case against the claim that the canonical Gospels used a passion tradition that is more accurately preserved in *Gos. Pet.* than in their versions.[60]

59. Helmut Koester, *Ancient Christian Gospels: Their History and Development* (Philadelphia: Trinity, 1990) 220-30.
60. See the detailed charts and analysis in Brown, *Death,* 1322-33.

Eusebius reports that *Gos. Pet.* was a local Gospel used by Christians in Syria. It was not known in the major churches such as Antioch. Bishop Serapion (ca. 190-211) initially permitted Christians to continue reading their local Gospel on his visit to Rhossus in Cilicia. When he was later informed that *Gos. Pet.* was being used to support the claim that Jesus only appeared to suffer, the bishop prohibited its use (*Hist. Eccl.* 6.12.2-6). Since it was an established part of the local church's public reading by century's end, *Gos. Pet.* was probably composed in the early to mid-second century. Although its author does not revise a Synoptic Gospel as his structural framework, he probably knew Matthew from reading or hearing it and perhaps had heard items from other Gospels as well.

Perhaps because *Gos. Pet.* was local tradition and not attached to a major urban center, it was not quoted by second- or early-third-century authors. The Gospel that we have is incomplete. Four fragments of Greek texts copied by two different scribes exist. A small seventh to eighth-century codex from a monk's grave in Egypt includes a version that begins in mid-sentence at the trial of Jesus and ends in mid-sentence by the sea. Presumably, the risen Jesus is about to appear to Peter, Andrew, and Levi, who are just setting out to fish. Since the scribe decorated the first page of the codex with a cross and began copying *Gos. Pet.* on the next page, he must have had only the incomplete text. Therefore we do not know whether the original was only somewhat longer, that is, was only a passion narrative, or included the life and ministry of Jesus. Other non-canonical Christian writings from the late first and early second centuries such as the *Shepherd of Hermas* show much greater variation from one copy to the next than is the case for the canonical Gospels. Therefore one must be cautious about concluding that our surviving fragments accurately represent the second-century *Gos. Pet.*, let alone some pre-Markan passion tradition.

Some items in *Gos. Pet.* suggest a redactional tendency to heighten the role of Jews in executing Jesus. The trial and guilty verdict take place before Herod and other Jews, who refuse to wash their hands. Pilate is present but not participating in the trial. Herod hands Jesus over for execution. Jews are depicted as pushing and dragging the Son of God along the way of the cross, mocking him as king of Israel, placing him on a judgment seat (*Gos. Pet.* 1.1; 3.6-9). A Jewish squad, not Roman soldiers, carries out the execution (6.21-23). Joseph of Arimathea appears as the "friend of Pilate and of the Lord." He requests the body prior to Jesus' death. Pilate must send the request on to Herod, who replies that Jewish Law would have required that they bury the body before sunset even if no one had stepped forward to claim it (2.3-5).

In an episode more dramatically detailed than Matthew's legend of the tomb guards (Matt 27:62-66), Jewish leaders actually secure a detachment of Roman soldiers to seal and guard the tomb (*Gos. Pet.* 8.28-33). The soldiers, commanded by a centurion, pitch camp and establish two-man watches. The watch sees two angels descend from heaven, roll back the stone, and enter the tomb (9.35-37). They have time to wake the centurion and a group of Jewish elders also present as a guard. The entire contingent sees Jesus brought out of the tomb with the cross following. A heavenly voice asks if Jesus has preached to the dead. The cross replies "yes" (10.38-41).

When the soldiers and Jewish elders appear before Pilate to report what has happened, he throws the guilt back on the Jews, saying, "I am clean from the blood of the Son of God; it was you who desired it" (11.46). This development brings the story into conformity with the paradigm story of the suffering righteous more closely than do the Synoptic accounts. Ordinarily, the "wicked" must witness the triumph of the person whose death they have engineered. In Wis 5:1-8, for example, the wicked are compelled to confess what they have done when they discover that the righteous are "sons of God." In *Gos. Pet.* those responsible recognize that Jesus is "Son of God" but, fearing that the people will turn on them if the truth comes out, they orchestrate a cover-up with Pilate. In so doing, the officials acknowledge accepting divine condemnation for the punishment of death in place of the stoning that the people would inflict if the truth were known (11.48).

Gos. Pet. also attaches a confession of guilt to the signs which accompanied the removal of Jesus' body from the cross. A terrifying earthquake occurs when the body is laid on the ground (6.21; contrast Matt 27:51: at the moment of Jesus' death). Then the sun reappears. The Jewish officials lament the judgment their evil deeds have brought on, namely, the destruction of Jerusalem (7.35). The author works the solar eclipse into the burial tradition by having the people concerned that the Torah has been broken, since it stipulates that the sun should not be permitted to set on a murder victim. Even the notice about those who gave Jesus gall and vinegar to drink in fulfillment of Scripture (cf. Matt 27:34, 48) has been turned into a mark of condemnation: "And they fulfilled all things and accumulated their sins on their head" (*Gos. Pet.* 5.17). Thus *Gos. Pet.* exhibits a consistent pattern of redaction that appears to be more legendary and apologetic expansion of passion traditions familiar from the canonical Gospels than evidence of a pre-Markan account.

Gos. Pet. provides a glimpse into the passion story as it was known to Christians outside such major centers as Antioch in the second century. The lack of a common sequence of episodes or vocabulary shared with the canonical Gospels indicates that it was not composed using one or more written texts. Some of the legendary elements have analogues in the canonical Gospels, such as the implication of Herod in the trial (Luke) or the guard set at the tomb (Matthew). Both appear in a more elaborated form in *Gos. Pet.* Both contribute to this Gospel's version of Jewish guilt for the execution of Jesus. By making the signs at Jesus' death and the resurrection evidence that even Jesus' enemies know they deserved divine punishment, *Gos. Pet.* completes the paradigm story of divine vindication. This development at the level of popular Christian story-telling confirms the hypothesis that Jewish story patterns influenced the way in which early Christians understood the events of Jesus' death and resurrection. One might infer from the differences in narrative sequence that there was not a fixed form of the passion narrative even in the early second century, let alone prior to Mark's version. *Gos. Pet.* could be partial evidence for the view that Mark assembled his passion narrative from a group of traditional materials. When the trial scenes of *Gos. Pet.* and Mark are compared, Mark's combination of a somewhat unclear proceeding involving the Sanhedrin, after which Jesus is remitted for trial and execution by Pilate, has a much stronger claim to historical plausibility than the scenario imagined by *Gos. Pet.*

That said, all conclusions about *Gos. Pet.* should come with a note of caution. Our only evidence derives from a late manuscript that was copied from an incomplete exemplar. Though it would appear to have ended with some story similar to John 21:1-14, the risen Jesus appearing to disciples who have returned to fishing, we have no clue about its original beginning. Unless a more extensive manuscript is discovered, we do not know how the peculiar trial scene is set up or what motivation is given for the hostility against Jesus. We do not know if clues about a social or historical setting could be found in *Gos. Pet.* that might explain its presentation of Jewish hostility to Jesus. Nor do we know if its author introduced Peter's voice as a first person narrator earlier than in the fragmentary scene at the conclusion (*Gos. Pet.* 14.58). Does "we the twelve disciples of the Lord wept and mourned" (14.59) reflect a bit of narrative forgetfulness or a passion story that was told without a Judas as betrayer? Without additional evidence such important literary, theological, and historical questions cannot be resolved.

Every newly discovered fragment of gospel material from the first three centuries will elicit the same mixture of inflated hopes of a pre-Synoptic date and skepticism that we have observed in *Gos. Thom.* and *Gos. Pet.* So far our only reliable evidence for the sources employed by the Synoptic Evangelists remains in the Synoptic Gospels themselves. Even sayings and parables from *Gos. Thom.* judged more primitive than the alternative versions known in the Synoptics have been stripped of their context in a second-century collection of sayings. As the analysis of the sayings material common to Matthew and Luke has become a specialized area, arguments about the origin and composition of *Gos. Thom.* have been like those concerning the canonical Gospels. Oral transmission is pitted against written levels of composition and redaction. Hypotheses about a Q community and christology are advanced. And in the process a new gospel portrait of Jesus emerges which its advocates suggest is closer to the "historical figure" than that found in any of the canonical Gospels. However, such proposals often depend upon a very thin collection of actual textual evidence and a great deal of speculative reconstruction.

While the hope of filling in the gap of some four decades between the execution of Jesus and Mark's Gospel is a powerful motivation for picking the Gospels apart, many interpreters question the value of the effort. The interest in the bits placed on display by source and form criticism can distract from reading a biblical book as a whole. Rhetorical analysis and various methods of literary criticism have come to play an important role in study of the Gospels. Form criticism has less to do with asserting a communal setting in which certain types of tradition were formulated than with comparing familiar types of sayings or story patterns from the surrounding culture to similar elements in the Gospels. Such parallels help modern readers train their ear to appreciate the distinction between creative innovations and familiar types. Rhetorical and literary analyses have suggested new approaches to the Jewish Scriptures as sources for indirect storylines or echoes in the Gospels. As we study the individual Gospels, observations from source criticism and form criticism will be part of this larger task of understanding each Gospel as a narrative whole.

CHAPTER FOUR

Reading Mark's Gospel

As we have seen, Mark's Gospel appears to have been the earliest written narrative to combine an account of Jesus' ministry with a report about his final days in Jerusalem. Modern scholars have no way of confirming the suggestion made in antiquity that the Evangelist employed notes or reminiscences jotted down by someone who listened to an aging Peter. Nor has it been possible to extract other sources that may have been available to the author from the text as we know it. Miracle stories, call stories, parables, sayings, and even stories about Jesus' death certainly circulated orally. Written collections of such materials may have passed from one community to another. If the author of John's Gospel was not familiar with the Synoptic Gospels, then such narrative sequences that coincide with Mark

---

Suggested Reading

Best, Ernest. *Mark: The Gospel as Story.* Edinburgh: Clark, 1983.

Collins, Adela Y. *The Beginnings of the Gospel: Probings of Mark in Context.* Minneapolis: Augsburg, 1992.

Evans, Craig A. *Mark 8:27-16:20.* WBC 34B; Nashville: Nelson, 2001.

Marcus, Joel. *Mark 1–8.* AB 27; New York: Doubleday, 2000.

Moloney, Francis J. *The Gospel of Mark.* Peabody: Hendrickson, 2002.

Vines, Michael E. *The Problem of Markan Genre: The Gospel of Mark and the Jewish Novel.* SBL Academia Biblica 3; Leiden: Brill, 2002.

might indicate a pre-Markan form of the story. Both John's Gospel and the sayings collection Q begin the story of Jesus with John the Baptist.

Mark's opening line invokes early Christian preaching about Jesus rather than identifying its subject by family and regional origins, as most ancient lives do. We have seen that some scholars object to treating the Synoptic Gospels as lives of Jesus because they diverge from the literary patterns found in biographies of famous political or philosophical figures. However the revisions introduced by Matthew and Luke include such items as genealogy, birth prodigies, and elements of chronology along with additional materials about Jesus' teaching. Such developments suggest that the later Evangelists were filling out what they took to be a life of Jesus.

Although most readers today think of Mark as a sacred written text, its first audiences would not have. Scripture for them meant the Greek version of Jewish sacred texts. That is why some scholars think that it would be better to imagine Mark as a performance script that enabled early Christian storytellers to recite the stories about Jesus than as a sacred book. The Evangelist has provided a narrative structure, taking what appear to have been separable episodic bits and fitting them into a compelling plot that ends with the death of his main character. Although Jesus does not begin to teach the disciples about his destiny until halfway through the story, the audience sees hints of danger from the opening verses. Jesus begins preaching after John's arrest (Mark 1:14). He soon has religious and political enemies plotting his death (3:6). The Evangelist interrupts the story of Jesus' ministry with a digression on the death of the Baptist (6:14-29).

From Beginning to End: Mark's Narrative Shape

Even if exegetes agreed on a single map of the sources and forms of every unit in Mark's Gospel, they might disagree over interpretation of the larger narrative that holds them together. Recent commentaries devote more attention to questions about how the individual episodes fit into the Gospel as a whole than to spelling out details of source and form criticism for each unit. A Gospel is not a rigid literary structure with rules that the author must follow. Readers would expect a life to include its subject's great exploits and/or wise teaching, something about the subject's origins, and the conclusion of his or her life. The larger narrative structures play an important role in determining how readers interpret the smaller units, whether actions or sayings, contained in a Gospel. The Evangelists sometimes provide a different reading of a shared parable, saying, or episode as much by its place in a larger section of narrative as by the changes introduced into the story itself.

Most people in antiquity, even those who could read, encountered a book by hearing it. Today that habit is making a return thanks to the CD player. Customers expect the bestsellers in fiction and nonfiction to be out in audio form almost as soon as the print version appears. These new listeners differ from their ancient counterparts in two important respects: the experience is solitary and usually involves only one trip through the book. The modern listener uses personal headphones and is not part of a group listening to the reading. Once finished, the modern listener puts the CD on the shelf or returns it to the library and goes for a new title. Ancient audiences would hear a book repeated many times. In both the modern and ancient listening situation, the person doing the reading will impart meaning while performing the text. No two readings are the same. Some modern listeners have favorites among the professionals who record books. Others only want to hear a book read by its author. It is impossible to recover the nuances of ancient reading in the case of the Gospels. But scholars do recognize the importance of oral performance as a key to the patterns used in constructing the narratives.[1]

Commentators often differ in where they place the breaks between major sections. For example, does Mark 1:1 function as a title, after which the reader comes to a full stop? Or should "as it is written in the prophet Isaiah" in v. 2 be linked to "beginning of the gospel"? Does the preliminary section end after Jesus' testing in the wilderness at 1:13 or after the summary report about Jesus' preaching in Galilee in 1:15? The final word of v. 15 is "gospel," which could be treated as ending the segment by picking up the second word of v. 1. On the other hand, Mark habitually attaches short sections to what precedes with the words "and" or "and immediately," so "after John was arrested" in v. 14 might be read as beginning a new section, with the "and" of v. 16 indicating that the story of Peter's call is second in a series. Listeners depend on clues from the reader such as pauses, changes in tone, or even gestures for a sense of where divisions fall. An author can provide verbal cues by describing departures and arrivals or change of

---

1. See Joanna Dewey, "Oral Methods of Structuring Narrative in Mark," *Interpretation* 53 (1989) 32-44.

place. The Evangelists also compose brief summary passages to mark a shift in the narrative (such as Mark 1:32-34).

Since the letters are run together in ancient manuscripts, a reader had to be familiar with a work before giving a public recitation. Modern students often fail to recognize that the layout of pages they study has decisions about the Gospel's structure built in. Printed translations insert breaks and sometimes even headings into the text. The NRSV leaves an extra space between vv. 15 and 16 in Mark 1, so a reader will infer that the opening section ends at v. 15 rather than v. 13, for example. Modern editors may introduce section titles or subtitles. The United Bible Societies edition of the Greek New Testament introduces each pericope with spacing, a content-related title and an indication of parallel passages in the other Gospels. Some translations, such as the New Jerusalem Bible, follow that practice of giving a title to each small unit of text. This division into smallest units, most beginning with "and" in Mark's Gospel, might give the impression of a narrative that lacks larger structural patterns to tie the episodes together. Sayings collections like Q or *Gos. Thom.* have very little internal organization or plot. Though Mark eventually has to end the story with the passion, an episodic arrangement prior to that point gives the impression that the Evangelist has strung together a random collection of stories about Jesus.

Closer reading of the Gospel indicates that the Evangelist has done much more than copy down assorted stories. For example, he employs the summary in 1:32-34 to emphasize the crowd appeal of Jesus' activity as healer and exorcist. By the next episode, the Evangelist has clued the reader in that celebrating Jesus the miracle worker is not the purpose of the story. At dawn, Jesus withdraws to pray in a deserted place. He then leaves Capernaum to begin the series of journeys around Galilee and neighboring territories (1:35-39). The distinction between the Judean territory and Galilee constitutes the main geographical division in the narrative. Jesus comes from Nazareth in Galilee to the Baptist in Judea (1:9) and returns to begin preaching in Galilee after John's arrest (1:14). He does not return to Judea again until the journey that ends with his death (10:1, 32, 46; 11:1, 11, 15, 27). Finally, the Gospel leads its reader to anticipate a return to Galilee that will reunite the risen Jesus with his disciples (14:28; 16:7), but the story comes to an abrupt conclusion at 16:8 with the frightened women fleeing from the empty tomb.

Such an ending provides something of a jolt to readers who antici-

pate a triumphant conclusion. Though some scholars think Mark's original ending has gone missing,[2] Matthew and Luke go in separate directions
after the women leave the tomb. It appears that their versions of Mark also
ended with 16:8. Matthew (28:16-20), John (21:1-14) and *Gos. Pet.* (14:59-60)
all bring the story of Jesus to an end with an appearance in Galilee. Since
there are no geographical tags attached to the witness list in 1 Cor 15:5-9,
we do not know if the Galilee appearance stories were in circulation well
before Mark wrote his Gospel. If so, then Mark's audience may have filled
in the rest as the later Evangelists did. If not, then the narrative concludes
on a note of unfulfilled prophecy. The tension generated by the ending is
heightened by the fact that all the other predictions Jesus makes about his
death and the actions of his disciples leading up to the passion are fulfilled
in the course of the narrative. Therefore some exegetes conclude that the
Galilee saying in Mark 16:7 refers not to the resurrection but to the second
coming. However, the saying lacks the trappings of glory, angels, or coming on clouds typical of parousia oracles (e.g., 14:62). Mark 14:28 associates
the return to Galilee with Jesus' resurrection. Therefore most exegetes conclude that Mark is referring to the period after the resurrection.

Near the midpoint of the narrative the story takes a major turn. The
miracles and teaching in and around Galilee have generated speculation
about who Jesus is. He takes an opinion poll through his disciples (8:27-
30). Peter's confession that Jesus is Messiah appears closer to the truth than
that of the crowds. However, as soon as Jesus predicts that he will suffer
and die at the hands of chief priests and scribes in Jerusalem, Peter objects.
Jesus' reprimand distinguishes human opinions from what God intends.
Furthermore, Jesus' followers must also be willing to take up the cross
(8:31-38). Each of the next chapters on the journey to Jerusalem contains a
passion prediction followed by resistance on the part of the disciples (9:31-
32; 10:32-34). Two healing miracles serve as bookends to a transitional section of teaching between Galilee and Jerusalem: Jesus heals a blind man
just before the messianic question (8:22-26) and another as he passes
through Jericho on the way up to Jerusalem (10:46-52).

Again commentaries will differ in where they situate the midpoint
break in the Gospel. Some begin the second section with the messianic

---

2. According to this hypothesis, v. 8 began a new section. The reader would have
paused after the angel's announcement in v. 7. The ending which Mark intended was either
lost or never composed by the Evangelist. So Evans, *Mark 8:27–16:20,* 538-39.

question at 8:27. The first cure of a blind man serves to conclude Part One. Others prefer to keep the two healing miracles together as a frame around the instruction of the disciples. They end the first section at 8:21.[3] Concluding the first half with 8:14-21 presents as much of a challenge to the audience as the ending of the Gospel does. The disciples are being accused of the same blindness and hardheartedness that was typical of unbelieving Israel. The unit ends with Jesus' question, "Do you not yet understand?" The dramatic difference between the two possibilities is evident if one imagines ending Act One with 8:21 or ending it with the healing miracle of 8:22-26. In the first instance, the curtain drops leaving the audience with a dilemma. In the second way of staging the Gospel, there is a proleptic promise that the lack of comprehension or blindness of the disciples will also be healed. Both options are plausible readings. The choice that an exegete or editor makes in arranging Mark's text already carries with it decisions about its meaning.

Turning to each of the main divisions, scholars have proposed varied strategies for discerning additional literary divisions within the two halves of the Gospel. One solution works from the three scenes in which Jesus calls a group of disciples (1:16-20), chooses the Twelve (3:13-19), and sends them out with the power to heal and preach repentance (6:7-13).[4] This series incorporates the Twelve into the activity of Jesus depicted in this part of the Gospel. They return from the mission flush with success (6:30). Jesus steps off stage after sending them on mission. Mark treats readers to a legendary account of the circumstances which led to John the Baptist's execution (6:16-29). He prefaces the tale with a survey of opinions about who Jesus is similar to the discussion Jesus has with his disciples at (or near) the beginning of the second part of the gospel (6:14-16; 8:27-28). In this instance, Herod pronounces the definitive judgment: the Baptist, whom he has beheaded, has been raised. Herod's comment (6:16) can be read as the Baptist's vindication over the wicked ruler. Though the fact of John's execution can be confirmed in Josephus (*Antiquities* 18.109-16), Mark's story has all the earmarks of popular legend. Form-critically it is a martyrdom story, but it is told with no direct confrontation between the martyr hero and his accusers or the king. Instead, his head enters at the end as though it

---

3. Marcus, *Mark 1–8*, 63.

4. Marcus, *Mark 1–8*, 63-64. Marcus also employs word counts to show that his outline produces sections of equivalent length.

were a course to be served at the banquet. Immediately after this banquet, Mark will narrate the feeding of the 5,000, an anti-type to the scene the reader has just witnessed. As we have seen, the introduction to this section insures that the audience will see an analogy between the Baptist's fate and that of Jesus.

Jesus had to call disciples before he could begin his public ministry (1:16-20). His initial success leads to conflict with Pharisees and Herodians who seek to kill him (3:6) despite the crowds from surrounding territories (3:8) who seek him out. Selection of the Twelve appears to be a response to that narrative development. Similarly, Jesus sends the Twelve out on mission following a scene of disbelief in Jesus' home village of Nazareth, which limited his ability to perform miracles (6:1-6a). If incorporating disciples into his mission is the narrative response to hostility and disbelief, the conclusion of Part One raises questions about how effective the strategy was. During the sea miracles (4:40; 6:52) the disciples exhibit a shocking lack of faith, which has not been healed.

The second half of the Gospel falls into three sections. The first takes Jesus and the disciples from the affirmations of Jesus' identity as Messiah (8:27-30) and Son of God (9:2-9), known only to his followers, to the outskirts of Jerusalem (Mark 8:27 [or, v. 22]-10:52). The second recounts Jesus' entry into Jerusalem and teaching in the Temple area during the days prior to his death (11:1–13:37). The account of Jesus' final meal and passion constitutes the final section in this part of the gospel (14:1–16:8a). Some commentators distinguish between the events which occur in northern regions of the Decapolis and Galilee (8:27–9:50, Caesarea Philippi, to Capernaum) and those which take place as Jesus moves through Perea across the Jordan through Jericho to Jerusalem (10:1-52). Others open section two with the healing of the blind Bartimaeus (10:46-52) because it introduces the title which links Jesus to Jerusalem, "Son of David." Rather than see the empty tomb story as a continuation of the burial narrative, some scholars detach 16:1-8a from the passion narrative to create an epilogue that is symmetrical with the opening section (1:1-15).

An important question underlies the issue of how to treat the empty tomb story. Some exegetes think that the empty tomb traditions were created by early Christians several decades after Jesus' death. The tale grew out of either liturgical veneration of a site or an apologetic interest in defending belief in resurrection. Consequently, they argue that there is no reason to think that the tomb story belonged to the pre-Markan passion traditions. On the opposite side of the historical debate, other scholars insist that the tomb tradition belonged to the early passion story. The "was buried" of the creedal affirmation requires a report about the state of the tomb as well. Or, if the passion was narrated as a story of a suffering and vindicated righteous one, then the empty tomb story could have been perceived as the divine response. The apocryphal *Gos. Pet.* created a full-fledged demonstration of the Lord's divine status before his enemies for its second-century audience.

Literary Features of Mark's Narrative

Modern readers often think of the four canonical Gospels as a single book. Because the Synoptic Gospels share sources in common, it can be difficult for students to notice details that make one different from the others. Scholars began isolating special characteristics of language and composition in hopes of distinguishing the Evangelist's editing from the sources employed. As difficulties with that project mounted, scholarly attention shifted to the Evangelists as authors rather than as editors of collected material. What literary devices does each Evangelist favor in composing the narrative? How do particular persons or groups function within the plot as allies or antagonists of Jesus? How does the author tie the small units of the story together in larger patterns?

Mark's Gospel appears to be very choppy on the surface. Phrases beginning with "and," "and immediately," "and it happened," or "and" plus a verb referring to some change of place are common introductions to the individual sections. To our ears that style sounds as though a young child were the narrator. Or it could give the impression that the Evangelist did not have the ability to compose a literary piece. He simply strung together traditional materials along with brief introductory comments and summary passages on the simple timeline: (1) Jesus' baptism and testing in Judea, (2) his ministry in Galilee comprised of miracles, a few parables, and teachings embedded in brief episodes *(chreiai)*, (3) predictions of his passion and teaching on the way to Jerusalem, (4) his arrival at Jerusalem and the Temple cleansing and teaching there, and (5) the passion narrative. Repetitions in the first section of the Gospel such as the doubled feeding miracles and sea rescue stories might suggest that Mark simply copied whatever traditions he could find. It would not seem appropriate to look for other literary features in such a naive representation of remembered oral stories.

Exegetical interest in literary analysis has challenged such judgments about Mark's narrative style. For example, the geographical plot can be further detailed by considering movements within each of the two areas. The Sea of Galilee serves as a key transit point in the first half of the Gospel. Jesus calls disciples along its edge (1:16; 2:13), instructs the crowds at the edge from a boat (4:1), and rescues his disciples from its violent storms twice (4:35-41; 6:45-52). By crossing the sea in a boat, Jesus ventures outside Jewish territory to the Gentile cities of the Decapolis (5:1, 20). In some instances Mark's sea crossings appear to go off course. The disciples set out for Bethsaida on the northeastern shore (6:45) but land at Gennesaret, the plain on the western shore between Capernaum and Tiberias (v. 53). As in other concluding summaries, Jesus cannot enter an area without sick people from the entire region flocking to him. Mark interrupts Jesus' travels for a dispute between Jesus and Pharisees from Jerusalem over purity regulations (7:1-23) before Jesus departs from Jewish territory for the region around Tyre on the Mediterranean coast. Even here, his reputation draws a Syro-Phoenician woman to seek healing for her daughter (7:24-30). The geographical notice by which Mark attempts to return Jesus to the Sea of Galilee (7:31) takes him north to another Syro-Phoenician city, Sidon, and then back through the Decapolis cities, all but one of which are to the east of the sea. These geographical mistakes suggest that Mark is not familiar with actual routes of travel. The Evangelist must be employing geography for another purpose. Although the Gospel only contains two miracles on behalf of Gentiles, the cure of the Gerasene demoniac (5:1-20) to the east of the sea and that of the Syro-Phoenician's daughter to the west, these geographical notes imply that Jesus has burst the boundaries which excluded non-Jews from God's people.

Some exegetes think that the feeding of 4,000 in 8:1-9 refers to Gentiles.[5] However, Mark's awkward transitional geography has put Jesus back along the Sea of Galilee, where he is again mobbed by crowds (7:32-37). The two Gentile episodes do not involve healing in the presence of a large crowd. Therefore the crowd of 4,000 is most likely Jewish, not Gentile. Once again, the Evangelist uses a boat to move Jesus and his disciples away from the crowd, this time to the region of "Dalmanutha." No town by

5. For example, Marcus, *Mark 1–8,* 492.

that name is known. Manuscripts of Matthew's Gospel show that ancient scribes — and perhaps Matthew himself — were also puzzled. Some have Magdala, others another unknown town, "Magadan" (Matt 15:39). Jesus encounters Pharisees as soon as he arrives (Mark 8:10-11), which suggests that the location is a Jewish town on the western side of the Sea of Galilee. After a brief exchange that ends with Jesus uttering a prophetic judgment against his generation for seeking a sign, he crosses the sea once more (v. 13). When Jesus and the disciples arrive at Bethsaida, the crowds bring a blind man for healing (v. 22). That encounter marks the end of sea voyaging for Jesus and his disciples. Thus the geographical patterning of the Gospel also suggests that the first major section concludes with 8:26.

Jerusalem forms the geographical center of the second half of the story. Although Jesus has not been to Judea since his baptism, the city has not been forgotten. People come to Jesus in Galilee from the southern territories, "Judea and Jerusalem, Idumea and Transjordan" (3:8). Authorities from Jerusalem appear in Galilee to challenge Jesus' activities (3:22 [scribes]; 7:1 [Pharisees? and scribes]). The transition between the Galilean ministry and Jesus' actions and teaching in Jerusalem prior to his death opens in Gentile territory, Caesarea Philippi; Jesus then moves about undefined areas of Galilee before a final stop in Capernaum. At 10:1, he and his followers leave Galilee and enter Judean territory. Once Jesus arrives in the vicinity of Jerusalem, the Temple constitutes the defining place in the narrative. Following his entry into the city, Jesus pays a brief visit to the Temple before leaving Jerusalem for the evening (11:11). On the following day, he engages in a prophetic condemnation of those engaged in selling items needed for offerings as well as those carrying things, perhaps ritual items, through the Temple area (11:15-17, citing Isa 56:7 and Jer 7:11). Once more Jesus leaves for the evening (11:19), and he returns to the Temple the following day. There Jewish authorities — high priests, scribes, and elders — demand proof that Jesus acts with God's authority (11:27-28). In a classic controversy story, Jesus defeats these opponents without explicitly answering. John the Baptist is mentioned for the final time in the Gospel. The officials decline to take a stand on the source of John's authority. Mark's audience is privy to their reasons. They cannot admit that John was one of God's prophets without condemning themselves for not believing him. They cannot say what they actually think, that John acted on his own, without angering the crowd (11:27-33).

A section of teaching follows this exchange. The wicked tenants of

Jesus' parable become the authorities who have challenged Jesus' authority. Their hostility toward the parable-teller and continued fear of the crowd set the stage for the passion even as they leave the scene (12:12). A group of four *chreia,* three teachings elicited by representative authorities (v. 13 [Pharisees and Herodians], v. 18 [Sadducees], and v. 28 [a scribe]) and the last by Jesus himself (v. 35, citing an opinion of the scribes) bring Jesus' teaching in the Temple to an end. Mark concludes the series with a note that the crowd was pleased to hear Jesus (12:37b). The Evangelist then attaches a saying warning an undefined audience against the hypocritical pretensions of the scribes.

Mark has Jesus move away from the Temple in two stages. First, he moves to the area in which offerings are collected. Jesus draws his disciples' attention to the sharp contrast between the complete devotion, "all she had to live on," of the poor widow and the extravagant display of the wealthy (12:41-44). Then he moves across the valley to the Mount of Olives. One of the disciples voices the tourist's view elicited by the structure, the largest religious sanctuary of its day, only to be shot down by Jesus' prediction that the Temple will be destroyed (13:1-2). Jesus' following words about the end of days foreshadow the doom which will overtake the entire city at the hands of invading forces (13:3-17). Mark's audience would easily recognize the Roman legions which responded to the Jewish rebellion of 66-70 C.E. At the same time, these prophecies are careful to disconnect the time of God's final judgment from the impending destruction of Jerusalem and its Temple.

Jesus leaves the city for the last time two days before Passover. While an anonymous woman anoints him during a meal (14:3-9), one of the Twelve, Judas, provides those plotting against Jesus with the opportunity they have been seeking to nab him away from the crowds (14:1-2, 10-11). The Temple prophecies from the discourse on the Mount of Olives return as the testimony of false witnesses during the Sanhedrin proceedings (Mark 14:58). These witnesses do not acknowledge Jesus as a prophet but assert that he put himself forward as one who would destroy the existing structure and raise another not built by human hands within three days. Though "not by human hands" could be given a pious interpretation, a Temple coming down from heaven, it also has a sinister tone. Jesus could be seen as one claiming to exercise magic arts. The Gospel's final reference to the Temple can be viewed as proleptic fulfillment of Jesus' words about its fate: at the moment of Jesus' death the sanctuary veil is torn in two from top to bottom (15:38).

From a narrative point of view, Jerusalem is defined by its Temple. Exegetes are uncertain which veil the Evangelist or his source envisaged, that at the entrance to the sanctuary building (Exod 27:16) or that separating the Holy of Holies from the rest of the inner space (Exod 26:31-37). In either case, an ancient audience well-attuned to portents of disaster attached to breaking or defiling something regarded as sacred would recognize the symbolism implied. God has deserted this temple and those associated with it. Juxtaposing the Temple emptied of God's presence with the empty tomb story a few verses later presents Mark's reader with another layer of ambiguity. If the two empty spaces are in some sense equivalent, then Jerusalem has no sacred significance for the followers of Jesus either. The risen One has abandoned it for Galilee. His disciples are to do likewise (16:7).

The Galilee-Jerusalem axis of Mark's narrative is easily established at the level of literary analysis. Whether or not it can be taken to reflect historical moments in early Christian history remains disputed. Most exegetes lean toward a date just after Titus had destroyed the Temple in 70 C.E. for the composition of the Gospel. In that case, Jesus' words as well as the symbolic destruction of the Temple at his death might be perceived as explanation for the disaster which has struck the city. Other exegetes see the same apocalyptic words about the Temple in Mark 13 as evidence that the Gospel was composed in the region of Syria-Palestine in the mid-60s, after the rebellion had begun but before its final days. The Evangelist has used every means in his power to persuade Christians that they have no stake in the fate of the doomed city. They should abandon it for Galilee and the surrounding Gentile regions.

The move away from Jerusalem may have been more traumatic than Christians today ordinarily imagine. Three bits of evidence indicate that Jerusalem was the spiritual home of the Jesus movement in its first decades: Paul's comments in Galatians 1–2, his efforts to gather money from his Gentile churches for their poor fellow Christians in Jerusalem, and the early chapters of Acts. A deity without sacred precincts would have been a strange concept in antiquity. Even non-Jewish Christians could point to Jerusalem as a place sacred to their God. As in the case of all attempts to draw historical conclusions from literary features in the Gospels, such attempts to link the story with other historical or cultural events remain speculative.

Another example of Mark's literary use of place involves movements between the public space in which Jesus and his disciples are among the crowds and the private space, often inside a house, to which Jesus withdraws to speak to the disciples alone (7:17, 24; 9:28-29, 33; 10:10-12). Further circles of the private sphere include Jesus with an inner group of disciples, usually Peter, James, and John (5:37; 9:2-12; 13:3; 14:33), or Jesus by himself in prayer (1:35; 14:35-36) or being tested (1:12-13). Jesus summons the Twelve up a mountain (3:13) and later is transfigured before Peter, James, and John on another mountain (9:2).

But the Evangelist appears to have introduced the distinction between public and private teaching into his sources somewhat awkwardly. Jesus privately explains why he speaks in parables and gives his allegorical interpretation of the sower to "those around him with the Twelve" (4:10-20, 34b) — before he has finished telling parables to the crowd (4:10-34a). The distinction between public and private teaching is not always clear. Why should allegorical interpretation of the parables be private (4:34b; 7:24) while the need to follow the example of the suffering Son of Man is addressed to "the crowd with his disciples" (8:34), for example? As the disciples exhibit both lack of understanding and lack of courage to stay with their master during his passion, Mark's audience must have been perplexed about the private instruction.

In a philosophical school or religious cult, private teaching implied higher wisdom. In private one learned the doctrines of a sect that were too complex for public teaching or was initiated into the mysteries of a cult. Such instruction or initiation would be required of anyone who would then pass the group's teaching on to others. The simple fact of having a group of disciples around him would imply that Jesus provided private instruction in addition to his public teaching. But Mark does not employ this motif in the conventional way. The places where such teaching occurs have been depicted as insecure. Neither houses nor out of the way deserted areas are proof against the crowds. The house as physical dwelling provides little protection from crowds gathered at its door (1:33; 2:2; 3:20). Similarly, crowds pursue Jesus into the wilderness areas (1:45b; 6:32-33).

Another literary feature of Mark's narrative which also distinguishes between private and public is the command to remain silent. These commands are often, though not always, attached to statements about Jesus' identity. Early studies of Markan redaction referred to this motif as the "messianic secret" and even used it as evidence that the historical Jesus had rejected or at least deflected messianic expectations attached to his person. More recent studies distinguish types of silencing within the narrative. Secrecy is to be considered a literary device employed by the author, not a report about how Jesus viewed the matter. In exorcism stories, demons attempt to deflect the power of Jesus by confronting him as "Son of God." Silencing the demon implies its expulsion from the human instrument through which it speaks (1:23-27). But Mark adds the note that Jesus silenced the demons because they knew who he was (1:34b, repeated in the summary at 3:11-12). This narrator's aside suggests to the reader that there is more at stake than routine exorcism. Jesus does not want what the demons know to become public. There are no instances in the story of witnesses to the exorcisms picking up on statements by the demons, however.

A second group of silence commands is addressed to people healed by Jesus (1:44 [a leper]; 5:43 [Jairus's daughter]; 7:36 [a deaf mute]). In two of the three cases, the command not to tell others about the miracle is immediately disobeyed. Commands in this set appear different from those associated with the "Son of God" phrase. From the opening episodes of the Gospel, Jesus has failed to control the exponential growth of his reputation as a healer. Mark has not consistently attached "tell no one" commands to miracle stories. Therefore an audience might treat the stories in which the healed disobey Jesus as further evidence for the extraordinary powers that Jesus possessed.

Only the third group of silence commands, those addressed to Jesus' disciples, refer to his identity as Messiah. The first occurs in response to Peter's confession at Caesarea Philippi (8:30). The disciples are to keep this knowledge to themselves. The second is addressed to Peter, James, and John. They are not to reveal what they witnessed at the Transfiguration until the Son of Man is raised from the dead (9:9). In both cases, the disciples fail to comprehend what Jesus tells them about his destiny. Jesus reprimands Peter sharply for opposing the divinely ordained suffering of the Messiah (8:31-33). At the Transfiguration "resurrection of the dead" proves to be the sticking point (9:10). Peter, James, and John appear even more obtuse than Herod, who had no difficulty concluding that Jesus' miraculous powers prove him to be the Baptist returned from the dead (6:14). Granted, Herod's hypothesis is not correct, but it demonstrates that a plausible interpretation of Jesus' words was culturally available to his audience. The possibility of identifying the Baptist with Elijah is picked up when Jesus responds to the disciples' implicit objection that Elijah has not yet returned (9:11-13). In the summary passage Mark composes for Jesus' second attempt to teach his disciples about the passion, they are not only unable to understand what he has said, but are also too frightened to ask a question (9:30-32). Once inside, Jesus challenges the pretensions to human greatness exhibited by his disciples. They remain silent (9:33-37).

Lest the audience miss the point, Mark repeats the pattern again in the next chapter. Jesus marches ahead of his frightened disciples. He then calls the Twelve for a final, detailed prediction of the passion (10:32-34), but they show no sign of comprehension. Instead, James and John seek a promise of lofty positions when Jesus comes to rule (10:35-40). Thus the silence commands at the beginning of this section in the Gospel appear unnecessary. The disciples are so frightened that they are hardly speaking to Jesus, let alone anyone else. Or the commands may serve to put the audience on notice that the truth about Jesus' messiahship is not what it appears to be at this point in the story.

All three types of silence command play a role within the world of the narrative. Mark's audience is no more ignorant of Jesus' identity and fate than theater-goers were of Oedipus's parentage. Ambiguities attend each group of silence commands. Silencing a demon who seeks to use the exorcist's name or identity as a counter-spell belongs to the exorcism story as a genre. Mark's redactional note that Jesus had to silence demons lest they make him known is more puzzling, since no other characters in the narrative appear to notice what the demons say. Mark does have Jesus confront the charge that control over demons proves him to be a practitioner of magic, not a God-empowered healer (3:22-30). Perhaps the note about why Jesus silences demons has less to do with their correct identification of the one facing them than with the dangers that being known as an exorcist posed for Jesus.

In the case of the second group of silence commands, those addressed to humans who have been healed, not even Jesus' direct command will keep some people quiet. Has Mark included silence commands because he disapproves of spreading stories about Jesus as miracle-worker? Or does he in fact think that those who frustrate Jesus' efforts to silence them are acting appropriately? Audiences have to decide. Finally, in the case of the disciples, given their failures to understand the significance of suffering as Jesus' destiny, keeping the Twelve quiet is certainly desirable. But Mark's use of the motif leaves us with an ambiguity in these cases as well. Does their silence reflect obedience to Jesus' instructions or fear?

Mark also employs another storytelling technique that brings individual units of tradition together by sandwiching one inside the other. Some scholars refer to it as intercalation, others simply speak of "sandwich technique." Four examples occur in connection with passages we have already discussed: 3:21, 31-35 and 3:22-30; 5:22-24, 35-43 and 5:25-30; 6:7-13, 30-31 and 6:14-29; and 11:12-14, 19-25 and 11:15-18. In two of these examples, the plot requires a time lapse. The disciples have been sent out to preach (6:7-13), so time must elapse while they are separated from Jesus. The story of Herod's opinion about Jesus and his murder of John the Baptist fills that space. When Jairus arrives his daughter is very ill, but not dead. The encounter with the hemorrhaging woman provides narrative space for others to arrive and tell the father that she has died.

In the other two examples, the relationship between the framing story and the episode within it is more complex. As we have seen, the scribes from Jerusalem bring a very serious charge against Jesus, that of being in league with Satan. Its frame story involves Jesus' relatives, who seek to bring him home because they think he is possessed in some way (3:21). The huge crowd makes it impossible for Jesus' mother and brothers to get near him. Jesus does not make room for his family members or go out to meet them. He announces the conditions for being part of the family of those around him (3:31-35). Juxtaposing the tradition about breaking with one's birth family to join those around Jesus and the accusation that Jesus is a magician adds dark tones to the family episode. They appear to be moved by something worse than natural concern about a relative who is so pressed by crowds that he cannot eat (3:20).

The frame to the Temple cleansing provides two key images. On the negative side, the withered fig tree indicates the fate awaiting the Temple, which has ceased to be a place of prayer for all nations. On the positive side, Jesus gives his disciples brief instructions on prayer, faith, and forgiveness (11:22-25). The Temple and its sacrificial rituals are not a necessity.

These examples show that attention to the literary details of a Gospel unlocks meanings that superficial readings often miss. Mark has taken care to put episodes together in particular contexts. He has also provided larger structures to the plot of the Gospel which shape the audience's understanding of the story. Although Mark's style does not come up to the standards of educated Greek prose, the Gospel bears out the conclusion of scholars who have approached it with a literary sensibility. It is much more than a loose collection of recollections and oral and written tradition. Mark's Gospel is a complex, deliberately crafted composition.[6]

6. Moloney, *The Gospel of Mark*, 16-22.

Characters in the Gospel

All stories require a cast of characters. Initially readers may be inclined to treat all the historical figures mentioned in the Gospel of Mark as simple images of themselves. We have run up against problems for that approach already. Ancient biographical accounts are intended to press a point of view about the subject's character or achievements. They also employ cultural archetypes of heroic, noble, or villainous behavior in presenting a life story that modern historians must disentangle to meet our standards of objective reporting. We have no first person, contemporary evidence from or about Jesus during his lifetime to serve as a control in evaluating later stories. Unlike the more learned biographers or historians of their time, the Evangelists stay out of their text. They do not tell us about themselves, their sources, or their personal evaluations of the persons and events described. So the coast is clear for scholarly disputes over how much is history and how much is legend or somewhere in the middle, a first century narrator's best guess about what happened. In addition, the scholarly desire to fill in the enormous gaps in our knowledge of early Christian history leads us to press the Gospels for information where it may not be present.

In addition to these larger methodological concerns, features of Mark's narrative also create problems for a naive reading of the persons mentioned. For example, the increasingly negative depiction of Jesus' disciples as the narrative proceeds creates a sharp outline for Jesus' impending death on the cross. No human understanding would accept that outcome for the Son of God. His miracles are ample proof that Jesus can call upon God's power to heal, defeat demons, feed the hungry, and quell raging seas. Peter, James, and John even witness a transfiguration of Jesus which places him in the company of Israel's greatest figures, Moses and Elijah. So how plausible is it that Jesus' disciples had no understanding of suffering and death as central to Jesus' mission until after the fact? Most historians would agree that there must be a kernel of truth to the tradition that Judas provided authorities with information about Jesus' movements and that the other disciples fled when Jesus was arrested. Neither giving information to authorities nor evading arrest by fleeing or denying any connection with the prisoner translates into the persistent misunderstanding and hardheartedness that Mark attributes to the disciples.

In addition, details in Mark's Gospel run contrary to the larger picture that he paints of the disciples. For example, when called, they are willing to abandon family and occupation to follow Jesus (1:16-20; 2:13-17). That action makes them part of the new family with which Jesus has replaced his own relatives (3:31-35). The story of the rich man who will not sell all to follow Jesus even provides a positive interpretation of their sacrifices. Jesus reassures Peter that they will recover more than they have given up to follow him even though they will suffer persecutions (10:23-31). Despite their flaws Jesus entrusts the disciples with the power to spread his message in the towns and villages of Galilee. Their efforts were so successful that even Herod became aware of Jesus (6:6b-14). In some summary statements, Mark comments that although Jesus' parables and deeds were not clear to the crowds, Jesus explained everything to his disciples (4:34). Finally, in his description of terrified, faithless disciples during the storms at sea, Mark conveniently forgets that a third of the group were professional fishermen who had worked those waters all their lives. They have been out in rough weather before. To frighten fishermen, the storm must be one of unprecedented violence.

Mark had certainly heard stories about Jesus' disciples. He did not invent his characters out of whole cloth. His sources probably painted a mixed picture of the group. But he uses the disciples as characters in telling the story of Jesus. Therefore it is important to consider literary models and theological concerns that have shaped his narrative. Some interpreters think that Mark was influenced by Paul's view of the cross as the key event in salvation. Paul insists that a crucified Messiah is so foreign to any human way of thinking that only faith can grasp this truth (1 Cor 1:18-25).[7] As Jesus' disciples struggle with his teaching about the passion in the second half of the Gospel, the difference between human understanding and God's gift of faith becomes clear. Some scholars who treat Mark as more imagination than history think that his flawed and failing disciples are taken from an earlier literary model. For example, Dennis MacDonald points to Homer's *Odyssey*. For all his courage, endurance, and native wit, there is one thing Odysseus cannot do: he cannot save any of his crew. They repeatedly fail to follow instructions which would have saved at least some of them.[8]

---

7. Marcus, *Mark 1–8*, 74-75.

8. Dennis R. MacDonald, *The Homeric Epics and the Gospel of Mark* (New Haven: Yale University Press, 2000) 18-19.

143

A less extreme view of Mark's literary activity holds that he reworks the material available to him in response to the concerns of Christians of his day. His audience would more naturally identify with the disciples than with any of the other characters in the story. By the time Mark wrote, Peter and several other apostles had died for their faith. Therefore the reader brings knowledge about the future activities and death of the disciples to the story. According to this view, the struggles and even lack of faith exhibited by Jesus' disciples are intended to encourage Christians when they are faced with persecution or other difficulties. In the allegorical interpretation of the parable of the Sower (4:13-20) some plants are lost to persecution of various sorts, others to the desire for wealth and cares of daily life. Mark's depiction of the disciples shows readers that individual failures are not the end. The readers can always find their way back to Jesus just as the disciples eventually did.

Another possible reading does not see Peter and the other disciples as an image of the readers' own struggles. Rather, the audience is to react with the same frustration that Jesus exhibits (see 8:21). With all the evidence of Jesus' authority before their eyes, his disciples should have accepted his words without question. At the same time, isolating the subject of a narrative from those who should be allies and helpers contributes to the heroic character of his achievement. A Jewish audience might think of patriarchs like Jacob or Joseph forced to make their fortune through hardship because of family conflict. Or one might be reminded of the failings of Moses' brother Aaron, who created the golden calf (Exod 32:1-8), and his sister Miriam (Num 12:1-16). Other readers might think of Socrates sending his weeping wife and children away before his death or chiding his old friend Crito for suggesting that he flee into exile rather than drink the hemlock. In these stories, the failures of relatives and friends only prove the greatness of the central figure.

Mark's readers learn that both the Baptist and the Pharisees have disciples (2:18). Jesus is asked why his disciples are not subject to the same rules of fasting that followers of these other teachers must observe. The reply indicates that his presence is different. No one fasts at a wedding feast. That *chreia* not only distinguishes Jesus as the one who inaugurates a time of salvation from teachers who prepare their disciples for its coming but also differentiates Jesus' disciples from other groups.

If a non-Christian were to pick up the Gospel, he or she might find Jesus' failure to provide rules governing the behavior of his disciples troubling. Stories of famous philosophers converting raucous youth to a philosophical way of life highlighted the moral rules which the teacher imposed on his followers, for example. A similar objection is played out from a Jewish perspective in 7:1-23. Jesus does not insist, like other teachers, that his disciples take care to observe the Sabbath rules. By that point in the narrative, readers know that Jesus places other concerns above strict observance of the Sabbath (3:1-6). In the private instruction that follows, Jesus advocates the sort of inner moral reform that a philosophically educated audience might anticipate (7:14-23). These two *chreiai* also explain why Christians no longer follow the pious customs of Jews that were familiar to most people in the ancient world.

Every story requires opponents. Jesus confronts two forms of hostility, demonic and human. Readers are introduced to demonic opposition first. Jesus has defeated Satan in the wilderness (1:12-13) before he begins driving out the demons who hold humanity in their grasp (1:21-28). By naming the demons who possess the man in Gerasa "Legion," the Evangelist hints at the connection between Satan's activity and that of the armies that occupy the land. This association between physical, social, and political evil and the operation of demonic powers was characteristic of the apocalyptic elements in Jewish thought, which came into prominence during the second century B.C.E. Daniel 7–12 provided a foundational text for many later authors. Two key sections in particular are repeatedly picked up in the Gospels — the vision of a human figure, the Son of Man, ascending to God's throne (Dan 7:13-14), and the promise of resurrection from the dead after the final defeat of Satan (Dan 12:1-3). In the sequence of evil empires described by Daniel, the righteous must hold fast to their faith despite suffering. The pious will face persecution from leaders of their own people, whose power depends on the foreign rulers. Many are led astray by false teaching. Each era is more riddled with evil than the last. Each world-ruler is more arrogant than the previous. Finally God sends Michael and angelic forces to defeat the evil powers that are behind the suffering and chaos of the human world.

Jesus' words about the end of the Temple and the end of the world in Mark 13:3-37 depend on such apocalyptic images. Some scholars have reconstructed a wisdom layer in the sayings of Jesus that would exempt the teaching of the historical Jesus from any apocalyptic speculation, but most scholars disagree with that reconstruction of Jesus' message. Apocalyptic understandings of the world were too common in first-century Palestine and are too deeply imbedded in the Jesus traditions to be the secondary creation of later Christian authors like Mark. When one reads Mark against an apocalyptic background, then the opening encounters between Jesus and the demons take on an additional meaning.[9] Jesus is not simply a more powerful exorcist than others. His appearance marks, rather, the beginning of the saving intervention of God that the pious had been anticipating for almost two centuries. John the Baptist's prophecy that a "stronger one" is to follow him (Mark 1:7-8) points forward to such an expectation. God's reign is about to replace that of Satan. The demons readily acknowledge that they are up against God's power, not the counterspells or coercion of human exorcists.

However, Jesus' claim to inaugurate God's reign does not match the inherited expectations in two regards. First, he is not the angel Michael wiping out demonic armies prior to divine judgment. The Son of Man appearing to judge the nations is still delayed. Second, instead of liberating the righteous who have held fast to God's Law and have suffered for it, Jesus changes the rules. He begins to seek out sinners, and, to make matters worse, he himself adopts the path of suffering and death. When Peter protests that suffering cannot be part of the plan, Jesus calls Peter "Satan" (8:33). That is the only case in Mark's Gospel where Satan is said to operate through a human opponent. Satan is not invoked as the cause of Judas's action in 14:10-11. Perhaps Mark understands Peter's objection as an episode of momentary demonic possession. (The Q version of the temptation story employed in Matthew and Luke has Jesus confront the possibility of becoming a Satan-backed world ruler before beginning his ministry.)

If Jesus only employs the term "Satan" for Peter because Peter would have Jesus evade death at the hands of the "elders and high priests," then how are readers to understand the Jewish opponents in Mark's narrative? While the masses follow Jesus from Galilee, Judea, and surrounding territories, Jewish religious authorities persistently raise objections intended to discredit Jesus in the eyes of the people. Jesus could be leading others into sin with his disregard for such basic elements of piety as observance of the Sabbath (2:23-28 [Pharisees]; 3:1-6 [Pharisees and Herodians]), keeping apart from the wicked (2:15-17 [scribes of the Pharisees]), purification rites (7:1-13 [Pharisees and scribes from Jerusalem]), and fasting (2:18-22 ["they" = disciples of John and of Pharisees?]). Along with this casual atti-

9. Marcus, *Mark 1–8*, 71-73.

tude toward practice, Jesus is confronted about his claim to pronounce sins forgiven (2:6-10 [scribes]) and about a familiarity with demons more appropriate to a magician than a holy man (3:22-30 [scribes from Jerusalem]). The religious teachers appear to have a *prima facie* case against Jesus' claim to be from God.

Mark's sources may have named the opponents for most of these *chreiai*. It is difficult to determine how much of the Evangelist's own redactional work is involved in the list of Jewish authorities who step forward to challenge Jesus. The Evangelist includes other traditional pieces that involve Jewish leaders who are well-disposed toward Jesus. Jesus heals the daughter of a synagogue ruler, Jairus (5:22-24, 35-43). When Jesus is teaching in the Jerusalem Temple, a scribe who has just heard him debate similar opponents understands that the greatest commands are love of God and neighbor. Jesus commends him as "not far from the kingdom of God" (12:28-34). Finally, a pious member of the council, "also himself waiting expectantly for the kingdom of God" (15:43), retrieves Jesus' body for burial.

Though some scholars assume that Mark's apocalyptic scenario requires that all human opponents are demonic agents, Mark's narrative does not support that conclusion. Although most Jewish authorities mentioned are hostile, the positive figures moderate the negative picture of Jewish officials. Some had faith in Jesus as healer (Jairus), acknowledged the truth of his teaching (a scribe), and stepped in for the absent disciples to bury their master (Joseph). John the Baptist is the most prominent Jewish figure to serve as a prophetic witness for Jesus (Mark 1:7-8) as well as an example of the death Jesus will suffer. Those scribes and elders who reject Jesus also failed to heed John as God's prophet (11:27-33). However, John and his disciples are associated with a piety no longer appropriate to the reign of God, which is present in Jesus, as we have seen. The parallel between the Baptist and Jesus provides a perspective on the passion narrative as well. Herod imprisoned John for religious reasons, for John's prophetic condemnation of Herod's marriage to a sister-in-law, but the Baptist's execution was the result of a drunken vow and palace intrigue. There was not even a pseudo-trial in John's case.

Similarly, the accusations made against Jesus in Galilee do not come up in the passion narrative. His prophetic word and action in the Temple spur the authorities into action, but the exact charges under Jewish law remain unclear. The hatred and intrigue of powerful individuals play a major part in bringing about Jesus' execution. Mark's description of "high priests, elders, scribes and the whole Sanhedrin" (15:1) conducting the prisoner to a trial before the Roman governor makes good fiction but is historically implausible. This group of prosecutors may have been part of the passion tradition that Mark inherited. The motif of the innocent brought to trial by raging enemies fits a familiar story pattern. Pilate acknowledges that the plotting of others ("jealousy") is responsible for Jesus' predicament (15:10). Mark's passion story leaves Pilate's role in condemning Jesus fairly neutral. He offers the possibility of a festal amnesty, only to have the crowd request Barabbas. He then insists that they confirm their opposition to an apparently harmless man. Pilate never attempts to remove himself from responsibility or declares the prisoner innocent as he does in the other Gospels. Mark's audience may not have distinguished between the Roman prefect and his soldiers who mock the prisoner as soon as he is turned over to them.

Crowds play a complex role in the Gospel. In the first sections their geographical diversity (3:7), size (6:54-56), and enthusiasm indicate the extraordinary impact of Jesus' ministry (7:37; 9:14-17; 10:46). Jesus teaches the crowd along with his disciples that one must be willing to accept physical suffering and death for Jesus and the gospel (8:34-38). At the same time, crowds pose physical dangers as they press in around Jesus and the disciples (1:45; 2:2; 4:1; 5:21, 31) or even make eating impossible (3:20; 6:31) or forego food themselves (6:34-36; 8:1-2). Jesus is teaching the crowds when the Pharisees challenge him with a question on divorce (10:1-2) However, in the passion narrative, the crowd plays a more volatile role. Rulers fear violent reactions on the part of crowds. Hence the high priests and scribes seek to arrest Jesus in secret so that the people will not engage in rioting (14:1-2). At the same time, they can manipulate the crowd in Pilate's court to agitate for Jesus' crucifixion (15:11-14).

Finally, the Gospel includes a number of minor characters whom Jesus encounters only once. Most of them are positive examples of faith. Many are petitioning Jesus to heal either themselves or a child (1:23-24 [a possessed man in a synagogue]; 1:40 [a leper]; 2:4-5 [a paralytic and his friends]; 5:1-20 [the Gerasene demoniac]; 5:21-24, 35-43 [Jairus]; 5:25-34 [a woman with a hemorrhage]; 7:24-30 [the Syrophoenician woman]; 7:32 [a deaf mute brought by others]; 8:22-26 [a blind man at Bethaida brought by others]; 9:17-27 [the father of a possessed boy]; 10:46 [Bartimaeus]). Most of these examples make an explicit connection between the petitioner's faith and the miracle. The stories involving the two women are unusual in the initiative which each takes to overcome barriers that would have prevented her from being healed by Jesus. One woman's hemorrhage makes her ritually impure. She was obligated to avoid all contact with men, but hopes that an unobtrusive touch in the middle of the crowd will bring healing. Jesus stops and makes her action public. The Syrophoenician woman has to overcome a rebuff by Jesus: his mission was to Israel, not Gentiles. She turns Jesus' image of dogs begging at table to her advantage. Dogs cannot have the children's dinner, but they do get the scraps. Once again, Jesus commends her extraordinary faith.

Two other minor characters approach Jesus for other reasons. A pious rich man asks what more he can do to inherit eternal life. He has observed the Torah's commandments since he was a young man. Jesus invites him to join the other disciples, but the man cannot part with his wealth in order to do so (10:17-22). On the other hand, an anonymous woman parts with valuable ointment to anoint Jesus before his passion (14:3-9). Unlike the other two women, she never speaks to Jesus. He interprets and defends her gesture as an appropriate recognition of his impending death. Another group of women emerges at the cross. For the first time, we learn that a group of Galilean women have followed Jesus and provided for him. They serve as witnesses to his death, his burial, and the empty tomb. 15:40 gives three names (Mary Magdalene, Mary the mother of James the less and Joses, and Salome). 15:47 has only Mary Magdalene and Mary mother of Joses see the burial. All three return to find the tomb empty on Easter (16:1). As we have seen the women disciples do not fare much better than Jesus' male followers. They do not carry out the instructions given by the angel, but flee in terror (16:8). Mark has no indication that any of Jesus' relatives were part of the entourage which came with him to Jerusalem. Mary Magdalene is one of a group of followers. She has no special connection to Jesus in this Gospel.

Jesus in Mark's Gospel

Many prominent features in the picture Mark draws of Jesus have already been mentioned. In the first verse some manuscripts read only "gospel of Jesus Christ" and others have "gospel of Jesus Christ, Son of God." Text critics are divided over including the "Son of God" title here. Even if it was not part of the original heading, God's voice informs readers of this special relationship in the baptismal vision (1:9-11). At that point, God speaks only to Jesus. Though the demons know who their opponent is (1:24, "the holy one of God"; 3:11; 5:7), humans do not. The privileged group, Peter, James, and John, witness a glorified Jesus and hear the divine voice at the transfiguration, "This is my Son, the Beloved; listen to him!" (9:7). How well the disciples follow the injunction to listen in the rest of the story is up for debate. The revelation on the mount of transfiguration plays no part in the subsequent narrative.

But the scene does remind the audience that Jesus is Son of God. That knowledge must shape the hearer's response to Jesus' teaching in Jerusalem. The murdered son in the parable of the Wicked Tenants (12:1-8) is not just any son or even any righteous person. The chief priests, scribes, and elders recognize that they are those tenants. To the audience, their determination to eliminate God's Son awakens all the revulsion that the scenario sketched out by the parable would if it appeared as actual news. With the threatened penalty pointing ahead to Jerusalem's destruction, the Jerusalem leaders are twice condemned: first for killing God's Son, second for bringing God's wrath down on their own people. They, not Jesus, have brought destruction on the Temple. At the end of Jesus' teaching in the Temple, he argues that the Messiah cannot be Son of David as the scribes teach. "Son of David" was the title first used by Bartimaeus as Jesus passed through Jericho (10:47-48). Those who hail his approach to Jerusalem do not use that title, but do speak of the coming kingdom of David (11:10). Jesus undoes all ordinary messianic expectations. The Holy Spirit taught David the truth, that the Messiah is not descended from him but is "Lord." When the high priest demands an answer at his trial, Jesus affirms that he is indeed Messiah and Son of God (14:61-62).

The "Son of God" acclamation emerges on the lips of the centurion at the moment of Jesus' death (15:39). On the one hand, that confession confirms Jesus' earlier attempts to explain that he came to give his life not to be a Messiah-king. Mark attributes the centurion's comment to what he saw as Jesus died. What did he see? The text is unclear. Does Mark infer that the centurion could see the Temple veil ripped from top to bottom? Is the loud cry Jesus utters as he dies the trigger for a divine response at the Temple? Perhaps. Mark is not necessarily familiar with the layout of Jerusalem. Most exegetes take the centurion's words at face value. He is identifying the crucified as Son of God in the same sense as Mark's Christian audience would have done. Other interpreters find such a reading implausible. The centurion belongs to the same Roman squad that had mocked the prisoner. A positive meaning that is not yet the Christian confession takes "son of god" in a more general sense to designate a semi-divine person or favorite of the gods. Another interpretation denies any positive meaning to the centurion's observation. It treats the expression as purely ironic. Just as the soldiers made fun of Jesus as "king of the Jews," so the centurion is pointing to the deceased as "Son of God" to make fun of that belief.

As Jesus hangs dying, his claims to inaugurate God's reign or to bring salvation form the basis for a game of verbal taunts. All jump on the bandwagon, those passing by, the chief priests and scribes who put him there, and even the two criminals dying with him. The cross makes the ordinary human expectations of saving power impossible to meet. The taunting "he saved others; he cannot save himself" (15:31) recalls Jesus the miracle worker. This juxtaposition of miracle worker with the crucified has continually perplexed exegetes. Does Mark's audience come away from the end of the story rejecting the faith in a miracle-working Jesus so firmly rooted in the miracle stories of the first section of the Gospel? Some scholars have understood Mark that way. They conclude that Mark has a christology based on the cross which is directly opposed to an alternate belief in Jesus as a miracle worker. After all, the disciples, who witness all the miracles in the story, fail miserably in understanding Jesus' mission. They also collapse before the events of the passion. Even before the arresting party arrives, Peter, James, and John are too weak to stay awake and pray with Jesus.

Miracles and prodigies occur so frequently in ancient storytelling that an author is not likely to include so much evidence for his hero's ability to work miracles only to pull the rug out from under his audience. The Evangelist has highlighted the need for faith on the part of a miracle's beneficiaries. When the disciples ask why they could not exorcise the epileptic boy, Jesus replies that prayer is required (9:29). The brief instructions on prayer in 11:22-24 insist that there is no prayer which it is in principle impossible for God to answer. Jesus' threefold prayer in Gethsemane underscores the fact that the cross is God's will (14:32-42). The disconnect between the cross and the miracles creates an obstacle for hostile unbelievers. Mark's Christian audience recognizes that Jesus has chosen God's will.

We have seen that Mark's narrative ends on an ambiguous note. The promise of seeing Jesus again in Galilee has not been fulfilled. The vision of Jesus transfigured in the company of Moses and Elijah anticipated his exaltation to heaven after the resurrection. The Gospel provides readers with an apocalyptic scenario that points toward events at the end of days. Some exegetes associate the transfiguration with the second coming rather than the resurrection. Jesus identifies with the human figure referred to as "Son of Man" in Dan 7:13-14 whose ascent to God's throne marks the advent of divine judgment.[10] The Son of Man prophecy addressed to the high priest and Sanhedrin in Mark 14:62 functions as a judgment saying. Mark's readers have already encountered such Son of Man sayings. Mark 8:38 warns that anyone who rejects Jesus and his teaching in this age will be condemned by the Son of Man at the judgment.

This identification between Jesus and the quasi-divine human figure who will vindicate the suffering righteous and vanquish the wicked at the end time provides an additional level of meaning to other sayings that use the phrase "son of man" but do not refer to the apocalyptic judgment. This layered meaning is hard to capture in translation. The expression "son of man" was as peculiar in ancient Greek as it is in modern languages. Hebrew and Aramaic can use the expression "son of man" in parallelism with "man," as in the familiar Ps 8:4. The NRSV translates: "what are human beings that you are mindful of them, mortals [= sons of man] that you care for them?" The NRSV translator has chosen to pick up on the contrast implied in the psalm between the mortal human beings and the angels mentioned in the next verse. In other instances, a speaker might use "son of man" as an indirect way of saying "someone" or "a person." The evidence for its use as an indirect first person, "I," belongs to Aramaic of a somewhat later period.[11] The same parallelism found in the psalm occurs in Jesus' saying about the Sabbath (Mark 2:27-28) but instead of translating "son of man" in v. 28 as "mortals," the NRSV infers that Jesus is only speaking of himself and so employs "Son of Man." That reading suggests that Jesus' statement about Sabbath observance will be confirmed at the judgment. Once the audience has the apocalyptic Son of Man image in view, then other statements in which Jesus asserts his authority by using a "Son of Man" phrase can be included. The claim to forgive sin (2:10) takes on an added dimension when the apocalyptic overtones of "son of man" are heard.

By using the expression "Son of Man" in sayings that refer to the cru-

---

10. See Marcus, *Mark 1–8*, 528-32, for an analysis of the use of Daniel in the Markan Son of Man sayings.

11. See the linguistic discussion in Joseph A. Fitzmyer, *Luke I-IX* (AB; New York: Doubleday, 1981) 208-9.

cifixion, Mark brings the apocalyptic imagery of a final judgment and defeat of evil and the authority of the earthly Jesus together with his death on the cross. Jesus, the Son of Man, does not simply pronounce forgiveness. He makes forgiveness possible by giving his life as ransom (Mark 10:45). All three passion predictions are formulated using "Son of Man" as their subject (8:31; 9:31; 10:33-34). In protesting, Peter clearly recognizes that Jesus is referring to himself (8:32). Once again the objection takes on additional meaning if "son of man" evokes the scenario from Dan 7:13-14. That figure represents God's intervention to bring the evil regimes that have dominated the world to an end. How could the "Son of Man" undergo suffering and death? On the human level, Peter and the others apparently reject the idea that Jesus as a person endowed with such miraculous powers would suffer and die. On the theological level suggested by the apocalyptic vision of Daniel, their lack of comprehension speaks to the problem of what God's plan for salvation is. This double layer of meaning can be found in the words of those who mock Jesus on the cross, "he saved others, but cannot save himself" (Mark 15:31). The chief priests and scribes who utter these words then promise to see and believe if Jesus performs the miracle of coming down off the cross. Mark's Christian audience knows the truth. Jesus is in fact saving others by giving his life on their behalf (10:45). His blood inaugurates a new covenant between God and humanity (14:24). Mark does not explain these convictions. They belong to the earliest Christian affirmations of faith, as does the assertion that the suffering Son of Man was predicted in Scripture (14:21; cf. 1 Cor 15:3b-5). The new community of the children of God, who will see the Son of Man's coming in glory as salvation (Mark 13:26) rather than as their condemnation, is constituted by its faith in Jesus' death as salvation.

The Community Implied in Mark's Narrative

Good news requires an audience to hear the word. The Evangelist opens with the word "gospel," that is, oral proclamation of the Christian message. Does the narrative provide any clues about the Christians for whom the Evangelist wrote? Some exegetes remain convinced that redaction criticism permits correlations between a Gospel's unique features and the historical circumstances of Christianity in a particular region. Other scholars object that the audience created by the reader's imagination has no direct link to historical persons or communities, that we do not have any other information about the Evangelists, the circumstances that led them to write, the first audiences, or how the Gospels were disseminated.

Those scholars who seek to locate a historical setting for the Gospel are divided into two groups. Some begin with the ancient Christian tradition that Mark collected reminiscences of the aged Peter in Rome, where the apostle would be martyred under Nero (ca. 62). The Gospel as we know it may have been written shortly after Peter's death. Christians had first arrived in Rome in the early 40s as a movement within Rome's Jewish community. Claudius expelled some for a riot that broke out over Christian evangelizing in the late 40s. We know from Paul's letter to Roman Christians that this community had become predominately Gentile by the mid-50s and that they could be counted on to follow an elaborate theological argument and were familiar with the Septuagint. Mark's Gospel would have been much easier to recall and even recite than Romans. Rom 13:1-7 suggests that Paul expected Christians to coexist within the larger society just as Jews did. The outburst of persecution under Nero may have been an unexpected and disorienting shock. Both Peter and Paul lost their lives at that time. So it is not implausible that Mark's preoccupation with suffering addressed the consequences of Nero's persecution.

A strongly argued alternative position locates Mark in the province of Syria during the years of the Jewish revolt against Rome and its immediate aftermath (66-73). After a long siege Roman legions stormed into the Jerusalem upper city, looting and burning the Temple in August, 70. Both the Roman historian Tacitus and the Jewish historian Josephus describe divine portents which should have warned the Jewish leaders and inhabitants that their city was doomed:

> Prodigies had indeed occurred . . . contending hosts were seen meeting in the sky, arms flashed and suddenly the temple was illumined with fire from the clouds. . . . Of a sudden the doors of the shrine opened and a voice greater than human cried: "The gods are departing"; at the same moment the mighty stir of their going was heard. (Tacitus, *Histories* 5.13)

> Thus it was that the wretched people were deluded at the time by charlatans and pretended messengers of the deity; they neither heeded nor believed the manifest portents that foretold the coming desolation,

but, as if thunderstruck and bereft of eyes and mind, disregarded the plain warnings of God. So there were a star resembling a sword which stood over the city and a comet which continued for a year. (Josephus, *War* 6.297-99)

Scholars who think that Mark was written for Christians coping with life during the rebellion emphasize the apocalyptic prophecies in Mark 13. On the one hand, Jesus' own words about the fate of Jerusalem and its temple are being fulfilled. On the other, Christians should not be taken up in the political and apocalyptic fervor of the revolt. The end of the Temple will not trigger the end of the world. Jesus' return as glorified Son of Man remains for the indefinite future (13:26-32).[12] This context provides an additional meaning to the geographical features of Jesus' ministry. The Evangelist has Jesus undertake those odd geographical journeys outside Galilee into Syria and into cities of the Decapolis in order to connect the gospel with the experience of his community, which had fled Judea after the revolt against Rome broke out.

What the Gospel itself says about Jesus' disciples in the future highlights suffering. The apocalyptic prophecy of 13:9-13 warns of persecution. Christians must expect to be dragged before Jewish and non-Jewish authorities because of their testimony to the gospel. But the conflict will not stop there. Family members will also turn against Christians. Jesus' followers must remain confident that the Spirit will be present. Their task involves bringing the gospel to all nations. But it will even cost some Christians their lives.

Additional references to suffering are tucked into the Gospel at other points too. Mark has expanded the reference to seed on rocky ground from lack of roots to "trouble or persecution on account of the word" (4:17). When Jesus assures Peter that the disciples will recover all they gave up to follow him, he tucks in the fact that they can also expect persecutions (10:30). With such a consistent emphasis on suffering for the gospel, the stories of how fearful Jesus' disciples were show that the Evangelist does not ignore the human difficulties involved.

---

12. These scholars make detailed correlations between items in Mark's Gospel and Josephus's descriptions of the city under Zealot leadership. For example, the "den of robbers" (Jer 7:11) which Jesus referred to in condemning the Temple (Mark 11:17b) could refer to the Zealot leaders who made the Temple their headquarters (Josephus, *War* 4.151-57; 5.5). See Marcus, *Mark 1–8*, 30-36.

Mark's awkward attempt to explain purification rules in Mark 7:3-4 suggests that neither he nor the readers he envisages have any personal experience of Jewish observance. Jesus has challenged the necessity of strict Sabbath observance and voluntary fasting. Mark 7:23 asserts that Jesus also abolished kosher rules. As we have seen, the Temple and its rites are considered doomed by the actions of the Jewish leaders. Mark 7:9-10 and 7:14-22 point to the way in which followers of Jesus are to be righteous. The Ten Commandments are more important than all the rules and pious practices of Pharisees or scribes. In addition, Mark employs a second argument from popular philosophical ethics that would be familiar to non-Jews: The key to goodness lies in transforming an individual's heart. That means virtuous actions and control of speech and even of emotions. The external rites of piety have little to do with the process of attaining such virtues. A similar emphasis on the fundamentals of righteousness in contrast to externals returns in Jesus' teaching on prayer (11:22-25). One Jewish scribe recognizes that the command to love God and neighbor is the point of the entire Torah (12:28-34). Clearly Mark does not envisage an audience with strong ties to Jewish faith and practice. At the narrative level, Jesus defies expectations by not forming his disciples into more religious or pious Jews in the mold of Pharisees or even disciples of John the Baptist. There are no hints in Mark's Gospel that its distance from Jewish practice of Torah was problematic for those who followed Jesus. For non-Jewish readers the disputes about piety and virtue would appear similar to arguments between philosophers of different schools.

Endings Added to the Gospel of Mark

The story told in the Gospel contains a number of references to the future. Christians will suffer and even die for their faith. The movement will not remain a religious party or way of life within Judaism. The risen Jesus lives in heavenly glory. He is to come again as the Son of Man figure foreseen by the prophet Daniel. The faithful who have been redeemed by Jesus' death on the cross will be united with him at the banquet in the kingdom (14:25). Despite all these positive hints about the future, the Gospel's narrative line does not depict any transformation of the disciples after Jesus' death. The women flee from the tomb in fear at its conclusion. Ancient manuscripts provide evidence for two attempts to remedy the situation created by this ambiguous conclusion.[13]

The shorter patch assumes that the failure of v. 8 was overcome. It asserts that Jesus later sent the disciples out to proclaim salvation throughout the world. This brief comment sounds as though a scribe sought to reassure readers that the story does not end as it might appear. It does not require any further gospel traditions, canonical or apocryphal. It may base the sending out of the disciples to east and west on the conclusion to Matthew's Gospel (Matt 28:18-20).

The short ending usually turns up in manuscripts which also contain a longer patch to the Gospel (Mark 16:9-20). Despite the fact that it is not part of the original Gospel, this longer ending serves as the lectionary gospel reading for the feast of St. Mark the Evangelist. Small Christian sects in rural parts of the United States practice handling poisonous snakes during services based on this passage. This ending echoes elements from the other canonical Gospels, Acts, and possibly apocryphal traditions. There is no canonical basis for drinking poison unharmed, but handling poisonous snakes might derive from the tale of Paul bitten by a viper on Malta (Acts 28:2-6).

This longer ending has very little connection with Mark's Gospel. The Acts of the Apostles as well as apocryphal acts traditions are the closest theological relatives of this bit of narrative. Miracles attract potential converts or confirm that an apostle is from God or rescue the believer from his or her enemies in most of the apocryphal acts just as they do in Acts. The scribe who penned this ending for Mark did not have to generate a list of passages from the canonical Gospels and Acts as we have done. The catalogue of items from the resurrection appearances through Jesus' ascension and the global mission of the apostles may have been a summary used in oral teaching or preaching. Presumably the sequence was so familiar to a second-century audience that it represents what everyone knew happened next. However peculiar Mark's abrupt conclusion at 16:8, the other canonical gospels, Acts of the Apostles and perhaps apocryphal acts have produced a strong tendency to assume that any account of Jesus' life would show his disciples making the transition from initial skepticism about the resurrection to successful world-wide evangelization.

13. Evans, *Mark 8:27–16:20*, 540-51.

Sources of Mark 16:9-20

v. 9	Jesus appears to Mary Magdalene from whom he cast out seven demons.	John 20:11-17 Luke 8:2
v. 10	She reports to the disciples, who are mourning;	John 20:18 John 20:11 (Magdalene)
v. 11	they do not believe her.	Luke 24:11
v. 12	Jesus appears to two disciples on journey into the country;	Luke 24:13-35
v. 13	their report is not believed when they report Peter has seen Jesus.	(Luke 24:11) Luke 24:34-35
v. 14	Jesus appears to the eleven gathered for a meal, chides them for not believing the earlier witnesses,	Luke 24:36-43 John 20:27 (Thomas)
v. 15	and commissions them to go out and preach to the whole world.	Matt 28:19; Luke 24:47
v. 16	Belief and baptism are the basis for salvation. Unbelievers are to be condemned.	Matt 28:19 (John 3:18, 36)
v. 17	Signs accompany believers: casting out demons using Jesus' name,	Mark 6:7 (9:38, a non-disciple using Jesus' name)
	speaking in tongues,	Acts 2:4; 10:46
v. 18	handling snakes,	Acts 28:3-5
	drinking poison,	—
	and healing by laying on of hands.	Acts 9:17, 40-41; 28:8; Mark 6:13; Luke 9:6
v. 19	The Lord Jesus is taken up into heaven and sits at the right hand of God.	Acts 1:9 Acts 7:55b (vision of Jesus standing at right hand of God)
v. 20	The disciples go and proclaim the gospel everywhere; the Lord confirms their message by signs that accompany it.	the theme of Acts

A Secret Version of Mark?

In 1973 Professor Morton Smith published a text he had photographed in the library of the monastery of Mar Saba fifteen years earlier. The final pages of an eighteenth-century codex containing a seventeenth-century edition of the letters of Ignatius of Antioch incorporated a letter alleged to be by Clement of Alexandria.[14] In this letter, Clement indicates that three versions of Mark's Gospel were known in Alexandria: the one used for public reading and instruction, that is, our canonical version; another edition for more advanced students, that is, an esoteric or "secret" Mark; and a further edition of the esoteric text by a sect of Gnostic Christians, followers of Carpocrates. The letter provides two examples of the expanded text in secret Mark, a long section following Mark 10:32-34 and a brief addition after 10:46a.

Although some scholars have remained convinced that this late text provides access to forms of Mark known in late-second-century Alexandria,[15] others have been skeptical since the beginning.[16] The manuscript, itself, was never made available for study or authentication. Although Professor Guy Stroumsa of Hebrew University saw the codex with the pages containing the alleged letter of Clement, those pages have since gone missing from the volume.[17] Is this letter really from Clement of Alexandria or the work of a clever forger, perhaps even the late Professor Smith himself?[18] With Smith deceased and the relevant pages gone, the truth will remain in doubt unless some other manuscript find preserves the letter in question or fragments of the alleged Gospel. The volume into which the partial letter was copied contains the letters of Ignatius after apparent interpolations had been removed. If genuine, the eighteenth-century monastic copyist may have included the letter of Clement because it demonstrated that even a canonical Gospel could circulate in corrupted textual variants.

The long quotation tells a story that begins much like the raising of

14. Morton Smith, *Clement of Alexandria and a Secret Gospel of Mark* (Cambridge: Harvard University Press, 1973); an English translation of the quotations from "Secret Mark" can be had in Elliott, *Apocryphal New Testament,* 149, and Schneemelcher, *New Testament Apocrypha,* 108.

15. For example, Helmut Koester, *Ancient Christian Gospels* (Philadelphia: Trinity, 1990) 295-303.

16. As is H. Merkel, the author of the section on Secret Mark in Schneemelcher, *New Testament Apocrypha,* 106-9; for a thorough discussion of the question, see Bart Ehrman, *Lost Christianities* (New York: Oxford University Press, 2003) 70-89.

17. Ehrman, *Lost Christianities,* 89.

18. For a forceful indictment of Prof. Smith as the likely author of a detailed hoax, see Stephen C. Carlson, *The Gospel Hoax: Morton Smith's Invention of Secret Mark* (Waco: Baylor University Press, 2005).

Lazarus in John 11:1-44. Instead of named figures, all friends of Jesus, Secret Mark has unnamed characters. A woman from Bethany persuades Jesus to restore her brother to life. The young man falls in love with his healer before they even emerge from the tomb. He is wealthy and presses Jesus to visit his house. John's Gospel has Jesus dine at the house of his friends, Martha, Mary, and Lazarus six days before Passover (John 12:1). Secret Mark has Jesus summon the young man to participate in a secret initiation ritual six days after his return from death. Wearing only a linen robe, he spends the night with Jesus, who teaches him the mystery of the kingdom of God. Scholars who consider the letter authentic point out that the initiation episode fits onto a peculiar detail in Mark's passion narrative: a young man who had been following Jesus flees naked, leaving his *sindōn* behind (Mark 14:51-52). By itself the image of the young man in flight could have been intended by the Evangelist as a repetition of the flight of the male disciples from Gethsemane and as an anticipation of the women fleeing the tomb (16:8).[19] Neither Matthew nor Luke retains the notice about the young man's flight.

The word *sindōn* can refer to a light linen garment. The baptismal rites of a later period call for clothing the newly baptized in such a white linen garment after they emerge from the pool. Professor Smith asserts that Secret Mark was derived from an Aramaic esoteric source earlier than canonical Mark. He constructs a picture of the historical Jesus as a magician who taught secrets in a baptismal initiation. The young man's nakedness is, in his view, evidence that the mystery initiation also had a homoerotic component.[20] The possibility that esoteric Christian truths were conveyed through unusual sexual practices and magic fits the profile of the Carpocratians given by their orthodox opponents (Irenaeus, *Against Heresies* 1.25). Even if the alleged letter of Clement is authentic, there is no good evidence for the assertion that Secret Mark reflects a pre-canonical Aramaic tradition. Its use to support the hypothesis that Jesus himself practiced and taught magic arts is even more speculative.

19. So Raymond E. Brown, *The Death of the Messiah* (New York: Doubleday, 1994) 303. Brown surveys the wealth of speculative interpretations attached to this episode (pp. 294-304).

20. Carlson, who thinks that Smith has created the whole document as a hoax, points out that as a wealthy young property owner the young man is a social equal of Jesus and an unlikely partner in a homosexual relationship. Carlson concludes that Smith's desire to advocate a modern sense of homosexuality led to this slip (*Gospel Hoax*, 68-71).

On the assumption that the letter copied in the seventeenth-century book was by Clement, Secret Mark is more likely a mid-second-century apocryphal work from someone familiar with the canonical texts. Its tale of the rich young man restored to life as well as Jesus' visit to his house and the baptism six days later might all derive from John's Gospel, its sources, or related oral traditions. It may reflect an emerging pattern of baptismal practice as initiation in Alexandrian Christianity. Second- and third-century texts from Gnostic sects exhibit considerable interest in baptismal initiations as the means to attain esoteric wisdom about the heavenly regions. Charges of deviant sexual practices in esoteric cults is such a standard item of polemic against deviants that such claims cannot be credited as historical without additional confirmation. The story of a rich, handsome young man falling for a wisdom teacher, whom he cannot provoke to engage in erotic activity despite spending the night with him naked, would have been familiar to the more educated Alexandrian Christians. It represents Alcibiades' complaint against Socrates (Plato, *Symposium* 219bc). Alcibiades accuses Socrates of loving all handsome young men but not engaging in the physical *erōs* that his attentions awaken in them.

It is more difficult to discern the significance of the brief phrase added in Secret Mark after Mark 10:46a, "And there was the sister of the young man whom Jesus loved and his mother and Salome; and Jesus did not receive them." It provides a bit of filler between Jesus and his disciples reaching Jericho and their leaving on the road up to Jerusalem. Despite the assertions of advocates for an early Secret Mark that the awkwardness of Mark 10:46a proves that something has been dropped, the geographical transition makes sufficient sense as it stands. Jericho serves as a mile-marker on the road to Jerusalem (10:32). Jesus' refusal to receive the women could be no more than an echo of the earlier distance between Jesus and his mother and brothers (3:31-35). Or it might serve other interests such as establishing that Jesus and his disciples were an all-male group like the young men gathered around Socrates. Or such a notice could have arisen to explain how the women became separated from Jesus and his male disciples despite the fact that a Passover meal involved entire families. Of the three women, Salome is the only one mentioned in canonical Mark (15:40; 16:1). As an apocryphal tradition, this list is unusual in not including Mary Magdalene, whose increasing prominence as a resurrection witness is already evident in John 20:11-18 as well as in the apocryphal long ending to Mark.

161

The additional endings to Mark demonstrate a process similar to that exhibited by Secret Mark. Material from the other gospel traditions including John was attached to the canonical story. The authors of such additions probably rely more on oral retelling of the stories in question or reminiscences of hearing those Gospels. Such adaptations may have sustained interest in reading and copying Mark's Gospel even as it was losing ground to the others in the public worship and teaching of Christian communities. However, all discussions of Secret Mark remain tentative. Unless the pages in question which have gone missing from the Jerusalem patriarchate, where they were last photographed,[21] are found, it will not be possible to determine when the Clementine letter was copied. It remains a distinct possibility that the "Letter of Clement to Theodore" is a modern forgery.

Modern readers find the tensions and ambiguities in Mark's Gospel a positive affirmation of a Jesus who shares the agony of the human condition. Despite Jesus' celebrated powers as healer and his popularity with the crowds, he finds himself unable to secure a loyal and understanding band of disciples. The enemies who have dogged his steps from the first controversies in Galilee succeed in bringing about the death Jesus anticipated. Surrounded by mockery, Jesus dies in despair, crying out to a God who has left him to his fate. Unlike other stories of righteous sufferers, there is no last-minute rescue. Nor is there any restoration of the band of disciples. It remains possible that Mark intended to continue his account beyond 16:8, but was unable to do so. Matthew, Luke, and the scribes who penned the short and long endings of Mark as well as any apocryphal versions that may have existed did not have a canonical text in front of them. Whether or not the Evangelist had completed his composition or left it unfinished, those who picked up his work considered it incomplete.

Unlike the apocryphal or forged Secret Mark which attaches to the text meanings its author never envisaged, Matthew and Luke retain most of the Evangelist's work. Their editing of some stories removes awkward phrases and transitions which may have seemed to them the consequence of an unfinished composition. Some scholars today treat the same ele-

---

21. Charles Hedrick, "The Secret Mark: New Photographs, New Witnesses," *The Fourth R* 13 (2000) 3-11, 14-16; for a discussion of the whole problem and review of recent books on both sides, see Paul Foster, "*Secret Mark:* Its Discovery and the State of Research," *ExpTim* 117 (2005) 46-52, 64-68.

ments as representative of the oral story-telling milieu for which the text was formulated. Certainly the existence of additional Jesus traditions would have indicated to Matthew and Luke that an expanded edition of Mark's account was needed for the churches in which the Gospel was circulating. Therefore students of Mark's Gospel will benefit from a close reading of how the other Evangelists retell the same stories. Those new versions provide our best clues to what first-century Christians thought was important in the Markan account.

CHAPTER FIVE

Reading Matthew's Gospel

Early Christians recognized the close similarity between sections of Matthew and the Gospel of Mark. Without the close reading and comparison of all three Synoptic Gospels facilitated by printed editions, they reached a different conclusion about the connections among the Gospels than modern scholars have come to. As we have seen, the fourth-century theories about Gospel authorship considered Matthew the first written Gospel. It was traced back to a Hebrew or Aramaic original. Mark was considered a

---

Suggested Reading

Betz, Hans Dieter. *The Sermon on the Mount.* Minneapolis: Fortress, 1995.

Davies, W. D., and Dale C. Allison. *A Critical and Exegetical Commentary on the Gospel According to Saint Matthew.* 3 volumes. International Critical Commentary; Edinburgh: Clark, 1988-97.

Harrington, Daniel J. *The Gospel of Matthew.* Sacra Pagina 1; Collegeville: Liturgical, 1991.

Luz, Ulrich. *Matthew 1-7.* Minneapolis: Fortress, 2007.

———. *Matthew 8-20.* Trans. James E. Crouch. Minneapolis: Fortress, 2001.

———. *Matthew 21-28.* Trans. James E. Crouch. Minneapolis: Fortress, 2005.

Saldarini, Anthony J. *Matthew's Christian-Jewish Community.* Chicago: University of Chicago Press, 1994.

Senior, Donald. *Matthew.* Abingdon New Testament Commentaries; Nashville: Abingdon, 1998.

later compilation based on Peter's reflections or an abbreviated version of Matthew.

Two literary features of Matthew's account appeared to favor this conclusion. First, Matthew exhibits a distinctly Jewish Christian orientation from its opening genealogy of the "son of David, son of Abraham" (Matt 1:1-17), through its demonstration that Jesus' life fulfilled oracles of the prophets (e.g., 1:23; 2:6; 12:17-21) and brought the Law to its completion (5:17-20) to the vigorous condemnation of the scribes and Pharisees whose teaching binds heavy burdens on the people quite unlike the yoke of Jesus' teaching (11:28-30; 23:1-7, 13-33). When Jesus sends the Twelve out on mission, he restricts their activities to Israel (10:5-6).

Second, one of the Twelve disciples is a tax official referred to as Matthew in this gospel (Matt 9:9), unlike Mark, whose "Levi, son of Alphaeus" (Mark 2:14) does not appear in the list of Twelve, which does include Matthew (Mark 3:16-19). Luke 5:27 also refers to the tax official as "Levi", not Matthew. Most contemporary exegetes would conclude that the call story originally referred to an individual not included among the Twelve. Some suggest that Mark himself formulated the call story in order to introduce the subsequent objection to Jesus' table fellowship with tax collectors and sinners (Mark 2:15-17). Convinced that a call story similar to those of Peter, Andrew, James, and John must refer to one of the Twelve, the author of Matthew's Gospel dropped the name "Levi" and identified the figure in question as Matthew. The phrase "tax collector" has been added to that name in the disciple list in Matt 10:3 (contrast Mark 3:18). As we have seen, identifying the Evangelist as "Matthew" provided a direct link to Jesus on the part of two of the canonical authors, Matthew and John. Some ancient manuscripts show that scribes even corrected the text of Mark 2:14 by substituting the "James son of Alphaeus" from the disciple list (Mark 3:18) for Levi. Other ancient exegetes concluded that the names "Levi" and "Matthew" must refer to the same individual.

The claim that Matthew composed his work in Hebrew or Aramaic for the instruction of Jewish Christians cannot be sustained by any surviving textual evidence, though claims to have discovered an "Aramaic Matthew" or its Greek translation pop up in the media from time to time. Studies of the Evangelist's Scripture citations indicate that the author uses both familiar Greek translations of the Hebrew and translations dependent on the Hebrew text, not the Greek. It is impossible to know whether the Evangelist himself was responsible for bringing his Greek closer to the underlying Hebrew or has employed a Greek translation which has done so. Still other citations in Matthew mix the Septuagint and Hebrew traditions. Where Matthew takes a quotation from Mark or Q, the rendering follows the Septuagint or has been adapted to conform with the Hebrew.[1] Thus it is probable that the Evangelist was responsible for translating or revising some of the Scripture quotations. However the Gospel as we have it was written in Greek, the language in which most of the Evangelist's sources were composed as well.

From Beginning to End: Matthew's Narrative Shape

Matthew has expanded the narrative outline found in Mark, following Markan order more closely in the second half of the Gospel than in the first. Why the Gospel exhibits this difference remains unclear. Even in the second half of the Gospel, Matthew shortens and adapts the Markan sequence. Mark divides Jesus' entry into Jerusalem into two days so that the crowd's acclamation occurs on the first, Jesus' prophetic sign in the Temple on the next (Mark 11:1-17). Jesus withdraws from the city for the evening and begins his teaching in the Temple area on the third day (Mark 11:19-28). Matthew has the entry, the Temple cleansing, and a verbal exchange between Jesus and the chief priests and scribes all take place on the first day (Matt 21:1-17). On the following day Jesus returns to the city, and he does not leave until he moves to the final discourse on the Mount of Olives (Matt 24:3; Mark 13:3).

We have seen that Mark often uses one episode to frame another. He had Jesus curse the unfruitful fig tree on the morning of the second day (Mark 11:12-14). On the third morning, Peter called attention to the fact that the tree was withered (11:21). This frame served as a striking comment on the fate of the Temple. Matthew's revised chronology has no place for this literary pattern. Instead the fig tree withers as soon as Jesus curses it, much to the disciples' amazement (Matt 21:18-20). By reshaping Mark's chronology Matthew drives his narrative forward to a much more vigor-

---

1. For a brief discussion of the Old Testament citations and allusions in Matthew, see Richard C. Beaton, "How Matthew Writes," in Markus Bockmuehl and Donald A. Hagner, eds., *The Written Gospel* (Cambridge: Cambridge University Press, 2005) 127-34; a detailed analysis for scholars which concludes that Matthew must have known Hebrew can be had in Davies and Allison, *Matthew* I, 32-58.

ous encounter between Jesus and the religious authorities. Jesus' words of judgment against them and the Temple will have the same effectiveness as the curse on the fig tree.

Although Matthew engages in careful editing of Mark's narrative, the turning points in Jesus' public ministry are familiar: John the Baptist appears (3:1-12); Jesus is baptized and tempted (3:13–4:11); he initiates his activities in Galilee after John's arrest by assembling a core group of disciples and teaching and healing (4:12–11:30; 12:46–13:53; 15:21-39); Jesus' activities elicit controversy with Jewish authorities (9:1-18; 12:1-45; 15:1-20; 16:1-12); his disciples acknowledge him as Messiah (16:13-20); he begins to instruct them about his impending death and resurrection as they head toward Jerusalem (16:21-28; 17:22-23; 20:17-19); he enters Jerusalem and carries out his prophetic action in the temple (20:29-34 [healing the blind before entry]; 21:1-22); he teaches publicly in the temple (21:23–23:39); teaches his disciples about the destruction of the Temple and the end of the world (24:1–25:46); he is put to death, and the empty tomb is discovered (26:1–28:8). Matthew provides a fuller biographical shape to his story by providing Jesus' family genealogy and stories about his birth (1:1–2:23), resurrection appearances, and sending of the disciples on mission (28:19-20).

Although Jesus draws the crowds with his teaching in Mark (e.g., Mark 1:22; 2:13; 6:34; 10:1), miracle stories occupy as much space in the narrative as teaching in that Gospel. By incorporating sayings material from Q as well as special traditions, Matthew redresses that imbalance in the story. The Evangelist highlights the teaching of Jesus by incorporating five discourses into his account of Jesus' ministry:

> a summary of Jesus' teaching, the Sermon on the Mount (5:1–7:29),
> instructions for the disciples on mission (10:1–11:1),
> parables about the Kingdom of God (13:1-52),
> instructions for relationships among members of Christian communities (18:1-35), and
> parables and instructions about the judgment (24:1–25:46).

Some exegetes hold that the five-discourse pattern was intended to reinforce the connection between Jesus and Moses, who is credited with the five books of the Pentateuch. However there are no parallels between the five discourses and the content of the Pentateuch. The Sermon on the Mount is clearly the most significant of the Matthean discourses, since it is a summary of Jesus' teaching. An earlier form of that summary probably came to Matthew in his version of Q. Since the final verse in the Gospel speaks of teaching all nations to observe Jesus' teaching (28:20a), an epitome such as this may have played an important role in instructing new Christians.

The Sermon on the Mount provides a foundation for the story which follows in another way. Much of its teaching will be exemplified in the person of Jesus.[2] Ancient moralists insisted that students learned as much from sustained observation of their teacher's way of life as from the formal teaching of a philosopher or rabbi. By presenting this summary of Jesus' teaching as the first event of the public ministry, Matthew invites the audience to apply its standards to Jesus. The obverse could be said of opponents. Matthew will repeatedly argue against Pharisees and scribes that their way of life does not conform to the teaching found in the Torah. It is important to remember that the accusation "hypocrite" (6:2, 5, 16; cf. 22:15-18; 23:13, 15, 23, 25, 27) does not represent an accurate picture of Pharisees. All five of Matthew's discourses contain editorial elements that are directed toward a specifically Christian audience. 7:15 and 7:21-23 pick up sayings from Q that warn against being deceived by external appearances. Even the ability to prophesy and do miracles in the name of Jesus does not guarantee entry into God's reign. Only those whose lives match the will of God as expressed in the teaching of the Sermon on the Mount will be saved at the judgment.

In order to move the Sermon on the Mount to the opening of Jesus' public ministry, Matthew puts all the stories about Jesus' actions in Galilee after the sermon except the call of four fishermen disciples (4:18-22). The Evangelist then employs a summary account of Jesus' teaching and healing activity to indicate how he gathered crowds from the entire area, including the Decapolis, Jerusalem, Judea, and the Transjordan (4:23-25). Thus the public audience for this discourse is drawn from all the areas into which Jesus' ministry will take him.

Matthew has taken similar care in crafting the instructions for Christians on mission, Jesus' next discourse. The Evangelist has revised the setting and expanded its content to serve the needs of the Christian community. To do so, he also changes its place in the narrative sequence inherited from Mark. Mark had Jesus respond to rejection at Nazareth by picking

2. Dale C. Allison, *The Sermon on the Mount* (New York: Crossroad, 1999).

the Twelve and dispatching them on mission to surrounding towns and villages. To fill the gap while they were gone, Mark inserted the story of John the Baptist's death (Mark 6:1-29). Matthew provides a different motivation for entrusting disciples with the message and ministry in which Jesus is engaged. After healing and teaching in the synagogues of towns and villages, Jesus looks on the crowds with compassion. Lost sheep or grain to be harvested, they desperately need a shepherd and laborers. (Matthew will situate the rejection at Nazareth and death of the Baptist much later in the story, at Matt 13:53–14:12, after the third discourse.) Matthew fills in this place with John the Baptist traditions from Q. The Baptist sends his disciples to inquire if Jesus really is the stronger one that John prophesied (in 3:11-12). Jesus' reply first points back to the preaching and healing activities of the previous chapters (11:2-8). Then Jesus speaks to the crowds about himself and John (11:9-19). John is the Elijah to come before the day of the Lord (Mal 3:1). In the end, a fickle generation will reject both John and Jesus. Matthew attaches a woe oracle against the cities that have witnessed Jesus' great works without repenting to the more benign parable of the children in the marketplace which concluded Jesus' remarks about himself and the Baptist (11:20-24).

Although Matthew's second discourse opens with calling and naming the Twelve as apostles to be sent on mission (10:1-5a), the Twelve do not leave Jesus' side. Instead, at the conclusion of this teaching Jesus gets up to go and preach in the towns (11:1). From a narrative point of view, that change makes the mission discourse instruction for later use, not for immediate action. Matthew's expansion of the discourse's content contributes to that perception by incorporating material from Mark's apocalyptic prophecies concerning the hostility that Christians will face in the future (Matt 10:16-25; Mark 13:9-13), sayings about the necessity to confess Christ before others (Matt 10:32-33, a variant of the "Son of Man" saying in Mark 8:38, also in Q [Luke 12:8-9]), and sayings about the hostility in families engendered by the gospel (Matt 10:34-39; Luke 12:51, 53). Matthew concludes the discourse with a note of consolation that promises rewards to all who assist those who come in Jesus' name. To receive one of these "little ones" (disciples) is to receive Jesus himself (Matt 10:40-41; Mark 9:41).

If these instructions are intended for the future activities of Jesus' disciples on mission, then a redactional element introduced into the opening becomes more troubling than it would be if Jesus were speaking only of a one-time expedition while Jesus is alive. The apostles are instructed not to go anywhere near Gentiles or Samaritans. They are to stick to "the lost sheep of the house of Israel" (10:5b-6). Matthew has edited out most of the references to Jesus journeying into Gentile territory to be found in Mark. "Tyre and Sidon" have been dropped from the territory list as it was reformulated to introduce the first sermon, and the woman whom Jesus meets when he enters the region of Tyre and Sidon is no longer a "Syrophoenician" but a "Canaanite." She addresses Jesus with the phrase already used by Jewish suppliants, "have mercy on me, Son of David" (15:22). Matthew makes another subtle shift in her reply which suggests a more profound acknowledgment of who Jesus is than in Mark's version (Mark 7:24-30). In Mark she counters Jesus' rejection with the remark that dogs get the scraps that fall from the children. Matthew has her say that dogs get scraps from the tables of their "masters" ("lords"). Where Mark has Jesus grant her healing because of her "saying," Matthew's Jesus grants the request because of her "great faith." There is no suggestion that Jesus might have lost a verbal contest to a non-Jewish woman!

Matthew's exclusion of Samaria from the mission territory also puzzles exegetes. Luke 10:25-37; John 4:4-42; and Acts 8:4-25 indicate that Samaria had been receptive to the gospel from an early period. Jesus himself may have found a positive response there or used Samaritans as a contrast to the negative responses encountered among fellow Jews. Yet if Matt 10:5b-6 articulates mission rules for later Christians, the two most vital areas of early missionary activity, Gentiles and Samaritans, are excluded. On the other hand, the Evangelist does have the risen Jesus commission his followers to go out to "all the nations" (28:16-20). The Greek word *ethnē* can be used in both a geographical sense of the "nations" that are not the land of Israel and an ethnic sense of the non-Jewish inhabitants of those nations, "Gentiles." Exegetes are divided over how to understand that final command. It could be a command to go to Jews in all those geographical places. Then the restrictions in 10:5b-6 would still stand. Or it could mean to go and preach to "Gentiles," in which case the risen Lord thus issues a retraction of the previous restriction.

By the end of ch. 11 the story has taken an ominous turn. Jesus utters a prophetic oracle against areas in which he has worked. They face a worse fate at the judgment than Sodom (11:24). His teaching will divide God's people. The wise and learned do not know the truth that God has revealed to mere children. Those who take up Jesus' way of life (his "yoke") will find rest (11:25-30). Ulrich Luz argues for a division in the narrative at this point, observing that 12:1–16:20 is marked by a series of withdrawals following conflict between Jesus and Jewish leaders (12:15; 14:13; 15:21).[3] The first two conflicts are occasioned by a plot to kill Jesus (12:14) and by Jesus' learning of the execution of John the Baptist (14:13). This proposal makes a useful observation about the changing tone of the plot at this point in the Gospel. But the suggested conclusion to the section has structural difficulties. Matthew's major restructuring of Markan material to allow the introduction of Q material and to foreground Jesus' role as teacher ends at Matt 14:1, where the Evangelist inserts the death of John the Baptist from Mark 6:14-29. From that point on, Matthew introduces some blocks of material from his special tradition and Q (e.g., Matt 16:17-19; 17:24-27; 18:21-35 [= M]; 18:12-13, 15 [= Q]) but in general follows the sequence found in Mark.[4] Therefore, the division in the chapters concerning Jesus' ministry should coincide with the Markan pattern.

A break at Matt 16:5-12 serves as a partial inclusio with 11:28-30 and thus marks the end of this section of the Gospel. The transition into this section encouraged readers to adopt Jesus' "yoke," that is, his way of life or teaching about what the Torah requires. The transition out of the section constitutes a sharp warning against the teaching of alternative Jewish authorities, Pharisees and Sadducees. To create this conclusion, Matthew has rewritten the boat episode from Mark 8:14-21 to mitigate the disciples' misunderstanding and substitute Sadducees for the Herod of Mark's account, since Herod was not representative of a school of Torah interpretation. Matthew understands the leaven as a reference to teaching. Objections to alleged Torah violations by Jesus or his disciples come from Pharisees and scribes.[5] Thus Matthew has structured this section of the Gospel as one in which the increased tensions between Jesus and the authorities are

---

3. Luz, *Matthew 8–20*, 177.

4. Davies and Allison, *Matthew* I, 71. Davies and Allison surmise that this shift in strategy of composition was the consequence of Matthew's using up most of his Q material by this point in the narrative. What remained, he intended to save for incorporation into the two remaining discourses, ch. 18 and chs. 24–25.

5. Matthew has first brought the Sadducees into the picture with his reformulation of the request for a sign (16:1-4; Mark 8:11-13 has only Pharisees) and has incorporated Pharisees and Sadducees into the crowd which received John's baptism (3:7). Sadducees will only appear once more, to challenge Jesus' teaching about resurrection (22:23-33; Mark 12:18-27). The retelling of that *chreia* concludes with the observation that the crowd was struck by Jesus' teaching (v. 33).

grounded in arguments over teaching, not simply his popularity as a miracle-worker as in Mark.

Matthew's expansion of Mark's narrative sequence has pushed the parables of the kingdom of God almost to the middle of the Gospel. This new position makes both the failed seed of the Sower parable and the use of Isaiah to make parable-telling a hardening of heart for some hearers more appropriate. The Gospel's audience has begun to witness negative responses to Jesus' teaching. At the same time, Matthew continues to shape the discourses to address the internal needs of Christian communities. He substitutes a trickster tale for Mark's parable of hidden growth (Mark 4:26-29): by refusing to clear his field of the weeds sown by an enemy, the farmer has a dual harvest, brush to burn and his wheat (Matt 13:24-30). The allegorical interpretation of this parable is only given to the disciples as part of a second round of teaching that occurs away from the crowds in the house (13:36-52). Therefore the parables discourse falls into two distinct parts. The initial address to the crowds is apparently intended to leave them without understanding. The second section opens with an apocalyptic scenario. At the judgment the Son of Man will divide the good seed, which he has sown, "the children of the kingdom," from the bad seed sown by the devil, "the children of the evil one."

Matthew may be using this apocalyptic scenario to explain why it is not necessary or possible for Christians to purify their ranks in the present age. The issues of sin and forgiveness within the Christian community will be a specific topic in the next discourse. Matthew adds three more parables to the private instruction of the disciples. In the first two, the reign of God is exemplified by a person's actions upon discovering a treasure buried in a field (Matt 13:44; *Gos. Thom.* 109) and a merchant's response to finding an extraordinarily valuable pearl (Matt 13:45-46; *Gos. Thom.* 76). The individual's swift, decisive action, which seems to be the point of the comparison, passes without comment. Presumably Christian listeners will acknowledge that they have had to give up everything they had before to follow Jesus. The final parable, a fisherman clearing his catch (Matt 13:47-48; *Gos. Thom.* 8) is provided with an apocalyptic reading. At the end of the age, the angels will separate the righteous from the wicked (vv. 49-50).

Matthew brings each of the five discourses to a conclusion with a reference to judgment. The Sermon on the Mount employed the image of house foundations, rock or sand, from Q. Only the rock, that is, putting Jesus' teaching into practice, can enable the house to withstand the storm

(Matt 7:24-27; Luke 6:47-49). Judgment language is not focused on believers in the missionary instructions. Instead it identifies the disciples on mission, the "little ones," with Jesus. It promises appropriate reward to outsiders who assist them in any way (Matt 10:40-42). This acknowledgment should caution readers against drawing the boundary too tightly around the community of believers. Others who are not self-identified followers of Jesus may be among "the righteous" or "the children of the kingdom." The famous parable of the sheep and the goats which concludes the final discourse, a set of parables about the judgment, develops that point in more detail (Matt 25:31-46). The fourth discourse, a set of instructions about sin and forgiveness addressed to followers of Jesus, concludes with a long parable: a servant turns his unexpected good luck into tragedy by refusing to extend the debt relief he has just received to another servant who owes him money (18:23-35). This parable takes readers back to Jesus' teaching on similar topics in the Sermon on the Mount (5:42; 6:12, 14-15).

Most of the fourth discourse concerns tensions that arise among Christians. Although the Evangelist follows Mark's sequence of episodes much more closely in the second half of the Gospel than in the first, a shift toward the needs of later Christian communities continues to be apparent in the Evangelist's presentation. This section of the Gospel runs from Peter's acknowledgment of Jesus as Messiah in Caesarea Philippi to the healing of two blind men at Jericho (16:13–20:34). It includes the three passion predictions found in Mark (Matt 16:21; 17:22-23; 20:17-18). Mark's sequence had Peter's confession followed by an equally sharp rebuff for protesting against Jesus' suffering (Mark 8:27-33). Matthew changes the picture. The Evangelist inserts sayings about Peter that point forward to his future role in the Christian community. God enabled Peter to recognize Jesus' true identity. In the future Peter will be the rock foundation for the church, an echo of the house built on rock from the Sermon on the Mount (7:24-25). Judgments that Peter makes about applying Jesus' teaching will be confirmed in the heavenly court.[6] This insertion shows Matthew's audience that Peter's objection to the passion was only temporary even though Jesus speaks of Peter as a "stumbling block to me" (16:23).

Special Matthean traditions have Jesus instruct Peter about paying the Temple tax (17:24-27) and about the unlimited possibility of forgiveness (18:21-22). Instead of treating each passion prediction as evidence of

6. See Luz, *Matthew 8–20*, 356-65.

increasing alienation between Jesus and the disciples, as in Mark, Matthew has the disciples beginning to grasp what Jesus has told them. After the second prediction they grieve (17:23). At the third, Jesus has the Twelve gathered with him privately on the road to remind them of what is about to happen (20:17). A final note added to the cure of the two blind men takes Matthew's audience back to the motivation for healing presented at the beginning of the public ministry, Jesus' compassion for the suffering people of God (20:34; see 9:36).

Matthew adds material to the Markan account of Jesus' teaching in Jerusalem. Some of the parables and sayings taken from Q appear earlier in Luke, such as the Great Banquet (Matt 22:1-24; Luke 14:15-24), the woes against the teaching of scribes and Pharisees (Matt 23:1-36; Luke 11:37-52), or the lament over the fate of Jerusalem (Matt 23:37-39; Luke 13:34-35). The final discourse in the Gospel expands the apocalyptic prophecies of Mark 13 with additional parables from Q (Matt 24:45-51/Luke 12:41-48; 25:14-30/Luke 19:11-27) and Matthew's special tradition (Matt 25:1-13; 25:31-46).

As we have seen, some exegetes think that the parable of the prudent and foolish servant girls is an allegory created by Matthew or his tradition as a warning against the danger of finding oneself excluded from the reign of God. The final parable in the group concludes the church year in the Christian lectionary. As we noted, its promise that those who aid the suffering "little ones" even without recognizing them as surrogates for Jesus will receive just reward picks up the conclusion to the instructions on mission (Matt 25:40, 45; 10:40-42). This parable has been a staple for Christian ethicists who wish to argue for a universal, divinely ordained standard of justice based on a person's treatment of the poor and oppressed that applies regardless of an individual's religious convictions or lack thereof. But exegetes have pointed out that Matthew's Gospel enables a slightly different interpretation. The designations "least of these" and "my brothers" in the parable could refer to Christians, who are referred to as "little ones" in both 10:40-42 and 18:6. In that case, the parable correlates the fate of non-believers with their treatment of persecuted and suffering Christians.[7] Davies and Allison reject this revisionist interpretation on the grounds that the opening judgment scene has the Son of Man on the throne judging "all the nations *(ethnē)*." They prefer to see the scenario as a reference

---

7. For a defense of this reinterpretation see John R. Donahue, "The 'Parable' of the Sheep and Goats," *Theological Studies* 47 (1986) 3-31.

back to the beatitude on those who show mercy at the beginning of the Sermon on the Mount (5:7).[8]

Their common sense argument that in a judgment of the nations all peoples would not have had the opportunity to respond to Christians on mission with the gospel is somewhat weaker than it initially appears. Matthew has built into his narrative the possibility that Jesus will not return to judge the nations until all have heard the gospel. The final commission of the risen Lord dispatches the disciples to "all nations" or "all Gentiles": the Greek can mean either. Their task is to teach the *ethnē* to observe Jesus' teaching. The final verse picks up the name that the angel revealed to Joseph at the very beginning of the Gospel. The child is to be "Emmanuel," "God with us" (1:22-23). Now Jesus promises his followers that he will be with them until the close of the age (28:20b). Therefore, one might infer that Matthew does intend his audience to imagine a confrontation between all the peoples of the world and the gospel message before the end of the age. Matthew also includes an explicit statement of that view earlier in the concluding discourse: "And this good news of the kingdom will be proclaimed throughout the world, as a testimony to all the nations; and then the end will come" (24:14). Since this verse is Matthew's addition to his Markan source, it must represent his own point of view.

Matthew's account of the passion follows Mark closely. He shortens and makes stylistic improvements in some episodes. Other changes, as in the words over bread and cup at the Last Supper (Matt 26:26-29/Mark 14:23-26), probably reflect the liturgical wording in Matthew's community. A few larger insertions of special Matthean tradition either reflect legends circulating among Christians or details intended to answer objections to Christian belief. We have seen how Matthew's assertion that Jewish officials obtained a guard for Jesus' tomb (Matt 27:62-66; 28:11-15) was further expanded in the second century *Gospel of Peter*. Matthew also contains a legend in which Judas attempts to return the money to the Temple authorities. In his despair, Judas goes and hangs himself. Thus he actually dies before Jesus does in Matthew's narrative (27:3-10). Luke also reports the death of Judas (Acts 1:18-19), but, just as Luke's infancy stories do not overlap with Matthew's, so his account of Judas's death cannot be harmonized with what we find in Matthew.

Matthew is responsible for another famous detail in the hearing be-

8. Davies and Allison, *Matthew* III, 428-29.

175

fore Pilate, the warning by Pilate's wife (Matt 27:19). Ancient readers took warnings conveyed in dreams more seriously than modern readers do. Pilate does not hand Jesus over for execution until the crowd begins to riot. Then he takes the step of washing his hands of the guilt for innocent blood and passes responsibility off on those agitating for Jesus' death (27:24-25). This account has generated dramatic expressions of Jewish guilt for the death of Jesus in representations of the passion down through the ages.[9] The Evangelist's shift from speaking of the "crowd" in v. 24 to the "people" in v. 25 could imply that he did intend a reference to the Jewish people as a whole. However, Matthew may have thought that the Jewish people had paid for Jesus' death when Roman soldiers destroyed the Temple in 70 C.E.

Careful analysis demonstrates the value of using the hypothesis that Matthew reworked Mark's Gospel by incorporating Q material and other early Christian traditions. We have seen that the five discourses, which are the most prominent structural changes in the account of Jesus' public ministry, serve as focal points in successive sections of the narrative. Unlike Mark, Matthew's conclusion is not ambiguous. Even the guard knows that the body is missing. The women initially leave the tomb both afraid and rejoicing. Jesus appears to repeat the commission they have received from the angels (28:7, 10). The eleven remaining disciples meet the risen Jesus in Galilee. Jesus dispatches them to spread the gospel and establish believing communities throughout the world.

Literary Features in Matthew's Narrative

The five discourses in Matthew play such a key role in the narrative structure of the Gospel as a whole that they were discussed in the previous section. The connections which the Evangelist draws between the discourses and the surrounding narrative demonstrate that Matthew is not a haphazard revision of Mark. The Evangelist has created new, well-constructed patterns in telling the story of Jesus. Although modern translations smooth out some of the roughness and chopped-up style found in Mark, readers can appreciate the stylistic improvements Matthew makes in retelling selections from Mark. He avoids the jumpy strings of episodes held together by "and" phrases. Matthew reformulates introductions to link epi-

9. See Luz, *Matthew 21–28*, 506-10.

sodes together as continuous narrative. Inserting the discourses into his account also breaks up the extended series of one short episode after another. Matthew also makes stylistic improvements in Mark by shortening and tightening up some of the stories. For example, it takes Mark twenty verses to tell the story of Jesus and the Gerasene demoniac (Mark 5:1-20). Matthew devotes only seven verses to the tale (Matt 8:28-34).

Matthew also modifies details in his sources which are incorrect or inappropriate. The leper who disobeyed Jesus' command to tell no one (Mark 1:40-45) no longer ignores the instructions (Matt 8:1-4). Matthew ends the story with Jesus commanding him to fulfill the Torah. Thus the audience must conclude that Jesus respects precepts of the Mosaic law and expects others to do so as well.[10] Mark's use of Gerasa, a town some thirty miles from the sea, for the healing of the demoniac has long troubled exegetes. Matthew recognized the inaccuracy. He shifted the location to Gadara, only a few miles from the sea. When Mark cites a mixture of Isaiah and Malachi as Isaiah (Mark 1:2-3), Matthew corrects the citation (Matt 3:3). Matthew removes some of the disrespect implied when James and John try to get Jesus to give them high places in the kingdom by having their mother solicit this favor for her sons initially (Matt 20:20), but as he continues the story Matthew forgets that change and reverts to the plural "you are asking" (v. 22). Thus Matthew knew the story as one in which James and John, not their mother, had requested influential positions.

Our earliest Christian statements of faith include the conviction that the death and resurrection of Jesus were "according to the Scriptures" (1 Cor 15:3-5). The passion narrative draws on images of the suffering servant of God from Isaiah and phrases from the Psalms to make the point. Mark's Gospel began with the quotation from Isaiah to introduce John the Baptist. Early Christians could show that the events of Jesus' life and death were the culmination of God's plan for humanity by correlating them with the Scriptures. Non-Jews also had an interest in oracles and prophecies attached to major historical figures and events. Readers today find it easy to claim Jesus' ministry and the rise of Christianity as central events in world history. When the Evangelists wrote the Gospels, things were quite different. How could a tiny splinter group that had grown out of what was itself a minority religion claim that the fate of their founder would shape the entire world?

10. Luz, *Matthew 1-7*, 48.

Matthew's use of prophecy provides ancient readers with a persuasive form of argument for Christian belief. He introduces prophetic passages into the narrative. Ten of them are marked by a formal introduction such as "so that the word of the prophet Isaiah might be fulfilled, saying" (12:17). Scholars refer to this collection of citations as Matthew's "formula quotations." The citation of Isa 40:3 referring to the Baptist belongs to this group (Matt 3:3). The discovery of a collection of messianic prophecies among the texts from the Jewish sect at Qumran (4QFlor = 4Q174) led scholars to suggest that Matthew might have drawn on a similar collection in use among Christians, though the Evangelist himself may be responsible for some of the prophetic texts he employs in the Gospel.

The Qumran material only illustrates the genre, not the content of a Christian collection. Its authors sought to show that the prophets had spoken about the events which would occur in the last days and about the emergence of their own community. Prophetic text and interpretation are generally linked with the phrase "this refers to. . . ." However, one also finds the expressions "as it is written" and "as it is written in the book of Isaiah the prophet for the last days." The Essene author then cites Isa 8:11 and Ezek 44:10 as pointing to the founding of his community: "This (refers to) the sons of Zadok and (to) the men of their council, those who seek justice eagerly, who have come after them to the council of the community."[11] As in Matthew, there is more at stake than attaching random prophecies to events in one's narrative. The assembly and interpretation of prophetic passages in 4QFlor could be used to reassure its audience that they belonged to that assembly of righteous ones in the last days. In other words, it locates their sect and its teaching in God's plan of salvation for the righteous and destruction of the wicked.

Matthew uses his formula citations somewhat differently. He does not begin with the prophetic text and say "this refers to. . . ." Instead, he takes the narrative about Jesus as primary. The formula citation provides the audience with a sense that this story was foreseen as part of God's larger plan.

The Evangelist acquaints readers with this motif at the outset. A number of formula quotations appear in the infancy narrative. Some scholars would include only prophetic quotations which are spoken in the

---

11. 4Q174 I 21.17; from Florentino García Martínez and Eibert J. C. Tigchelaar, *The Dead Sea Scrolls Study Edition* (Leiden: Brill/Grand Rapids: Eerdmans, 1998) I, 353-55.

narrator's voice using a fulfillment phrase. It seems more appropriate to incorporate other prophetic citations that appear in the narrative as well. Matthew's audience would certainly have perceived them all to be part of the same presentation.

Formula Quotations in Matthew

1:22-23	"all this took place to fulfill what had been spoken by the Lord through the prophet"	Isa 7:14
2:5-6[12]	"for so it has been written by the prophet"	Mic 5:2
2:15	"this was to fulfill what had been spoken by the Lord through the prophet"	Hos 11:1
2:17-18	"then was fulfilled what had been spoken through the prophet Jeremiah"	Jer 31:15
3:2-3[13]	"this was the one of whom the prophet Isaiah spoke when he said"	Isa 40:3
4:14-16	"so that what was spoken through the prophet Isaiah might be fulfilled"	Isa 9:1-2
8:17	"this was to fulfill what had been spoken through the prophet Isaiah"	Isa 53:4
11:10[14]	"this is the one about whom it is written"	Mal 3:1
12:17-21	"this was to fulfill what had been spoken through the prophet Isaiah"	Isa 42:1-4
13:14-15	"with them indeed is fulfilled the prophecy of Isaiah that says"	Isa 6:9-10
13:35	"this was to fulfill what had been spoken through the prophet"	Ps 78:2
15:7[15]	"Isaiah prophesied rightly about you when he said"	Isa 29:13 (LXX)

12. Some exegetes would not treat this passage as a formula citation, since it is placed in the mouths of the scribes informing Herod about the birthplace of the messianic child.

13. Also not included in some lists of formula quotations, since this citation is drawn from Mark, not the Evangelist's own redaction.

14. Also omitted from some lists of formula citations because it is in the mouth of Jesus rather than a narrator's comment.

15. This citation occurs in the mouth of Jesus during a controversy story taken from Mark. Since the Qumran example includes prophecies about the "wicked" at the end of days, we are including it in the catalogue.

21:4-5	"this took place to fulfill what has been spoken through the prophet saying"	Isa 62:11; Zech 9:9
21:16[16]	"have you never read"	Ps 8:2
27:9-10	"then was fulfilled what had been spoken through the prophet Jeremiah"	Zech 11:12-13 (from Jeremiah 18–19)

Psalm texts can be included as prophetic testimony, since their fictive author, David, was also considered a prophet (so Mark 12:36/Matt 22:43). The texts of Matthew's citations follow various textual traditions. Some are derived from the Septuagint (e.g., Isa 7:14 in Matt 1:22-23); others appear to be independent translations of a text closer to the Hebrew version (e.g., Isa 53:4 in Matt 8:17) or a mixture of the Septuagint and Hebrew text types (e.g., Ps 78:2 in Matt 13:35). The mixture of text types in the citations leads some scholars to conclude that Matthew has accepted some quotations from Mark or Q as he found them and is responsible for the others, selecting for them the version whose wording best suited his context.[17]

The majority of these quotations appear in the early chapters, especially Matthew's infancy narrative, and in the final chapters connected with the passion. Formula quotations practically disappear from the second half of Jesus' ministry. As noted above Matthew ceases major restructuring of the Markan sequence at the beginning of ch. 14. The decline in proof-texts at the same point confirms the hypothesis that Matthew was responsible for introducing them into the narrative. Their frequency in the infancy narrative suggests that the Evangelist has more in mind than collecting legends about the subject's family genealogy and birth to fill out the biographical form. Matthew has indicated that we have reached the conclusion of God's plan by organizing the genealogy into fixed patterns of years between defining events in Israel's history: Abraham to David, Solomon to Babylonian exile, exile to the Messiah (Matt 1:2-17).

Both the stories about Jesus' birth and the formula quotations introduced into them confirm the divine destiny of the child. The dream vision which reveals his destiny to "save his people from their sins" and his name Jesus ("Joshua" in Hebrew) resolves the first of a series of threats to the in-

---

16. Not quite in form, but so close to the earlier citation that Matthew's audience is likely to perceive Jesus' reference as part of this larger genre.

17. Davies and Allison, *Matthew* III, 574-76.

fant's life. Without divine intervention, Joseph would have had to divorce an unfaithful fiancée. Popular etymology attached the name "Joshua" to the word "salvation." Each of the threats to the child or those associated with him also has a formula citation marking the geographical points in the story. Ancient readers would have been impressed by the heavenly sign that a great ruler had been born. One might even expect signs in such a context. If the audience was familiar with stories about the declining years of Herod the Great's reign, the king's murderous paranoia in the story of Jesus would be considered quite realistic.

The citation of Hos 11:1 in association with the flight into Egypt introduces a different figure in the background of the story. To this point, the promise of a Messiah from the royal line of David dominated the narrative. With the flight into and return from Egypt, the image of the people coming out of Egypt under Moses enters the frame of reference. Though the divine child has escaped, others will pay the price (Matt 2:16-18). That motif also evokes the story of Moses being rescued from the slaughter of Israelite infants in Exodus 2. The final quotation in the infancy narrative incorporates the death of the infants from Bethlehem into the divine plan. Matthew introduces Jeremiah by name three times: twice in formula quotations (2:17 and 27:9) and once adding his name to the popular opinion about Jesus' identity (16:14). The second formula citation attributed to Jeremiah mixes Jer 32:6-9 with Zech 11:12-13. It has been attached to the "field of blood" that Temple authorities purchased with the money that Judas returned. Thus the two Jeremiah quotations indirectly refer to the impending death of Jesus himself. The death which the infant Jesus escapes will overtake the adult. Both stories evoke the malice of authorities willing to shed the blood of innocent victims.

By quoting four different prophets early in the story, Matthew provides support for his claim that Jesus came to fulfill "the law and the prophets" (Matt 5:17). The Evangelist does not rely on just one prophet to make the case. Instead, this group of four could suggest to readers that all the prophets anticipated the story that is about to unfold concerning Jesus the Messiah.

Characters in the Gospel

Matthew inherits a cast of characters from Mark's Gospel. The infancy narrative adds some figures who do not appear in Jesus' adult life. Jesus' adoptive father Joseph, the descendent of David, was never mentioned in Mark. Mark 6:3 speaks of Jesus as a "carpenter, the son of Mary." Matt 13:55 revises that notice to read "the son of the carpenter, . . . his mother called Mary." Even in Matthew, Joseph only appears in the infancy narrative. There he is the key figure. He receives the revelation about the baby's name and divinely appointed destiny. The murderous king of the infancy narrative, Herod the Great, died in 4 B.C.E. The Romans agreed to divide his territory among three surviving sons. Archelaus, who received Judea, would be removed in 6 C.E., after which time that region would be governed directly by Roman prefects. Matthew has Joseph decide not to return to Judea because he is afraid of Archelaus. However, Antipas, who rules Galilee, will turn out to be as dangerous as his father and brother. He imprisons and later beheads John the Baptist (14:1-12).

Matthew shines the spotlight on Jesus as teacher from the beginning of his public ministry. He often abbreviates miracle stories taken from Mark so that the sayings or teaching embodied in the episode becomes the central point. Compare his pared down version of the healing of the ruler's daughter and the cure of the hemorrhaging woman sandwiched in between (Matt 9:18-26) with Mark 5:21-43 or the quick healing of two demoniacs in Gadara (Matt 8:28-34) with the elaborate scenario provided by Mark 5:1-20. As a consequence of such abbreviations, the demons do not function as opponents for Jesus. Audiences hearing Matthew's Gospel would not have the same sense of Jesus engaging apocalyptic forces of evil that can be derived from Mark. The Gadarene demons in Matthew do not put up much of a fight. They accuse Jesus of "coming before the appointed time *(kairos)* to torment us" (Matt 8:29). Readers may take the word *kairos* ("appointed time") in one of two ways. If it refers to the day of judgment, then the demons are complaining that Jesus is something of an advance party. If it refers to the plan to save God's people, then the reader knows that Jesus' arrival on the scene is in fact the right time to get rid of demons.

Matthew also makes the role of the crowd less complex than it is in Mark. During Jesus' public ministry, the crowds are drawn to him for healing and teaching as in Mark. Unlike those in Mark, the crowds never press up against Jesus and his followers in a way that is physically dangerous. Jesus has compassion for the crowd as lost sheep in need of leaders (Matt 9:36-38). Similarly, the miracles of healing and feeding are performed out of compassion (14:14; 15:30-32). Matthew also sets up a progressive series of crowd reactions to the miracles that they witness. Simple amazement at something not seen in Israel before (9:33) becomes the hopeful anticipation that Jesus is "Son of David" (12:23; 21:15) and praise given to the God of Israel (15:31). Therefore, the crowd has an appropriate understanding of the source and significance of Jesus' miracles even though they do not become believers. Jesus goes inside the house away from the crowd to instruct his disciples about the parables (13:36).

Just as the crowd held John the Baptist to be a prophet (14:5), so those accompanying Jesus into Jerusalem identify him as "the prophet Jesus from Nazareth in Galilee" (21:11). Just as Antipas feared the Baptist's popularity with the crowd (14:5), so also the chief priests and Pharisees. They wanted to seize Jesus after he told the parable of the Wicked Tenants against them, but feared the crowd (21:45-46). The crowd only becomes dangerous when they are manipulated by the chief priests and elders to demand amnesty for Barabbas and death for Jesus (27:20-26).

Matthew casts the Pharisees as the primary opponents in his story. Where Mark has an indefinite "they" as the party offended by the parable of the Wicked Tenants (Mark 12:12), Matthew identifies them as "chief priests and Pharisees." Matthew then rewrites the introduction to the pronouncement story on taxes to Caesar so that the Pharisees are engaged in a formal plot when they dispatch their disciples with Herodians to interrogate Jesus (Matt 22:15-16). Mark 12:13 has an indefinite "they" send some Pharisees and Herodians. Similarly, at the beginning of Jesus' controversies with Jewish opponents, Matthew narrows the focus to Pharisees in a number of instances (Matt 9:11/Mark 2:16: "scribes and Pharisees"; Matt 9:34 and 12:24/Mark 3:22: "scribes from Jerusalem"; Matt 12:14/Mark 3:6: "Pharisees with Herodians").

Matthew also adds comments about the Pharisees to his narrative. In the dispute over purification, the disciples point out to Jesus that the Pharisees are offended (Matt 15:12). In reply, Jesus excoriates the Pharisees as blind guides leading the blind on to disaster and threatens that God will uproot what God has not planted (15:13-14). After that digression, Matthew brings the story back to its Markan conclusion with Peter's question (Matt 15:15-20/Mark 7:17b-23). Matthew makes the Pharisees the addressees of Jesus' argument that the Messiah is greater than a "son of David" (Matt 22:41). In Mark the audience is not specified (Mark 12:35). This modification would lead an audience to infer that the phrase "no one was able to answer" (Matt 22:46) refers specifically to the gathering of Pharisees. Despite this repeated emphasis on the Pharisees, Matthew does not insert

INTRODUCTION TO THE SYNOPTIC GOSPELS

them into the actual trial proceedings against Jesus, events in which they had no part. However, the Evangelist is able to bring them back on stage one last time. They are associated with the chief priests in requesting that a guard be posted at Jesus' tomb (27:62). The pairing was introduced in 21:45. It is no surprise that casual readers of this Gospel often assume that the Pharisees were implicated in the proceedings which cost Jesus his life, despite their absence from the passion narrative itself.

The phrase "scribes and Pharisees" appears so frequently that many readers think the terms almost synonymous (5:20; 12:38; 15:1; 23:2, 13, 15, 23, 25, 27, 29). The programmatic statement in 5:20, "unless your righteousness exceeds that of the scribes and Pharisees, you will never enter the kingdom," sets up the point of conflict between this group and Jesus. Jesus teaches a way of righteousness that is in competition with Pharisaic *halachah*. Matthew follows this programmatic statement with a series of antitheses in the form "you have heard that it was said to those of ancient times . . . but I say to you that if . . ." (5:21-48).[18] The series culminates in non-retaliation and love of enemy, which defines God's own perfection, exemplifies the command to love one's neighbor from Lev 19:18 (Matt 5:43), and is the meaning of the golden rule (Matt 7:12).[19] Nothing in the ethical intensity of the proposals Jesus makes in the Sermon on the Mount contradicts Torah observance as practiced by Pharisees or other Jews. Matthew 5:17-19 says as much when it insists that Jesus did not come to abolish the law.

Jesus condemns the Pharisees for a way of life that does not match their teaching (Matt 23:2-3). Matthew treats their concern for the details of external observance as an unnecessarily heavy burden on a suffering people (23:4). Jesus rejects emphasis on external rites and practices which the scribes and Pharisees know are not mandated in the Law. He insists on that inner, moral conversion, which is God's intent in giving the Torah (23:23-28). Jesus heals the blind as the compassionate "Son of David" (20:29-34) in contrast to the Pharisees and scribes, who are blind guides leading the blind (23:16-23).[20] The most devastating attacks against the Pharisees are not in the disputes about what principles should guide practical imple-

18. Betz, *Sermon on the Mount*, 198-214. Betz holds that the antitheses were already found in the version of the inaugural sermon which Matthew found in his version of Q (p. 214).

19. Betz, *Sermon*, 210.

20. Luz, *Matthew 8–20*, 48.

mentation of Torah or even in the charge that they lack compassion for ordinary folk. Both accusations are typical of disputes between opposing schools of interpretation. The most shocking statements about scribes and Pharisees to modern ears, which hear in them the seeds of later anti-Semitism, imply that the Pharisees are liable to divine condemnation. When the crowd thought Jesus might be "Son of David," the Pharisees countered that he was in league with Beelzebul, an accusation which makes them guilty of sinning against the Holy Spirit (12:22-37). There is no forgiveness for that sin.

At the end of a catalogue of woes against the scribes and Pharisees, Jesus charges them with the ancestral crimes of murdering God's prophets (23:29-36). Again the evidence for such a charge is a bit ambiguous. The pericope opens by suggesting a false self-confidence. If the scribes and Pharisees had lived in earlier times, would they not have murdered the prophets (v. 30), whose tombs they now venerate? The evidence given against them seems to refer to the future, not the past (Matt 23:34-36): "I send you prophets, sages and scribes, some of whom you will kill and crucify, and some you will flog in your synagogues and pursue from town to town, so that upon you may come all the righteous blood shed on earth" (vv. 34-35a). Is Matthew's animus against the scribes and Pharisees as characters perhaps a reflection of his own experiences in the decades after the Jewish revolt? Much of the accusation itself appears in a Q saying spoken by the Wisdom of God (= Luke 11:49-51). Matthew has introduced "and crucify," "flog them in your synagogues," and pursue "from town to town." These additions suggest that the charges have been formulated with an eye toward both the death of Jesus and the subsequent persecution of disciples who went out on mission in his name (Matt 10:17-23).

Therefore it would appear that Matthew has two motives for casting the Pharisees as villains in his Gospel. First, their considerable influence over the people made it difficult to gain an audience for what Jesus taught about righteousness. Second, they had spearheaded actual efforts to persecute Christians and run them out of town. A generation before Matthew, Paul had been a zealous Pharisee attempting to wipe out the church (Gal 1:13-14). As a consequence of such experiences, Matthew may even have thought that the Pharisees were implicated in the crucifixion even though his sources do not support that interpretation. Thus the Evangelist positions this sharp woe oracle as part of the words of judgment in Jerusalem before the passion rather than as part of Jesus' Galilean ministry, as in Luke (Q).

Matthew employs Q traditions about John the Baptist to fill out Mark's portrait of that character. A judgment saying taken from Q serves as the Baptist's prophetic condemnation of the many Pharisees and Sadducees who came to be baptized (Matt 3:7-10). The Baptist warns that being a descendant of Abraham is not enough. It is necessary to "bear fruit worthy of repentance" (vv. 8-9). By the end of Matthew's Gospel the audience knows that the Pharisees and Sadducees have not heeded the prophetic warning. Just as the Baptist knows the true character of the Pharisees when they appear, he also recognizes that Jesus does not need baptism. Matthew adds an exchange between the Baptist and Jesus to explain why Jesus received baptism (3:13-15). It was a well-established conviction among early Christians that Jesus was without sin (see 2 Cor 5:21). Therefore Jesus did not need to participate in a ritual of repentance for sin. Instead, Matthew crafts the scene to show that the Baptist acknowledged his inferiority to Jesus.

As we have seen, Matthew moves the execution of the Baptist further into Jesus' ministry than in Mark's sequence of events. He incorporates an extensive block of Q material earlier in Jesus' ministry. Matthew retains the tradition that John was imprisoned before Jesus began his public activity (Matt 4:12). John had told the crowds that an apocalyptic figure would come after him. This figure would inaugurate divine judgment (3:11-12).[21] Upon hearing about Jesus, the Baptist has his disciples come to inquire whether or not Jesus is that person. Modern readers are often surprised by the tension between this inquiry and the clear recognition of Jesus at his baptism. Rather than invoke a psychological crisis of doubt on the Baptist's part, one should accept the arrangement as Matthew's way of presenting evidence for Jesus' messianic identity. The narrative is arranged so that readers have seen Jesus perform the deeds of healing which now serve as evidence that Jesus is fulfilling the prophetic promises (Matt 11:2-6/Luke 7:18-35). Matthew does not suggest a loss of faith on the Baptist's part. Rather the question is necessary to introduce the evidence. Jesus follows his reply to the messengers with a long speech to the crowds about John that explicitly identifies John and the Elijah who is to come before God's Messiah (Matt 11:11-15). The violence suffered by the kingdom will soon claim both the Baptist and Jesus (11:12). Finally, the parable of Children Ar-

---

21. Possibly a reference to the Son of Man figure from Daniel (so Luz, *Matthew 8–20*, 131).

guing over What to Play (Matt 11:16-19/Luke 7:31-35) illustrates the fickleness of a generation that rejects both the Baptist and Jesus. Matthew has told readers that the crowd considered both men prophets. Unfortunately their reputation does not produce a lasting conversion of Israel, the "fruits of repentance" mentioned in the Baptist's opening words to the Pharisees and Sadducees.

It is hardly surprising to find Matthew softening the rough edges that Mark has associated with Jesus' disciples. The three passion prediction scenes which structure the ministry from Peter's confession at Caesarea Philippi to the point of arrival near Jerusalem show the disciples slowly coming to terms with Jesus' words. That process is closer to what one might anticipate, growing acceptance of a difficult truth, than the downward slide into hardness of heart, fear, and misunderstanding found in Mark. Mark also uses two sea rescue miracles and a teaching episode in a boat to castigate the disciples for having "no faith." When Matthew takes over those stories "no faith" becomes "little faith" or a failure to understand that is corrected by explanation. For Mark, the Walking on the Sea (Mark 6:45-52) rescue puts the disciples in a worse light than the Storm at Sea (Mark 4:35-41) because "their hearts were hardened" (v. 52). Matthew's account disagrees. He adds an earthquake (Matt 8:24) to explain the extraordinary danger in the first account and changes "fear" to "amazement" at the end (8:27).

The second sea miracle has been expanded with special Matthean material about Peter's attempt to walk on water (14:22-33). Had he maintained a steady confidence in Jesus, the apostle would have been able to complete the transit from the boat to Jesus (14:28-31). Peter's wavering constitutes "little faith" (v. 31). Matthew provides a new conclusion to the story in v. 33. The disciples worship Jesus, confessing him to be Son of God. Therefore the disciples have made progress in comprehending who Jesus is by the conclusion of the second incident.

Matthew's emphasis on Jesus as teacher requires disciples who are capable of learning as well. Lest readers think that Jesus failed to communicate to them the meaning of his parables, Matthew has Jesus check their understanding at the end (13:51). The disciples reply that they do understand. Matthew shifts the final episode in Mark's sequence (Mark 8:14-21) out of the boat. He agrees that the disciples did not at first understand the metaphor of leaven as referring to teaching. By the time Jesus concludes the explanation there is no doubt about his point. But

187

again Matthew explicitly states that the disciples understood what Jesus meant (Matt 16:5-12).

Peter was already singled out as a spokesperson for the group of twelve disciples in Mark. Matthew expands the picture of Peter with traditions from his own special tradition. The most famous are the beatitude and promises addressed to Peter after he recognizes that Jesus is the Messiah (Matt 16:16-19). God has revealed Jesus' identity to Simon (16:17) just as God has given the secrets of the kingdom to infants, not the learned (11:25-26). Jesus interprets Simon's nickname Peter (= "rock" or "stone," 16:18). Jesus will build his community on this foundation. Readers may recall the parable of the houses built on sand or rock at the conclusion of the Sermon on the Mount (7:24-27). In the earlier instance, the rock foundation was hearing and living by the teaching of Jesus. Matthew's audience would have understood that Peter's faith and practice as the foundation to which Jesus is referring. Peter does not succeed Jesus in a formal role as the heads of philosophical schools did when a founder passed away. Matthew may be reminding his audience of the role that Peter had played in the earliest decades of the Jerusalem community (see Gal 1:18-19). Peter had been dead for thirty years by the time the Gospel was written.

The concluding sayings in Matt 16:19 refer to the keys and an authority to bind and loose that will be confirmed in the divine court. The keys could refer to a form of communal discipline. The community rules of the Dead Sea sect provided for a trial period in which candidates for membership were examined. Each member had an assigned rank in the community. Violations of communal rules could lead to exclusion from the communal meal or even permanent expulsion. Matthew's discourse concerning relationships within the Christian community mentions expelling an individual who will not be reconciled with a fellow Christian or accept the community's decision (18:15-17). The rules in Matthew are followed by a variant of the "binding and loosing" saying (18:18). In this instance the power to make such decisions rests with the community (plural "you"), not with a single individual.

However, "bind and loose" can refer to decisions about conduct required by Torah *(halachah)* as well. Matthew's oracles against the Pharisees assert that their teaching both shuts up the kingdom for others and demonstrates a refusal to enter it themselves (23:13). Therefore these sayings may refer to Peter as an authoritative voice in interpreting the teaching of Jesus. Someone must fill this role as Jesus has just cautioned his disciples against the teaching of Pharisees and Sadducees (16:5-12).[22] Other episodes in which Peter elicits instruction from Jesus on specific points confirm this possibility. Peter is being prepared to provide such guidance (15:15; 17:24-27; 18:21-22). At the same time, Peter's abortive attempt to walk on water has shown Matthew's audience that Peter is just as weak in faith as the other disciples. Without a Jesus who could reach out and rescue him, Peter might have drowned in the storm. The promise of Jesus' presence to his followers repeated in 18:20 is confirmed at the conclusion to the Gospel (28:20).

Matthew distinguishes between divine inspiration and simple human motives in describing Peter's actions. God showed Peter that Jesus is Messiah. The all-too-human Peter resists Jesus' words about his passion (16:22-23). Matthew retains the traditional story that Peter would deny knowing Jesus (26:31-35, 58, 69-75) as well as the tradition that Jesus rebuked Peter by name for failing to stay awake in Gethsemane (26:40). After Peter denies knowing Jesus and recalls Jesus' prediction (26:75), he vanishes from the narrative. Matthew has dropped his name from the instructions given the women (28:7, 10; contrast Mark 16:7). Thus Peter has a dual function as a character. On the one hand, he provides a link between the teaching of Jesus as it is remembered and practiced in the church of Matthew's day and Jesus himself. On the other hand, Peter also appears as an everyman figure possessing the weaknesses and strengths that any disciple might possess. At the conclusion to the story, Peter is not singled out by the risen Lord. He remains one of the eleven commissioned by Jesus to take the gospel to the nations (Matt 28:16-20).

Jesus in Matthew's Gospel

As was true of other characters in the Gospel, Matthew's depiction of Jesus is both more extensive and less ambiguous than Mark's. Modern readers may be drawn to the uncertainties of Mark's characterization, but the ancients would consider the consistency of purpose found in Matthew and Luke more impressive. A great public figure should exhibit larger-than-life virtues. Or, in stories intended to blacken a subject's memory, say of a despised emperor like Caligula or Nero, the vices will be just as clearly drawn.

---

22. For a detailed discussion which selects this option as the most plausible reading, see Davies and Allison, *Matthew* II, 635-39.

Though vices may be represented as a fall from a promising youth or wise teaching imparted by a philosopher tutor, the virtues of a great individual should be evident from an early age. Matthew has no stories about Jesus himself prior to his public ministry. Instead he uses the figure of Joseph to indicate that Jesus belongs to a family that is righteous. The major notes in the infancy narrative are explicitly christological. Jesus will be a figure comparable to Moses in bringing salvation to God's people. His adoptive father Joseph is directly descended from the royal house of David, which can trace its ancestry back to the founding patriarch Abraham. Heavenly portents acknowledged by wise men from the East herald the birth of this great figure, whose life has been foreseen by Israel's prophets. Despite these divine signs, Jesus will not be embraced by the leaders of his people. The local king recognizes the infant as a threat to his regime and tries to have him killed. Only flight into Egyptian exile saves the family. Thus Matthew's audience comes to the story of Jesus' public life with extensive information about who he is.

This beginning poses a question for the reader: How will Jesus actually fulfill his destiny? The military or political coup that would make the book's hero a new Moses or a king over all Israel does not occur. Herod's sons and their Roman overlords remain firmly entrenched in power at the end of the story. The social and religious elite as well as the crowds also remain unchanged. These bare facts might seem to undermine the claims made for Jesus established at the beginning of the Gospel. Of course, an audience that remembers the disasters of the Jewish revolt in Judea some fifteen years before Matthew was written might agree that the nation made a bad call in sticking with such leaders rather than listening to Jesus. Jesus prophesied doom for the city (Matt 23:37-39). Matthew has crafted his story to demonstrate that everything that happens to Jesus fits the divine plan. Through the disciples God's reign will be extended to all nations. Because the risen Jesus is exalted with God, Jesus can fulfill the promise of the name Emmanuel, "God with us" (28:16-20).

Matthew does not present the cross as a contradiction to God's plan. Only Jesus' enemies see it as evidence against Jesus' claim to be the Messiah. By incorporating early legends about Jesus' death and resurrection, the Evangelist suggests that even Jewish leaders suspected the truth. Crucifixion is not the end of a life if its victim is God's Suffering Servant. God can and will vindicate the Servant by restoring his life. The chief priests and Pharisees are worried enough to get a guard posted at the tomb. Since

Jewish expectations for resurrection of the dead considered it to be part of the end-time judgment (Dan 12:1-3), Matthew adds end-of-the-world motifs to the crucifixion scenario. Mark's cosmic signs of darkened sun and torn Temple veil are supplemented with an earthquake, tombs opened, and holy ones rising from the dead (Matt 27:51-53). This last bit of staging creates an awkward time lag. The resurrected righteous have to wait in their tombs until Easter, at which point they appear to many people around the city. Such legendary details would not be out of place in an ancient biography, however peculiar they appear to modern readers. They indicate to the audience that Jesus has triumphed over his enemies.

Matthew also strengthens the link between the life of Jesus and the Suffering Servant figure of Isaiah through the use of formula quotations. He sees the prediction that the Servant will bear the weaknesses of the people as fulfilled in the healing ministry of Jesus (Matt 8:14-17, citing Isa 53:4). After the Pharisees seek a way to kill him, Matthew incorporates a long quotation of Isa 42:1-4 into a transitional episode (Matt 12:15-21). Jesus is the beloved servant of God who bears God's Spirit. Matthew also incorporates a command not to make Jesus known into this transitional passage (v. 16). The Evangelist retains some of the secrecy commands from Mark, especially in association with Peter's confession (Matt 16:20) and the Transfiguration (17:9). The transitional passage in 12:16 leads the reader to surmise that Jesus' need to steer clear of his enemies was the reason for such restraint.

Matthew also reshapes the political overtones of the title "Son of David" by introducing it on the lips of persons seeking healing. The title does not appear in Mark until the encounter with a blind man as Jesus approaches Jerusalem (Mark 10:45-52). Matthew employs it throughout the healing ministry of Jesus (Matt 9:27-31; 20:31-33; 21:9). The exorcisms lead the crowd to hope that Jesus is Son of David (12:23). Even the non-Jewish Canaanite woman cries out to Jesus, "Have mercy on me, Lord, Son of David" (15:22). Biblical antecedents for connecting David with healing are weak though scholars have found a bit of first-century C.E. evidence in Josephus (*Antiquities* 6.166, 168).[23] Matthew may have created this interpretation of Son of David to explain that Jesus' role as Messiah was in bringing healing to God's suffering people.

Matthew retains the titles "Son of God" and "Son of Man" from his

---

23. Luz, *Matthew 8–20*, 47-49.

sources without much change in how they are used. He does clarify the ambiguity created when Mark has a Roman centurion refer to the crucified Jesus as Son of God by reshaping the scene. The centurion as well as his squad are terrified by the earthquake which occurs at the moment of Jesus' death (Matt 27:54). When they cry out as a group "truly this was a son of god," they are speaking as any pious Roman would have done. They have seen the portent and recognize that a divine or semi-divine being has just died. Of course Matthew's Christian audience recognizes the deeper meaning of the expression. Jesus is the Son begotten through God's Spirit. He has shown himself to be Son as the beloved servant of God suffering for the sins of God's people. Jesus as the apocalyptic Son of Man, judge of the nations, appears in the great judgment parable which concludes his final discourse (Matt 25:31-46).

Matthew's most significant development in the characterization of Jesus presents him as authoritative teacher. He is the guide to a righteousness greater than that of the official teachers in Israel, scribes and Pharisees (5:17-20). The Evangelist has shaped the narrative around the five discourses which embody Jesus' teaching. He has set Jesus over against the Pharisees, who are depicted in the Gospel as the embodiment of false teachers. They are blind to what God's Torah really requires and are hypocritical, leading lives that do not exemplify virtue or compassion for others. Jesus, by contrast, represents the perfect embodiment of God's love. He twice directs the words of Hos 6:6, "I desire mercy, not sacrifice," at his critics (Matt 9:13; 12:7). Both citations are prefaced by phrases that suggest a lack of real knowledge on the part of these opponents. "Go and learn," Jesus says (9:13). Non-Jewish readers might miss the significance of that expression. Learning is not an abstract, theoretical activity. Rather the sustained inquiry into the meaning of the Torah and the prophets involves practicing its precepts. Hence the harshness which emerges in Jesus' critique of the scribes and Pharisees. It implies that their learning has gone astray because it has not produced a lifestyle that conforms to God's will.

The conclusion to Matthew's Gospel makes Jesus' teaching applicable to all nations, not just Israel. This shift marks a striking change of course. The Jesus who will appear as Son of Man at the end time holds all people responsible for their actions. Even those who are not believers will be called to account for their treatment of the lowly, suffering ones with whom Jesus identifies.

The Community Implied in Matthew's Narrative

Matthew is the only Gospel in which the word "church" *(ekklēsia)* occurs. It appears in the reference to Peter as the rock foundation (Matt 16:18) and in the rules for dealing with a member who will not heed communal advice (18:17). The final instructions in the Gospel provide the ritual formula for admission to the community through baptism (28:19b). Thus it is easy to see that the Evangelist had the needs of established Christian communities in view when he composed the Gospel. The epitome of Jesus' teaching in the Sermon on the Mount as well as the other discourses provide material for the instruction in Jesus' teaching mandated in 28:19. Matthew has also embedded in the story references to the persecution awaiting those who preach the gospel (10:16-25). In its broadest sense, Matthew depicts the church as continuous with the community of disciples that formed around Jesus during his ministry. It is a community of those who put his teaching into practice. That much is obvious on the surface of the narrative. Two areas create problems for interpreters: the relationship between Christians and the larger Jewish community and the emergence of false teachers or prophets within the Christian assembly (7:15-23).

Does Matthew expect Christians to identify themselves as "Jews" in some sense? However peculiar the question might seem to Christians or Jews today, it was reasonable in the first century. Communities of Gentile converts were thriving by the mid-first century. Both Paul (Gal 2:1-14) and Luke (Acts 15) present the crisis that accepting Gentile believers without requiring that they adopt Jewish practices posed for the Jerusalem apostles, Peter among them. The conflicts that Paul faced when Jewish Christian missionaries arrived in churches he had established among non-Jews in Galatia, Philippi, and Corinth show that not everyone took the same meaning from the earlier Jerusalem agreement to accept both Paul's apostleship to the Gentiles and Peter's to the Jews. Such debates indicate that the problem of how to identify followers of Jesus was more complex than most Christians realize today. Even though most of the New Testament writings are directed to non-Jewish audiences, many first-century readers would still have thought of their religious beliefs as a sort of Jewishness. After all, faith in Jesus required conversion to the God of the Hebrew Scriptures (1 Thess 1:9-10).

Matt 5:17-20 affirms that Jesus did not come to abolish the Torah and

prophets but to fulfill or complete them. Christians can claim a righteousness greater than that of scribes and Pharisees (v. 20). Matt 23:2 even hints
that one can learn Mosaic teaching from the scribes and Pharisees as long
as one does not imitate their way of living out the teaching. Finally the instructions to disciples on mission in ch. 10 explicitly limit their activities to
Israel (vv. 5-6, 23). Apart from rare exceptions, Jesus restricted his own
ministry to the lost sheep of Israel (15:24). Matt 13:52 even suggests that
some Christians functioned as scribes for their community. Like the Evangelist himself, they could bring their knowledge of the Torah and the
prophets to bear on understanding Jesus' life and teaching. The controversies which pit Jesus against Pharisees over Sabbath, purity, and food rules
do not imply repudiation of Jewish practice. They involve disputes over
principles honored by such activities. The principle must trump the rules.
Matt 23:23-24 even accepts the practice of tithing as long as it remains sub-
ordinate to the weightier concerns of Torah, namely justice, mercy, and
faithfulness.

So far the evidence that Matthew's narrative envisages readers who
would identify their group as a Jewish sect seems compelling. However another set of details found in the Gospel pose difficulties for that reading.
The risen Jesus sends his disciples to evangelize "the nations" or "the
Gentiles" (28:19). The Greek term can mean either and both meanings occur in the Gospel. In 18:17 the adjective *ethnikos* clearly means "Gentile"
with the added implication that members of the church are not *ethnikoi*.
In the judgment scenario of 25:32, the gathering of "all the nations" before
the glorious Son of Man clearly refers to all humanity whether Jews or
non-Jews. Therefore a universal meaning should be attached to the final
commission. Both Gentiles and Jews living in the Diaspora are the object
of the mission envisaged. Some smaller details indicate that Matthew assumes a distinction between the church and the synagogue. Matthew repeatedly speaks of "their" synagogue (4:23; 10:17; 12:9).

In a puzzling episode, Peter first tells Jewish authorities that Jesus
does pay the tax required of Jewish males for the upkeep of the Temple. He
then receives instruction from Jesus on the matter. On the one hand, the
instruction affirms that in principle those who belong to the kingdom are
free from tax. On the other, one should pay to avoid scandal (17:24-27).
The attached folktale motif of the tax money turning up in a fish's mouth
is something of a distraction. At the time of Jesus, most Jews understood
Exod 30:11-16 as an annual half-shekel applicable to adult males. The

Essene sect had a different view. They argued that Exodus referred to a tax paid only once in a man's life, when he came of age (4QOrd). Therefore it is possible to situate this debate in tradition earlier than Matthew's Gospel. After the Romans destroyed the Temple in 70 C.E., they imposed a punitive tax on all Jews to be paid to the "Jewish treasury" in Rome. If Matthew's community still considered itself part of the larger Jewish community, then their participation in this tax may have been important to Jewish leaders who were responsible for gathering the tax revenue. It is not possible to tell from the story as told in the Gospel whether the Evangelist has simply repeated an earlier controversy story in order to show that Peter received special instruction from Jesus or is telling his audience to pay the Roman tax voluntarily.

Though the evidence is less clear than one might like, most scholars have concluded that Matthew writes from a church that has recently made a difficult transition from being an all-Jewish movement to incorporating non-Jewish believers. Its origins and traditions remain strongly rooted in Jewish Christianity. However, in the years after the fall of Jerusalem, their opportunities for successful missionary efforts in the Jewish community have declined. The Evangelist's sharply drawn polemic against Pharisaic teaching may be in response to the consolidation of Jewish communities around Pharisaic leadership after the Temple was lost as a religious center. Their influence may have been felt even in Jewish Christian communities. Including Gentiles in the global mission of the community does not mean that appeals to Jews had come to an end.[24]

The picture of Christian communities projected by the Gospel becomes even more complex when the allusions to internal divisions and false teachers are added to the mix. One set of charges refers to a growing spirit of "lawlessness" (24:12-13). This accusation applies to persons who claim to be Christians, even to have prophesied and worked miracles in Jesus' name (7:22), not simply to the conduct of scribes and Pharisees (23:28). Both groups accused of lawlessness are also charged with hypocrisy. To the external observer they appear pious, but the inner reality is quite different. The scenario presumed in 7:21-23 has Jesus acting as advocate in the judgment for those who have been faithful to his teaching. The lawless Christians find themselves rejected. Matthew 16:27 employs a Son of Man saying to make a similar point: everyone will be judged according

24. Davies and Allison, *Matthew* III, 684.

to his or her conduct.[25] By making Jesus' teaching in the Sermon on the Mount the required norm, Matthew can include Gentile Christians as believers without implying that they must adopt a Jewish way of life.

Those excluded as false Christians appeal to spiritual gifts practiced in the name of Jesus. They have engaged in prophecy, exorcism, and other miracles. 1 Cor 12:6-10 indicates that such gifts were familiar to Christians there. Some interpreters have read into Matt 7:21-23 a clash between a Gentile Christianity focused on spiritual gifts and a Jewish Christian Christianity that emphasizes "works of the Law," that is, conduct according to Torah. Paul creates a rhetorical form of that opposition in Gal 3:1-5. The spiritual gifts which his Gentile converts received in baptism should be, he says, sufficient. They should not seek out "the flesh," that is, circumcision and a life governed by Torah.[26] Matthew's text, however, admits a simpler reading, a warning against substituting external, dramatic signs for lived obedience to Jesus' teaching. It is impossible to tell from the previous warning against false prophets, wolves in sheep's clothing (Matt 7:15-20) what form their activities took. Other first-century Christian writings point to the existence of prophets who wandered from one community to the next (*Didache* 11:3-12). Because they offered instruction in local communities, such prophets could be as dangerous in their false teaching as the scribes and Pharisees.

Matthew also warns that some Christian leaders may emulate the objectionable behavior of scribes and Pharisees. They may prefer the public recognition which accompanies positions of authority over the example of service given by Jesus (Matt 23:8-12). The objections to honors gained from public acts of piety are similar in form to those voiced in 6:1-6, 16-18.[27] There Jesus instructs his followers to engage secretly in the three requirements of piety in the Jewish tradition, fasting, almsgiving, and prayer. Human rewards for such deeds render compensation from God unnecessary. Matthew's insistence on Christ as the only one who should be called teacher (23:10) underlines the difference between various rabbis or philosophers and Jesus. Ordinarily the founding teacher or rabbi selects a favor-

25. Betz, *Sermon,* 546-56.

26. So Betz, *Sermon,* 528: "If the picture drawn in that passage is right, prophecy along with exorcism and miracle-working is typical of Gentile Christians. Their prophecy is false because they have separated themselves from what belongs together: the law and the prophets (5:17; 7:15-20)."

27. Davies and Allison, *Matthew* III, 266.

ite student to assume responsibility upon his death. The particular philo-sophical or rabbinic school would then continue through a succession of teachers. Even though Matthew has Jesus single out Peter as the guarantor of stability and reliable teaching in the church (16:17-19), Peter does not re-place Jesus as sole head of a Christian school or sect. No one can be a suc-cessor to Jesus in that sense. Comments about concern for the "little ones" and those in the community who stray are addressed to future leaders at the beginning of the discourse in ch. 18 (vv. 1-5, 10-14). Thus the virtues of humble service required of community leaders are opposed to the posi-tions of social prestige enjoyed by the scribes and Pharisees. Christians are warned against any leaders who depart from that model. Jesus himself pro-vided the model as the Son of Man who both spent his life in serving and gave his life as ransom for sinners (20:24-28).

Jewish Christian Gospel Traditions

The Gospel of Matthew as we know it was written in Greek. It quickly be-came the most widely used Gospel in the early Church. Though most of its quotations from Scripture are from the Septuagint, some of them reflect Hebrew text traditions. Its author has Jesus hint that Christian scribes will combine what is new, Jesus' teaching, with the old (Matt 13:52). Early Christians noticed another small detail in Matthew. The tax collector who becomes a disciple was named "Levi, son of Alphaeus" in the other Gos-pels (Mark 2:14; Luke 5:27), but his name in this Gospel is "Matthew" (Matt 9:9). This detail suggested that the author of the Gospel was in fact one of the Twelve, "Matthew the tax collector" (10:3).

The hypothesis that a Hebrew or Aramaic Matthew tradition has been detected in new Gospel fragments continues to surface on the fringes of scholarship today. It was first proposed by the second-century Christian author Papias, who asserted that Matthew compiled sayings in Aramaic that others translated as best they could (Eusebius, *Hist. Eccl.* 3.39.17). In the same context, Eusebius indicates that Papias took a story about a woman falsely accused (a variant of the story found in some manuscripts at John 7:53-8:11?) from the "Gospel of the Hebrews."

Confusion over the connections among an Aramaic proto-Matthew, a later Aramaic translation of Matthew, and a text referred to as "the Gos-pel of the Hebrews" already existed in the fourth century. It was exacerbated when modern scholarship adopted the category "Jewish Christian Gospel" for editions of New Testament apocrypha and divided the patristic references among three lost Gospels, *Gospel of the Hebrews, Gospel of the Ebionites,* and *Gospel of the Nazareans,* assigning all three to the early second century.[28] Although the categories still appear in collections of New Testament apocrypha, scholars have come to doubt the existence of second-century Gospels appropriate to the last two designations.

The first references to a so-called "Gospel of the Nazareans" are medieval.[29] A number of Greek manuscripts in cursive script contain notes indicating textual variants from "the Jewish copy."[30] The evidence in patristic citations, most of them from Jerome, indicates that a group called Nazareans employed a Gospel "according to the Hebrews" or a version of Matthew that was either in Hebrew or in Aramaic/Syriac written in Hebrew characters. Jerome claims that the same Gospel is used by the Nazareans and another sect known as the Ebionites:

> In the Gospel that the Nazarenes and Ebionites use, which I recently translated from Hebrew into Greek and which most people designate as the authentic text of Matthew, we read that the man with the withered hand was a mason, who asked for help with these words, "I was a mason, working for my bread with my hands. I pray to you, Jesus, restore me to health so that I do not eat my bread in disgrace."[31]

Elsewhere Jerome also speaks of a copy of the Hebrew Matthew preserved in the library at Caesarea. He says that he obtained a copy from the Nazarenes of Beroea in Syria. In this edition, Jerome observes that the citations from the Scriptures are not taken from the Septuagint but from the Hebrew version. The two specific examples that Jerome mentions are the quotations in Matthew's infancy narrative (Matt 2:15 = Hos. 11:1; Matt 2:23 = Isa 11:1?[32]).

---

28. Bart Ehrman, *Lost Christianities* (New York: Oxford University Press, 2003) xi; Elliott, *Apocryphal New Testament,* 3-16; Hans-Josef Klauck, *Apocryphal Gospels: An Introduction* (London: Clark, 2003) 36-49.

29. Klauck, *Apocryphal Gospels,* 43-49.

30. Elliott, *Apocryphal New Testament,* 13-14.

31. Jerome, *Commentary on Matthew* 12.13, from Elliott, *Apocryphal New Testament,* 12.

32. Since there is no citation in Matt 2:23, identifying the scriptural passage implied remains problematic. For an analysis of the options that in the end concludes that a variant of the LXX of Isa 4:3 in which "Nazarite" has been substituted for "holy one of God" is most plausible, see Davies and Allison, *Matthew* I, 274-81.

Thus one finds in the citations from Jerome two alternative gospel traditions, a "Gospel of the Hebrews" sometimes referred to by other titles, and a Hebrew or Aramaic version of Matthew's Gospel. The latter is not a sayings collection or proto-Matthew as the Papias tradition suggests. Instead it is a translation and revision of a Greek text. The additional variants in stories found there reflect the fluidity of gospel traditions circulating in the early centuries.

Since the Hebrew/Aramaic translation of Matthew contains some expansions or variants of episodes in the Greek version, it is difficult to distinguish it from the "Gospel of the Hebrews" mentioned in some patristic references. Some scholars argue that in the latter the expression "Hebrews" designates ethnic origins, as in the canonical "Epistle to the Hebrews," not the language in which that Gospel was composed.[33] Jerome in his Matthew commentary (398 C.E.) appeals to *Gos. Heb.* to explain the unusual adjective *epiousios* (Latin *supersubstantialis*) in the bread petition of the Lord's Prayer (Matt 6:11). He says that he found the Hebrew word *mḥd*, "tomorrow's," which means that the petition reads "bread for tomorrow." Elsewhere in a commentary on Psalm 135, Jerome attributes the same translation to the Hebrew Matthew.[34] Thus it is not even possible to be certain which of the two second-century gospel traditions Jerome has employed.

Clement of Alexandria and Origen read a "Gospel of the Hebrews" in Greek. Clement twice cites a saying about seeking and finding that is similar to *Gos. Thom.* 2, once attributing it to "the Gospel of the Hebrews" (*Stromateis* 2.9, 45). Origen has a saying in which Christ claims that his mother, the Holy Spirit, carried him by the hair to Mount Tabor (*Commentary on John* 2.12). None of the early patristic authors consider *Gos. Heb.* heretical. It was not composed by an author advocating a deviant christology, as *Gos. Pet.* was said to, for example. Nor was it a variant of canonical Matthew that was adapted by a heretical sect. What little information our sources provide about its content suggests that *Gos. Heb.* had adopted a standard gospel narrative pattern that related the life and teaching of Jesus from infancy traditions through encounter with the Baptist to public teaching, crucifixion, and resurrection appearances. There are no

---

33. Dieter Lührmann, *Die apokryph gewordenen Evangelien. Studien zu neuen Texten und zu neuen Fragen* (Novum Testamentum Supplements 112; Leiden: Brill, 2004) 239.

34. Lührmann, *Evangelien*, 241-42.

patristic references to miracle traditions from this Gospel, but the evidence is too slight to know whether miracles had been dropped from the work as a whole.

The third category, the "Gospel of the Ebionites," was a hypothesis of nineteenth-century scholars. Epiphanius is our main source of information about Gospel usage in this Jewish Christian sect, which insisted that Christ was born of human parents and held its members to strict observance of Torah. Epiphanius repeatedly claims that they employed a mutilated form of Matthew translated into Hebrew which they called "Gospel of the Hebrews" (*Panarion* 30.3, 13).[35] Similar remarks without any citations from the Gospel in use among the Ebionites can be found in Eusebius (*Hist. Eccl.* 3.27.4) and Irenaeus (*Adv. Haer.* 1.26.2). Some scholars have suggested that the Gospel being employed by the Ebionites in the second century was a gospel harmony, not the Hebrew or Aramaic translation of Matthew that appears in the third century.[36]

The limited survival of gospel traditions from second-century Jewish Christian communities shows that those groups who identified themselves as pious Jews were moving to the margins of Christianity. The Acts of the Apostles directs its attention to the spread of Christianity from Jerusalem and Syrian Antioch west to Rome. Greek was the *lingua franca* for this expansion. As a result we know little about how the followers of Jesus who moved eastward, where Aramaic and Syriac were spoken, presented their story of Jesus.

Even though Matthew retains much of the Jewish Christian tradition, the Evangelist chose to revise an earlier account of Jesus composed for a Greek-speaking audience. The occasional scholars who repeat claims to an Aramaic (or Hebrew) proto-Matthew have failed to recognize the significant turn toward the wider, non-Jewish world intended by the Evangelist. By putting the story of Jesus as Jewish Messiah and Son of David in Greek and indicating how Jesus' teaching represented a greater righteousness, Matthew makes the Jewish heritage of Christianity available to both Jewish and non-Jewish believers. Matthew's shaping of discourses of Jesus acknowledged the need for concise summaries of Jesus' teaching which could be used to instruct new converts without the prior formation in Jewish piety that Jewish Christian communities could assume. The wide-

35. Elliott, *Apocryphal New Testament*, 5-6.
36. Lührmann, *Evangelien*, 231-33.

spread adoption of Matthew's Gospel by early Christians is evidence enough for the practical wisdom of the Evangelist's decision.

At the same time, the rhetorical strategies employed to carve out a space for Christians as disciples of the Messiah Jesus, who fulfilled the law and the prophets, have left a troubling linguistic heritage for twenty-first-century believers. The language of hypocrisy, false teaching, and malicious responsibility for the death of God's servants that Matthew uses to secure allegiance to Jesus' teaching fits the normal parameters of warring schools of interpretation. Remove such phrases from the world of sectarian polemics within a shared faith, and they become general condemnations of Judaism as a religion. Matthew calls down a divine judgment on those responsible for refusing to accept God's Son (e.g., 22:7). But his readers easily recognized what later interpreters forgot, that the price had been paid when Roman legions destroyed Jerusalem. It was not a judgment to be enacted by future Christian rulers. In fact, it is hard to imagine that Matthew, who warned against becoming like the powerful and insisted on servant leadership (20:25-27), could even have foreseen Christian rulers or even a Christian majority. His church is made up of the "little ones" who will survive by the kindness of outsiders and their faithfulness to Jesus until the final judgment.

CHAPTER SIX

Reading Luke's Gospel

Luke's Gospel opens as a more sophisticated reader might expect a book to begin. The author dedicates his book to a prominent patron and explains why his effort is superior to that of his predecessors (Luke 1:1-4). We have seen that his claims to be familiar with earlier accounts and to have created an order for the sources he incorporates have been confirmed by source criticism. Luke proves to be a gifted stylist who can shift into the Semitic idioms of the Septuagint to give his narrative a biblical tone in key scenes.

Although Luke addresses a patron in the prologue, he does not identify himself. Unlike Matthew and John (John 21:24), there are no internal hints by which later readers identified the Gospel's author. This departure

---

Suggested Reading

Bovon, François. *Luke* I. Trans. Christine M. Thomas. Minneapolis: Fortress, 2002.

Brown, Raymond E. *The Birth of the Messiah.* Garden City: Doubleday, 1977.

Fitzmyer, Joseph A. *The Gospel According to Luke I-IX.* AB 28; Garden City: Doubleday, 1981.

———. *The Gospel According to Luke X-XXIV.* AB 28A; Garden City: Doubleday, 1985.

Johnson, Luke Timothy. *The Gospel of Luke.* Sacra Pagina 3; Collegeville: Liturgical, 1991.

Tannehill, Robert C. *Luke.* Abingdon New Testament Commentaries; Nashville: Abingdon, 1996.

from literary convention is not surprising in the somewhat rough compilation of Jesus material in Mark's Gospel, but it is more puzzling from an author of Luke's sophistication. Has Mark established a precedent for anonymity on the part of a Gospel's author? The sayings collection employed by Luke (Q) may also have been anonymous in contrast to the second-century *Gospel of Thomas,* which opens with a clear statement of its line of transmission. The "living Jesus" spoke the words and Didymus Jude Thomas wrote them down. Or perhaps Luke considered this suppression of authorial identity to be characteristic of biblical narrative. Early Christians might have given a somewhat different account of the matter. They distinguished between the Gospels of Matthew and John, attributed to disciples of Jesus, and those of Mark and Luke, whose authors had heard the apostles Peter and Paul respectively. Luke's preface makes it clear that the Evangelist is not an eyewitness to any of the events recorded in the Gospel.

The criterion for setting out the events that Luke presents in the prologue is not investigation of the various sources to determine what happened, as we expect a biographer to do. Luke tells readers that he is beginning with what Christians of his day are preaching. This Gospel will provide a secure foundation for that message. Along the way many of the most beloved characters and stories about Jesus are found in Luke's special material. Even the most casual churchgoer will recognize such famous stories as The Good Samaritan (Luke 10:25-36), Martha and Mary (10:38-42), The Prodigal Son (15:11-32), The Rich Man and Lazarus (16:19-31), The Pharisee and the Tax Collector (18:9-14), Zacchaeus (19:1-10), The Good Thief (23:40-43), and The Disciples on the Road to Emmaus (24:13-35). We even refer to people as "a good Samaritan," "a Martha type," or "a prodigal son" without thinking twice about it. Luke has etched the picture of the mild-mannered, compassionate Jesus who seeks to bring back the sinner, lift up the poor, and heal the sufferer in our imaginations. His Gospel has the story of the Annunciation to Mary, Jesus in the manger, the angels on high, and the shepherds. So without Luke's Gospel our visual images of the Christian story would be impoverished as well.

In addition Luke has incorporated poetic celebrations of salvation into his infancy stories. Salvation will be experienced when God unseats the powerful and lifts up the lowly, a key motif in the gospel story. These canticles became established pieces in the daily round of Christian prayer, the Benedictus (Luke 1:68-79) recited at morning prayer, the Magnificat (1:46-55) at evening prayer, and the Nunc Dimittis (2:29-32) at night prayer. For Roman Catholics, the first part of the Hail Mary comes from this source as well (1:42). The complex biblical echoes of these canticles suggest that Luke may have taken them from Jewish Christian sources. It is their place in his Gospel that has established these words as fixed elements in the Liturgy of the Hours. Luke concludes the Gospel with the disciples returning to Jerusalem with joy and repeatedly praising God in the temple (Luke 24:52-53). He may have expected the audience to recall these words of Zechariah, Mary, and Simeon in that context. So one might even think of Luke's Gospel as the aesthetic teacher of Christian senses in hearing and speech through story and song and in sight through the many artistic renderings of his stories.

From Beginning to End: Luke's Narrative Shape

The emergence of a four-Gospel canon separated Luke's account of Jesus from that of the apostles. None of our ancient manuscripts has the Gospel and Acts in sequence even though the preface to Acts (Acts 1:1-2) reminds readers of the previous book. Therefore the Gospel is only the first half of a two-volume composition.[1] Such prologues are common in ancient historians whose works extend over multiple volumes (scrolls). The intention stated at the beginning of the Gospel, to "set down an orderly account of the events that have been fulfilled among us" (Luke 1:1-4) still governs the story of the apostles. Luke's concerns are not primarily historical but theological, to confirm the truth of Christian preaching. The Evangelist has arranged the long periodic sentence which constitutes the prologue to his Gospel so that it ends with the word *asphaleia* ("reliability"). That word can be used in historical and legal contexts as it is in Acts 25:26. Festus must conduct an inquiry so that he will have something reliable to send along with the accused for trial in Rome.[2]

Literary convention dictates that an author refer to the sources. Luke mentions both oral traditions from eyewitnesses and earlier written mate-

1. David E. Aune, *The Westminster Dictionary of the New Testament and Early Christian Literature and Rhetoric* (Louisville: Westminster/John Knox, 2003) 280, insists on treating Luke-Acts as a single work for the purposes of a rhetorical and literary analysis. Also, working from a literary perspective, see Robert Tannehill, *The Narrative Unity of Luke-Acts: A Literary Interpretation* (Philadelphia: Fortress, 1986).
2. Bovon, *Luke* I, 23.

rial as the basis of his information. This combination of oral tradition with earlier written accounts situates the author and his readers at some temporal distance from the events that Luke is going to narrate. But these events are not from a bygone age. It is still possible to speak of them as having occurred "among us." Josephus' introduction to his history of the Jewish revolt also opens an account of fairly recent events that have been told by others. Unlike Luke, though, Josephus himself was a participant in some parts of the story:

> The war of the Jews against the Romans — the greatest not only of the wars of our own time, but, so far as accounts have reached us, well nigh of all that ever broke out between cities or nations — has not lacked its historians. Of these, however, some having taken no part in the action have collected from hearsay casual and contradictory stories which they have then edited in a rhetorical style; while others who witnessed the events, have, either from flattery of the Romans or from hatred of the Jews, misrepresented the facts, their writings exhibiting alternatively invective and encomium, but nowhere historical accuracy. In these circumstances, I — Josephus, son of Matthias, a Hebrew by race, a native of Jerusalem and a priest, who at the opening of the war myself fought against the Romans and in the sequel was perforce an onlooker — propose to provide the subjects of the Roman Empire with a narrative of the facts by translating into Greek the account which I previously composed in my vernacular tongue [Aramaic] and sent to the barbarians in the interior.[3]

Josephus continues attacking earlier accounts as either flattery or fiction for several more paragraphs. He considers it a nobler task to write history of recent events than to compile ancient history. He defends his claim that the war he is about to describe is among the greatest by suggesting that the fate of the eastern half of the empire hung in the balance and that the tragic fate of the Jewish people led to ruin by tyrants and thugs. This should elicit some sympathy from his readers in Rome. By contrast, Luke's prologue is quite formal and provides little information.

Joesphus anticipates an audience that has heard the story from other authors, some hostile to the Jewish people. He wishes to persuade readers

---

3. Josephus, *Jewish War* 1.1, tr. H. St. J. Thackeray (LCL 203; Cambridge: Harvard University Press, 1927).

to adopt a different viewpoint. Josephus also sketches the topics to be treated in the book that follows. Luke does not provide us with such a carefully worked out agenda. Scholars have often sought to discern what Luke's apologetic or rhetorical purpose might be from the content of the combined work, Luke-Acts. Since the narratives in Acts frequently depict wealthy individuals or Roman officials responding positively to the apostles, scholars often propose that Luke intends to quell suspicions about the Christian movement by showing that those Roman officials who dealt with Jesus and his followers recognized that they were victims of malicious persecution. Christians are not a seditious lot but heirs of an ancient faith whose God has planned the course of human history. Luke traces Jesus' genealogy back to Adam (Luke 3:23-38). Although the Gospel ties the birth of Jesus into the reign of Augustus (2:1), its story begins and ends in Jerusalem. Acts becomes a critical piece in the assertion that God sent Christ for all people, since it deals with the transition from the Jewish traditions of Israel to a message for the entire civilized (Roman) world. Paul is cast as the divinely chosen agent to make that momentous journey.

Luke appears to be more constrained by sources in the Gospel than in Acts. He follows Mark for sections of narrative, though his Gospel has no parallels to Mark 6:45–8:26. The Evangelist may have considered that material repetitious or may have had a version of Mark that did not contain that section. Luke also appears to have done much less rearranging in the sayings material found in Q than Matthew did. Luke incorporates several blocks of special material, including

traditions in the infancy narratives	1:5–2:52
poetic compositions	1:47-55, 68-79; 2:29-32
a section of the Baptist's ethical advice to the crowds	3:10-14
a genealogy that traces Jesus back to Adam	3:23-38
a variant on the call of Peter which resembles John 21:1-4	5:1-11
additional miracle stories and *chreiai*	7:11-17, 36-50; 8:1-3; 9:51-56; 10:1-12, 17-20, 38-42; 11:27-28; 13:1-5, 10-17; 14:1-6, 7-14; 17:11-19; 19:1-10

a number of parables or example stories	10:30-37; 11:5-13; 12:13-21; 13:6-9; 15:8-10, 11-32; 16:1-8, 9-13, 19-31; 18:1-8, 9-14
appearances of the risen Jesus to followers in Jerusalem and the vicinity	24:1-48

It is easy to see from this list that most of Luke's special material has been added in three discrete sections of the narrative: the infancy narratives, a major block from ch. 10 to ch. 19, and the resurrection stories at the end of the Gospel. Luke's passion narrative differs from the Mark/Matthew mold at a number of points such as Jesus before Herod (23:6-12) and the repentance of one of the criminals crucified with him (23:39-43). Scholars continue to debate whether Luke depends on another source for his passion account or has made the changes himself, rewriting Mark and adapting some non-Markan material that probably circulated orally.[4]

The Evangelist composes a coda at the very end to tie the Gospel to his next volume. Jesus commands the disciples to remain in Jerusalem until they receive the Holy Spirit and then is taken up into heaven. His followers return to the city rejoicing and begin assembling in the Temple for prayer (Luke 24:49-53). Thus Luke's traditions about the resurrection and post-Easter movements of the disciples contradict Mark and Matthew, which postulate a return to Galilee and encounter with the risen Lord there (narrated in Matt 28:16-20). The contradiction may have been less obvious to Luke if he knew the Galilee tradition only as represented in Mark. Since the women flee in fear and do not report to anyone in Mark, he might have assumed that the Galilee promise was negated and that the resurrection appearances began in Jerusalem. Matt 28:9-10 has a Jerusalem appearance to the women outside the tomb, John an expanded version of that tradition attached to Mary Magdalene (John 20:11-18) as well as appearances to the disciples at a meal (John 20:19-29) such as one finds in Luke (24:28-49). Therefore Luke probably has some form of oral or written sources for that element in his conclusion. But the explicit order to remain in Jerusalem until the coming of the Spirit at Pentecost (Luke 24:49b) ap-

---

4. R. E. Brown, *The Death of the Messiah* (New York: Doubleday, 1994) 64-75, reached the latter conclusion on the basis of his monumental study of the passion but admitted that the evidence was far from conclusive. He, like other scholars, had changed his opinion on the matter during his career.

pears to be an intentional correction of the tradition that the disciples fled back to Galilee (Mark 16:7).

By opening the Gospel with the angel's appearance to Zechariah as he is serving in the Temple (Luke 1:5-25) and concluding with Jesus' disciples blessing God in the Temple (24:53), Luke begins and ends his story in the same place. Zechariah and his wife Elizabeth, a descendent of Aaron, are perfect models of Jewish piety (1:6). Rejoicing and praising God in the Temple represents the ideal piety of the Jerusalem church during the first days of its existence (Acts 2:46).

Given this focus on Jerusalem, it is not surprising that Luke has expanded the segment from Mark's narrative sequence in which Jesus teaches his disciples on the road to Jerusalem. Luke has largely followed Mark's sequence and added material from Q in chapters 3 to 9. But at Luke 9:51 the traveling around Galilee comes to an abrupt end. It is time to head for Jerusalem. Jesus has predicted what would happen there twice (Luke 9:22, 44-45). During the Transfiguration, Jesus discussed "his exodus which was to be fulfilled at Jerusalem" with Moses and Elijah (9:31). The final passion prediction occurs at the end of this journey narrative just as the group is approaching Jericho (18:31-34). Though Luke usually softens the sharp edges of Mark's portrait of the disciples, he does not do so here. The Twelve are unable to comprehend what Jesus has said to them.

Easily the most accomplished Greek stylist among the Evangelists, Luke revises the quick entry to and exit from Jericho found in Mark 10:46 by providing a number of events associated with the city. Jesus cures the blind man upon nearing the city (18:35-43) and meets Zacchaeus and stays at his house on the way through (19:1-10). Before entering Jerusalem, Jesus tells the parable of the Owner Entrusting Servants with Money (19:11-27/ Matt 25:14-30) as a response to expectations that the kingdom would arrive along with Jesus' entry into the city. Despite his triumphal entry, Luke has Jesus weep over Jerusalem's fate. The enemies pressing around the city destroying her people would remind Luke's audience of the siege and fall of the city (19:41-44). The journey ends with Jesus' entry into the Temple. Luke pares the Temple cleansing story down to two verses (Luke 19:45-46/ Mark 11:15-19). Luke presumes that this action was preliminary to Jesus taking up the role of teaching the people there daily (Luke 19:47-48). Once again the narrative takes its audience back to the Temple motifs of the opening chapters. That section of the Gospel concluded with a tale of Jesus as a precocious twelve-year-old staying behind after Passover to debate with teachers there (Luke 2:41-52).

Scholars have suggested that the correlations between infancy narratives and the account of Jesus' ministry represent the second stage in a two-part process of composition to create the two-volume work. Several features in the combined work suggest that initially Luke may have composed a single volume that began as Mark does with John the Baptist and continued into the opening chapters of Acts.[5] First, the divided work has two ascensions: one on Easter at the end of the Gospel (Luke 24:50-52a), the other forty days later at the beginning of Acts (Acts 1:6-11). The command to remain in the city until the coming of the Spirit in Luke 24:49 is a more generalized form of the one found at Acts 1:4-5, which recalls a prophetic word of John the Baptist about a baptism with fire (Luke 3:16/Mark 1:7-8). Luke has crafted an introduction for the saying which he found in Mark to make it a refutation of speculation that the Baptist is the Messiah (Luke 3:15). Thus Luke's reader already expects a Pentecost-like demonstration of Jesus as Messiah. Without the doubling found at the end of the Gospel and the brief prologue now attached to Acts, Acts 1:3 or 1:4 could be read as continuing the Gospel from 24:48. With the risen Christ, the plot carries forward into Acts (Acts 1:8).[6]

The summary reference to the first volume in Acts 1:1-2 is a second piece of evidence that at an earlier stage in its composition the Gospel was conceived as beginning with the ministry of Jesus. Acts 1:1-2 assumes that the prior volume began with what Jesus did and taught and ended with an ascension. A third bit of evidence for an earlier version that began with Jesus' ministry is found in the formal, historical introduction which Luke provides to open ch. 3 of his Gospel. Luke 3:1-2 lines the story up with the reigning emperor, the local Roman governor in Judea, two sons of Herod the Great who governed the surrounding territory, and the high priests in Jerusalem. Luke also employs a prophetic call formula to initiate the Baptist's ministry (v. 2b; cf. Jer 1:1 LXX). Luke also includes a patronymic identifying the Baptist as "son of Zechariah," hardly necessary in the Gospel as we now have it since the account of John's birth focuses on his father.[7] Luke 3:23-38 adds a genealogy of Jesus' legal father Joseph, which a biogra-

---

5. Joseph A. Fitzmyer, *The Acts of the Apostles* (AB 31; New York: Doubleday, 1998) 192.
6. Bovon, *Luke* I, 25.
7. Fitzmyer, *Luke I-IX*, 458-59.

phy would attach to the birth as in Matthew. If an earlier version of the Gospel lacked the birth and childhood stories, then Luke would have reason to provide the genealogy when his subject first steps onto the stage.

The Gospel as we now have it falls into four major sections:

1. Birth stories about John and Jesus plus legends about the child Jesus. These stories have the Jerusalem Temple as a geographical focus (1:1–2:52).
2. Jesus' inaugurates a public ministry in Galilee after the imprisonment of John the Baptist. His teaching and healing demonstrate that the prophesied time of salvation is at hand (3:1–9:50).
3. A journey from Galilee to Judea and Jerusalem, where Jesus will meet his destiny. Parables and example stories make up much of this section of the Gospel (9:51–19:27).
4. Jesus' teaching, death, and resurrection in Jerusalem (19:28–24:53).

The story begins in the Jerusalem Temple and reaches its climax when Jesus returns there some thirty years later. In the second act, the apostles endowed with the same divine Spirit that had been at work in Jesus will take the message to the world from that center. Jerusalem or its environs form a key point in journeys. In the first section, Mary makes the trip from Galilee to the Judean hill country shortly after Jesus' conception. There the slightly older babe in the womb, John the Baptist, rejoices at the presence of the Messiah (Luke 1:39-45). As a consequence of the shift to direct Roman rule in Judea, Jesus' parents must travel from Galilee to David's city Bethlehem, so that Jesus is born in the messianic city despite his Galilean origins. He is circumcised and brought to the Temple as an infant. Once again the baby is recognized as redeemer and made known to others (2:22-38). Jesus first makes the annual Passover pilgrimage with his parents at age twelve. As appropriate to an ancient biography the youth of a great man anticipates the task that will be his as an adult. His divine Father's business requires that he take over teaching in the Temple.

Jesus returns to Judea to receive John's baptism and be tested by the devil before he begins his own ministry. Though Luke usually remains close to Q's order, he appears to have introduced a shift in the order of challenges posed by Satan. The version in Matt 4:1-11 ends on a high mountain with the offer of world dominion. Jesus rejects it by citing Deut 6:13. Luke shifts that exchange to second place in the series so that the temptation story ends with Jesus and the devil standing on the parapet of the Jerusalem Temple (Luke 4:1-13). Luke picks up the Jerusalem-Nazareth axis that belonged to these journeys of Jesus' childhood and so changes the Markan order of Jesus' activity in Galilee. He no longer begins with calling fishermen who live in Capernaum only to reach Nazareth when he has disciples and a considerable reputation as healer (as in Mark 6:1-6). Luke asserts that Jesus had gained a considerable reputation for teaching in synagogues (4:14-15). The first detailed story about Jesus takes place with a programmatic sermon in Nazareth announcing the time of salvation (4:16-30). Jesus has to flee hostility in Nazareth. Only then does he begin traveling between Capernaum and other towns and villages in Galilee. In contrast to Mark's account, Jesus does not make boat journeys in and out of Jewish territory or back and forth across the sea. Luke has only the first of Mark's sea rescue miracles (Luke 8:22-25/Mark 4:35-41). The storm takes Jesus across into Gerasa, where he heals a local demoniac, as in Mark (Luke 8:26-39/Mark 5:1-20).

In a solemn gesture with overtones of biblical phasing, Jesus makes the turn to journey toward his destiny in Jerusalem in Luke 9:51. Once again, Jesus meets brief hostility. A Samaritan village refuses hospitality because Jesus and his disciples are bound for Jerusalem (9:52-56). Jesus warns potential disciples that they would have to give up everything to follow him (9:57-62). He sends out seventy (or seventy-two) followers on a mission matching that in the previous section of the Gospel (10:1-12, 17-20; 9:1-6, 10). Most of the journey is taken up with teaching largely derived from Q or Luke's special material. It can be divided into sections at the points where the narrator reminds readers of the destination toward which Jesus is moving (13:22; 17:11). In 17:11 "between Samaria and Galilee" suggests that Luke is not familiar with the regional geography. The expression may have been generated by the presence of a Samaritan in the attached story about ten lepers. Like the Good Samaritan earlier (10:30-37), this Samaritan also serves as an example of virtue. When Luke rejoins the Markan narrative order as the group approaches Jerusalem, he omits the request for positions of authority in the kingdom (Mark 10:35-45/Matt 20:20-28). This omission brings together the third passion prediction with its reference to the road up to Jerusalem (Luke 18:31/Mark 10:32) and the healing of the blind man on the road through Jericho (Luke 18:35/Mark 10:46). Luke keeps the reader's attention on the journey by adding the Zacchaeus story in Jericho (19:1-10).

Luke's account of Jesus in Jerusalem falls into three sections:

Jesus' teaching in Jerusalem prior to the passion (Luke 19:28–22:38),
the passion narrative (22:39–23:56), and
the Easter events (24:1-53).

In each of these sections, Luke has expanded Jesus' role as a teacher. The first section includes the Last Supper. Luke moves a dispute over who is the greatest (22:24-30/Mark 10:42-45; Matt 19:28) and a retraction of earlier limits on mission (Luke 22:35-38, contrast 9:1-6) into the meal setting. Ancient readers would have recognized in the expanded discourse a familiar type of meal, the symposium. After the food was cleared, wine was brought out and participants turned to literary or philosophical discussion. Though the passion narrative might seem an unlikely occasion for teaching, the exchange between Jesus and the criminal who appeals to him for salvation (23:39-43) has Jesus continue to teach up to the moment of his death. The exchange instructs readers about the saving power of the cross. Finally, each of the resurrection stories incorporates an element of instruction. The angel reminds the women of the predictions of his death and resurrection that Jesus made in Galilee (24:6-7). The disciples on the road to Emmaus include the women's report in explaining their despair to the mysterious stranger. Jesus responds by giving them a Scripture lesson. Moses and the prophets predict that the Messiah must suffer before entering his glory (24:25-27). When Jesus appears to his disciples at a meal, he repeats that instruction (24:44-46). Readers wishing to know the content of such instruction need only consult the sermons of Peter and Stephen in the opening chapters of Acts (Acts 2:14-36; 3:11-26; 7:1-53).

Jesus arrives in the city of destiny to great acclaim (19:28-40), but laments its fate (19:41-44). The story takes on a tragic edge. Had its leaders acknowledged God's Messiah, Jerusalem would not be lying in ruins as it has for almost two decades by the time Luke composes his story. All those who suffered and died in the conflict so thoroughly detailed by Josephus might otherwise be alive. Josephus might have agreed with Luke that the city's tragedy was to be blamed on the malice of some who employed a rhetoric of apocalyptic violence to cause rebellion. But he would not have seen the execution of Jesus as the crucial turning point, of course.

Before the passion, Jesus spends an indefinite period teaching in the Temple. Luke has moved Mark's story of the scribe's question about the greatest commandment into the journey narrative (Luke 10:25-29/Mark 12:28-34). As a result, all the stories of Jesus teaching in the Temple involve opposition. The "chief priests, scribes and leaders of the people" (19:47) remain consistently opposed to Jesus (20:1, "chief priests, scribes, elders"; 20:19, "scribes and chief priests"; 20:20, "their spies"; 20:27, "Sadducees"; 20:39, "scribes"; 22:2, "chief priests, scribes"). They make up the council which condemns Israel's Messiah (22:66, "the council of elders, chief priests, scribes"). The tragic note does not persist through the end of the story. Jesus' final words on the cross open salvation to others. Then the risen Jesus sets all these events firmly within the context of a divine plan whose final act has yet to be played out. The disciples will carry the forgiveness of sin to all the nations (24:47).

Literary Features of Luke's Narrative

Luke's two-part composition with its formal prologue to a patron immediately indicates that the Evangelist intends to elevate his work to a more educated level. The vocabulary of the prologue would not be out of place in any secular author. Yet where it suits his narrative, Luke adopts the style of the Greek version of the Hebrew Scriptures. His audience might have heard such passages much as modern Christians capture the biblical overtones in a speech, particularly if the speaker adopts phrases from the King James Version. Luke probably employed existing Jewish Christian material for the canticles (Luke 1:47-55, 68-79). Both of these poetic compositions use biblical antecedents such as Hannah's song in 1 Sam 2:1-10, phrases from the Psalms and the prophets, especially Isaiah. John the Baptist's birth story draws upon an archetype exemplified in the story of Hannah: a son born to an aging, barren mother will play a key role in Israel's history.

This jump from a learned prologue back into the language and imagery of Israel's story illustrates the two worlds that Luke brings together. In the Gospel, much of Luke's content comes from earlier sources shaped by the social and religious culture of Syria and Palestine. Luke appears to have a much freer hand in composing the stories found in Acts. There the sociocultural atmosphere of the educated, prosperous, non-Jewish inhabitants of the Greco-Roman cities comes to the fore. Many of the literary features that Luke employs in reshaping his sources for the Gospel are best understood in that setting. For example, Luke does not leave his readers back in the biblical past for long. The birth of Jesus in Luke 2:1-2 introduces the familiar world of the Roman Empire. Though Luke's facts about the census in Judea in 6 C.E. are a bit off, the rhetorical significance of his scenario is not. The census under Quirinus only involved inhabitants of Judea and occurred when the region was transferred from Herod's son to direct Roman rule. Only those who actually resided in the province were counted. Joseph would not have had to come from Galilee, which was ruled by Herod Antipas. But as a rhetorical framework, Luke's introduction underlies the significance of Augustus's achievement. One can now imagine that all nations are inhabitants of a single civilized world.

Despite attempts fueled by twentieth-century liberation theology to enlist Luke as a critic of imperial powers, the narrative in Luke-Acts comes much closer to the view that Paul expresses in Rom 13:1-1-7: God establishes political power for the good of humankind. Even though Roman authorities do not worship the one true God, believers should remain obedient to the authorities' decrees. Because Jesus' parents were obedient to an imperial decree, their son was born in the city of David, Bethlehem. Quite apart from the conscious intentions of those involved, the prophecy was fulfilled. This distinction between God's plan and human intentions becomes evident in the legend about the angelic chorus (2:13-14). Urban inhabitants of the Roman Empire would have been familiar with the Augustan claim to have established an age of peace. In his *Fourth Eclogue* the poet Virgil celebrated Augustus's birth as a child destined to return the world to its golden age. Therefore Luke's audience would hear the angelic song as contrary to such mythic descriptions of Augustus. Only God can restore the world to a golden age without disease, famine, violence, or war. Jesus, not Augustus, is the divine child.

Luke also brings the Christian story into line with Roman chronology at the beginning of Jesus' public ministry. Luke 3:1-2 begins with the year of Tiberias's reign and the name of the Roman governor in Judea before listing all the relevant Jewish authorities and their respective territories. Such historical notices serve an apologetic function. The narrative arc of Luke's story embraces the entire civilized world even though its beginnings lie in a distant city, the religious capital of a minority group, Jerusalem. In his final speech before the journey to Rome, Paul stands before Festus, the Roman governor, and the Jewish King Agrippa. He insists on the public significance of the rise of Christianity: "for this has not happened in a corner" (Acts 26:26). Luke incorporates the spread of the gospel from Jerusalem and its Jewish roots to the Gentiles and cities of the Roman Empire into God's plan. He edits the apocalyptic prophecies concerning Jerusalem and the end time so that the delay of the parousia has a purpose: "until the times of the Gentiles are fulfilled" (Luke 21:24).

An educated Gentile audience would have been less concerned with whether Jesus had an appropriate understanding of Jewish Torah than with the virtues extolled in his life and teaching. To a Jewish Christian reader, the infancy narratives demonstrate that Jesus' entire family were pious Jews who observed every requirement of Torah. The Gentile reader could view the same stories as evidence of a key Roman virtue, piety. Josephus distances himself and most Jews from those responsible for the revolt against Rome by suggesting that the Zealot leaders were not faithful followers of their God. God punished such impiety by permitting the Romans to destroy the Temple. Josephus even depicts the Roman commander Titus as so filled with piety that he did not want his men to burn the Temple. Historians doubt the truth of that view, but it demonstrates that piety could be extended to sacred places dedicated to gods not one's own. Another example of Luke's emphasis on piety comes in his report about Jesus' cleansing of the Temple. There is no narration of the actions taken such as one finds in Mark 11:15-19. No tables are overturned or animals removed or activities interrupted. Luke simply says that Jesus got rid of those engaged in commerce (Luke 19:45). There would be no reason to suspect Jesus of impiety in the sacred precincts on the basis of Luke's account. As they await the coming of the Spirit, Jesus' followers spend their time praising God in the Temple (Luke 24:53).

Luke's Gospel combines two points of view concerning wealth. On the one hand, the wealthy are the wicked responsible for the plight of the poor. Salvation can be perceived as turning the tables. The poor and oppressed are exalted, the wealthy reduced to nothing (Luke 1:47-55). Luke's beatitudes and woes are formulated on this principle (6:20-26). On the other hand, the wealthy can act as generous benefactors to the poor and make reparations for any injustice done, as with Zacchaeus (19:1-10). The parables of the Rich Fool (12:13-21) and Rich Man and Lazarus (16:19-31) both depict the rich as overwhelmed with greed rather than generosity. Both protagonists are extraordinarily wealthy but reject the obligations to serve as benefactor which ancient society demanded of such persons. Luke has Jesus' command to lend to any who ask (6:30) in the exhortation to love enemies. Sharing wealth is one way of imitating God's mercy

(6:36). The time and resources that the Good Samaritan (10:30-37) expends on the robbery victim is equivalent to what friends or family might demand.

Jesus' immediate disciples give up family ties and wealth in order to follow him (Luke 5:1-11; 9:57-62; 18:18-30). On the other hand, a group of elite women use their wealth to provide for Jesus and his disciples (8:1-3). The same dual message appears in the early chapters of Acts. On the one hand, the community replicates the classical ideal of friendship by having all possessions in common (Acts 2:43-47). On the other, some wealthy persons sell property that they contribute to the community coffers, but do not give up all their property (Acts 4:32-37). What the Gospel requires of a prosperous Christian is an openhanded generosity toward others — even toward those who are not bound to the donor by ties of family or friendship. It warns of the danger that one can be overwhelmed by the desire for money (16:1-13), but does not demand voluntary poverty of all disciples.

Scenes that involve hospitality or the behavior of hosts and guests at meals figure prominently in the Gospel. Some come with a straightforward positive or negative evaluation of the behavior involved. The hospitality which the disciples exhibit on the road to Emmaus occasions Jesus' self-revelation (Luke 24:28-31). On the negative side, the ostentatious luxury of the rich man's daily banquets while a diseased, poor, starving Lazarus is at his door being licked by feral dogs sets a tone of moral revulsion at the very opening of that parable (16:19-21). Other scenes are more complex. Some persons who appear to be engaged in socially appropriate or commonly accepted behavior come in for criticism. The brief scene involving Martha and Mary (10:38-42) remains a thorn in the side of interpreters. On the one hand, Jesus appears to be following one of his mission rules, accepting the hospitality of whatever house offers a welcome (10:7). Martha's efforts to provide hospitality would have seemed appropriate for such an honored guest as Jesus. On the other hand, Jesus said that his family are those who hear and do the word of God. Mary has abandoned the social role expected of her in order to hear the word of the Lord. Jesus rebukes Martha and praises Mary. Jesus suggests that Martha has made the wrong choice in serving. She should join her sister. Yet Jesus' mode of itinerant preaching leaves him dependent on the hospitality of others. Luke has already told readers that Jesus and his disciples are dependent upon the patronage of a group of wealthy women (8:1-3). Providing for the needs of Jesus and his disciples could be passed on to slaves by the wealthy, but

Martha's demand for her sister's help suggests that there are no slaves to do the work in their house.

A more dramatic story of Jesus taking on his host's objection to socially inappropriate behavior by a female occurs earlier in the Gospel. The setting is a formal banquet in a Pharisee's house. Since Jesus has been invited and is reclining on a couch, he must be one of ten or so important guests at the meal. For a woman known as a sinner to come up weeping, anoint Jesus' feet, and dry them with her hair is offensive at least — and perhaps even sexually shocking (Luke 7:36-50). As the story unfolds, Jesus excoriates his host for failing to show suitable hospitality to his guests. A man wealthy enough to have a dining room in which guests recline could have provided water to wash their feet. Thanks to her faith and love the woman's sins are forgiven. This tale appears to be a distant relative of one found in the other Gospels in which a woman anoints Jesus at a dinner shortly before the passion. There Jesus must defend her use of valuable ointment against the objection that it should have been sold for the poor (Mark 14:3-9). Luke does not have that episode in his Jerusalem section. Perhaps he dropped it, since he had already used this story from his special tradition.

The journey narrative has meal scenes in each of the three sections. The first section contains another dinner with a Pharisee (11:37-38). The dinner setting is Luke's creation since his source had the lapse in hand washing as an observation made about the behavior of some of Jesus' disciples (Mark 7:2). Luke has Jesus himself break the local Pharisaic customs and follow that up with a set of judgment sayings against Pharisees and legal experts (vv. 39-52). The hostility aroused by such behavior and speech (vv. 53-54) cannot be entirely unexpected.

A block of meal traditions in the second section of the journey to Jerusalem (14:1-24) opens with another case in which the Evangelist transposes a traditional episode to a meal setting. The dispute over healing a man with dropsy takes place as Jesus is on his way to a Sabbath meal with a prominent Pharisee (14:1-6). The same argument over Sabbath healing was presented at the end of the previous section. The setting for that story was a synagogue and the patient a paralyzed woman (13:10-17).

The remaining meal traditions in ch. 14 play off social conventions attached to banqueting in the ancient world. Seating order demonstrates an individual's place in the local hierarchy and the host's esteem. Jesus speaks in the mode of a wisdom teacher against pushing oneself forward.

Better to be moved up by the host than sent down (14:7-11). Ordinarily a host expected reciprocal hospitality from those invited. Jesus sets a different standard of hospitality that makes hospitality part of the Gospel's teaching on proper use of wealth. Invite those who are poor, crippled, and blind, that is, persons who have nothing to offer in return. God pays their "social debts" (14:12-14). Luke has Jesus drive that point home with the parable of the Great Banquet (vv. 15-24). In addition to the feasting that opens the parable of the Rich Man and Lazarus, this section also contains another parable that includes a banquet. The elder brother in the parable of the Prodigal Son reacts with anger to the celebration their father orders up when his brother returns. The elder son perceives the feasting as a mark of honor that he has never enjoyed and that his brother does not deserve (15:23-30). As in the case of the Pharisee and the sinful woman, this parable justifies the priority which Jesus places on seeking out the sinner.

The last stop on Jesus' journey up to Jerusalem is also the setting for the final public demonstration of hospitality. Jesus invites himself to be the guest of Zacchaeus, a tax collector. Zacchaeus responds by giving half his wealth to the poor and paying restitution to those he has defrauded. Stories of notorious wastrels converted to virtue by hearing a famous philosopher may have been familiar to Jesus' audience. This type of conversion is the point of Jesus' entire ministry (19:10). Thus Luke has used the cultural conventions surrounding banqueting to illustrate such important facets of Jesus' teaching as generosity to the poor, forgiveness of sinners, humility rather than social power, and the priority to be given to the word of God.

Luke is a storyteller on two levels: the narrative about Jesus and the stories that Jesus tells within that narrative (the parables). Since many of the best-known parables are found in the special Lukan material that the Evangelist has placed in the travel narrative, it is difficult to know which features of these parables derive from the literary activity of the Evangelist and which came to him. *Gos. Thom.* 63 has a parable of the Rich Fool, but that version appears to be a later redaction of the story. It displays the anti-business animus found in other *Gos. Thom.* sayings. Luke's parable has a more direct link to the agricultural setting characteristic of Jesus' parables. The abundant harvest is clearly God's gift for which the fool ought to return thanks by generous giving to others. *Gos. Thom.* 63 does include the character's inner dialogue, which also adds a dramatic touch to several of the special Lukan parables (Luke 12:16-21; 15:32; 16:1-8; 18:1-8; 18:9-14). Its use across a number of Luke's parables suggests that the Evangelist may have introduced or highlighted this element when he found it in his sources.[8] Luke exhibits a literary penchant for direct speech rather than reported speech in other parables. The Rich Man and Lazarus involves an extended though fruitless negotiating session between the rich man burning in hell and Abraham (16:19-31). The Prodigal Son (15:11-32) has both inner dialogue, the prodigal with himself, and direct speech, the exchanges between the father and each son.

Luke often uses parables as example stories. He can situate a parable in a context which indicates the virtue that it is intended to exemplify. The parable of the Rich Fool follows Jesus' refusal to mediate a dispute between two brothers over an inheritance (12:13-14/*Gos. Thom.* 72) and an introductory warning against greed (12:15). The Prodigal Son is the last in a collection of three parables which serve as reply to grumbling about Jesus' practice of receiving and eating with tax collectors and sinners (15:1-2). Luke uses the Good Samaritan (10:30-37) to fill out the "love your neighbor as yourself" side of the great commandment. In the parables of the Unjust Steward (16:1-8) and the Rich Man and Lazarus (16:19-31) the sayings placed between the two parables show that the Evangelist considers them example stories warning against greed.

Luke 16:13 insists that it is impossible to combine love of God and love of money, and 16:14 accuses the Pharisees of being "lovers of money," although there is no historical basis for such a charge against the Pharisees as a group. Nor do the sayings that follow in the Gospel substantiate the assertion (16:15-18). The Evangelist may have inferred that greed was a characteristic vice of the Pharisees from something in his sources. The version of Mark known to Matthew includes a controversy story in which Jesus

---

8. The inner dialogue may be typical of "fool" stories. *1 Enoch* 97:8-10 has a similar version of this story that like *Gos. Thom.* assumes the rich have set out to gain their wealth unjustly: "Woe unto you who gain silver and gold by unjust means; you will then say, 'We have grown rich and accumulated goods, we have acquired everything we desired. So now let us do whatever we like; for we have gathered silver . . . it shall take off from you quickly for you have acquired it all unjustly and you shall be given over to a great curse" (*OTP* I, 78). This version is not identical to Luke's parable. It lacks the element of false use of what has been given by God the benefactor. The imagery of a God who is not selective in his benefits also occurs in Matthew's version of the injunction to love one's enemies (Matt 5:45: God makes the sun shine and sends rain on just and unjust; Luke 6:35-36 lacks this imagery but has "kind, merciful" as an attribute of God).

charges the Pharisees and scribes who object to a lack of purity rites among the disciples with traditions in violation of the obligation to care for one's parents (Mark 7:1-13/Matt 15:1-9). A non-Jewish reader unfamiliar with dedication of goods to the Temple (corban) might conclude that Jesus is accusing his opponents of manipulating religious rules for personal greed. However, one cannot be certain that Luke knew this story, as it falls in the section of Mark from which there are no parallels in his Gospel. Luke does retain the charge which Jesus made against scribes in Jerusalem that they "devour widows' houses" (Mark 12:40/Luke 20:47) and may have thought that what was true of scribes also applied to Pharisees. Or Luke may be treating the term "mammon" in 16:13 as a cipher for any concern that displaces single-hearted devotion to God.[9] In the case of the Pharisees, what displaces genuine love for God is not desire for money per se, but a concern to maintain the appearances of righteousness. Luke's parable of the Pharisee and the Tax Collector turns this issue into one of self-deception. The Pharisee's regard for his own piety alienates him from others and even from the God he thinks he is serving (Luke 18:10-14).

Luke provides the two parables in ch. 18 with brief sentences that suggest how each parable is to be applied: "it is necessary to pray always and not become discouraged" for the Widow and the Unjust Judge (18:2-5). He follows that parable with comments by Jesus. God is not like the judge, so God's concern for the elect is genuine, not compelled as in the story. This correction on Luke's part highlights an important question facing interpreters of the parables. Does every master, king, host, and father stand as a direct image of God? Or are the characters all types of human beings who will either discover a way of acting appropriately to God's reign, as in the case of the father welcoming his prodigal son, or fail to do so, as did the rich man who ignored the starving Lazarus at his door? Or, in a somewhat more complex literary construction, the central figure in a parable may be an example of a kind of prudence and decisive action that disciples can emulate in the proper context, but not in the actual, self-serving context of the story, like the unjust steward who pulls a fast one on his master to secure his future. In the Prodigal Son, the father's words make it clear what the elder brother ought to do — come inside and join the party, but the story does not tell us what he did do. Thus even among the parables that Luke presents

---

9. So Fitzmyer, *Luke X-XXIV,* 1112. Fitzmyer points out that Jesus is still replying to ridicule directed against him by the Pharisees.

as example stories there is room for differences in interpretation. Expectations that the hearer brings to the story may be challenged or may determine the conclusion reached about those stories which have ambiguous main characters or open-ended conclusions.

Characters in the Gospel

The characters in Luke's most famous parables are so etched in Christian imagination that readers often forget that they belong to stories within the story. In the overlap between parables and the larger narrative in the various meal and hospitality scenes the setting with its focus on a central typical figure seems very close to the example story type of parable. Jesus and the sinful woman at the Pharisee's dinner or Jesus visiting Martha and Mary or getting Zacchaeus out of his tree to act as host often function as mini-parables in Christian preaching. Luke's interest in the individuals around Jesus provides a richer cast of characters than in Mark, for example. In the birth legends which introduce the Gospel the reader meets a number of characters who never appear in the story again. Aside from Jesus, only his mother and the Baptist figure in Jesus' adult life. Even they are somewhat at the margins. His mother appears again only in the saying about Jesus' true family (Luke 8:21). She is not explicitly mentioned at the cross. Because Luke has recast the "rejection at Nazareth" into an inaugural sermon in the synagogue there, she does not appear there either. The crowd merely refers to his father Joseph (4:22; contrast Mark 6:3). One might think that Luke forgot about her, but he is careful to include her among the disciples gathered in Jerusalem to await the coming of the Spirit (Acts 1:14).

Although Luke gives the Baptist a major role in preparing for Jesus, he actually mentions John's arrest before indicating that Jesus was baptized by John (Luke 3:21). In fact, the brief notice about John's arrest in Luke 3:19-20 is all the reader will hear about the matter. Luke has a version of Herod's suspicion that Jesus might be the Baptist back from the dead (Luke 9:7-9/Mark 6:14-16), but he omits the tale of why Herod beheaded the prophet. He has inserted the Q material about the Baptist sending disciples to ask Jesus if he is the Messiah between the healing of the widow's son at Nain and the story of the sinful woman at the Pharisee's dinner (Luke 7:18-35/Matt. 11:2-19). This block of material is independent of the infancy narrative traditions about the Baptist with which Luke opened the Gospel. Because of the peculiar way in which Luke reports that Jesus was baptized by John (3:21a), there is no narrative depiction of contact between the two men earlier in the Gospel. Thus Luke avoids the problem created by a narrative such as Matthew's in which the Baptist acknowledged Jesus when he came for baptism but later has doubts. As Luke tells the story, Jesus came along with the crowds for baptism and was not singled out by John at that time.

Luke may have added 3:21 to his Q source so that Jesus performs the miracles to show the Baptist's emissaries that he is the one who was foretold in the prophets. Several Isaiah texts may be invoked as the basis for the list. Luke's reader already knows Isa 61:1 as the key text for Jesus' ministry, since Jesus employed it for his inaugural sermon in Nazareth (Luke 4:18-21). Jesus is the one anointed with God's Spirit to bring healing and peace to the people. The Baptist remains a prophetic figure, albeit the final appearance of the great Elijah sent to prepare them for the day of the Lord (7:27-28, citing Mal 3:1). Luke adds another redactional note here. John's preaching had divided the people between those who accepted his message and were baptized, "the people and the tax collectors," and those who did not, Pharisees and Torah experts (7:29-30). The final section of this episode contains Jesus' parable of Children Squabbling over What to Play. In the end, both the Baptist and Jesus have their critics. Jesus will be repeatedly condemned as "a friend of tax collectors and sinners" (v. 34).

Luke's representation of John the Baptist has occasioned considerable discussion about John's place in salvation history. On the one hand, without the forerunner, Jesus could hardly claim to be the one who would inaugurate God's reign. On the other, Luke appears to set the Baptist more squarely in the time of Israel as the final prophet than Mark and Matthew do. Not only does he fail to narrate the tale of the Baptist's death, which anticipates Jesus' own execution in the other two Gospels. Luke also drops the discussion about the Baptist as Elijah that occurs during the descent from the Mount of Transfiguration (Mark 9:11-12). The Evangelist's final reference to the Baptist is an enigmatic saying (Luke 16:16) that has something of an analogue in Matthew's version of the Q speech (Matt 11:12-14). Matthew has the Baptist as Elijah on the kingdom side of salvation history with the Torah and the prophets on the other. Luke's formulation shifts the balance. The Baptist is on the edge of the kingdom, but still a figure anchored in the past, in the story of Israel. This perspective anchoring John in Israel's story of salvation is reinforced when the Evangelist adds the infancy narratives as the opening chapters of his Gospel. Although the chronology of Luke 2:1 situates the birth of Jesus in the reign of Augustus eighty or ninety years before Luke wrote, the language and images used in the birth stories evoke more distant times depicted in Israel's sacred texts.

The Baptist's father is in the midst of his sacred duties as priest in the Temple when the angel appears to him. Josephus treats his readers to an elaborate description of the Temple buildings and of the High Priest in full regalia in his account of the Jewish revolt (*War* 5.184-237). The high priest only officiated on the Sabbath and other special holy days. Josephus's audience, like Luke's, knows that the Jewish sanctuary was destroyed in 70 C.E. A non-Jewish audience may not have been sympathetic to the Jewish people. Vespasian and Titus had employed the triumph in Judea for their own political purposes. But Roman religious practice involved scrupulous attention to the details of sacrificial rituals and careful inspection of omens. Any flaw in the rite could require beginning again from the beginning. Josephus remarks in passing that Jewish priests avoided strong drink lest they make some mistake in performing their ritual duties (5.229). The atmosphere of scrupulous ritual piety that pervades the stories in Luke 1–2 would have been familiar to Luke's readers. Although Zechariah would not have been alone while performing his duties, Luke sets the scene as though he was. The audience would be familiar with the tension in a crowd when an officiating priest did not appear as expected. Has some procedural flaw invalidated the rite? The Evangelist has the crowd give Zechariah's delay and subsequent dumbness a benign interpretation: it is the consequence of an encounter with a divine messenger, not an omen of impending disaster. Zechariah continues to fulfill priestly duties for the rest of his allotted term of service (1:23).

If Luke was responsible for bringing together birth legends about John the Baptist with other legends about the birth of Jesus, as seems to be the case, he must have devised the chronological framework that coordinates the two births. Gabriel does not visit Mary until Elizabeth is in her sixth month (1:26). The announcement of Jesus' birth is similar to that of the Baptist but involves both a new, special relationship to God on the part of the infant and the fulfillment of Israel's hopes for a Davidic Messiah. Unlike Zechariah, Mary is favored by God. She responds appropriately to learning of God's plan. Elizabeth's pregnancy becomes a sign that Gabriel's word to Mary is true. Luke may have invented the kinship relation between the young girl from a Galilean village and the aging woman of priestly lineage who lived in Judea in order to bring the two together as a culminating event in the announcement cycle. There are no other hints of a genealogical tie between the Baptist and Jesus in the tradition. Both Elizabeth and the child in her womb acknowledge that Mary is carrying the long-awaited Savior. Luke has Elizabeth use the christological title "Lord" (1:43). Mary is overshadowed by God's Spirit in conceiving her child. Elizabeth is inspired by the Spirit as she acknowledges that child (1:41).

Two other minor characters encounter the infant and his parents in the Temple, Simeon and Anna. Both are archetypes of aged, faithful, pious persons who pray and wait for God's salvation. Simeon also possesses the Holy Spirit (2:25-27). It is possible that these recognition stories were originally independent of the annunciation cycle, since Simeon's canticle declaring Jesus to be God's salvation for God's people (2:29-32) causes his parents amazement (v. 33).[10] Simeon's prophetic oracle about the infant and his mother is more ominous. She will suffer as a consequence of the opposition to her son (2:34-35). Luke does not dramatize the meeting with the second figure, the elderly widow Anna, who lives fasting and praying in the Temple. The audience is informed that as she not only praises God but begins telling other worshipers about him, Anna, too, is inspired by the Holy Spirit (2:36-38).

All the characters in the infancy narratives differ from those that readers encounter in the story of Jesus' adult life in that they are archetypal examples of piety and recipients of God's Spirit. Mary can be included as the exemplar for those who hear the word of God and do it (Luke 8:21). Zechariah's slight lapse aside, he is a model of ancient, priestly piety. Luke also incorporates briefer notices indicating that both the Baptist (1:80) and Jesus (2:40, 52) assimilated the ancestral piety of their families as they grew up.

After this extensive account of John the Baptist's conception and birth, his minimal role in the story of Jesus' ministry is somewhat surprising. Luke compensates for that reduction somewhat by adding to the Q tradition about John the Baptist's preaching. John shifts away from apocalyptic prophecy to provide the crowds with moral instruction (3:10-14). Though the Baptist is a figure in the line of the Hebrew prophets in Luke's picture of salvation history, the moral precepts he teaches could have come from almost any teacher in the Greco-Roman world. The first two fit

10. So Bovon, *Luke* I, 104.

Luke's interest in generosity and proper use of wealth. Disciples should share their excess with persons who lack clothing and food. Tax collectors are to refrain from the usual method of enriching oneself, which was collecting more than is owed. John's advice to soldiers does not have as obvious a tie to teachings of Jesus in the Gospel. Luke may have included this example of moral conversion to demonstrate that John the Baptist did in fact accomplish the change of heart predicted by Gabriel (1:17) and mentioned again in Zechariah's canticle (1:77). Luke's characterization of the Baptist is similar to that of Josephus: "He was a good man and exhorted the Jews to practice virtue, with both justice (or righteousness) toward one another and piety toward God" (*Antiquities* 18.117). Josephus is careful to present the Baptist as more a moralist than a populist prophet by insisting that John's baptism was a physical sign of the individual's ethical conversion. Luke is not as touchy on the subject of baptism. He knows that disciples of the Baptist continued to teach and baptize after John's death (Acts 18:25). Like Josephus, Luke appears to be recasting the populist appeal for repentance in categories that an educated, non-Jewish audience would readily understand.

Gabriel told Zechariah that his child would be a source of joy and gladness not only to his parents but to many people (1:14). This mood of rejoicing and praising God dominates the infancy stories (1:64; 2:20, 28, 38) and continues to be the response of individuals or crowds throughout much of the Gospel. It is the proper response to miracles (5:25b-26; 7:16-17; 10:17; 13:13; Acts 3:8). Jesus' parables of finding what is lost also conclude with celebration (Luke 15:6, 9, 22-24, 32). The quick turn from joy to violence at Jesus' inaugural sermon in Nazareth fulfills Simeon's prophecy and points to the darker side of the story (4:16-30). Luke 7:29-30 adds a narrator's note to remind readers that those who went out to hear the Baptist were divided. Some who were sinners like revenue collectors repented; Pharisees and others learned in the Torah did not. Those who refused to repent were disobeying God's will (7:30). The story of a sinful woman who is forgiven and the Pharisee who has failed in his basic obligations as host follows closely upon that statement as if to illustrate the point. The Baptist may be off the scene but repentance and forgiveness are available in Jesus (Luke 7:36-50).

Pharisees and scribes or Torah scholars (lawyers) generally appear as the ones who are out to spoil the party. Yet Luke's characterization of the Pharisees is not quite as flat as Matthew's. Pharisees invite Jesus to dine with them (7:36; 14:1) and warn him that Herod wants to kill him (13:31). Where Mark implicates Pharisees and Herodians in a plot to kill Jesus early in the story (Mark 3:6), Luke moderates the end of that scene. They consult with each other over "what they might do to Jesus" (Luke 6:11). Though Luke attributes a mindless anger to the Pharisees, their anger is not murderous. The last time the Pharisees appear in Luke's Gospel they ask Jesus to silence the crowds as he enters Jerusalem (19:39).

Luke retains the picture of Pharisees as a group concerned over details of legal observance and purification found in Mark (Luke 5:30/Mark 2:16, "scribes of the Pharisees"; Luke 5:33/Mark 2:18; Luke 6:2/Mark 2:24; Luke 6:7/Mark 3:6; Luke 11:37-39/Mark 7:1-3). He also adds Pharisees to his Markan source (Luke 5:21/Mark 2:6) and repeats the woes against them from the Q material (Luke 11:42-43/Matt 23:6-7, 23-25). The Pharisees and scribes protest Jesus' association with sinners and tax collectors (5:30; 7:39; 15:2). The parable of the Pharisee and Tax Collector allows Luke's audience to see the disastrous consequences of a Pharisee's commitment to keeping himself separate from sinners, a delusional self-congratulation that has cut him off from God as the source of righteousness (18:9-14).

In Acts, the Pharisees are presented as a sect or school. Paul exploits his own membership in that group to set Pharisees against Sadducees in the Sanhedrin (Acts 23:6-9). Christians who were also Pharisees seek to require circumcision and Torah observance from non-Jewish converts (Acts 15:5). The Pharisee Gamaliel encourages the Sanhedrin to let Peter and John go. If they are engaged in a human fabrication, it will die out soon enough. If they are from God, nothing can stand in the way (Acts 5:33-40). Thus Luke provides a mixed picture of the Pharisees. Some serve as characters to whom moral lapses can be attributed such as self-righteousness, a harsh attitude toward sinners, and condemnation of Jesus, who enacts God's own desire to seek out and rescue the sinner.

Luke's mixed picture of the Pharisees fits a general pattern in his narrative. He usually mitigates opposition and misunderstanding. That makes the murderous outbreak at the end of Jesus' inaugural sermon in Nazareth (Luke 4:28-29) all the more striking. In many of the episodes Jesus is received by the people as one who brings salvation. Luke also pushes Satan to the margins for most of the story. Luke ends the scene of Jesus being tested by Satan with the comment, "the devil left him until the opportune moment (kairos)" (4:13). That special moment comes when it is time for the passion. At that moment, Satan enters Judas Iscariot (22:3).

226

Thus although Jesus heals those afflicted by evil spirits (6:17-19), it is possible to see the public ministry as a Spirit-filled time when the forces of evil are well in check. Luke has no sense of the apocalyptic conflict in which the power of Jesus is on the offensive against that of Satan such as one finds in Mark.

Since Luke's narrative carries the story of Jesus' disciples forward into Acts, his readers know that the disciples will go on to preach the gospel even when imprisoned, dragged before the Sanhedrin, and threatened with death. Once the disciples have received the Holy Spirit, all the weakness and uncertainty that they exhibit during Jesus' public ministry vanishes. Judas, on the other hand, has been infected by evil. Luke defers an account of Judas's death until the opening chapter of Acts (1:16-20) unlike Matthew, who inserted a different legend about Judas' suicide into the passion narrative itself (Matt 27:3-9). Luke's Judas purchases a field with the blood money and suffers a gruesome accident there, which every ancient reader would recognize as divine retribution. The Twelve are a symbolic group selected from a larger contingent of eyewitnesses and followers. They do not represent a permanent communal structure whose members are replaced as they die off. But Judas's place does have to be filled before the disciples receive the Spirit and commence the mission entrusted to them (Acts 1:21-26).

Luke anticipates the larger group of disciples at three points in the Gospel: in a notice that a group of prominent women accompanied Jesus and provided for the group out of their resources (Luke 8:1-3), in the commission of seventy-two to preach and heal (10:1-12, 17-20), and in the addition of unnamed male followers to the group of women who witness Jesus' crucifixion (23:49). The two disciples on the road to Emmaus presumably belong to that larger group (24:13-35). By establishing the existence of such a large group of women and men around Jesus, Luke changes the tenor of the passion story. Jesus does not die abandoned by all except a few women as he does in Mark. Although the Twelve may have fled Gethsemane, Jesus' followers remain firmly in place in Jerusalem.

Given this tendency to present more ambiguity in some of the minor characters, it is no surprise that Luke's descriptions of the Twelve remove the harsh edges that make them appear alienated from Jesus in Mark's account. Luke does not have a parallel to the second storm at sea miracle in Mark (6:45-52), which ended with the accusation that the disciples had become hardhearted. When Luke rewrites the first sea miracle (Mark 4:35-41;

Luke 8:22-25), Jesus issues a milder rebuke: "Where is your faith?" (v. 25). He does not accuse them of having "no faith" as he does in Mark. Luke drops Peter's negative response to Jesus' first passion prediction altogether (Luke 9:21-26/Mark 8:30-38).

The disciples continue to be much closer to Jesus as he moves toward Jerusalem. Luke edits the transfiguration scene so that Peter, James, and John are overcome with sleep as Jesus speaks with Moses and Elijah about his impending departure (Luke 9:28-32a) and drops the discussion of Jesus' impending death and resurrection found in Mark (Mark 9:9-13). Instead of having Jesus order the disciples to remain silent about these events, Luke merely states that they did not tell anyone about them at the time (Luke 9:36). Mark has an ironic twist in which James and John ask Jesus for the top positions of authority in his kingdom immediately after Jesus has predicted the passion for the third time (Mark 10:35-45). Luke drops that episode. Instead he incorporates into the symposium part of Jesus' final meal a general debate over which of the disciples was greatest. Jesus intervenes with the sayings about greatness that form the conclusion of this *chreia* (Luke 22:24-27). Luke also supplements the prediction that Peter will deny Jesus with sayings which point to a future beyond that disaster. The denial itself represents a winnowing by Satan — who rejoined the story when he entered Judas a few verses earlier. In Peter's case Jesus has prayed so that the apostle will not lose his faith. Eventually Peter will turn and strengthen the rest (22:31-34). Luke also changes the narrative order so that Peter's denials occur at the high priest's house before anything has happened to the prisoner. Jesus is able to look at Peter just after the third denial, which sends Peter out weeping (22:54-62).

Just as the inappropriate request of James and John was shifted to the disciples as a group, so the whole group, not just Peter, James, and John, is told to pray in Gethsemane. Luke attributes their falling asleep to grief (22:45-46). When Jesus wakes them after his own prayer, he repeats the command to pray not to enter into temptation or testing (vv. 40, 46). At that moment the arresting party arrives on scene. The disciples' failure is not rubbed in by repetition as it is in Mark 14:32-42. Despite their weaknesses during the passion in Luke, the disciples, both men and women, remain a cohesive group throughout the events. The women can report their experience at the tomb to the larger group. The disciples know where to find the others when they hurry back to Jerusalem from Emmaus. Thus Luke's portrayal of the disciples guarantees that continuity of eyewitness testimony to the events of salvation stipulated in the selection of Matthias: "who have accompanied us during all the time that the Lord Jesus went in and out among us, beginning from the baptism of John until the day when he was taken up from us — one of these must become a witness with us to the resurrection" (Acts 1:21-22).

Any reader who comes to Luke after reading Mark and Matthew will immediately notice that many more women appear in this Gospel. Stories in which women are important actors occur in all sections of the Gospel. Luke's special material supplements the stories that he has from Mark. Luke's source for the announcement and birth of John the Baptist was centered on the father, Zechariah, just as Matthew's legends about Jesus are centered on Joseph. However, all of Luke's material about the annunciation, birth, and childhood of Jesus centers on his mother Mary. She is the one who exemplifies "hearing and doing the word of God." She is the one addressed by Simeon's oracle. It was her purification after childbirth that brought the family into the Temple. Mary's canticle matches that spoken by the Baptist's father in length and poetic resonances. Mary is the one who keeps and ponders in her heart the events surrounding her son's birth. These scenes are so familiar, particularly in Christian churches that celebrate feasts in honor of the Virgin Mary, that they hardly seem unusual. But this picture is in striking contrast to the other two Synoptic Gospels where Mary is a very minor character. Perhaps most astonishing to an ancient audience is the small detail in which the one who rebukes the twelve-year-old boy for staying behind in the Temple is not his father but his mother (2:48).

Given this focus on Mary at the beginning, her near invisibility during the public ministry of Jesus is somewhat surprising. The people in the Nazareth synagogue identify Jesus as "the son of Joseph" (4:22). Perhaps Luke wishes to indicate that there were no rumors about Jesus' conception in the village. Mary's objection to the angel's initial words about her son and her three months with Elizabeth have made it clear to the reader that Joseph was not the biological father of the child. To those in the village, however, Jesus is nothing out of the ordinary. Luke clued his readers in on this distinction between the public perception of Jesus' origins and the truth at the beginning of the genealogy in 3:23-38: "he was the son (as was thought) of Joseph."

Luke first introduces women characters as recipients of gifts of salvation. Jesus comes upon a widow burying her son and restores life to the youth without being asked (7:11-17). Since the previous story involved healing a slave who was near death (7:1-10; Matt 8:5-13), the second story demonstrates greater power on Jesus' part than the first. After the interlude on John the Baptist (Luke 7:18-35), the story of the sinful woman who anoints Jesus in a Pharisee's house draws on the contrast between "the people and tax collectors," who respond enthusiastically to the message of salvation, and "the Pharisees and lawyers" (7:29-30). The verbal exchange in the *chreia* does not involve the woman directly. It pits Jesus against the Pharisee, who needs to be converted to the will of God. But both his character flaws as host and the previous statement about "Pharisees and lawyers" make that outcome unlikely, though the episode itself never gives the Pharisee's final word on the matter. Instead, Jesus turns to the woman and announces that her sins are forgiven. Since the Pharisees as a group find Jesus' association with sinners a stumbling block (15:2), the question these words elicit from the other guests should probably be treated as a negative reaction. None of Jesus' appeals, whether in argument or parable, appear to have changed their minds.

This section of the Gospel contains three more references to women, two taken from Mark. Jesus' mother and brothers cannot reach Jesus because of the crowd (Luke 8:19-21/Mark 3:31-35). Luke has moved that episode so that it follows Jesus' teaching on parables and dissociated it from accusations that Jesus employs the powers of Beelzebub to which it was attached in Mark. The exemplary faith of the woman who had suffered hemorrhages for twelve years is also from Mark (Luke 8:42b-48/Mark 5:24b-34). Luke adds to these traditional scenes the notice about women disciples who are accompanying Jesus (8:1-3). Luke gives this group two attributes. First, they have all been healed of either illness or demonic possession by Jesus. Contrary to much later tradition, Mary Magdalene belongs to this group. She is not a prostitute or a sinful woman. Nor does she have a particularly close relationship with Jesus. Second, the women in this group, unlike Mary or Elizabeth, apparently have independent financial resources. They are acting as patrons for Jesus and the Twelve. The women who are mentioned in the crucifixion and resurrection stories belong to this cadre of female disciples.

The women encountered during the journey to Jerusalem as well as the women characters in parables of Jesus provide additional examples of women as hosts, as hearers of God's word (Martha and Mary, 10:38-42), as recipients of healing (13:10-17), and even as widows forced to exist on their own. Anna did so by adopting a biblical archetype of the pious widow living a life of fasting and prayer. When Jesus restored life to the widow's son at Nain, he may have thus spared her the fate of the widow in his parable of the Unjust Judge. In that story, the widow has to badger the judge almost to the point of physical blows to obtain her rights (18:2-5). Luke matches the parable of the Lost Sheep (Luke 15:3-7/Matt 18:12-14) with another in which a woman seeks a lost coin (Luke 15:8-10). Both parables are part of an attempt to persuade Jesus' critics that seeking out sinners is God's plan. The two short parables are a prelude to the extended drama of the Prodigal Son.

Luke's eschatological sayings about the sudden appearance of the Son of Man add the story of Sodom and Gomorrah (Luke 17:27-30, 32) to that of the flood (17:26-27/Matt 24:37-39) as an example of sudden, catastrophic judgment. After picking up Mark's warning to flee without even going inside (Mark 13:14-16/Luke 17:31), the Evangelist remembers that Lot's wife made the crucial mistake of looking back (17:32). While on the road during the travel section, Jesus responds to a woman in the crowd who shouts out a blessing on his mother with a phrase similar to that used earlier of his true family, "blessed are those who hear the word of God and keep it" (Luke 11:27-28; cf. 8:21). Luke may have found the exchange in his special material. A variant occurs in *Gos. Thom.* 79, which combines the reply to a beatitude on Jesus' mother with a prophecy that Jesus makes to the mourning women in Jerusalem on his way to the cross in Luke's Gospel (23:28).

The dramatic encounter between Jesus and the women of Jerusalem (23:26-30) serves as a final lament over the fate of the city. Luke's audience has already heard two such laments. The first (13:33-35) makes Jesus' death there — not at Herod's hands in Galilee — a divine necessity. Jerusalem has a sorry history of killing prophets and emissaries of God. The second (19:41-44) foresees destruction for the city, not peace. Luke incorporates words from the prophet Hosea into the final lament (23:30; Hos. 10:8). A proverbial saying at the end of the scene (v. 31) invites readers to view the events which put Jesus on the cross as part of a much greater tragedy to overtake Jerusalem. The two previous laments link the fate of the city with its refusal to accept Jesus as way to peace. The city's opportunity does not end with the cross. Luke presents the first sermons of the disciples in Jerusalem as a second opportunity (Acts 2:22-36; 3:17-26). Though Jesus tells the women that it is inappropriate for them to lament his death (Luke

23:28), their presence demonstrates that not all of Jerusalem's inhabitants are implicated in the actions of those who put him on the cross. This motif is further expanded as some of the crowds who have seen Jesus die return home lamenting what has happened (23:48) This episode also serves as a partial replacement for the anonymous woman who anoints Jesus in anticipation of his death in Mark 14:3-9 (also Matt 26:6-13). Luke does not repeat that meal story perhaps because he has told a story about the woman who washed Jesus' feet with her tears earlier.

Jesus' women disciples play the same role in Luke's account of Jesus' death, burial, and resurrection as they do in Mark. The Evangelist modifies only a few details. Just as there are additional male followers who witness the crucifixion, so the group of Galilean women is larger than the few names mentioned in Mark 15:40. Luke does not give any women's names until after the encounter with the angel (24:10). Even there he adds "and others." Another modification in detail picks up the tone of observant piety with which the Gospel began. The women had begun preparing the spices, but the Sabbath interrupted their part in the burial process. Luke gives a biblical solemnity to the interruption: "On the Sabbath they rested according to the commandment" (23:56b). They return to the tomb as soon as it is possible to resume their activities (24:1). Thus the entire sequence has almost obliterated any hint that Jesus might have died abandoned, alone, or left in the hands of strangers. He is mourned by his own followers from Galilee, by the women of Jerusalem, and by others in the city. A pious member of the Sanhedrin said to have dissented from the council's actions provides a burial place. The Galilean women disciples make all the appropriate preparations to bury a revered figure.

Jesus in Luke's Gospel

Since Luke has adopted the literary conventions of ancient biography, readers would expect the infancy narratives to provide evidence of the subject's future greatness. The disciples' question after the sea miracle, "Who is this?" (Luke) and that posed by the Baptist, "Are you the one who is to come?" (7:19) have already been answered for the reader in the opening scenes. Jesus is more than a prophet like Elijah or the Baptist and greater than a divinely chosen king like David because God has formed this child through the Spirit working in his mother's womb. An audience attuned to biblical language, as Luke expects his readers to be, might even detect a remote echo of Genesis in Gabriel's answer to Mary's question, "How can this be?" (1:35). If they miss the allusion the first time, Luke's genealogy, progressing backward from Joseph to Adam (3:23-38), will pick it up again.

As we have noted, Luke's fidelity to his diverse sources creates some tension between the legends of divine birth and the beginning of Jesus' public life at age thirty (3:23). Jesus' official descent as far as anyone knew had nothing miraculous about it. He was considered Joseph's offspring. By ancient standards thirty suggests a mature man, not the young man so often represented in Christian art. Between the twelve-year-old, on the verge of adulthood in ancient terms, who was so anxious to be about his life's work, and the mature adult, who finally steps onto the public stage, there is nothing to report. He lived an ordinary life shaped by the meticulous piety that is exhibited by his family in the infancy narratives (2:51-52).

By coordinating Jesus' story with that of John the Baptist, Luke provides an answer to the natural question: Why such a long interval? John must complete his prophetic mission of preparing a people for the Lord's coming. Chronological notices like those Luke gives to John's prophetic call (3:1-2) were the ancient counterpart of a date in a modern biography, though most scholars today doubt the accuracy of the dates suggested in Luke's material.[11] A best guess, given the considerable problems in determining the regnal years for Tiberius, has his fifteenth year beginning in August-September of 28 C.E.,[12] though Luke may have taken his chronological markers from different sources. The census which he connects with Jesus' birth is usually dated around 6 C.E. Add on thirty years and Jesus does not begin his public ministry until sometime in 36, too late for a crucifixion under Pilate in a year when Passover coincides with a Sabbath. Perhaps Luke did not know that Pilate was removed in 36 C.E. The Baptist has a well-established core of disciples and has been imprisoned by Herod before Jesus emerges on the scene, so he appears to have been active for several years before Jesus comes to be baptized. By inserting the genealogy

---

11. Fitzmyer (*Luke I-IX*, 453) treats it as a theological note (the story of salvation belongs in a particular part of human history) and a signifier of the "Roman and Palestinian ambience" of Luke's story. While both observations are true, one should not let the historical problems over whether or not Luke has an accurate chronology (probably not) override the function of such a notice as dating in a first-century biographical or historical work.

12. Fitzmyer, *Luke I-IX*, 455.

between the baptism and temptation stories, Luke creates a time lapse between those two events, though Jesus is said to go from the Jordan to the desert. Jesus acts because he is filled with the Spirit. He is not driven into the desert immediately after his baptism as in Mark 1:12.

Jesus' official public declaration of his ministry occurs in the synagogue at Nazareth, where he claims to be the one anointed with God's Spirit mentioned in Isa 61:1-2. Luke reminds readers throughout the Gospel that Jesus is led by the Spirit (Luke 4:1, 14; 10:21). In instructing his disciples about prayer, Luke modifies the saying that God certainly answers requests. Matt 7:11b has "your Father in heaven will give good things to those who ask him." Luke 11:13 reads "the Father from heaven will give the Holy Spirit to those who ask him." This saying is one of the few cases in which Luke clearly has departed from the Q source.[13] The Holy Spirit, which this instruction makes the object of a disciple's request, comes to be a key factor in Acts.

The infancy narrative creates a problem which will explode during the trinitarian debates of later centuries: When did Jesus receive the Holy Spirit? The answer is quite straightforward in the narrative sequence that begins with Jesus' adult ministry: the Holy Spirit descends on Jesus at his baptism (3:21-22) and is directing his activities from that point forward. Not so, if the infancy narratives are taken into account. The Holy Spirit overshadows his mother at his conception and is the basis for the special status of the infant as Son of God. So there is a distinction between Jesus' connection to the Spirit and a more transient "filling with the Holy Spirit," as evident in Elizabeth's recognition that Mary's baby is her Lord (1:43) or in the relationship with a prophetic figure like the Baptist who is also full of the Spirit from his mother's womb (1:15).

This distinction between the way in which Jesus possesses the Spirit and how other humans receive the Spirit is not explained. Nor does the Gospel explain the difference between the role of the Spirit inspiring figures from the biblical past, including the Baptist, and the new descent of the Spirit on humanity inaugurated by Jesus' death and resurrection (3:16; 24:49). Traditional christological titles are used of Jesus from the opening chapters of the Gospel. In addition to "Son of God" (1:32, 35), "Son of David" (1:32b-33), "Lord" (1:43), and Messiah (2:11), Luke has the angelic choir

---

13. J. M. Robinson, et al., eds., *The Sayings Gospel Q in Greek and English* (Leuven: Peeters, 2001) 104.

introduce another epithet, "Savior." The term is first used of God (1:47) and then of Jesus (2:11; also in Acts 5:31; 13:23). This title occurs in only one other Gospel, at John 4:42, "Savior of the cosmos." Its use by Samaritan villagers in John's narrative points toward the origin of "Savior" as a christological designation among non-Jewish believers. Luke expects readers to bring these affirmations forward into the account of Jesus' ministry.

Although Luke retains some passages from Mark in which Jesus commands silence of demons or of the disciples, there is no necessity for Jesus to evade dangerous crowds or keep his messianic claims under wraps in the story as Luke tells it. As we have seen, Luke converts Jesus' command not to tell anyone about the transfiguration until after the resurrection found in Mark 9:9 into a simple statement that they did not do so (Luke 9:36b). Jesus' question, "Who do the people say that I am?" is a check to see if the disciples are on track. Peter indicates that the disciples recognize Jesus to be "the Messiah of God," unlike the crowds (9:18-21). This does not mark the central transition in the Gospel, as in Mark, or elicit the indication that Peter has been given this knowledge by God, as in Matthew.

Luke's Jesus does not withdraw to flee the crowds as in Mark. He frequently goes apart from them or from his disciples to pray. Once again, the piety so firmly established in the infancy narratives marks Jesus' adult life as well (5:16). He spends the night praying on a mountain before selecting the Twelve (6:12-13). He has been praying alone, with his disciples nearby, when he asks what the crowds are saying (9:18-20). The disciples observe Jesus praying and ask for instruction, and the Lord's Prayer and other teaching on prayer is his response (11:1-13). His prayer will protect Peter from the ravages of Satan's testing during the passion (22:32). Luke's revision of the Gethsemane prayer scene has Jesus recommend the final petition of the Lord's prayer, "not enter into temptation," rather than to "remain and watch" to his disciples (22:40, 46). Luke's Jesus does not come to his final hours in agony of soul (contrast Mark 14:34). He will tell the women of Jerusalem not to mourn for him (Luke 23:28). Throughout the Gospel, Jesus has acknowledged that his death in Jerusalem is a necessary part of God's plan (9:22, 44; 13:33). Jesus' prayer expresses a hope that the eschatological trial of the passion might somehow be avoided. This prayer should not be understood as an expression of concern for himself. The laments have already indicated that the tragedy of Jerusalem is at stake here (13:34; 23:28). Nothing less than an unlikely conversion of the leaders responsible for those events would be required.

Some manuscripts of Luke's Gospel contain an addition to Jesus' prayer in Gethsemane that often appears in artistic depictions of the scene (22:43-44): a comforting angel and drops of bloody sweat fall to the ground as Jesus engages in agonized prayer. The angel represents God's answer to Jesus' prayer. The plan will not be aborted, but God does not leave his chosen one without assistance. Those scholars who see this passage as Luke's own composition treat it as the culmination of a minor motif in the earlier references to Jesus' death. Jesus is compared to the martyred prophets from Israel's past (11:47-51; 13:34; 6:23). The Greek word *agōn* does not suggest mental anguish as in the English word "agony" but the extreme exertion of an athletic event. Both Jewish and Christian martyrdom stories use the language of the athletic arena of the martyr's triumph over the fear of death that enemies have tried to inspire in him or her. Thus these additional verses do not detract from the steady resolve to accept death in Jerusalem as part of his fate that Jesus has shown throughout the Gospel.[14]

But the case for seeing these two verses as an addition to Luke's account by second-century scribes seems marginally stronger than that for Luke's authorship. They do not appear in the earliest surviving manuscripts or in the Alexandrian traditions. By the middle of the second century the tradition was known to Justin Martyr (*Dialogue* 103.8) and slightly later to Irenaeus (*Adv. Haer.* 3.22.2). Both patristic authors cite this tradition against the tendency of some Christians in the second century (Docetists) to argue against the full humanity of Jesus. A similar theological objection was made against the *Gospel of Peter,* composed in the early second century as we have seen. Therefore some text critics suggest that scribes introduced this passage into Luke's Gospel to support an orthodox picture of Jesus.[15] It may have originated as part of the oral telling of the story before finding its way into the text of the Gospel. In some later manuscript traditions it even turns up in Matthew (after Matt 26:39). Luke himself would certainly have sided with the orthodox against any attempt to treat the humanity of Jesus as mere appearance like the appearances of gods and goddesses in Greek and Roman myths. He has made it clear that those who knew Jesus in Nazareth never saw anything but the human son

---

14. Brown, *Death,* 179-90.

15. Bruce M. Metzger and Bart D. Ehrman, *The Text of the New Testament: Its Transmission, Corruption, and Restoration* (fourth edition, New York: Oxford University Press, 2005) 286.

of Joseph. When the risen Jesus appears to the disciples at a meal in Luke 24:39-43, he demonstrates the physical reality of his risen body and even eats a piece of broiled fish. For ancient readers, Jesus' stoic determination in the face of death represents the virtue one would expect of a great man. His words to the mourning women of Jerusalem could be compared to the philosopher Socrates, who excluded his wife and child from his jail cell because of their weeping (Plato, *Phaedo* 60a).

The image of Jesus as heroic prophet/martyr fits the explanation that it was only because authorities were offended by his teaching that Jesus was executed. Luke's Gospel has toned down other disruptive elements in the Jesus traditions such as his activities as an exorcist, his ability to draw crowds that could be a source of civic disturbances, and his cleansing of the Temple. The response of those from his hometown to the first sermon and the death of the Baptist demonstrate that prophetic speech itself is sufficient to endanger one's life. Most of the central section of the Gospel, Jesus' journey to Jerusalem, is taken up with teaching. The only persons who find Jesus' words offensive are Pharisees and Torah experts. They object to his policy of extending God's forgiveness to sinners. Even such a dramatic example as the conversion of Zaccheus cannot sway Jesus' critics (19:1-10). By turning the Last Supper into a formal symposium in which the meal is followed by discussion and teaching and by adding the story of the repentant criminal to the crucifixion, Luke has Jesus continue to function as a teacher right up to his last breath. As we have noted, the risen Jesus also teaches his disciples how the Scriptures anticipated his death and resurrection.

Luke is aware that a Roman governor would hardly execute someone for the sort of teaching that Jesus engages in. He even shortens the Sanhedrin proceedings by putting most emphasis on Peter's denial at night. The prisoner is abused prior to his appearance before the council, not during its deliberations. In the Jewish investigation no formal charges are lodged against Jesus at all. A claim to be "Son of God" is said to be sufficient evidence, but of what? When Jewish officials bring Jesus to Pilate, the charges are patently untrue. Jesus is not a zealot or a Messiah king who stirs up the crowd to resist Roman rule. Luke frames their accusations so that it mirrors the zealot cause which destroyed Jerusalem some forty years after Jesus' death. Jesus is accused of first preaching rebellion in Galilee and now importing it to Jerusalem (23:5). The reference to Galilee allows Herod an opportunity to see Jesus. His interest in and possible malice toward Jesus were mentioned in 13:31-34. But Herod cannot get anything out of Jesus. Pilate announces the official verdict for both rulers: there is no evidence to substantiate the charge that Jesus was fomenting rebellion (23:13-16, 22). Any reader of Luke's Gospel would have to agree, but Pilate finally grants the wishes of those who have asked for a death sentence (vv. 23-25).

Jesus remains aloof and silent through most of the proceedings. He has always known that God's plan required him to die in Jerusalem. Not only does he accept that fate, he does so without any signs of fear or weakness. Unlike most criminals, he does not carry his cross beam to the place of execution. Luke does not explain why the execution squad conscripted Simon to do the job. Most readers and moviemakers have assumed that Jesus had become too weak to carry the beam, but Luke's audience may have drawn a very different conclusion. Notice the shift in details as Luke tells the story: the first mockery Jesus suffered was during the night after his arrest. He was blindfolded and struck, but not necessarily beaten (22:63). The second round of rough treatment, also not described as beating, came from Herod's soldiers (23:11). It ends with Jesus clothed in an elegant robe and sent back to Pilate. Pilate twice proposes flogging and release as the alternative to crucifixion (vv. 16, 22). Since this alternative is rejected, Jesus has not been flogged by the Roman guard. He still has the fine robe acquired during the visit to Herod. Luke's audience knew that important people did not receive the same treatment as common people, even when condemned to death. So they probably saw something very different as Jesus walked toward his death. The execution squad got Simon to carry the cross beam, not because Jesus was too weak but because he is an important man, not a criminal.

To demonstrate that Jesus retained his composure even at the moment of death, Luke drops the citation of Ps 22:1 which represents Jesus' last words in Mark 15:34. He substitutes a simple expression of confidence in God from Ps 31:5 (Luke 23:46). Having witnessed the noble death of his victim, the centurion draws the correct conclusion about Jesus' character: "Certainly this man was just" (Greek *dikaios;* 23:47). When used in a Jewish context the Greek term might also be translated "righteous." The NRSV translation "innocent" limits the point of the centurion's remark to a judgment about the charges discussed. But ancient readers would expect the manner of a person's death to correspond to his character. *Dikaios*, whether translated "just," as most Greek speakers would hear it, or "righteous" as Jews would understand it, refers to an individual's character. Of course, such a person would not be guilty of the absurd charges brought by Jesus' accusers, but that is not the only point made by the centurion's remark. Luke also avoids the problem of having the centurion use the christological title "Son of God" found in Mark 15:39. Luke defers mentioning the charge posted on the cross, "king of the Jews," until the execution squad has mocked Jesus (23:37-38), thus again indicating that Jesus' death was that of a noble martyr. By connecting the accusation with mockery, the Evangelist makes it even clearer that no one participating in the events which led to Jesus' death ever thought that there was a case to be made against him.

Luke picks up the language of Jesus as Savior introduced in the first chapter when he retells the crucifixion story. He reformulates an expression used by the religious officials to mock Jesus, "he saved others, he cannot save himself" (Mark 15:31), to remove the hint that perhaps Jesus *cannot* save himself. Luke writes, "he saved others, let him save himself" (Luke 23:35). Unlike his Markan source, Luke uses the verb "save" in the next two statements as well. The soldiers say, "If you are king of the Jews, save yourself" (v. 37). Finally, one of the two criminals says, "Aren't you the Messiah? Save yourself and us" (v. 39). It is the other criminal who acknowledges their guilt, castigates his associate for not recognizing that Jesus is not a criminal, and asks Jesus to remember him. Jesus promises that man paradise. Thus Luke symbolically presents the cross as a source of salvation.

Some manuscripts contain an additional statement by the crucified Jesus at the beginning of v. 34: "Jesus said, 'Father, forgive them, for they do not know what they do.'" Jesus seeks forgiveness even for those who put him to death. Again this sentiment would not surprise Luke's ancient readers. Socrates refuses to be perturbed by the injustice of those Athenians who secured his death. Those who do evil to a just person are worse off than a just person who suffers harm, in Socrates' view. Thus Jesus' acknowledgment that his enemies act in ignorance confirms his own superiority to them. Not only is the Roman execution squad ignorant of what they are doing, the responsible Jewish authorities are ignorant as well. The "they do such things" of Jesus' words to the Jerusalem women (23:31) refers to Jewish leaders. Speeches in Acts also speak of the Jewish people and their rulers having acted in ignorance (Acts 3:17; 13:27). Of course Luke's readers will also recall Jesus' earlier teaching about love of enemies (Luke 6:27-36).

The text-critical question of 23:34 remains problematic. The verse is found in some ancient manuscripts but not in others, including early papyri. It also disrupts the description of the activities of those around Jesus. The words appear in Stephen's prayer in Acts 7:60b as well as in a later story about the stoning of James the Just (Eusebius, *Hist. Eccl.* 2.23.16). Some scholars treat the verse as a later addition to the story.[16] Others incorporate it as Luke's composition, since it reflects a positive attitude toward the Jewish authorities responsible for Jesus' death whereas later Christian authors pass a harsher judgment on the Jewish people. That tendency suggests that ancient scribes would have more reason to omit such a prayer than to attribute these words to Jesus.[17] Even if the verse is not original to Luke, it fits the character of Jesus as Luke has depicted him throughout the Gospel.

The Community Implied in Luke's Narrative

Luke's preface introduces the ideal audience for his narrative, an individual named Theophilus. The name, which means "loved by God," was used by both Jews and non-Jews in this period. The epithet *kariste* ("most excellent") is a Greek equivalent for such Latin phrases as *egregius,* which was used of members of the Roman equestrian order, or *optimus,* used for anyone who belonged to the aristocracy rather than the common people. Luke applies the term to the Roman governor Felix in Acts 23:26. Consequently many of the older books on Luke-Acts concluded that Luke had such Roman magistrates in mind as his audience. Just as Josephus wishes to correct some slanderous accounts about Jews circulating among the educated in Rome, so Luke knows that Theophilus has heard bad reports about Christians. The simple fact that their founder had been crucified like the lowest criminal by order of a Roman governor would be a major hurdle to getting a hearing from an elite audience. Therefore some commentaries suggest that the agenda of Luke-Acts is to persuade such mid-level Roman officials that Christianity is not a subversive movement or a superstition of the lower classes. It merits the same respect that Romans have extended to the ancient religious traditions of the Jewish people.

More recent commentaries have adopted an alternate interpretation

16. Fitzmyer, *Luke X-XXIV,* 1503.
17. Brown, *Death,* 975-80; Metzger and Ehrman, *Text,* 288.

of Luke's preface. They agree with the earlier view that Theophilus is an actual person, not some idealized patron. The epithet means that he also enjoys some degree of social prominence either as a member of the local elite in a major city such as Antioch or as a Roman functionary. Sometimes persons named in a preface were expected to act as patrons for the work in another sense. They would become the "publishers" in a sense. The patron would host public readings of the author's book and either pay for copies to be circulated or make a copy available for use by those who wished to make a copy. Though it is possible that Theophilus could provide such resources, the fact that the author does not use his own name in the preface suggests that Luke is not close enough to Theophilus to make such a request. Instead, Theophilus appears to be a catechumen or interested inquirer who has already received some instruction in the basic Christian beliefs. Some scholars see the early sermons in Acts as examples of the preaching new converts would encounter in Luke's day.

Luke presents himself as a generation removed from those who were "eyewitnesses and servants of the word" (1:2). It is not clear whether he intends to distinguish the apostolic eyewitnesses to the events of Jesus' ministry (Acts 1:21-22) from subsequent preachers of the word or has the two phases of activity by the Twelve in mind. Luke also refers to earlier written accounts consulted in the process of providing his own more thorough, complete, orderly, and accurate version. He does not indicate whether Theophilus has heard or read any of these sources, but that appears not to be the case. Similarly, there is no trace of any of the Pauline letters in Luke's portrayal of Paul in Acts. Therefore some scholars argue that Luke-Acts must have been composed before Pauline letter collections had begun to circulate.[18] Luke's use of both citations from and echoes of the Jewish Scriptures does suggest that his readers would be familiar with the Septuagint. Luke's description of the general content of his work, *pragmata*, "things, affairs, business" which "have been fulfilled among us," suggests some reference back to the Jewish Scriptures. Luke is not simply narrating events from the recent past. The perfect participle "have been fulfilled" suggests that there are consequences of those events to be observed by his readers in the present. Thus the significant story of God's deeds of salvation does not end with the resurrection of Jesus.

Neither Luke nor his imagined audience are concerned with the de-

18. Fitzmyer, *Luke I-IX*, 57 (ca. 90-95 C.E.).

241

tails of Jewish religious practice. Although Luke includes traditions that have Jesus take on elements of Jewish observance, Luke himself has simplified the matter. His Pharisees are not so much teachers and custodians of Torah as a self-righteous, status- and money-loving elite who refuse Jesus' teaching because it requires extending forgiveness and hospitality to sinners. Luke is not at all familiar with the geography of Galilee, Samaria, and Judea. He sometimes uses Judea as a generic term for the whole region. He also assumes that the story takes place in cities, not the towns and villages of Galilee. Luke imagines that Elizabeth lived in a city in the Judean hill country (1:39). He even refers to Nazareth as a city (1:26)! When the paralyzed man's friends let him down through the roof in Luke 5:19, they have to remove the standard tiled roof of Hellenistic houses, not the mud thatch of a Palestinian village house as in Mark 2:4. Luke has also gone upscale in the various dinner or symposium arrangements that recur throughout the story. Jesus is reclining on a dining couch in Luke 7:36, for example.

Such shifts in small details may not involve deliberation on Luke's part. He may instinctively set stories in the world that is familiar to his audience. Similarly, he has adopted the style and literary conventions that such readers expect in prose narrative. However inaccurate Luke's chronological indicators are by modern standards, the Evangelist and his readers probably considered them the real dates. By the time a reader comes to Acts, Luke provides an explanation of how educated, urban Gentiles came to be the heirs of a tradition that had belonged to a people whose great Temple was lying in ruins and who had rejected their Messiah (Acts 13:46). That, too, was part of a grand design, God's plan for humanity since Adam. God would gather a people from among the nations (Acts 15:15-21).

Acts refers to the religion which Paul preaches as a *hairesis,* that is, a sect or school (24:5; 28:22). Luke's educated audience would have been familiar with disputes among teachers from different philosophical schools. They would have been less suspicious of a philosophical school than of a new religious sect, since the introduction of new deities or cults could result in civic disturbance in ancient cities (see the Ephesus riots in Acts 19:21-40). Luke addresses that suspicion in various trial scenes. As employed in charging Jesus before Pilate, the accusation is patently trumped up. Not only are statements that Jesus has threatened to destroy the Temple (Mark 14:58) omitted from Luke's Jewish proceedings, Jesus' earlier confrontations in the Temple involve nothing more violent than teaching (Luke 19:45-47). Paul faces similar trumped-up charges at Ephesus (Acts

19:21-40) and Jerusalem (24:5-9). Roman intervention saves Paul's life. Rome's governors provide the prisoner with several opportunities to defend himself, and the appeal to Caesar saves his life from fanatical Jewish opponents. Presumably these positive sentiments about Roman authorities reflect the sociopolitical integration of Luke's audience.

The virtues taught by Jesus and exemplified in his life were familiar to ancient moralists. Piety and prayer suffuse the narrative from the opening pages of the Gospel. Jesus teaches a way of peace, not discord. Rules for conduct at a banquet/symposium in ancient society warned participants against the kind of discord that breaks out among the disciples (Luke 22:24). Jesus intervenes immediately. The challenge of his ethic asks people to renounce the cultural habits of struggles for position and power (22:25-27). Meal hospitality becomes a key setting in which to make this point and is expanded to teach the elite audience a lesson about charity. Luke's readers were familiar enough with the ethic of benefactors and patrons. The poor were expected to return honor, public support in various ventures, and the like to their benefactors. Jesus makes a more radical demand: charity toward those who have nothing to give in return (14.7-24). Although Luke retains the traditions in which Jesus calls for renouncing possessions, he provides his audience with an alternative: generosity with no expectation of repayment.

Some scholars suggest that Luke is employing comic stereotypes to promote generosity in the parables of the Unjust Steward and the Rich Man and Lazarus. In both instances the central figure exhibits behavior so extreme that it is more suited to stock figures than to actual persons. The steward is the shifty slave overseer of a master's property. The master is fairly easily duped, so the slave escapes the punishment his wastrel behavior deserves. Similarly, the rich man is a caricature in his excessive feasting and luxurious dress, is completely oblivious to the geography of punishment, and persists in trying to drive a bargain with Abraham for some advantage. The moralizing lessons to be drawn from these stories about greed, justifying oneself by human appearances, and neglect of God's law have been sandwiched between the two stories. The rich man in torment is the sort of friend acquired by "unjust mammon" with whom the greedy can expect to spend eternity (16:9). For Luke there is no Dickens *Christmas Carol* ending for the rich man's brothers. No ghost from the dead will engender reform for those who have no regard for the teaching of Moses. The stock comic elements along with the concluding allusion to "one returning from the dead," which for a Christian audience can only imply the resurrection of the dead, could be greeted with amused superiority. These folk are quite unlike Luke's readers.

Alongside these fictional characters, one finds a note that troubles readers today. As we have seen, Luke asserts that the Pharisees are "money-lovers" and that "they made fun of him" (16:14). Although Luke has more diverse characterizations of the Pharisees than Mark or Matthew, this sequence of parables and sayings comes dangerously close to typecasting Pharisees as Shylock figures. Gentile readers who only know Pharisees from what they read in Luke's work might conclude that they possess all the vices condemned in this section of the Gospel.

Luke's narrative introduces figures of women from all levels of society. Widows at the margins of poverty appear along with women followers who are wealthy enough to be patrons for the whole group. The story of Martha and Mary encourages women to learn and practice the teaching of Jesus. This mix of female figures in the Gospel, continued to some extent in Acts, may represent their participation in local communities. However one cannot enlist Luke-Acts as an advocate of gender equality. All the leadership roles in the churches of Acts are held by men. Women pray, participate in communal meals, prophesy, give and receive charity, and serve as patrons. Acts 18:26 suggests that Priscilla may have played a more substantive role in evangelization than the roles Luke provides for women followers suggest. She appears to be engaged in preaching and instructing new converts along with her husband Aquila. Just as the women in the infancy narratives were exemplary in their piety, so the women in the rest of the narrative run the gamut of female social roles. The Jesus movement had not changed cultural perceptions of gender.

Mary Traditions and Other Infancy Gospels

The stories of family origins, birth announcements, divine conception, birth, and childhood found in Matthew and Luke are just the beginning point for an explosion of legends about Jesus' family, especially his mother, and about his childhood exploits. Christian devotion to the figure of Mary led to new emphasis on her upbringing and virginity and created the need to explain those referred to as brothers and sisters of Jesus in the canonical Gospels (e.g., Mark 6:3; John 2:12; Acts 1:14; also Gal 1:19). The Evangelists saw no need to maintain Mary's virginity after the birth of Jesus. They consider the brothers and sisters Jesus' younger siblings. A second-century Gnostic text that describes the risen Jesus appearing to his brother James (1 Cor 15:7) has Mary explain the relationship between the two boys. Unfortunately the surviving text is quite fragmentary:

> Once when I was sitting and deliberating, [he] opened [the] door. That one whom you hated and persecuted came in to me. He said to me, "Hail, my brother, hail." As I raised my [face] to stare at him, (my) mother said to me, "Do not be frightened, my son, because he said, 'My brother' to you. For you were nourished with this same milk. Because of this he calls me, 'My mother.' For he is not a stranger to us. He is your [step-brother . . .]." (2 *Apocalypse of James*, NHC 5.50.1-23; *NHLE*, 271-72)

Since this text assumes that Mary nursed both boys, James cannot be a stepbrother from a previous marriage of Joseph, as the *Protoevangelium of James* concluded (25.1). Nor can James and others be cousins of Jesus, as St. Jerome later insisted. Jerome's view became the official teaching of the Latin West. His opposition to *Protoevangelium of James* may be the reason that no copies of a Latin translation survive, despite numerous Greek manuscripts and translations into other languages.[19]

The *Protoevangelium of James* combines elements from the infancy narratives of Matthew and Luke with echoes of 1 Samuel. It pushes the story of Mary back to her miraculous birth to a wealthy, pious couple, Joachim and Anna, her dedication and life in the Temple from age 3 to 12, her betrothal to Joseph, the annunciation, the scandal caused by her pregnancy, and Jesus' miraculous birth. Instead of her suffering the ordinary pains of childbirth, a great light shines in the cave. When the blinding light fades out, a child is present already able to nurse at the breast (19.2-3). Because there is so much controversy over Mary's pregnancy, the midwife who announces that the virgin has borne a child agrees to let another woman, Salome, subject Mary to a gynecological exam. Mary is found to have remained a virgin. God strikes Salome's hand but agrees to heal her when she holds the newborn infant (20.1-3). The story of the wise men paraphrases Matthew's Gospel but without the flight into Egypt. Mary protects her baby by hiding him in a manger. Elizabeth flees to the hill country, where a mountain splits to shelter her and John (22.1-3).

19. Elliott, *Apocryphal New Testament*, 50-51.

Like most apocryphal texts, the *Protoevangelium of James* survives in a number of variations. Stories were more easily incorporated into copies of apocryphal texts than into the canonical Gospels. Even our third-century manuscript, Papyrus Bodmer V, has a legend about the death of Zechariah at the end of the story that seems to have been unknown to readers such as Origen earlier in the same century. The *Protoevangelium* casts the Baptist's father as the high priest. He prays about what to do with Mary when she reaches age 12, and an angel appears to him in the Holy of Holies with the instruction to have a group of widowers from Judea draw lots for her (8.1-3). At the end of the Papyrus Bodmer V version, he dies a martyr's death in the Temple. Herod has ordered his men to kill Zechariah if he refuses to reveal where his son is hidden. A miraculous sign accompanies the martyr's death. His body disappears, but his blood remains congealed rock-hard beside the altar. A voice warns that the blood will not be wiped away until Zechariah's avenger comes. At the end of the martyrdom story, the aged Simeon takes over as high priest (22–24). The fictive author of the work, James the "brother" of the Lord, claims to have written it during the period of turmoil that accompanied Herod's death. He has withdrawn into the Judean wilderness at that time (25.1).

The designation "Protoevangelium" was given to this work by sixteenth-century scholars in their Latin translations. They claimed that it was the proto-Gospel from which the infancy traditions of Matthew and Luke were derived. On closer reading it is clear that the author of the *Protoevangelium* has built up the tale by adding legends to a Gospel harmony created from Matthew and Luke. The scribe who copied the Papyrus Bodmer V version provides the following title at the end: "Nativity of Mary. Apocalypse of James."

Some of the details of a birth story found in the *Ascension of Isaiah* 11 match additions from the *Protoevangelium of James*. Mary herself is said to be descended from David, not just Joseph as in the canonical texts. The baby emerges miraculously from Mary's womb leaving her virginity intact, though in *Asc. Isa.* the surprise arrival of the infant meant no labor pains and no midwife. *Asc. Isa.* also lacks any contact with the Matthean traditions about the wise men's arrival and Herod's slaughter of the infants. Its author does not explain why the family moved from Bethlehem to Nazareth, but suggests that the move may have facilitated the complete obscurity of Jesus' life until he began his public ministry. Thus the legends which make up the *Protoevangelium of James* were widely circulated in different forms.

The *Protoevangelium* not only contributed to establishing the tradition that Mary remained a virgin after the birth of Jesus, but also expanded on childhood legends to demonstrate her unusual holiness. As soon as baby Mary can walk, at the early age of six months, her mother declares that Mary's feet will never touch ground again. The bedchamber becomes a miniature sanctuary where the baby is cared for by pure young virgins (6.1). On her first birthday, Joachim brings his daughter to the priests for a special blessing and then she returns to the bedroom sanctuary (6.2). Though Joachim wants to dedicate her to the Temple at age two, Anna asks to wait a year so that the child will not be pining for her parents (7.1). As further evidence for Mary's purity, the lot falls to her to weave in the scarlet and purple threads for a new veil for the Temple. Only pure virgins of the tribe of David were permitted to participate in the weaving project (10.1-2). Thus Christian imagination is transforming the Temple piety of Luke's infancy narrative into an elaborate system that guarantees the purity and holiness of the virgin. She has no contact with anything that is impure or sinful.

The imaginative elements in *2 Apocalypse of James, Asc. Isa.*, and the *Protoevangelium of James* remain chronologically bounded by the canonical infancy narratives in regard to the life of Jesus. Nothing is known about Jesus' childhood or early adult life in Nazareth. Luke's account of the twelve-year-old Jesus among the teachers in the Temple anticipates a key aspect of Jesus' adult life (Luke 2:41-52). In addition to outshining any official teachers, the adult Jesus also performs miracles. Another set of legends from the second or third century, the *Infancy Gospel of Thomas*, no relation to the *Gospel of Thomas* sayings collection, contains a series of miraculous deeds of the child Jesus, ending with the scene in the Temple. Some of the stories turn up elsewhere. The manuscript traditions for this material are complex since all the Greek versions are late. Attempts to construct an early text using the Syriac, Latin, Georgian, Old Church Slavonic, and Ethiopic versions require a more complete collation of all the variants than presently exists. Such a loose collection of individual tales may never have been very stable in its content. "Gospel" may not have been in its original title. The expression "childhood deeds" found in the introduction is more appropriate, since the *Infancy Gospel* is more a collection of episodes than a narrative.

Unlike *Ascen. Isa.* 11, which follows the canonical Gospel traditions by insisting that Jesus' life in Nazareth appeared completely ordinary, in the *Infancy Gospel* Jesus begins creating havoc at age 5. The first episode has the child magically purify pools of water that he has created. He then goes on to make some clay sparrows. No surprise to those familiar with the adult Jesus, this happens to be the Sabbath. A Jew notices and pushes Joseph to reprimand the boy for breaking the Sabbath law. In response, Jesus claps and the sparrows fly off alive. The child Jesus constitutes a danger to his playmates, since any angry word or curse from his mouth will cause injury (3.2, withering the son of Annas the scribe; 5.1, blindness to those who accuse him) or death (4.1, a child who has bumped into Jesus). Scolded by Joseph, Jesus eventually restores those his words have injured. Jesus quickly proves more advanced than the local teacher, who has asked Joseph to send the youth to him for instruction. The teacher infers that Jesus must have more than human origins:

> This child is not earth-born; he can even subdue fire. Perhaps he was begotten even before the creation of the world. What belly bore him, what womb nurtured him I do not know. . . I am filled with shame, that I, an old man, have been defeated by a child. . . . Therefore I beg you, brother Joseph, take him away to your house. Whatever great thing he is, a god or an angel, I do not know what I should say. (7.2-4; Elliott, *Apocryphal New Testament*, 77)

The child's bad reputation becomes an occasion for suspicion when one of his playmates dies after falling from a roof. Once Jesus has restored the boy to life, the miracle comes to the positive conclusion often found in Luke's Gospel, praise of God. However, in this situation only Jesus' parents "glorified God . . . and worshiped Jesus" (9.2). But this response extends to the crowd when Jesus cures a man who has cut his foot open with an ax: "Truly the spirit of God dwells in this child" (10.2). Sometimes Jesus performs miracles to assist his parents with daily tasks, collecting water in a garment when his mother stumbles and breaks her pitcher (11.1-2) or lengthening a board that is too short (13.1-2). The story that his seed yielded a hundred measures more than his father's seems to be based on Jesus' parable of the Sower (Luke 16:7). What Jesus does with the excess picks up another Lukan theme — excess wealth should be shared with the poor. Unlike the rich fool in the parable (Luke 12:13-21), the eight-year-old Jesus calls the poor of the village to come and get the grain (12.2).

The *Infancy Gospel of Thomas* contains a paired variation on the earlier teacher stories. First, a teacher who gets annoyed with the child's challenge to explain the hidden meaning of the alphabet strikes Jesus on the head. Jesus curses the man, and he dies (14.1-2). When a second teacher permits the lad to teach Torah thanks to the inspiration of the Holy Spirit, the situation improves. That teacher admits that Jesus does not require schooling because he already has grace and wisdom. As a reward, Jesus restores life to the first teacher (15.2-4). Jesus also manages to elicit praise from the crowds with two more examples of his power to restore the dead to life. First, when he restores a dead child the amazed crowd responds, "Truly this child is either a god or an angel of God, for every word of his is an accomplished deed" (17.2). Then a man killed at a building site elicits a confession that Jesus possesses saving power: "This child is from heaven, for he has saved many souls from death, and is able to save them all his life long" (18.2). In another episode, the child Jesus cures James of a viper's bite. The narrator opens with "Joseph sent *his son* James. . ." (16.1). The author evidently shares the view that James was Joseph's son by a previous marriage.

The final episode is a paraphrase of Luke's story of the twelve-year-old in the Temple. It adds only a few details. Jesus is "elucidating the chapters of the law and the parables of the prophets" (19.2). After Mary reprimands Jesus and he replies (Luke 2:48-49), the scribes and Pharisees ask if she is the child's mother. Learning that she is, they reply using Elizabeth's words (Luke 1:42), "Blessed are you among women and blessed is the fruit of your womb. For such glory and such excellence and wisdom we have never seen nor heard" (19.4). In contrast to the more distant echoes of Luke found in some of the earlier stories, this last is almost identical to its Lukan archetype. Thus the author would appear to expect his audience to infer that the stories he has told could be part of that tradition. The miracles that result in some positive affirmation, glorifying God or acknowledging the more than human identity of the child, at least fit a pattern of miracle use in Luke. However, the vindictive speech miracles that make Jesus a danger to those around him seem indebted to a different cultural world. In that world, Jesus could be confused with someone who employs magic powers. But he is not like other practitioners of the dark arts. He does not need the spells that we find on ancient curse tablets, since the very words out of his mouth are effective.

The Reception and Revision of the Gospel of Luke

Modern readers are captivated by Luke's talents as a storyteller. Christian imagination would be much poorer without him. The apocryphal Gospels that depict the life of the virgin Mary or repeat folk tales about the child Jesus depend on clues from Luke, though they lack his stylistic ear for biblical language. Even when a later author is indebted to Matthew more than to Luke, one cannot imagine such interest in Jesus' parents, conception, birth, and childhood without the initial impetus provided by Luke. That said, why did Luke's Gospel lag behind Matthew in popularity during the second century C.E.?[20] One reason may have been the ancient view of its authorship. Unlike Matthew, the Gospel of Luke was not associated with one of the Twelve. Nor could an alleged Aramaic Gospel be attributed to him. Luke's work was referred to as ". . . from hearsay. For he himself had not seen the Lord, but insofar as he was able to follow. . . ," according to an ancient Latin canon list of the second to fourth centuries. Luke's Gospel was said to represent that proclaimed by Paul (Irenaeus, *Adv. Haer.* 3.1.1; 3.14.1-3).[21] The other Evangelist who can only record what he heard from the apostles, Mark, fell into near obscurity in the second century.

From another perspective, the second-century reception of Luke's Gospel may reflect the approach which the Evangelist set out in his own preface. Although he claims to have revised those who preceded him to give the church's preaching a secure foundation, Luke has no authority by which his own work could be secured from such a fate. Quite the contrary. We have two bits of evidence for substantial revisions of Luke-Acts in the second century. The first comes from the work of text critics. As we noted in Chapter Two, the bilingual Greek and Latin Codex Bezae (sixth century) represents a version of the New Testament text known for its paraphrases, rephrasing, and additions. Although referred to as the "Western text" because it is often found in early Latin translations, this text type was not limited to that region. It is contained in some papyri from the end of the second century and underlies some Syriac versions. The order of the Gospels in Codex Bezae demonstrates that some early Christian scribes considered the apostolic Gospels more important than

---

20. See David P. Moessner, "How Luke Writes," in Markus Bockmuehl and Donald A. Hagner, eds., *The Written Gospel* (Cambridge: Cambridge University Press, 2005) 149.

21. For other early Christian examples of this tradition, see Fitzmyer, *Luke I-IX*, 36-40.

those by later followers. One finds the sequence Matthew, John, Luke, and Mark.

The Western text of Luke's Gospel contains a few important changes. It breaks into the dispute over plucking grain on the Sabbath (6:1-5) to include another incident at the end of v. 4: "That same day, seeing someone working on the Sabbath, he said to him, 'Fellow, if you know what you are doing, you are blessed. If you do not know, you are thoroughly accursed and a transgressor of the law." With this insertion, Jesus' next remark to a "them," "The Son of Man is Lord of the Sabbath" (v. 5), must be to his disciples rather than to the Pharisees of v. 2. The Western text also exhibits a tendency to harmonize by adding to the opening "Father" in the Lord's Prayer (11:2) the liturgical elements found elsewhere: "Our Father, who art in the heavens." To the petition "your kingdom come" Codex Bezae adds "upon us." And as a final harmonizing with the Matthean version, this text tradition has "may your will be done on earth as it is in heaven."[22]

The addition of an angelic presence to comfort Jesus during his agony in Gethsemane along with the drops of blood-like sweat (22:43-44) is so familiar in Christian art that most Christians are surprised to learn that they might be apocryphal coloring added to Luke. Although the manuscripts that omit them generally are preferred to those which include these verses, both text critics (so the Nestle-Aland twenty-seventh edition) and translators (so NRSV) have them in double brackets and put the option of a text without them in a footnote. Since the nineteenth century some text critics have argued that these verses were composed by the Evangelist. For many other scholars, the combination of marginally better manuscript attestation for the version without the scene and its interruption of Luke's depiction of Jesus' progress toward his destiny is enough to tip the balance in favor of another example of second-century interpolation in Luke.[23] Justin Martyr (ca. 155 C.E.) knows the tradition that Jesus' "perspiration poured out like drops of blood" as he prayed in agony (*Dialogue with Trypho* 103.8). However, there is no angelic response to Jesus' prayer. Justin attributes this information to "the memoirs of the apostles and their successors," not to a particular Evangelist. And he provides a clue to the dogmatic point being scored with a more expansive description of Jesus' suf-

22. These variants in the Lord's Prayer are included among the "other ancient authorities" in the NRSV.
23. See Fitzmyer, *Luke X-XXIV,* 1443-45.

251

fering, which serves to demonstrate that even though God called Jesus "Son" God did not spare him the pain of what happened to him during the passion. In other words, the addition defends belief in the human suffering of Jesus during his passion against docetic and Gnostic accounts that insisted that the divine Savior never suffered on the cross.

An even more puzzling set of variants surrounds Jesus' words about the cup(s) and the bread in 22:17-20. Liturgical tradition as well as our oldest witness to the formula, 1 Cor 11:23b-26, have a fixed order, bread first and then the cup. Luke 22:17 has Jesus take a cup, give thanks, and command his disciples to share it without any words interpreting the cup in relationship to his own blood. Then 22:18 echoes the prediction that Jesus will not drink from the cup until he does so in the kingdom from Mark 14:25. In Mark that saying follows the interpretation of the cup as blood of the new covenant. Luke has a second cup after the dinner and attaches the new covenant in Jesus' blood to it (22:20). Some manuscripts of Luke lack some or all of the words in vv. 19b-20. One would expect a scribe attempting to harmonize the Gospel with liturgical practice to drop the first cup, not the second. Faced with an awkward text which mentioned a shared cup only before the bread, later scribes may have patched in the second cup with the traditional formula. But bread then cup, each with an interpretive word, was received tradition well before Paul wrote 1 Corinthians. Therefore text critics generally present the longer text as Luke's version.

A final bit of disputed text appears in the concluding verses of the Gospel. Should "and he was taken up into heaven" (Luke 24:51c) be retained? Or were they added to explain what happened to Jesus once the Gospel was being copied and read without reference to its continuation in Acts? There is an extensive early Christian tradition of Jesus ascending into heaven on Easter as implied in John 20:17 and stated explicitly in such second-century texts as *Epistle of Barnabas* 15:9 and the *Gos. Pet.* 55-56. But in this instance the clause is present in most of the early ancient witnesses and missing in the Western text, so it appears more likely that they were omitted by a scribe who viewed them as contrary to the opening of Acts, where Jesus does not ascend for forty days.

Just as Luke himself appears more restrained in the modifications introduced into sources in the Gospel than in Acts, so the Western text adds much more to Acts than to the Gospel. Its version of Acts is some 10% longer than that found in the other textual traditions. These examples from the textual history of Luke's Gospel combined with Justin Martyr's appeal to "memoirs of the apostles" for an expanded text show that the text of Luke's Gospel was not a finished or stable entity in the mid-second century.

Our second piece of evidence for the revisor's hand at work also stems from the mid-second century, namely the revision of Luke and a collection of Paul's letters by Marcion. Convinced that the loving Father revealed by Jesus could not be identified with the wrathful deity of the Jewish Scriptures, Marcion claimed the authority of Paul's law-gospel dichotomy for his version of Christianity. As we have seen, Luke as we have it presents Jesus as a figure within the tradition of the pious humble ones of Israel. Marcion argued that a Judaizing corruption of both Paul's letters and Luke's Gospel was responsible for the apparent continuity between Christian faith and its Jewish sources. He adopted a familiar tactic in dealing with ancient texts, excising those accretions which had been added. Unfortunately anti-Marcionite authors such as Tertullian do not provide extensive quotations from Marcion's version of the Gospel. It is impossible to know how extensive his revisions were. That such a text was created for use in Marcionite churches is certain.

These clues indicate that Luke's Gospel remained something of a work in progress well into the second century. It could be expanded, as in the examples from the Western text tradition. It could be subject to a restoration by editing, as Marcion claimed to provide. Combination of this textual fluidity and the acknowledged difference between its author and the apostolic authors of two Gospels left Luke third after Matthew and John. Until the status of the four-Gospel group became firmly established as canon, Christians of limited means may not have sought to obtain copies of all four. Our dearth of early papyrus evidence shows that Mark was least often copied. The revisions of Luke do not approach the work of adding material and reshaping the narrative that both Luke and Matthew undertook with regard to Mark. Nor, as far as we can tell, did Tatian's harmony comprise a major rewrite of the gospel story. The fanciful expansions into new territory, whether in the *Gospel of Peter* for the passion and resurrection or in the *Protoevangelium of James* and the *Infancy Gospel of Thomas* for tales of family and childhood, inhabit a very different literary and imaginative world from Luke or the other canonical Gospels. In our final chapter, we will explore some of the other writings from the second and third centuries that carry the designation "Gospel."

CHAPTER SEVEN

Gospels from the Second and Third Centuries

The media hype which accompanies discovery or publication of new manuscripts often promises that the materials in question will rewrite our understanding of Jesus. Sometimes it is suggested that early Christian authorities intentionally suppressed apocryphal Gospels. When the smoke clears, marginal presses that specialize in alternative spirituality put out a paraphrased edition with a commentary suited to their views. Scholars situate the new textual remains among the known materials from the second and third centuries. Mainstream churches find their worship and spiritual-

---

Suggested Reading

Ehrman, Bart D. *Lost Christianities: The Battles for Scripture and the Faiths We Never Knew.* New York: Oxford University Press, 2003.

King, Karen L. *The Gospel of Mary of Magdala: Jesus and the First Woman Apostle.* Santa Rosa: Polebridge, 2003.

Klauck, Hans-Josef. *Apocryphal Gospels: An Introduction.* Trans. B. McNeil. London: Clark, 2004.

Koester, Helmut. *Ancient Christian Gospels: Their History and Development.* Philadelphia: Trinity, 1990.

Perkins, Pheme. *Gnosticism and the New Testament.* Minneapolis: Fortress, 1993.

Porter, Stanley E., and Gordon L. Heath. *The Lost Gospel of Judas: Separating Fact from Fiction.* Grand Rapids: Eerdmans, 2007.

ity unchanged. Some of the stories about Jesus which circulated in oral tradition may have provided more entertainment than instruction. The
childhood miracles in the *Infancy Gospel of Thomas* include harm inflicted
by a enraged child, for example. Community and parents must intervene
to get Jesus to watch how he uses his powers. Stories about the virginity of
Mary were fabricated to remove any doubts about the conception of Jesus.
Even they are oriented more toward popular entertainment than the infancy narratives of Matthew and Luke. Both of those Gospels focus on the
messianic destiny of the child. They are replete with echoes of earlier biblical stories which also provide the basis for God's special intervention in
the birth of the child.

Luke's preface stated the purpose of his Gospel to provide support
for what was being preached. By the end of the second century, Irenaeus
made a similar claim about the relationship between the four canonical
Gospels and what he refers to as "the rule of faith." Against Marcion's attempt to purge Christian belief of its Jewish heritage, Irenaeus also insisted
that the God revealed in the Jewish Scriptures is identical with the Father
proclaimed by Jesus and his disciples. Although some modern authors
have imagined that Irenaeus was bringing down the heavy hand of episco-
pal authority on free-spirited Christians and their creative Gospel writing,
the real situation was less dramatic. Christians were still a suspect, poorly
understood, and persecuted minority in the second century. Neither
Irenaeus from Lyons nor the bishop of Rome could compel the myriad
house churches and study circles that made up the church to conform to a
single pattern of faith and practice. We know that mid-second-century
Rome encompassed orthodox Christians who had different views over
when to celebrate Easter, philosophically inclined groups represented by
figures like Justin Martyr, groups gathered around Gnostic teachers like
Valentinus and Ptolemy, and the emerging challenge posed by Marcion's
radical form of Paulinism. Legend has it that both Valentinus and Marcion
made a run at being elected bishop.

With such a diverse Christian community, there is no surprise in
finding different views of Jesus and his message. One can see the combination of a basic creed with a four-Gospel canon comprised of texts known
to have originated in the previous century as a useful way of setting the
standard that most Christians would agree on. It was not until the late
fourth century, after Christianity had become the official religion of the
Roman Empire, that actual lists of a full canon of Old and New Testaments

are adopted. Given the relatively weak social and economic status of most second- and third-century Christians, one should be impressed by the energy that they committed to writing divergent, often fairly local traditions as in the case of *Gospel of Peter*. In this chapter we will survey a few more of the remains from the second and third centuries that often crop up in books about early Christianity.

A Mixture of Traditions: Oral and Written

As the global Internet has loosened the controls on ownership of texts, photos, films, and music, tracking down an original or authoritative version of a work can be quite difficult. Proposals being circulated to create new tags for ownership reflect our modern understanding of individual property rights. On the one hand, the multiplication of versions and the weaving together of items from diverse sources on the Web provide some analogy to the production of new Gospels in the second century. On the other, modern ideas about individual creativity, ownership, and property make it difficult to appreciate the ancient cultural context. Communal listening and even participation in creating the story as it was being performed were the norm in antiquity. Some scholars have analyzed Mark's Gospel as the written reflection of oral performances that occurred over a period of time.[1] Contemporary use of digital technology has been moving modern audiences further away from communal experience. Each individual creates programming for himself or herself or for a virtual audience with like-minded tastes. The Web-cast audience views that performance in isolation. Best-selling books appear on CDs as soon as they are released in print. Yet hearing the spoken performance is often less communal than book club discussions of printed texts. Thus speaking about oral and written gospel traditions has a very different feel for twenty-first-century Christians than it would have for early Christians.

Writing, memorizing, repeating, and paraphrasing stories, fables, and maxims was a standard part of schooling for the literate segment of an ancient audience. From monumental inscriptions down to individual dedications, graffiti, and amulets, those who lived in ancient cities had been

---

1. Whitney Shiner, *Proclaiming the Gospel: First-Century Performance of Mark* (Harrisburg: Trinity, 2003).

surrounded by writing for centuries. Therefore oral transmission of information was not contrary to writing, as anthropological discussions of preliterate cultures might suggest. The combination of written text with the kinds of variations that derive from oral performance means that a saying or episode may be derived from one of the written Synoptic Gospels without being a close copy of its source. Often details from more than one version may have been worked into a new telling of the story. Therefore it would be anachronistic to treat the varied Gospels from the second and third centuries as though their authors or audiences intended to distort the Christian message.[2] Irenaeus's defense of the four canonical Gospels and Acts as the only witnesses to apostolic traditions grounded in the rule of faith created that perception once the rich oral environment of second-century Christianity had been forgotten.[3]

When we speak of "apocryphal" Gospels of the second and third centuries, we do not mean that these were either secret traditions given only to the elect or that they were intended to be fraudulent replacements for the canonical Gospels. The designation simply indicates that one is dealing with early Christian texts that were composed to be similar to the Gospel writings incorporated into the Christian canon.[4] Since we use the designation "Gospel" for elements of a life of Jesus, infancy narratives, sayings of Jesus, stories about miracles and other deeds of Jesus, controversies with authorities, and passion and resurrection narratives, the term shows up in the titles of works which contain only one type of Jesus material. Some scholars even think that it stretches the point to speak of the canonical Gospels as though they were literary "lives" of Jesus. They would prefer to see them as a kind of handbook of materials about the founder of a school and his teachings.[5] Certainly some of the additional second- and third-century Gospels such as the sayings collection *Gospel of Thomas* fit that profile of what Gospels were thought to be.

Fixing a narrative story about Jesus that concluded with his death and resurrection in writing takes a step beyond the handbooks of sayings,

---

2. Klauck, *Apocryphal Gospels*, 2-3.

3. Winrich A. Löhr, "Kanongeschichtliche Beobachtung zum Verhältnis von mündlicher und schriftlicher Tradition im zweiten Jahrhundert," *ZNW* 85 (1994) 248-58.

4. So Ehrman, *Lost Christianities*, 11.

5. Loveday Alexander, "Ancient Book Production and the Circulation of the Gospels," in R. Bauckham, ed., *The Gospels for All Christians: Rethinking Gospel Audiences* (Grand Rapids: Eerdmans, 1998) 105.

discourses, *chreiai,* and miracles. Mark made narratives about Jesus the centerpiece of an emerging written tradition in Christianity. Prior to Mark, we have no evidence of an attempt to lay out the sequence of events in Jesus' life. Contrast the letters of Paul or even the reconstructed sayings collection Q with Mark's Gospel. Matthew follows Mark's lead by creating "handbook" discourses out of the sayings traditions but putting them within the framework of the story about Jesus. Luke's prologue demonstrates an even more explicitly literary concern in collecting and shaping both oral and written testimonies into a narrative account. Many if not all of the second- and third-century Gospels will have readers who are already familiar with the storyline about Jesus as it was found in one or more of the canonical Gospels. In some instances one sees the early Christian imagination filling in the gaps in a familiar account. The written version of new episodes involving Jesus that one finds in a Gospel fragment from the second or third century probably reflects some elements of oral storytelling in Christian communities.

None of the canonical Evangelists treats his account as an individual literary work to be claimed over against others. The author never gives his name or credentials or specifies his relationship to the persons and events being narrated. Luke only lets us know indirectly that he is not one of the "eyewitnesses and servants of the word." The Papias traditions suggest that some concern to attach identities to the authors of the Gospels had arisen by the early second century (Eusebius, *Hist. Eccl.* 3.39). Eusebius corrects the claim in Irenaeus that Papias had heard John and then been an associate of Polycarp by quoting from the preface to Papias's five-volume work, *The Sayings of the Lord Interpreted.* Papias, like Luke, describes the procedure used to compile his information. He sought out those presbyters who had known any disciples of the Lord, Andrew, Peter, Philip, Thomas, James, John, and Matthew. He also asked what Ariston, allegedly the author of the present ending of Mark, and the presbyter John, that is, the Evangelist rather than the son of Zebedee, were still saying (3.39.3-4). Eusebius does not provide quotations to back up his statement that Papias's book contained some parables and teachings of the Savior that were otherwise unknown. He objects to Papias's belief in a literal thousand-year reign on earth and thinks that Papias misunderstood some teachings of the Lord and misled others, including Irenaeus, into holding that false viewpoint.

Papias already has stories about Mark's unsystematic record and

Matthew's record of sayings (3.39.15-16). Neither of these references describes the Gospels as we know them. Mark, he says, wrote down Jesus' sayings and doings written from what he could remember from Peter's teaching. Matthew, he says, wrote in Aramaic, apparently recording no deeds of Jesus. Others had to translate the Aramaic as best they could. But the identity of the authors means that it is still possible to recover something of the original teaching of Jesus, despite the multiple channels of both oral and written tradition through which it has passed. For Papias, the "living voice" of the apostles is the key to authenticity, so he perceives the contents of the canonical Gospels of Mark, Matthew, and John in those terms.

During the second century, the terms of the debate changed from questions about genuine oral tradition to designating written texts of apostolic origin. The conventional title "Gospel according to. . ." requires the name of an apostolic figure to indicate the authority behind the text. Consequently, *Gos. Thom.* has the title "Gospel according to Thomas" at the conclusion even though the opening describes it as "secret sayings which the living Jesus spoke and which Judas Thomas wrote down."

Individual books, whether Gospels or collections of sayings and anecdotes, can only be partial representations of the oral or remembered tradition. Luke's preface as well as the concluding statement about the purpose of John's Gospel (John 20:30-31) acknowledge that reality. Even Matthew's concluding "teaching them to observe everything which I have commanded" (Matt 28:20) does not equate "all things" with the content of that Gospel. Since Serapion initially presumed that *Gospel of Peter* was suitable public reading for the church at Rhossus, it is clear that second-century Christians did not draw sharp distinctions between the four which became canonical and other Gospels that we call apocryphal.

Once the codices of the fourth century established a reasonably stable text for the canonical Gospels, deviations from the sayings and anecdotes found there become more obvious than would have been the case in earlier centuries. It is easy to forget that all of the written gospel material prior to the fourth century is fragmentary. Papyri that resemble one of the textual traditions found in fourth- and fifth-century codices are generally described as being from one of the canonical Gospels and find their place in the text-critical apparatus of the Greek New Testament. But there are some identification problems. Patristic citations that deviate from the familiar textual traditions may represent a different text type from those seen in the later codices. Or they may represent a local oral tradition, a

259

memory that has assimilated more than one version, or even use of some other Gospel or collection. For example, 2 *Clement* 12.2 has a saying that appears in *Gos. Thom.* 22 and 37 as well as in Clement of Alexandria (*Stromateis* 3.13), who attributes it to a "Gospel of the Egyptians." That Gospel cannot be identified with a "Gospel of the Egyptians" found in Coptic. 2 *Clement* gives no indication of its source beyond the brief introduction to the saying, "when the Lord himself was asked by someone when his kingdom would come, he said. . . ." Some patristic citations do appear in the text-critical apparatus of modern Greek texts, especially if the citation matches some minority textual tradition or a translation version.

Classification of papyrus fragments or of pages from a damaged codex becomes more difficult if the contents do not match one of the canonical Gospels or an apocryphal work which survives in a more complete text, either in Greek or in a translation. It is impossible to know whether smaller fragments containing sayings, miracle stories, or other anecdotes are from apocryphal Gospels, collections such as that of Papias, Tatian's *Diatessaron* or another Gospel harmony, or citations in a writing that was not a Gospel at all. A text published in the early twentieth century, *Papyrus Egerton 2*, combines both Johannine and Synoptic-sounding material. It cannot be read as a simple expansion of one of the canonical Gospels with material from the other. But still it is cited as a textual variant in the apparatus to John 5:39 in the Nestle-Aland twenty-seventh edition. In addition to the original two papyrus leaves with bits of a third, a further fragment from among the Cologne papyri was published in 1987 (P. Köln 608). This fragment filled out readings in the existing papyri but did not resolve the question of whether the four episodes from the life of Jesus found there were derived from an "unknown Gospel" or from some other source.[6] Originally the first fragments were dated approximately 150 C.E., making *P. Eg.* 2 one of the oldest surviving copies of gospel material. More recently most scholars favor a date somewhat later in the second century, though the minority view which treats all apocryphal texts as sources for canonical counterparts still argues for a first-century date.[7]

Pushing *P. Eg.* 2 later into the second century increases the probabil-

6. Ehrman (*Lost Christianities,* xii) employs the designation "Gospel." Dieter Lührmann, *Die apokryph gewordenen Evangelien. Studien zu neuen Texten und zu neuen Fragen* (Novum Testamentum Supplements 112; Leiden: Brill, 2004) 139, urges more caution.

7. Elliott (*Apocryphal New Testament,* 37) still lists 150 C.E. as the date for the codex fragments.

ity that its amalgam of Johannine and Synoptic traditions represents an oral or written tradition that had conflated details from stories found in the canonical Gospels. Divisions between episodes may have been marked by scribes using abbreviations for "Jesus" or "Lord" at the opening of a unit.[8] It is possible to understand the fragments as a series of episodes from Jesus' ministry rather than a connected narrative. Not enough survives to indicate if the text had a larger narrative holding them together:

Fr. 1 verso   Discourse in Johannine style: Jesus tells lawyers to punish transgressors, not him. Then turns to rulers of the people: their search for life in Scriptures should lead them to Jesus of whom they speak. Moses will be their accuser — echoes of John 5:39 and 45. Their reply: they acknowledge where Moses is from but do not know that about Jesus — echo of John 9:29. Jesus reply: this is proof of their disbelief. To believe in Moses requires belief in Jesus, to whom Moses bore witness — echo of John 5:46.

Fr. 1 recto A   Jesus is threatened with stoning but is able to walk through the crowd "because the hour of his betrayal had not yet come" — echo of John 7:30; cf. 10:39.

Fr. 1 recto B   Variant of Jesus healing a leper, whom he sends to the priests to fulfill the offering commanded in Torah — as in Mark 1:40-44; Luke 5:12-14; Matt 8:2-4. Adds the injunction "sin no more" to the end of the story — as in John 5:14, to the paralytic — as well as detail that the man contracted leprosy by eating with lepers in an inn. Perhaps the sin in question was associating with lepers.

Fr. 2 recto   Variant of the controversy story over paying tribute to Caesar — Mark 12:13-15; Matt 22:15-18; Luke 20:20-23 — rephrased as giving kings what belongs to their rule. Instead of the reply in the Synoptics, this version expands Jesus' attack on the hypocrisy of his challengers with a citation from Isa 29:13 (LXX), found in the controversy over plucking grain on the Sabbath — Mark 7:6-7; Matt 15:8-9.

Fr. 2 verso   fragmentary beginning has Jesus walking by the Jordan and posing a riddle to those with him that they cannot solve. He then sows seed on the river which produces a miraculous harvest of grain.

8. Lührmann, *Evangelien*, 133.

Further discoveries might fill out more of the context for these bits of story. Without the echoes of familiar gospel stories, the fragments would be even more difficult to read. It is not possible to tell from these examples how thoroughly echoes of Johannine discourses or debates were combined with episodes from Synoptic Gospel traditions. As they stand, only a few phrases bleed over from one type to the other. *P. Eg.* 2 could represent isolated incidents from Synoptic and other sayings or stories. Ehrman has argued that nothing in the way in which *P. Eg.* 2 tells its stories suggests an author claiming to make an authoritative or canonical reading of Jesus material.[9]

Apocryphal Gospels and Reading the Synoptics

A number of these second- and third-century gospel traditions have already been introduced in our study of the Synoptic Gospels. The most significant, a Coptic translation of a Greek collection of sayings of Jesus, the *Gospel of Thomas,* enabled scholars to identify Greek fragments as part of that text. These Greek fragments had been among the earliest published Oxyrynchus papyri (P. Oxy. 1, 654, and 655).[10] P. Oxy. 1 is a leaf from a papyrus codex dated around 200 C.E. It contains sayings 26-28, a bit of 29, 30-32, and the opening of 33. P. Oxy. 654 comes from the back of a third-century papyrus roll. (On the front is a survey list.) It contains the introductory saying and variants of sayings 1-6 and a bit of 7. P. Oxy. 655 originally consisted of eight pieces from a papyrus roll. Two have been lost. Two others do not have enough text to reconstruct. What remains is also fragmentary but can be seen as representing sayings 36-39. Since P. Oxy. 654 contains the opening, "these are the [secret] words which . . . the living Jesus spoke" followed by the sequence of sayings found in Coptic *Gos. Thom.,* there is no question about the sayings collection represented in this material. Similarly P. Oxy. 1 and P. Oxy. 655 have sayings in the same order that one finds in Coptic *Gos. Thom.* Each represents a separate copy of *Gos. Thom.* in Greek.

9. Ehrman, *Lost Christianities,* 50.
10. See Harold Attridge, "Appendix: The Greek Fragments," in Bentley Layton, ed., *Nag Hammadi Codex II,2-7* (Nag Hammadi Studies 20; Leiden: Brill, 1989) 96-128; Lührmann, *Evangelien,* 144-81; Elliott, *Apocryphal New Testament,* 123-47.

Detailed comparison of the overlapping sayings in the Greek and Coptic versions shows some differences which indicate that another form of *Gos. Thom.* was translated into Coptic a century or so after the composition of the collection. Coptic *Gos. Thom.* 36 is an abbreviated version of the longer versions in Q (Luke 12:22b-31/Matt 6:25-33) and P. Oxy. 655, "Jesus said, 'Do not be concerned from morning until evening and from evening until morning about what you will wear.'" P. Oxy. 655 retains part of the imagery employed to support the injunction in Q. It preserves the series "food, eat, robe, clothe yourself" (Q: life, eat, body, clothe yourself), the comparison with lilies that do not spin, and the paradox of adding to one's stature. In another case, *Gos. Thom.* 30 (Coptic) has an opening which disagrees with the Greek P. Oxy. 1 and lacks the further sayings added to the conclusion. For Coptic *Gos. Thom.* 30 ("Where there are three gods, they are gods. Where there are two or one, I am with them") P. Oxy. 1 has "if there are three, they are godless (Gk. *atheoi*), and where there is one only, I say, I am with him." Then P. Oxy. 1 attaches sayings which appear elsewhere in Coptic *Gos. Thom.* 77b: "Lift the stone and there you will find me; split the wood and I am there." In *Gos. Thom.* 77b, the order is reversed, wood and then stone. The first part of the saying resembles Matt. 18:20, "for where two or three are gathered in my name, there I am in their midst." Matthew has attached the saying to another assuring God's favorable response to those so assembled. The added sayings in P. Oxy. 1 suggest a different interpretation, the presence of Jesus everywhere.

A number of other differences between the Coptic and Greek versions may have been introduced by translators or may be scribal errors in the archetype used by the translators. The Greek witnesses are so fragmentary as well as limited to opening logia in *Gos. Thom.* that one cannot draw certain conclusions about how the versions are related. Isolated sayings admit varied interpretations. Thus 2 *Clement* 12.2 has a very different understanding of the saying it shares with *Gos. Thom.* 22 (see the comparison on p. 264). Though both authors agree that the saying has something to do with the kingdom of God, 2 *Clement* understands its meaning in terms of the ethical conduct required of Christians. For the Gnostics who transmitted and read the Coptic *Gos. Thom.* the saying had a different meaning. To "make the two one" referred to a process of self-transformation. Through the esoteric knowledge conveyed in Gnostic groups one could recover the primordial unity of the person which existed before Adam and Eve were divided. This unified human possessed immortality and the eternal glory

Gos. Thom. 22	*2 Clement* 12
Jesus saw infants being suckled. He said to his disciples, "These infants being suckled are like those who enter the kingdom." They said to him, "Shall we then as children enter the kingdom?"	For this reason, we should await the kingdom of God with love and righteousness every hour, since we do not know the day when God will appear. For when the Lord himself was asked by someone when his kingdom would come, he said, "When the two are one, and the outside like the inside, and the male with the female is neither male nor female."
Jesus said to them, "When you make the two one, and when you make the inside like the outside and the outside like the inside, and the above like the below, and when you make the male and the female one and the same, so that the male not be male nor the female, female; and you fashion eyes in place of an eye, and a hand in place of a hand, and a foot in place of a foot, and a likeness in place of a likeness, then will you enter [the kingdom]."	Now "the two are one" when we speak truth to one another and when one soul exists in two bodies with no hypocrisy. And "the outside like the inside" means this: the "inside" refers to the soul and the "outside" to the body. Just as your body is visible, so too your soul should be clearly seen in your good deeds. And the words "the male with the female is neither male nor female" means this, that a brother who sees a sister should think nothing about her being female and she should think nothing about his being male. When you do these things, he says, "the kingdom of my Father will come."

of the true God. The fluidity of such sayings of Jesus and their application did not end with their incorporation into narratives of Jesus' ministry. Papias's interest in sayings and their interpretation along with the four versions of *Gos. Thom.* show an active interest in such traditions during the second and third centuries.

As we have seen, sayings were not the only form that apocryphal gospel traditions took in the second and third centuries. Where we have only the titles and quotations in patristic authors, very little can be said about these works. There appears to have been a Gospel used among Jewish Christians that began with the story of Jesus' baptism, "the Gospel of the Hebrews." Unlike the title conventions which came to dominate both canonical and non-canonical Gospels, this work did not employ the pattern of "according to" plus an apostle's name. Instead the name represents those who made use of it. Other alleged Jewish Christian Gospels, "of the Nazareans" or "of the Ebionites," were not independent works, contrary to the impression given in some collections of New Testament apocrypha.[11] Whether this Gospel and its variants reflect an amalgam of materials from the canonical Gospels and other sources, a revision of a canonical Gospel such as Matthew, or another Gospel with only loose ties to other Gospels cannot be decided without better evidence than we currently possess.

It is not clear how patristic authors came by the citations which they label "from the Gospel of the Hebrews." Clement of Alexandria twice cites a saying about seeking, finding, being disturbed/astonished, reigning, and finding rest. The first time he introduces it with the words, "As it is also written in the Gospel of the Hebrews" (*Stromateis* 2.45.5). The second time he only says that the word he is about to cite is like others (5.96.3). The first citation contains only the second half of the chain: be astonished, reign, and find rest. The same saying occurs as the second saying in *Gos. Thom.* The Coptic version lacks the final reference to finding rest. P. Oxy. 654 contains the reference to finding rest but omits "astonished" from the chain, as does the second citation in Clement of Alexandria. Perhaps Clement is correct in attributing the saying to "the Gospel of the Hebrews." Injunctions to seek and find wisdom are commonplaces of Jewish wisdom traditions (Sirach 6:27-28).[12] On the other hand, Clement may not know the source of an often used saying. "Gospel of the Hebrews" could be a guess on his part.

Because Clement and Origen are the earliest witnesses to the *Gospel of the Hebrews,* Klauck infers that it was composed in Alexandria. However, he acknowledges a legend with Alexandrian ties that would push for an origin elsewhere. Eusebius reports (*Hist. Eccl.* 5.10.3) that the Christian teacher Pantaenus found a copy of Matthew's Gospel in Hebrew during a

---

11. Such as Elliott, *Apocryphal New Testament,* 5.
12. Klauck, *Apocryphal Gospels,* 38-40.

visit to India and brought it back to Alexandria.[13] If the *Gospel of the Hebrews* appeared to be a translation of the legendary Hebrew version of Matthew, then it must have been closely related to the canonical Gospel of Matthew. Papyrus fragments that contain only partial texts would then be identified as Matthew even if they came from this Gospel. Therefore one would have to find a manuscript which preserved a title in order to identify it as the *Gospel of the Hebrews*. But it may not have circulated widely enough to be translated into Coptic, as *Gospel of Thomas* was. The erudite Alexandrians had an interest in collecting and comparing multiple versions of texts that was not common everywhere. Hence an interest in Gospel material from a distant land would be natural for them. Despite its implausibility, the Hebrew Matthew legend shows no signs of vanishing. News flashes keep popping up in which a scholar, usually not a well-trained New Testament text critic, claims to have found fragments of the "original Hebrew or Aramaic Matthew" among the holdings of some library. So far no such candidates have withstood expert scrutiny.

Scholars also try to supplement the surviving sixth-century copy of the *Gospel of Peter* with other Gospel fragments from the earlier period, including *Papyrus Egerton* 2. Where Greek fragments overlap the Akhmimic text, as in the case of P. Oxy. 2949, reconstruction of the fragmentary text is fairly straightforward.[14] There is no reason to attach *Papyrus Egerton* 2 to *Gos. Pet.* other than its mixture of Synoptic and Johannine materials.

Lührmann has proposed that another very fragmentary second-century papyrus (P. Oxy. 4009) is part of *Gos. Pet.* In order to reconstruct the text, he first detects an echo of the saying in Matt. 10:16 (also found in *Gos. Thom.* 39/P. Oxy. 655). That saying serves to open a dialogue between Jesus and Peter in 2 *Clement* 5.2-4. Peter objects that the wolves will tear the sheep to pieces. Jesus replies that "you (plural) should no more fear those who can kill you without harming you than sheep do wolves. Only fear those who have the power to throw soul and body into the fire of Gehenna." On the basis of this 2 *Clement* text, Lührmann has reconstructed a short dialogue between Jesus and Peter that was, he speculates, on the recto side of P. Oxy. 4009. He admits that the clue to filling out the few Greek letters per line on the other side has not been found.[15] If this fragment is part

---

13. Klauck, *Apocryphal Gospels*, 38.
14. See Lührmann, *Evangelien*, 60-73.
15. Lührmann, *Evangelien*, 73-86.

of *Gos. Pet.* and if the exchange with its echo of Matthew's mission discourse occurred during an account of Jesus' ministry, then we would have evidence for more than the passion-resurrection section which survives in the later manuscript. However, as Lührmann points out, one cannot be sure. The Akhmimic text breaks off with what appears to be the beginning of a tradition similar to that in John 21. So such a mission discourse could have been associated with the appearance of the risen Jesus as well.[16] Jesus instructs Peter to "feed my lambs" in John 21:15-18, for example. Lührmann proposes additional possibilities for tracking down second-century remains of *Gos. Pet.* Since one passage of *2 Clement* has proven so fruitful, other Gospel quotations found in that writing could have come from *Gos. Pet.* It is unlikely that *2 Clement* only used that Gospel once. In addition, other familiar Peter traditions such as the allusion to the transfiguration in 2 Pet 1:16-18 and a third-century fragment from the Fayum (P. Vindob G 2325) containing an exchange between Jesus and Peter similar to Mark 14:27-30 could also qualify, though *Gos. Pet.* and 2 Pet 1:16-18 might be independent examples of early-second-century Peter tradition.[17]

Without a surviving manuscript of a Greek version or translation, it is difficult to assess such proposals. The Coptic codices copied in the fifth century that included the *Gospel of Thomas* contain three apocryphal Peter texts. Two of them employ the figure of Peter as recipient and guarantee for a Gnostic understanding of the crucifixion. The heavenly being, the true Savior, does not suffer on the cross (*Apocalypse of Peter*, NHC 7.3; *Letter of Peter to Philip*, NHC 8.2). The third is an allegorical tale of the Twelve on mission to the city of a mysterious pearl-seller (Jesus). When they find him, Jesus sends them back to heal the poor of the city (*Acts of Peter and the Twelve Apostles*, NHC 6.1). The allegorical tale may come from Gnostic Christians as well, but it contains no specifically Gnostic motifs. Unlike the other two, it has only a very distant echo of the canonical Gospels or Acts. However, these examples show that there is no a priori reason to reduce apocryphal Peter traditions to a single Gospel. Had we found only fragments of *Apocalypse of Peter* that refer to the crucifixion scene, we might even have classified them as from an "unknown Gospel." Caution remains the watchword in assigning fragments to a particular Gospel. The evident interest in composing, circulating, and translating such apocryphal works

16. Lührmann, *Evangelien*, 85-86.
17. Lührmann, *Evangelien*, 87-88.

in the second and third centuries also undercuts theories that would push *Gos. Pet.* back into the first century, prior to the composition of the canonical Gospels.

The most imaginative developments in retelling stories about Jesus occur where the first-century authors have not laid any groundwork, at the beginning of Jesus' life. Bits and pieces from Luke's infancy narrative were familiar enough to provide some characters and the Temple location for the *Protoevangelium of James.* Its narrator addresses other concerns, especially protecting the virginity of Mary before and after the birth of her son. The *Infancy Gospel of Thomas* picks up a different motif, Jesus as miracle-worker. Though some of the miracles reflect the beneficial actions of his adult life, others are merely the consequence of the power of his words. The young child is either unable or unwilling to rein in his tongue. Both of these infancy narratives allow the imagination free play with legends of conception, birth, and early childhood. But Luke's story of the twelve-year-old in the Temple is the cutoff in the *Infancy Gospel of Thomas.* There is no further account for the period between ages twelve and thirty. Such a gap would not be unfamiliar to the audience. Exodus jumps from the birth and adoption of Moses to the dramatic episodes which precipitate his flight and encounter with God in the wilderness. The legends in the infancy Gospels do not provide any historical clues about their origins. They tell us even less about the infancy narratives found in Matthew and Luke. By the fourth century, Jerome will reject the *Protoevangelium of James* because it presents James as an older step-brother of Jesus. Nevertheless, its Marian traditions became so inscribed in the Latin West that many Roman Catholics today still assume that the names of Mary's parents and stories about her sinlessness are to be found in Scripture.

Gnostic "Gospels" from the Second and Third Centuries

The thirteen codices containing Coptic translations of Gnostic and other early Christian works found near Nag Hammadi in Egypt contain a number of texts that have "Gospel" in their colophon. Other writings in which various apostles individually or as a group present Gnostic rites, mythologoumena or doctrine as the true teaching of Jesus have such titles as Apocryphon, Apocalypse, Letter, Teaching, or Book. The latest edition of Schneemelcher's *New Testament Apocrypha* lumps all of these Nag Hammadi finds, along with other patristic references to Gnostic writings, into two sections: "Dialogues of the Redeemer" and "Other Gnostic Gospels and Related Literature." However, two of them also find their way into separate sections, "Gospel of Thomas" and "Gospel of Philip." Elliott's collection, *The Apocryphal New Testament,* only includes the sayings collection "Gospel of Thomas." That distinction properly reflects the difference between *Gos. Thom.* and the other items in the Nag Hammadi collection. Because *Gos. Thom.* represents a compilation of sayings that was employed to support a Gnostic understanding of Jesus' kingdom preaching, it also provides valuable evidence for the transmission of sayings material, as we have seen. Attempts to contort the sayings from the dialogues between the risen Jesus and the disciples found in other works from this collection such as *Dialogue of the Savior* (NHC 3.5) are not persuasive.[18]

Designations such as "secret book," "revelation," "dialogue," or "discourse" reflect the literary genre of these other writings. They claim to represent teaching that Jesus gave to one or more of the disciples after his resurrection. In some cases the text is too fragmentary to be certain whether or not the setting is post-resurrection, though analogies of form and content with other Gnostic texts indicates that that is likely the case. Another Coptic codex (Berlin 8502) contains additional copies of works in the Nag Hammadi collection *(Apocryphon of John, Sophia of Jesus Christ)* along with parts of a post-resurrection dialogue in which Mary Magdalene plays a key role. She strengthens the Twelve, who hesitate to go out to preach as the Savior ordered, and relates a private revelation that she has received from the Savior. The colophon entitles this work "The Gospel According to Mary" even though the first half appears to have been a dialogue between Jesus and a group of disciples.

Most of the first half of *Gos. Mary* has been lost. The first surviving page includes a question from Peter which mentions the Savior's previous explanation to "us." As in the case of *Gos. Thom.,* Greek fragments from *Gos. Mary* have subsequently been identified (P. Oxy. 3525 and P. Ryl. 463). The first picks up the section in which the disciples are grieving and frightened, through Mary's intervention and Peter's request that she make known

---

18. See Helmut Koester and Elaine Pagels in Stephen Emmel, ed., *Nag Hammadi Codex III,5: The Dialogue of the Savior* (Nag Hammadi Studies 26; Leiden: Brill, 1984) 1-17, and the doubts about Koester's view expressed by Beatae Blatz in Schneemelcher, *New Testament Apocrypha,* 300-303.

to them words of the Savior, which they do not know. The second fragment contains the conclusion and title of the work. It begins as Mary completes her revelation. Andrew and Peter protest this strange revelation. Peter objects that the Savior would not have told a woman secretly something that he would not reveal to all his disciples openly. Then Levi defends Mary's revelation. Peter should not contest the Savior's judgment that she was worthy of this teaching. At this point the Greek and Coptic versions diverge significantly. In the Greek, Levi is the only one who goes off to preach the gospel as the Savior has commanded.[19] In the Coptic, the entire group does so.

The content of both the revelation dialogue with the disciples and of Mary's revelation has no explicit link to Gospel traditions of Jesus' life and teaching. The former deals with the final dissolution of matter and the nature of sin. The explanation for sin does not refer to Gospel traditions but to Gnostic mythology: "There is no sin, but it is you who make sin, when you do the things that are like the nature of the adultery which is called sin" (BG 7.13-16; NHL 525). For Gnostic readers "the adultery" designates the fall of the lower Sophia figure away from the divine Father. Mary Magdalene's revelation in the second half of the work concerns the ascent of the soul past the powers which seek to prevent its return to the divine. Upon successful completion of the journey, the soul attains rest in the silence of an aeon beyond time (15.1–16.7). This journey is another familiar motif in Gnostic texts. Since the opening pages of both sections are missing, one cannot tell if the content was tied to well-known sayings of Jesus in some way. The protest by Andrew and Peter suggests that that was probably not the case for Mary Magdalene's revelation.

Since the colophon survives in the early-third-century Greek fragment, we know that the formal designation "Gospel according to . . ." had been applied to this work by that time. The puzzle remains in what sense this is a "Gospel according to Mary." Was she set up as the source for both revelatory episodes by the introduction in some way? The revelation which she provides appears after the Savior has commanded the disciples to go and preach the gospel. Therefore it would appear to be distinct from the task undertaken at the end of *Gos. Mary.* Only discovery of a manuscript that filled in the missing pages could resolve these difficulties. The resurrection ap-

---

19. For a reconstruction of both Greek fragments, see Lührmann, *Evangelien*, 105-10. Schneemelcher (*New Testament Apocrypha*, pp. 392-95) is aware of both fragments but only incorporates P. Ryl. 463.

pearance, dialogue with the disciples, commission to preach the gospel, and the Savior's departure are intended to remind readers of traditions found in the canonical Gospels. Mary Magdalene's revelation may refer to a version of her solitary encounter with the risen Lord such as one finds in John 20:11-18. Its laconic conclusion, "she announced to the disciples that she had seen the Lord and that he had said these things to her," provides a hook to expand "these things" beyond the brief exchange in the Johannine episode.

The dispute over the authenticity of Mary's revelation which pits Mary Magdalene and Levi against Andrew and Peter has raised several exegetical questions. It appears inappropriate to the earlier depiction of Mary Magdalene's relationship with the other disciples. At the conclusion of the revelation dialogue, when the disciples do not depart to preach the gospel as one would anticipate but are afraid and dispirited, she is the one who intervenes. The effective speech demonstrates her understanding of the Savior's teaching:

> Then Mary stood up, greeted them all, and said to her brethren, "Do not weep and do not grieve or be irresolute, for his grace will be entirely with you and will protect you. But rather let us praise his greatness, for he has prepared us and made us into men." When Mary said this, she turned their hearts to the Good, and they began to discuss the words of the [Savior]. (9.12-23; NHL 525)

When Peter then requests that Mary share her revelation, he states that she has knowledge of words of the Savior which the others do not (10.1-6). Therefore his objection that Jesus would not have taught her privately what he had not taught his other disciples seems out of order (17.16-22). In addition, the opening exchange between Mary and the Savior as she reports it would inform the ancient reader that Mary had attained a high degree of spiritual or intellectual insight. She is able to endure a vision of the Lord without wavering (10.14-16). The ability to stand unmoving in the presence of the divine serves as an image of philosophical or spiritual perfection across traditions in the ancient world.

At this point, Peter acknowledges Mary's understanding and relationship to the Savior. Seeking to learn the Savior's private teaching can be understood as a guarantee that when the disciples finally do disband to preach the gospel, they too will have full knowledge of Jesus' words. We have seen that Mark's abrupt conclusion left both Matthew and Luke with the problem of showing that Jesus' fearful and flawed disciples were able to convey his teaching. Luke employs a forty-day period between Easter and the Ascension and the descent of the Holy Spirit as advanced instruction. Second- and third-century Gnostic authors latched on to that suggestion of instruction by the risen Jesus. Some even extended its duration. One would anticipate that the lost opening to *Gospel of Mary* contained a setting for this occasion of Jesus' teaching at some time after the resurrection. The mission instructions at the conclusion indicate that this is the final revelation.

The very different Peter at the end of Mary's revelation could be the result of the composition history of the work as we have it. In that view, *Gos. Mary* combines a familiar revelation dialogue genre that ends with the revealer's departure and the actions of the recipient of the revelation with a second act in which teaching about the soul is at stake. As part of the combined work, Peter's behavior demonstrates a lack of spiritual insight. Levi accuses Peter of irrational anger and urges that they "put on the perfect man" and undertake what the Lord told them to do (18.6-20). In the Greek version, only Levi goes forth to preach. Thus the reader is led to infer that Peter has an immature soul and a flawed understanding of Jesus. The group departure in the Coptic version suggests a more benign view of the apostle. However, other Gnostic revelation dialogues show a concern that may have been spared by polemic against Gnostic teaching. Instead of relying on the private teaching that Jesus gives to a single disciple, as in the opening of *Gos. Thom.*, texts such as the *Sophia of Jesus Christ* or the *Pistis Sophia* have the risen Jesus instruct all the disciples, male and female, as a group. Therefore the Gnostic author could represent this teaching as the true teaching of all the apostles.

The Coptic *Gospel of Thomas* ends with a saying (114), which many scholars suggest belongs to the final redactional stage of that collection. It too involves an attempt by Peter to force Mary Magdalene out. He asks Jesus to exclude her, "for women are not worthy of life." Jesus refuses. Instead, he promises to "make her male so that she may become a living Spirit resembling you males." The transformation is then generalized: "Every woman who will make herself male will enter the kingdom." The meaning of this promise remains hotly contested. *Gos. Mary* referred to a similar transformation for all of Jesus' disciples, "make us men," "put on the perfect man."[20] Clearly a spiritual transformation that restores the di-

20. Lüdemann, *Evangelien*, 116-17.

vine image is at stake in such traditions. Other sayings in *Gos. Thom.* hint at a return to the unity before Adam and Eve were divided. Various teachings about such a restoration can be found in Gnostic texts. Whether the transformation is achieved by mystic enlightenment, by baptismal rites, by ascetic practices, or in the case of the Valentinians by a sacramental rite, the "marriage chamber," depends upon the context. A sayings collection like *Gos. Thom.* does not provide information about how it was used. *Gos. Thom.* 13, an echo of Peter's confession at Caesarea Philippi, demonstrates the superiority of the insight of the Gospel's authority, Jude Thomas, to that of Simon Peter (Jesus = righteous angel) and Matthew (Jesus = wise philosopher). After Thomas has correctly refused to give a comparison for Jesus, Jesus gives Thomas a private revelation. When the others ask him to reveal what Jesus said, Thomas refuses lest they attempt to stone him.

Esoteric traditions are not for the spiritually immature or for public reading. The argument at the end of *Gos. Thom.* determines that it is possible for women as well as men to attain such maturity. The argument in *Gos. Mary* has shifted focus. Mary's spiritual maturity is demonstrated both in her words and in her vision of the Savior. The problem lies in the esoteric teaching about the soul conveyed to her. The Greek text lacks four lines found in the Coptic text that give Mary's reaction. Only the last word of her reaction to Peter survives. Mary does not pick up Peter's disparaging remark about Jesus giving such a teaching to a woman. She fastens on the suggestion that she has made it all up and is lying about the Savior (BG 18.1-5). Thus *Gos. Mary* is engaged in defending the authenticity of esoteric teachings of the Savior against the claim that only those teachings given publicly to Peter and the other male disciples are authentic.

It is possible that this public teaching was represented by Matthew's Gospel in particular. This proposal cannot be definitively established but several observations suggest such a possibility. The two flawed opinions are expressed by Peter and Matthew in *Gos. Thom.* 13. Levi, the tax collector called by Jesus in Mark 2:14 (and Luke 5:27), is replaced by Matthew in Matt 9:9. Levi also appears in *Gos. Pet.* 60 as the companion of Peter and Andrew, who are setting out to fish. (John 21:2 has a different list: Simon Peter, Thomas, Nathanael, the sons of Zebedee, and two other disciples.) Levi's reprimand reminds Peter that the Savior had instructed them to preach the gospel "without determining anything or making laws" (P. Ryl. 463.12-13). Just as the Coptic version changes the ending so that Peter finally obeys the Savior's command, so it also adds to Levi's words prohibiting legal determinations the phrase, "beyond what the Savior said" (BG 9.1-2; 19.20-21). The Peter of Matthew's Gospel has the authority to make such determinations. The Father revealed to Peter that Jesus is Messiah (Matt 16:15-19). Thus it is possible that the second-century Greek version of *Gospel of Mary* had Matthew's representation of Peter as custodian of Jesus' teaching in its sights. Contrary to the conclusion of that Gospel, in which the Eleven go out to establish "all that Jesus taught" among "the nations/Gentiles" (Matt 28:16-20), they did not follow the Savior's instructions willingly in *Gos. Mary*. Either the Coptic translation or its Greek version has shifted the conclusion. Jesus does not insist on a law-free mission, only one that does not add to his teaching. Peter does not remain unconverted. All the disciples preach a gospel which incorporates the teaching Jesus gave to Mary Magdalene. However, the missing pages at the beginning and middle of the Coptic text render conclusions about its redaction tentative.

Three other texts from the Nag Hammadi codices are referred to as Gospels: the *Gospel of Truth* (NHC 1.3 and 12.2 [fragments]), the *Gospel of Philip* (NHC 2.3), and the *Gospel of the Egyptians* (NHC 3.2 and 4.2). *Gospel of Truth* was given that title by modern scholars because it opens with "The gospel of truth is joy for those who received from the Father of truth the grace of knowing him through the Word that came forth from the pleroma, the one who is in the thought and mind of the Father, that is, the one who is addressed as the Savior, that being the name of the work he is to perform" (1.16.31-39; NHLE 40). The word "gospel" clearly refers to the proclamation of salvation, in this case the knowledge of God, not to the literary genre of the written text. There is no title provided for *Gos. Tr.* in the codex itself. Only two of the five writings contained in that volume have titles, an opening prayer attributed to the Apostle Paul and a treatise concerning the resurrection. *Gos. Tr.* is a homiletic piece that draws on the full range of the emerging Christian canon for its biblical allusions — Genesis, John's Gospel, Pauline epistles, and perhaps Revelation. There are very few references to sayings traditions or the Synoptic Gospels.

Because Irenaeus claims that the Valentinians had written a "Gospel of Truth" that did not conform to the Gospels of the apostles (= the canonical Gospels; *Adv. Haer.* 3.11.9), scholars often treat this Nag Hammadi text as though it were composed by Valentinus. One should recognize the rhetorical cast of Irenaeus' argument. The accusation presumes that a recently composed work can be shown to diverge from apostolic tradition by comparison with the four-Gospel canon. Recent composition by a known presbyter was one of the reasons given for removing *Gos. Pet.* from public reading as well. However the text that scholars are calling "Gospel of Truth" has no intention of replacing the Christian canon. In fact, it depends on the reader's ability to detect the rich texture of allusions to that canon for its rhetorical effectiveness. It weaves in familiar bits of Valentinian myth and theology in much the same way as it does the canonical material. In addition, the opening sentence demonstrates that the author is familiar with the debates about the divinity and redemptive mission of Christ as they were formulated in the second and third centuries. It defines the Father as unknowable because God cannot be encompassed in human categories. Therefore the Word or Son emerging from the Father is a necessary condition for any knowledge of God. The problem was how to characterize the relationship between the two. Identifying the Son with the Father's thought/mind or will was a fairly common strategy.

Although it is possible that Irenaeus had seen a different Valentinian work that could be described as a "Gospel," he may in fact have had casual familiarity with a second-century Greek version of *Gos. Tr.* A brief glance at its opening words could have been sufficient ammunition for his rhetorical purposes. He had already devoted most of book 2 of *Adv. Haer.* to refuting Valentinian mythology and teaching about God. His aim at this point in book 3 is to establish the authority of the four-Gospel canon and Acts. What is not clearly taught by the apostles in the Gospels cannot have been revealed by Jesus. Valentinian exegetes were much more interested in the symbolic language of John's Gospel and the Pauline epistles than in the Synoptics. However, *Gos. Tr.* does contain fairly direct references to a few sayings from that tradition. Given the extent of its canon, these parallels are probably derived from Matthew's Gospel rather than from an independent form of the sayings tradition.

Gos. Tr. 20.13-14	Matt 20:28	"his death is life for many"
Gos. Tr. 27.23-24	Matt 5:48	"the Father is perfect"
Gos. Tr. 31.35-32.4	Matt 18:12-13	parable of the Lost Sheep
Gos. Tr. 32.17-22	Matt 12:11	sheep in a pit on the Sabbath
Gos. Tr. 33.4-5	Matt 11:28	rest for those who labor
Gos. Tr. 33.16-20	Matt 6:19	"do not be moth-eaten, worm-eaten"
Gos. Tr. 33.37-39	Matt 7:16, 20	known by their fruits

275

Gos. Tr. incorporates these sayings into its understanding of salvation. That process of interpretation does not require the Valentinian author to create a different Gospel from that being read in the churches.

The *Gospel of the Egyptians* has a long colophon (NHC 3.69.6-17) in which the phrase "the gospel of the Egyptians, the God-written, holy, secret book" occurs. But after introducing himself and invoking a blessing on his fellow enlightened spirits, the scribe gives another title, "the holy book of the great, invisible Spirit." The title of the text which follows (69.18-20) uses the latter title. Scholars have reconstructed the opening lines as "the holy book of the Egyptians about the great invisible Spirit" (3.40.12-13; 4.50.1-2). The work presents itself as a primordial revelation of Seth, the ancestor of the Gnostic race. It contains a Sethian Gnostic mythological view of the origins of the world and what appear to be formulas employed in baptismal initiation rites by which Seth's seed can be returned to its place in the heavenly world. Insofar as Jesus figures at all, Christ is identified as the third descent of the heavenly revealer into the created world to rescue the Sethians. There is no link between this work and any canonical or apocryphal Gospel traditions. Nor does it appear to be the "Gospel of the Egyptians" quoted by Clement of Alexandria (*Stromateis* 3.45.64-68)[21] and mentioned by Origen (*Homily on Luke* 1.1).[22]

The *Gospel of Philip* follows *Gos. Thom.* in Nag Hammadi Codex 2. Unlike *Gos. Thom.* or *Gos. Mary*, it makes no claim that Philip is the source for all or part of the teaching contained in it. Philip is the only apostle mentioned by name in this collection of excerpts on various aspects of Gnostic teaching (2.73.8). Most of the selections deal with Valentinian sacraments. For example, the saying attributed to Philip reports a legend that Joseph made the cross on which his offspring was crucified. The author contrasts the cross with the olive tree, which provides oil for chrism, which is necessary for resurrection. Early editions of *Gos. Ph.* divided its selections into numbered sections as with *Gos. Thom.* That numbering scheme has been retained in Schneemelcher, *New Testament Apocrypha*, 118-206. Because the paragraphs are not marked as sayings as in *Gos. Thom*, most recent treatments of *Gos. Ph.* have employed the codex page and line references used for the other Nag Hammadi texts. Once again the citation provided from a "Gospel of Philip" by the fourth cen-

---

21. Schneemelcher, *New Testament Apocrypha*, 209-211.
22. Schneemelcher, *New Testament Apocrypha*, 44-46.

tury heresiologist Epiphanius (*Panarion* 26.13.2-3) does not match this work. However, its genre as a collection of excerpts would make it easy for there to have been quite different versions in circulation under the same title. On the other hand, the title "Gospel of Philip" may have been created by the scribe who copied it into Codex 2. It is not set off as a subscript in the manner of other titles in the codex, but appears as the last line of the text.

Quotations from the canonical Gospels are used in some of its selections to underscore the truth of a particular teaching or the necessity of receiving the sacramental initiation described.

Gos. Ph. 55.33-34	Matt 16:17	"my Father in heaven"
Gos. Ph. 57.4-5	John 6:53	"whoever does not eat my flesh. . ."
Gos. Ph. 68.8-12	Matt 6:6	on praying in secret
Gos. Ph. 68.26-27	Matt 27:46	"My God, my God, why have you forsaken me?"
Gos. Ph. 72.23-73.1	Matt 3:15	"thus fulfill all righteousness"
Gos. Ph. 83.12	Matt 3:10	"already the ax is laid at the root"
Gos. Ph. 84.7-9	John 8:32	"truth will set you free"
Gos. Ph. 85.5-20	Matt 27:51	"veil torn from top to bottom"
Gos. Ph. 85.29-31	Matt 15:13	"Father not planted, rooted out"

The citations in *Gos. Ph.* are introduced either as "he/Jesus/the Lord said" or with the formula "the word (Greek *Logos*) said." In addition to citations, other selections explain a scene from the Gospels. For example, *Gos. Ph.* 57.28–58.10 explains how Jesus presented himself in the world. He had to appear in a form that recipients could receive. Consequently, the Word had to hide his true nature. Some thought they were seeing another human being. In order for the disciples to see Jesus transfigured on the mount (Matt 17:1-6) Jesus had to make them great. In addition to the canonical examples, *Gos. Ph.* attributes other sayings to Jesus of unknown provenance. Some may have been maxims popular among Gnostic Christians (55.37–56.3; 58.11-17; 59.23-27; 63.25-30; 64.10-12; 67.30-35; 74.25-27). *Gos. Ph.* incorporates other sayings and parable-like comparisons in its collection without providing any attribution.

A pronouncement story provides Jesus' response to the (male?) disciples who object to his preference for Mary Magdalene:

As for Wisdom who is called "the barren," she is the mother [of the] angels. And the companion of the [. . .] Mary Magdalene. [. . . loved] her more than [all] the disciples [and used to] kiss her [often] on her [. . .]. The rest of [the disciples. . . .] They said to him, "Why do you love her more than all of us?" The Savior answered and said to them, "Why do I not love you like her? When a blind man and one who sees are both together in the darkness, they are no different from one another. When the light comes, then he who sees will see the light, and he who is blind will remain in darkness." (63.30–64.9; NHL 148)

Earlier in *Gospel,* three women are named as always accompanying Jesus: Mary his mother, her sister Mary, and Mary Magdalene (59.6-10). The sacred kiss was part of ritual practice. As was the case in *Gos. Thom.* and *Gos. Mary, Gos. Ph.* defends the tradition that credits Mary Magdalene with special insight into the Savior's teaching. It does not support such twenty-first-century inventions concerning Mary Magdalene as Jesus' wife and mother of his offspring as popularized in Dan Brown's *The Da Vinci Code.*

The Gospel of Judas

In April 2006 the National Geographic Society announced its acquisition of a badly damaged ancient codex that contained copies of two previously known writings, the *Letter of Peter to Philip* (also found in NHC 8.2), the *First Apocalypse of James* (NHC 5.3), a previously unknown *Gospel of Judas,* and a work that refers to an "Allogenes" but is not a version of the *Allogenes* from the Nag Hammadi codices (NHC 11.3). A preliminary transcription of the Coptic text was made available on the society's web site along with an English translation subsequently published as a book. Further analysis of fragments from the codex turned up a page number 108. Therefore the original volume would appear to have contained closer to 100 pages of text, not the 60-plus received by the purchasers. At what point pages were removed, perhaps by one or more parties who attempted to sell the codex in the mid-1980s, cannot be determined.

Since the Judas of this gospel is Judas Iscariot, not the Judas Thomas of *Gos. Thom.,* the public anticipated an account of Jesus' passion from Judas's perspective. *Gos. Judas* does exalt Judas Iscariot over the other disciples of Jesus. He, not Peter, comprehends the true divine origin of Jesus. Jesus is not the son of the Jewish creator god whom the disciples worship with their "thanksgiving" *(eucharist)* over bread, but of an unknown divine power and his wisdom consort Barbelo. Because Judas has this insight, Jesus instructs him in the higher mysteries of the kingdom, which include an extended Gnostic account of the origins of the material world and humankind and of the enlightened soul's ascent back to the Father. Though the text is very fragmentary, Judas appears to have a vision of his own return to his heavenly guardian angel along with a vision of Jesus' ascent to glory. Salvation as the soul's ascent or return to heavenly glory appears in other apocryphal Gospels from the second and third century and is not limited to Gnostic Christians (see the description of the *Gospel of the Savior* below).

Because later Christians treated Judas as an archetypal symbol for the evil Jew, some initial publicity hinted that *Gos. Judas* would provide a perspective on the passion free of anti-Semitism. The Judas of the Gospel follows Jesus' own instructions when he hands Jesus over to authorities, since Jesus must leave this body behind to return to his Father. The actual text exhibits extreme hostility toward the god of Jewish Scriptures, toward such rituals as the Passover meal, and toward the sacrificial cult at the Temple. Despite Jesus' repeated command, his other disciples, the Twelve, remain devoted to that God and to the demonic powers that control creation. Judas has a vision in which the others appear to be stoning him. Jesus tells Judas that he will be replaced to complete the number of the Twelve. The cosmology of *Gos. Judas* has Twelve symbolize the demonic astrological powers that seek to prevent the soul from reaching the true God. The Twelve also represent mainstream Christians of the second and third centuries, who remain devoted to the Jewish god and rituals such as baptism and the Lord's Supper.

Unlike many of the apocryphal Gospels we have surveyed, *Gos. Judas* has very few direct allusions to the Jesus traditions or passion narratives of the canonical Gospels. Of course readers would not be able to figure out what is going on without knowing something of that part of the story prior to Jesus' arrest. But the primary "back story" required to understand this work is to be found in the speculations of second- and third-century Gnostic circles. Readers of the codex in which *Gos. Judas* is found encounter two other examples of the genre, a dialogue between Jesus and various disciples. During these revelations, Jesus teaches the true wisdom which leads to salvation. Suffering on the cross is a vain counter-move by demonic powers against the heavenly Savior. In the first tractate of the codex, the *Letter of Peter to Philip,* the scenario invokes the end of Luke's Gospel and the opening chapters of Acts. By its conclusion, Peter and the rest of the Twelve are fully enlightened and set out to preach this message to the world. In the second, *1 Apocalypse of James,* Jesus provides similar instruction to his "brother" James in two episodes. The first takes place, as does *Gos. Judas,* just before the passion and the second after Jesus' resurrection. Thus James, the leader in the Jerusalem church, has been claimed for the Gnostic cause as well.

We have seen that the canonical Gospels expanded the brief notices about Judas Iscariot found in Mark to include legends of his death and comments on his motivation. *Gos. Judas* does the same. The text is too badly preserved to give details, but the visions and Jesus' interpretations suggest that Judas will suffer a martyr's death. Jesus makes a similar prediction to James in *1 Apocalypse of James.* In both documents, the real agents of hostility are demonic powers. However the enlightened soul will be able to escape their clutches thanks to the Savior's teaching. Unlike the previous two tractates in its codex, *Gos. Judas* does not seem to have provided interpretations of details in the story of Jesus' passion.

Its final scene sums up the handing over of Jesus in a few enigmatic lines. Jesus has withdrawn into a room with the Twelve. Some scholars suggest that this room is thought of as attached to the Temple precincts, since high priests and scribes are looking to arrest him "during the prayer." As in the Synoptic accounts, they are worried about seizing someone the crowds regard as a prophet. When they find Judas outside, the scribes approach him. After receiving money, "he handed him over to them." Perhaps readers of *Gos. Judas* filled in the gaps by imagining that Judas was sent out of the Last Supper room, as in John 13:27-29, without the negative elements of demonic possession and greed in John's account. This scenario actually reduces Judas's role in the whole proceeding. There is no dramatic encounter in Gethsemane. Judas simply has to show the authorities the room in which Jesus and the disciples have gathered.

Based on the surviving evidence, the category "Gnostic Gospels" should be retired. The patristic heresiologists followed Irenaeus's lead in charging their opponents with the fabrication of false Gospels bearing the name of the apostles but not their teaching. Given the fluidity of sayings traditions as well as legends and stories about Jesus in the second century, none of the apocryphal elements in these texts is necessarily a corruption of canonical tradition for nefarious purposes. The only Gnostic text with a title "Gospel" which has some claim to belong in the category, the *Gospel of Thomas,* is a sayings collection that passed through various redactions. The Coptic version contains some sayings which have been reformulated to accommodate a Gnostic view of salvation. The *Gospel of Philip* and the *Gospel of Truth* provide examples of the ways in which Gnostic teachers could interpret both canonical and apocryphal Jesus traditions to the same end. In addition to composing commentaries, sermons, and theological treatises, Gnostics composed apocryphal works that provided esoteric revelations set either in the primordial period between Adam and Noah or in the period of post-resurrection encounters between Jesus and his disciples, as in the example provided by the *Gospel of Mary.*

P. Berol. 22220: The "Gospel of the Savior"

In the 1990s, scholars studying fragments of a Coptic manuscript from about the sixth century C.E. that the Berlin museum had acquired in 1967 recognized that it represented an apocryphal Gospel. Because its preferred term for Jesus is "the Savior," the initial editors called this work "the Gospel of the Savior."[23] This decision does not reflect any of the ancient scribal practices for naming such works. Other scholars prefer to retain either the museum number, P. Berol. 22220, or a generic designation such as "Unknown Berlin Gospel."[24] Initial enthusiasm produced claims that the Gospel represented in this sixth-century copy had been written in the early second century. A more sober look at what survives of its content and its relationship to both *Gos. Pet.* and another Coptic Gospel fragment, the *Strasbourg Fragment,* suggests that it was composed later in the second or in the third century. Page numbers permit scholars to place some of the P. Berol. 22220 fragments in sequence. The placement of some of the remaining fragments is disputed. Remains of about thirty pages survive. The original codex contained about one hundred pages. Like the Nag Hammadi codices, the Berlin codex which contains *Gos. Mary,* or the codex in which part of *Gos. Pet.* was found, there probably were other

23. Charles W. Hedrick and Paul A. Mirecki, *Gospel of the Savior: A New Ancient Gospel* (Santa Rosa: Polebridge, 1999).

24. So Klauck, *Apocryphal Gospels,* 27-28.

texts in the same volume. Therefore it is impossible to know whether or not P. Berol. 22220 extended beyond the passion account to include either resurrection material as in *Gos. Pet.* or some account of the ministry of Jesus prior to the passion.

The intelligible fragments present a discourse between Jesus and his disciples prior to the crucifixion on the model of the Johannine farewell discourses. Use of the transitional "arise, let us go" (John 14:31 at 98.47-51) and the narrator's comment from John 19:35 (at 108.61-64) indicates that the author was familiar with the Fourth Gospel. Matt 5:13-15, the identification of Jesus' disciples as the light and salt of the world, appears at 97.18-23. So Matthew's Gospel also appears to have been part of the author's repertoire. In addition, apocryphal sayings of Jesus such as *Gos. Thom.* 82 (107.43-48) turn up in the composition. The initial address to the disciples is replete with echoes of the Fourth Gospel:

"I will reveal to you"	98.25-26	John 16:25, 29-30
joy	98.27, 30	John 15:11; 16:20; 17:13
"Arise, let us go"	98.47-48	John 14:31
"One hand me over near"	98.49-51	= Matt 26:45
"You flee, leave me alone"	98.52-57	John 16:32a
"Am not alone, Father"	98.59-60	John 16:32b
"I and Father are a single one"	98.61-62	John 10:30
"It is written + quote"	98.63–99.3	= Matt 26:31
"I am the good shepherd"	99.3-4	John 10:11, 14
"I lay down my life for you"	99.5-6	John 10:11
"You lay down lives for friends"	99.6-9	John 15:13-14
"No greater command . . . lay down life"	99.12-15	John 15:12-14
"Because this Father loves me, I completed his will"	99.15-18	John 10:17; 17:4
"Though I was divine, I became human"	99.18-20	John 1:14

Apparently the transition from this Johannine discourse segment was followed by questions that also relate to its motifs. "How much time?" (99.33-34) could refer to Jesus' use of the expression "little while" also questioned in John 16:18. The follow-up, "take us out of the world" (99.37-39), alludes to the prayer of John 17, in which Jesus, who is no longer "in the world" because he is coming to the Father (17:11), prays for the disciples, whom he will leave in the world, though they are not "of the world" (17:11-17).

With so much of the intervening text missing, it is difficult to know how the next intelligible section, the disciples' vision of Jesus' ascent into the heavens and their own participation in a heavenly journey (100.33-51), was connected to the discourse. It may have also been generated by an allusion to John 17 as well as to the affirmation "we have seen his glory" from John 1:14. In John 17:22a Jesus asserts that he has given the disciples the glory that the Father gave him, and in 17:24 that they may be with Jesus in order to see the glory God has given him. P. Berol. 22220 mentions a mountain as the location for the visionary ascent by the disciples (100.33). Presumably the group has moved to the Mount of Olives. In order to ascend with Jesus into the heavenly regions, the disciples "become like spiritual bodies" (100.35). Such ascents appear in a number of ancient sources. Mary's revelation in *Gos. Mary* included a vision of Jesus as well as of the soul's ascent past demonic powers. Such powers are assumed in P. Berol. 22220. They perceive the ascent as an end to their dominion (100.42-48; 113.1-59). Earlier in the work Jesus has informed his disciples that he will descend into Hades to free those trapped there (97.59-63; compare 1 Pet 3:19; 4:6; *Gos. Pet.* 10.41-42). The *Strasbourg Papyrus* has lines on the fragmentary second page that promise such a revelation of Jesus' glory. The disciples are apparently able to see Jesus visually in divine glory as Stephen does in Acts 7:55: "Our eyes penetrated all places. We beheld the glory of his Godhead."[25] But that vision may refer to a post-resurrection ascension story similar to Acts 1:6-11 since it is followed immediately by anointing with apostleship in the *Strasbourg Papyrus*. The fragmentary state of P. Berol. 22220 as well as the separation between the two references to the disciples making their ascent makes it difficult to locate when the disciples are invested with apostleship (113.11-12). It would appear to occur at some point during their ascent to view Jesus enthroned in glory (113.38-41; cf. Rev 4:10).

---

25. *Strasbourg Papyrus* 6 verso; Elliott, *Apocryphal New Testament*, 42.

P. Berol. 22220 picks up with an extended prayer by Jesus prior to his death that presumably is set in Gethsemane. The *Strasbourg Fragment* also contains such a prayer punctuated with repeated Amens as in P. Berol. 22220. Both prayers are closer to the confident address to the Father that one finds in John 17 than the anguish of the Synoptic Gethsemane prayers. The *Strasbourg Fragment* combines Johannine echoes with the anticipated triumph over death derived from 1 Corinthians 15.[26] As far as one can make out, P. Berol. 22220 includes a vision of the impending events of the crucifixion such as mockery and mourning by those crucified with Jesus (106.39-46; cf. Luke 23:39-43; *Gos. Pet.* 4) along with Jesus' own ecstatic address to the cross. A number of the smaller fragments also mention the cross and include "Amen" phrases. *Gos. Pet.* has the cross follow the risen Jesus out of the tomb. When the heavenly voice asks if he has preached to the dead, the cross replies "yes" (*Gos. Pet.* 10). Just as Luke's Gospel moderates the anguish of the Gethsemane prayer and John's Gospel has replaced it with Jesus' acknowledgment of his hour earlier in the narrative (John 12:27-28), so the Jesus of P. Berol. 22220 suffers no anguish before the events of the cross. He rejoices at the prospect of shedding his blood for humanity. The anguish Jesus feels is over the condemnation he will issue as judge against those of his people who rejected him (114.2-63). Again the poor state of the text makes it impossible to tell if the author has employed sorrow at the fate of his people to explain why Jesus would ask the Father to spare him the cup if possible.

This prayer and vision of future events is interrupted by another section of Johannine-style dialogue between Jesus and his disciples (plural "you," 107.2–108.64). This discourse includes Jesus sending them out as he has been sent (108.31-32; John 20:21). The sequence of pages in Hedrick and Mirecki creates a problem, since the disciples have allegedly already been transformed into spiritual beings and begun the ascent process (100.33-51). Now they are asking Jesus when he will manifest himself to them and in what sort of body (107.2-9; cf. John 14:22). John actually asks that Jesus not manifest himself in his full glory, but something less. The full glory would be too much for the disciples to bear (107.10-23). This objection may reflect a theological caveat. The full glory of the Son is his divinity, but human beings are incapable of comprehending God's being, hence the need for Jesus as revealer (John 1:18).

26. Elliott, *Apocryphal New Testament*, 41-42.

The second set of Johannine echoes concludes with testimony about the consequences of piercing Jesus' side with a spear. Since P. Berol. 22220 is set prior to the events it reports, the indicative "he has testified" of John 19:35 now appears as an imperative, "let him bear witness."

"see and believe"	107.28-30	John 20:8, 29
"not touch until I go to the Father"	107.31-33	John 20:17
"my God and your God"	107.35-38	John 20:17
"whoever is near me, is near fire"	107.39-45	= *Gos. Thom.* 82a
"whoever is far from me, is far from life"	107.46-48	= *Gos. Thom.* 82b; John 1:4; 3:15-16 etc.
"I am in your midst as a child"	107.59-60	= Matt 18:5; (John 16:21)
"little longer I am in your midst"	107.62-63	John 16:16-17
"suffer for the sins of the world"	108.5-8	John 1:29
"I rejoice over you, continued well in the world"	108.9-16	John 17:13-18
"I am sent, send you"	108.30-32	John 20:21
"announce to you joy . . . you not in the world"	108.35-42	John 15:19; 17:6, 13-18
"not weep, now, rejoice"	108.42-44	John 16:20-22
"I have overcome the world"	108.45-46	John 16:33
"I am free from the world, you"	108.49-51	John 8:32, 36
"give me to drink"	108.54	John 19:28
"pierce my side with lance"	108.59-60	John 19:34
"he who saw, let him witness"	108.61-63	John 19:35

The fragmentary state of the text as well as uncertainty in placing and ordering fragments that are not numbered pages make all proposals about the style and content of P. Berol. 22220 very speculative. The editors,

Hedrick and Mirecki, discount many of the allusions included in our analysis of the discourse material. Unless there is a high degree of verbal overlap between the phrase in P. Berol. 22220 and the Sahidic Coptic New Testament, as in the case of the final references to the crucifixion scene above, they prefer to speak of oral traditions shaped by the author's familiarity with the written Gospels of Matthew and John.[27] However, the existence of canonical Gospels circulating widely among Christians and regularly read in liturgical settings creates what Klauck describes as a "secondary orality."[28] The canonical Gospels — or in this instance the Johannine discourses and passion account — provide an underlying script for the emergence of apocryphal Gospels.

Both *Gos. Pet.* and P. Berol. 22220 were popular enough to survive in copies made some three centuries after their original composition. At least some of their acceptance by later generations of Christians must have been the result of such a creative reuse of established gospel traditions. To the listening audience *Gos. Pet.* and P. Berol. 22220 would have sounded familiar, much as most Christian moviegoers accepted the publicity claim that Mel Gibson's *Passion of the Christ* was based on John's Gospel and were unable to sort out its harmonizations, distortion, and pure invention even on a second viewing. Both John and at least Matthew and Luke figure in the mix of canonical echoes employed by P. Berol. 22220. However, the Johannine-like discourse style which appears to have inspired sections of P. Berol. 22220 is sufficiently different from that found in *Gos. Pet.* that it does not appear plausible to argue that P. Berol. 22220 employed *Gos. Pet.* directly.[29]

P. Berol. 22220 may have been drawn to the Johannine discourses as a key to understanding the passion by an interest in the divinity of Christ. *Gos. Pet.* was removed from public reading in a local church because it was suspected of promoting docetism. What we find in surviving sections of *Gos. Pet.* does not advocate a theory in which the divine Christ or Savior withdraws, leaving his human husk to die on the cross, as one would expect in a Gospel advocating docetic views. The move toward removing all ambiguity or anguish from the Jesus who goes to the cross can be discerned as early as the first century in the canonical Gospels of Luke and John. P. Berol. 22220 certainly shares a picture of the divine Jesus as com-

27. Hedrick and Mirecki, *Gospel of the Savior*, 21-23.
28. Klauck, *Apocryphal Gospels*, 3.
29. Contrary to Klauck, *Apocryphal Gospels*, 28.

pletely above the fear and passions with which ordinary human beings face death. On the other hand, the death itself is embraced as an opportunity to shed blood for the sins of the world. Prior to or as part of his resurrection Jesus triumphs over death by entering its realm and releasing those imprisoned in Hades, a tradition linked to Jesus' death as atonement for sin in 1 Pet 3:18-20.[30] We do not know what else they may have contained, but these apocryphal reflections on the passion from the second and third centuries confirm an intuition that lay at the beginning of historical-critical study of Mark: the passion narrative lies at the core of the Christian impulse to retell the story about Jesus of Nazareth.

The Question of Genre Revisited

This brief look at other Gospel traditions from the second and third centuries reopens the question of genre with which we began this book. What is a Gospel? Since so many of the forty or so candidates for inclusion survive only as fragments, in later translations, or, as in the case of Tatian's *Diatessaron* or Marcion's edition of Luke, as works about which others made comments, the comparative problems are immense. One often feels a bit like the paleontologist confronted by an array of fossils. Which ones belong to the same animal? How does one fill in the missing pieces to create a virtual image of the animal to accompany the museum exhibit? Anyone who has followed the changing morphology of dinosaurs over the past half century should not be surprised to find similar shifts and arguments among students of early Christianity.

It is important to remember that there are three very different stages in how the material is presented. At the strictest level, there is the collection of physical remains, whether fossils or texts. Those remains are investigated for what the contexts in which they were found or the bits themselves can tell us. When did a fossil die? When was a manuscript copied? What other fossils or texts are around in the same region at that time? Are

---

30. The 1 Peter text has a complex history of interpretation. Since it refers to the time of Noah it is possible that the spirits in question were the rebellious angels who had corrupted humankind. Originally the victorious Christ would have been announcing their condemnation. However, from the end of the second century on, this text is treated as bringing the deceased of Noah's generation to salvation. For a detailed discussion see John H. Elliott, *1 Peter* (AB 37B; New York: Doubleday, 2000) 638-709.

there other fossils or manuscripts already published from museum collections around the world that are similar?

The second level requires that the scientist or scholar fit the data into something of a virtual reality model. Scholars will employ a number of assumptions based on what they know about the animals or texts in question, about similar phenomena and even models from other investigators to fill out their picture. Naturally there will be disagreements over the model building. A good presentation will make it easy to distinguish the bits of data from the parts that have been filled in. Sometimes a scholar is so anxious to put the new fossil or text into a particular hole in the known data that differences between the reconstruction and what is really there in the record are fudged. Such tendencies have been exhibited by scholars who rushed to claim that very small fragments of Gospel material are from missing parts of *Gos. Pet.,* for example. More cautious scholars insist that these fragments be referred to by their museum numbers and considered as separate examples of apocryphal Gospel tradition until such time as more secure evidence for the alleged connection is discovered.[31]

Finally, movies like *Jurassic Park* and *The Passion of the Christ* or mass-market books in the same vein represent the third type of presentation. Some bits and pieces from a scientifically based virtual reality have been woven together with heavy doses of imagination and arresting visual images. Teachers find themselves battling the false ideas generated by these films constantly. Perhaps the emergence of a four-Gospel canon by the end of the second century can be viewed as the response to a similar situation. The proliferation of Jesus traditions coupled with contending views about who Jesus was and what he taught threatened to leave Christian communities without any common center. At the same time, the emergence of an authoritative collection solved the problem of definition: Members of the species "Gospel" must resemble Matthew, John, Luke, or Mark. They must be attributed to an apostle or one of his followers. Their teaching must be congruent with that found in this collection.

31. For a thorough treatment of the exaggerated claims made about small papyrus fragments as witnesses to *Gos. Pet.,* accompanied by photographs of the material in question, see Paul Foster, "Are There Any Early Fragments of the So-Called *Gospel of Peter?" NTS* 52 (2006) 1-28. Foster insists that as we find even more apocryphal Peter material, as in the Coptic Gnostic material from Nag Hammadi, even the identification of the Akhmimic text of the seventh to ninth centuries with the *Gospel of Peter* read by Serapion in the second century should be treated as problematic (pp. 27-28).

On that basis, some of the oral traditions and free-floating stories about Jesus that one finds in fragmentary texts of the second and third century look very much like Gospels even if they may not have been part of an account of Jesus' ministry and passion similar to the four canonical works. Sayings collections with minimal narrative elements such as Q, a reconstructed first-century source, and *Gos. Thom.*, represented by second-century fragments and a third- (or fourth-) century translation, could be considered Gospels on the basis of their contents. However, the collection of sayings and teachings of a sage does not incorporate the elements of biographical narrative typical of canonical Gospels. Therefore some scholars would prefer to treat them as representing a separate genre. The Jewish Christian Gospels, *Gos. Pet.*, and Tatian's *Diatessaron* have survived not at all or only in part. On the basis of comments by ancient writers, they appear to have had a closer structural resemblance to the canonical Gospels than the sayings collections.

The so-called infancy Gospels belong in the category of entertainment or pious legend. They show no interest in informing audiences about the ministry, death, and resurrection of Jesus. Nor are they presented as "memoirs of the apostles," the phrase Justin Martyr used for those books read during Christian worship (1 *Apology* 67.3-4).

The assorted Gnostic texts which have been transmitted with the title "Gospel" pose additional problems of classification. As we have suggested, the titles are not a particularly good clue to genre. The group of post-resurrection dialogues between Jesus and his followers embraces one text with "Gospel" in its title, *Gos. Mary,* and a number of others which do not use that designation but share a similar narrative framework and make a comparable effort to attribute teaching to the risen Jesus which differs from his public instruction during the earthly ministry. Such works include the *Apocryphon of John,* the *Apocryphon of James* (which has an additional epistolary opening), the *Dialogue of the Savior,* the *Wisdom of Jesus Christ,* the *Apocalypse of James,* the *Letter of Peter to Philip,* and the *Apocalypse of Peter,* which includes a docetic interpretation of Jesus' crucifixion. Although a few scholars have attempted to wrench early pre-canonical sayings traditions from some of these writings, especially the fragmentary *Dialogue of the Savior,* most scholars agree that they depend on canonical Gospel traditions for the Christian framework used to encompass new forms of teaching. Although its lack of opening and middle pages makes it impossible to put the details of *Gos. Mary* together, the Christianizing frame story about Jesus' encounter with his bewildered, frightened, and reluctant disciples is based on canonical motifs. The content of the two sections of revelation has no discernable anchor in the public teaching of Jesus, however.

In addition to these texts which exploit the lack of specific teaching by the risen Jesus in the canonical material, scribes attached the title "Gospel" to other writings which have no ties to the "Gospel" genre at all. The *Gospel of Philip* and the *Gospel of Truth* are closer to sermons or reflections largely inspired by Valentinian teaching. Both incorporate echoes of familiar motifs and sayings from the canonical Gospels, which presume an audience able to attach this new spiritual teaching to the Jesus already known in that context. The *Gospel of the Egyptians* reflects ritual, baptismal practices of another line of Gnostic teaching, which modern scholars have named Sethian because the heavenly Seth functions as the ancestor of the enlightened and source of revelation. To what extent are the colophons attached to these works by second- or third-century scribes indicative of judgments about the genre of the texts? Often none at all. Some scribes may have been able to read what they copied sufficiently to reach such a conclusion. Others, as we learned from *Shepherd of Hermas* in Chapter Two, struggled to make letter-to-letter transcriptions. Second- and third-century Christians composing and distributing texts for private and even public use are more likely to have had scribes who could barely get the job done than scribes who could evaluate the genre of what they had been asked to copy. Thus the title "Gospel" may be attached for fairly extrinsic reasons, such as use of a phrase like "gospel [= message] of truth" in an opening line or recognition of the name of a familiar figure like Thomas, Philip, or Mary.

Once again Eusebius's report (*Hist. Eccl.* 6.12) about Serapion first accepting the Gospel being read in a local church, *Gos. Pet.*, is instructive. The bishop's initial impression of the text was that it looked like a Gospel. Only after complaints forced him to engage in actual reading of the work did Serapion prohibit its public use in the church. That objection did not bring an end to the circulation of *Gos. Pet.* Nor did the growing acceptance of the four-Gospel canon as the authoritative written embodiment of apostolic tradition sound a death knell for Gospel-telling among early Christian communities. Quite the contrary. One might say that as these Gospels gained a place alongside the Jewish Scriptures in Christian worship, they provided the basic material for new oral and written Gospels in their characters, speech patterns, story lines, and variations and gaps in the narrative. A brief look through the contents of any one of the collections devoted to the apocryphal Gospels will turn up such later works as the *Gospel of Nicodemus,* also known as the *Acts of Pilate* (Elliott, 164-204), the *Questions of Bartholomew,* referred to by ancient writers as the *Gospel of Bartholomew* (Elliott, 652-72), and patristic comments on the *Gospel of Judas (Iscariot)* (Schneemelcher, 386-87).

Since our ability to date ancient manuscripts is not precise and many of the longer texts for apocryphal Gospels come from later manuscripts and translations, even those claimed for the second century may have relied on the wide circulation of the canonical Gospels, especially Matthew and John. Of the four, Matthew was not only the most widely known but also the one Gospel not claimed by a marginal or heretical group. Valentinian Gnostics had a particular affinity for John's Gospel. The *Gospel of Truth* opens with the Word coming forth from the Father to enlighten those trapped in the "darkness of oblivion [= ignorance of the true God]," for example (*Gos. Tr.* 16.13-18.21). The first known commentary on John was written toward the end of the second century by the Valentinian teacher Heracleon. Long quotations from that work appear in the commentary of the famous third-century theologian and exegete Origen. As we have seen, Marcion took over Luke's Gospel to promote his revised version of Christianity. Some authors assert that docetists favored Mark. If that is correct, the stark human portrayal of Jesus in Mark's passion narrative must have been used to drive a wedge between the human being and the divine Son, associated with the Spirit descending upon Jesus at his baptism.[32]

Students often wish that either a Gospel harmony such as Tatian's or a single Gospel such as Matthew had emerged as the winner from the mix of traditions old and new swirling about in the first three centuries. Parishioners often are taken off guard by the practice in many churches of devoting a year to each of the Synoptic Gospels. The first Sunday of Lent in the year devoted to Mark produces the brief notice about Jesus' temptation (Mark 1:12-13), not the familiar question and answer with Satan from Q

32. For a discussion of the development of the four-Gospel canon which rightly points out that Irenaeus's defense of that collection mirrors a trend already in progress at the end of the second century, see Ronald A. Piper, "The One, the Four and the Many," in Markus Bockmuehl and Donald A. Hagner, eds., *The Written Gospel* (Cambridge: Cambridge University Press, 2005) 254-73.

(Luke 4:1-13). As the pastor was reading the Gospel, an elderly friend and lifelong parish member leaned over to me and said, "Boy, they've sure messed that one up, haven't they?!" When she didn't hear the story that she expected, she presumed that modern scholars or liturgy experts had decided to mess with the Gospel! Kidding her for having missed Tuesday's Bible study, I assured her that what was read was Mark's Gospel. So far she hasn't lobbied to ditch Mark, though it's not high on her list of favorite Bible reading.

Even second- and third-century theologians like Irenaeus, Clement of Alexandria, and Origen knew that there were disagreements among the four canonical Gospels. Of course such differences may not have troubled those educated in ancient Alexandria. The city's Museum (a scholarly library) had been known for collecting ancient manuscripts since its founding. We have seen that the Greek translation of the Hebrew Torah was alleged to have been funded by Egypt's ruler. Jewish legend had it that all the translators agreed, a claim not borne out by the manuscripts and the New Testament citations. Before learning the more erudite forms of textual commentary, students would have learned how to deal with apparent contradictions between passages in Homer. Resolving similar questions in the Gospels would not have been any more difficult.

Of course there were other reasons for attributing a special status to these four Gospels. They could claim an antiquity and origin in the apostolic generation that none of the second-century attempts at revising, expanding, or changing the story could. The claim to apostolic testimony was repeatedly debated when various groups of Gnostic Christians asserted that the risen Jesus had taught one or more of the disciples something different from what ordinary Christians believed. If the four most ancient witnesses could be shown to have a unified message that was coherent with the basic beliefs of Christians everywhere, then alternate theological views that their advocates said were the true Christianity could be discredited. What the theologians debated at a more abstract level may have been won on the ground among the faithful at a simpler level. The four canonical Gospels were more readily available. Given the difficulties of reading and performing an ancient text, familiarity has an important function. Both the one who reads or performs and the audience that listens depend on their prior knowledge of set bits in order to understand what is going on.

Students today often experience a similar disorientation when they attempt to read one of the apocryphal texts after being inspired by a talk on the open-ended creativity of such second-century alternatives to official Christianity. Unless they buy one of the editions in which a modern author has paraphrased and explained one of the Gnostic gospels in a way that fits modern notions of spirituality, non-specialists often find them unintelligible. A process of private instruction and, in some groups, ritual initiation was presumed by Gnostic teachers. Whenever someone comes up in the parking lot or the parish hall and wants to know if the church should open up its canon to admit these exciting new Gospels, the simplest response is, "Take a copy of the *Gospel of* (whatever the news flash of the week is) home. Try reading it silently and out loud to someone in your family. Then tell me." So far there are no votes to install one or another of these texts as a regular feature of Sunday worship. Although bishops like Serapion and Irenaeus played a role in determining which Gospels would be the basis for worship and instruction in churches under their care, they were not imposing an order of belief and worship from above that lacked a basis in the community. Nor did they have the power to shut down groups that gathered around teachers whose views the bishops considered distortions of the faith. The survival and translation of apocryphal Gospels and other writings used by such groups show that there was a receptive audience for them as well.

Index of Modern Authors

Index of Subjects

Index of Ancient Sources